Bjørn K. Myskja

The Sublime in Kant and Beckett

Kantstudien

Ergänzungshefte

im Auftrage der Kant-Gesellschaft
herausgegeben von
Gerhard Funke, Manfred Baum, Bernd Dörflinger
und Thomas M. Seebohm

140

Walter de Gruyter · Berlin · New York

2002

Bjørn K. Myskja

The Sublime in Kant and Beckett

Aesthetic Judgement, Ethics and Literature

Walter de Gruyter · Berlin · New York

2002

♾ Gedruckt auf säurefreiem Papier,
das die US-ANSI-Norm über Haltbarkeit erfüllt.

Die Deutsche Bibliothek – CIP-Einheitsaufnahme

Myskja, Bjørn K.:
The sublime in Kant and Beckett : aesthetic judgement, ethics and literature / Bjørn K. Myskja. – Berlin ; New York : de Gruyter, 2002
(Kantstudien : Ergänzungshefte ; 140)
ISBN 3-11-017126-0

Printed in Germany
Einbandentwurf: Christopher Schneider, Berlin
Druck und buchbinderische Verarbeitung: Hubert & Co., Göttingen

Contents

Acknowledgements

I want to thank *The Research Council of Norway*, *The Ethics Programme* for a three year Fellowship that made this work possible. The colloquiums and meetings of *The Ethics Programme* have been a source of inspiration, and I have received many helpful comments and suggestions from the participants. I also want to express my gratitude to the Department of Philosophy at NTNU Trondheim for an inspirational and friendly work environment. The Faculty of Arts, NTNU, supported a visit to Princeton University in the fall 1998. I am very grateful to Béatrice Longuenesse for inviting me and to the Department of Philosophy at Princeton for allowing me to visit. This gave me the opportunity to participate in Longuenesse's seminar on the Kant's Critique of Judgement from which I learned a lot.

Truls Wyller and Thomas Pogge have read drafts of the entire manuscript in different stages of completion. I have learned very much about Kant's philosophy from both of them, and their comments led to many improvements. Pogge saved me from several serious mistakes and has been an invaluable source of inspiration and encouragement. Béatrice Longuenesse commented on drafts to chapters two and three, which resulted in a major reworking of these chapters. Hannah Ginsborg commented on drafts to the same chapters. Many of her comments are reflected in these chapters that from the outset was inspired by her interpretation of Kant's third Critique. Tom Eide and Petter Aaslestad read drafts to chapter one and six. I hope to have done some justice to their patient explanations and suggested improvements. David Sussman read a draft to chapter four, and his thorough comments led to several changes. Helge Høibraaten commented on chapter one and helped me find the right approach to the project in its early stages. Martin Frank has proof-read all the citations in German, and many times helped me to make sense of difficult passages of Kant's German. I have learned a lot from discussing philosophy with him. I have also benefited from discussing Kant's aesthetic theory with Brit Strandhagen. Jonathan B. Beere proof-read the English of chapters one to six and suggested several improvements of the argumentation, as well. Any grammatical error found in this work is most likely due to changes in the manuscript after he checked the language.

Trondheim, October 2001 Bjørn K. Myskja

Citations and abbreviations

I have chosen to cite Kant in German to avoid discussions of the adequacy of the selected translations of key passages. The existing translations all have certain strengths and weaknesses connected to their different interpretations of the work, so I found it difficult using any of them without comparing them directly with the original. Providing my own translation of the text would not be an acceptable solution, either. The reader should be given the opportunity to check the interpretation of the text with the original. Werner Pluhar's translation is used as support for my choice of words and expressions when paraphrasing Kant's text. I follow the same practice when quoting or paraphrasing passages from other works by Kant. The English translations I have consulted are listed in the bibliography.

All references to the novels of Beckett's *Trilogy* and to Kant's works are inserted in parentheses in the text. Other references are given in footnotes. The first time I refer to a work I give the name of the author and the title without subtitles. Unless the title of the work already is short, I shorten it in subsequent references, so that 'H. Ginsborg, *The Role of Taste in Kant's Theory of Cognition*' becomes 'Ginsborg, *Role of Taste*'. Complete references are given in the bibliography.

The three novels of Beckett's *Trilogy* are published in the same edition. Contrary to common practice, I have chosen to indicate which of the three works I am citing, instead of just referring to the *Trilogy*. Since my argument primarily concerns *Molloy*, the reader should know when I gather support for my arguments from other parts of the *Trilogy*. So I abbreviate the novels in the following way:

M Molloy
MD Malone Dies
U The Unnamable

Kant's works are abbreviated as follows:

A Anthropologie in pragmatischer Hinsicht
B Beobachtungen über das Gefühl des Schönen und Erhabenen
EE Erste Einleitung in die Kritik der Urteilskraft
G Grundlegung zur Metaphysik der Sitten

KpV Kritik der praktischen Vernunft
KrV Kritik der reinen Vernunft
KU Kritik der Urteilskraft
MS Metaphysik der Sitten
P Prolegomena zu einer jeden künftigen Metaphysik
R Die Religion innerhalb der Grenzen der bloßen Vernunft
SF Der Streit der Fakultäten

All references to Kant's works are to the pagination of the *Akademie* edition. Where neither the German edition I have used nor the translation I have consulted has running pagination from the *Akademie* edition, I have consulted *Kants Werke. Akademie Textausgabe*, Walter de Gruyter & Co., Berlin 1968.

Introduction

The sublime, literature and ethics

Some of the most influential literary works of the twentieth century can aptly be classified as sublime works of art due to the effect they have on the reader. Although the sublime is an aesthetic category, it is connected to morality in a way that can explain why sublime novels can be morally significant despite their resistance to ethical interpretations.

An object or event is sublime when it evokes a particular feeling of combined repulsion and attraction connected to cognitive failure. Both nature and art is experienced as sublime when it resists cognition in a way that elicits this particular kind of feeling in the subject. The cognitive failure is not of the kind where something is experienced as merely meaningless, but rather one where the existence of something that is inaccessible to ordinary cognition is indicated. One can say that the experience of sublimity is closely related to the religious experiences of the mystics. Still it is a purely aesthetic experience, without religious import. Feeling is our only access to this experience, which means that the experience is an aesthetic experience, or aesthetic judgement, as Immanuel Kant would say. The most significant characteristic of this feeling, according to Kant, is that it is simultaneously positive and negative. To experience something as sublime, then, is to experience it as having elements that defy cognition in a way that give rise to a complex feeling of pleasure and displeasure.

Employing Kant's theory of the sublime in an interpretation of Samuel Beckett's novel *Molloy* implies that this theory developed in the eighteenth century can be illuminating when seeking to understand the impact of literature of the twentieth century. This is one of the claims of this book, although it is true that the novel as an art form is not a subject for Kant in his analysis of the arts, and the literary form and narrative world of Beckett probably would be inconceivable for Kant and his contemporaries. Kant's theory, although being developed in a completely different time with the experience of certain natural phenomena in mind, provides an important theoretical framework for analysis for one of the most significant features of Beckett's *Molloy*. The novel is sublime in the sense that its systematic negation of the meaning of the text denies the reader a coherent meaning which gives rise to the complex feeling described by Kant as the main element in a judgement of sublimity. In addition, if Lyotard is correct in saying that the sublime is the sensibility characteristic of modern art[1], this Kantian approach is significant both for other novels, as well as for other forms of modernist art.

Another argument of this book is that the aesthetic experience of the sublime is morally significant in the sense that it may contribute to moral conversion and to the cultivation of character. This explains the paradoxical fact that the novels of Beckett have an amoral or even immoral content and still they are generally regarded to have a positive moral value. According to Kant, the aesthetic judgement of sublimity not only presupposes man's moral nature but also serves morality. Kant himself does not specify how the sublime can serve the purposes of our moral selves, so I reconstruct this connection by reading his analysis of the sublime in connection with his main works of ethics. The main focus of this reconstruction is on Kant's theory of moral character as developed in his later works.

By combining this interpretation of Kant's theory of the aesthetic judgement of the sublime and the application of this theory on Beckett's *Molloy* with the reconstruction of Kant's theory of the moral import of the judgement of sublimity, an account is presented that can explain why the reader is emotionally affected by Beckett's work in a way that promotes rather than inhibits moral cultivation. If we follow Kant's general line of argument in his Critique of Judgement, they claim will be that not every reader is affected in this way when reading Beckett's *Molloy*, but every reader ought to be.

Background: The ethics of literature

The work with this book did not start out with an interest in Kant's aesthetic theory, but with the general question of how the reader of fictional literature is morally or ethically[2] affected. This is also the reason for formulating my questions

---

1 J.-F. Lyotard, *Om det sublime*, 52.

2 I take these words to be synonymous. Both words deal with the cluster of questions concerning human actions which include "How should one live?", "What is the good life for human beings?", "What is a good person?", "What are my obligations, and what am I not permitted to do?" and so forth. So I do not use 'morality' in a more limited sense than 'ethics', as B. Williams does in *Ethics and the Limits of Philosophy*, 6 ff. I do not hold that one word concerns practical questions and the other theoretical questions concerning these practical questions, either. In that case I distinguish between 'ethics' or 'morality' and 'ethical theory' or 'moral theory'.

in relation to the reading of a literary work rather than by starting out with an interpretation of aesthetic theories. The assumption that literature does something to us for good or for bad, and also affects the way we look at the world and how we behave, was once common among the literate population of the Western world. This view fell in disrespect for several reasons. One significant reason was the separation of aesthetics from morality and epistemology usually accredited Baumgarten and Kant[3]. I will argue that Kant's theory not only severs but also reunites the connections between these forms of judgement. Still, the historical consequence of his theory was an emphasis on the autonomy of pure aesthetic assessments of art. This led to the suspicion that criticising a work of art for moral reasons might fail to pay due credit to the aesthetic qualities of the work, a suspicion more often than not supported by prejudiced moral condemnation of novels not considered proper from the view of conventional morality.

A related development reinforcing this critical attitude to ethical interpretation was the predominant occupation with theoretical frameworks excluding such moral perspectives on literature. The effect was that moral concerns were more or less removed from the accepted agenda of literary criticism because they could not fit in with these formally occupied approaches. Here New Criticism[4] and Structuralism[5] were the more influential theories, followed by the many-faceted Post-Structuralist movement[6]. These approaches are arguably necessary for the exploration of those aspects of literature that form the basis for interpretations of meaning and for the determination of the restrictions that must apply to such interpretations. But they do not exhaust the field of literary theory. Very few would deny that reading literature is an important factor of human life in almost all literate cultures, and several commentators have argued that these theoretical frameworks cannot explain this assumption in an adequate way[7].

The reasons for this experienced importance of literature are not restricted to moral preoccupations, and I will not attempt to discuss all of them, although I present an open-ended list of the different perspectives we can lay on fictional narratives in chapter one[8]. The focus in this book will be the ethical significance of literature, based on the assumption that literature affects the reader in a way that

3 J. H. Zammito, *The Genesis of Kant's Critique of Judgement*, 20 and 45 ff.
4 T. Eagleton, *Literary Theory*, 48 ff.
5 Ibid. 96 ff.
6 Ibid. 143 ff.
7 For an example, see A. Danto, *The Philosophical Disenfranchisement of Art*, 142 ff.
8 See below, p. 31 f.

does something with how she[9] perceives the world. In this context what is called *moral* perception, i.e. the ability "to single out the ethically salient features of the particular matter at hand"[10], is important, although not in isolation. Moral perception is the ability to single out the elements that are relevant for deliberation and for making the correct decision on how to act. It neither influences my motivation for good deeds nor tells me how to act, unless we from the outset assume that it is through moral perception we discover what is a good deed in particular circumstances. But literature can function motivational and contribute to the discussion on what ends to pursue, too. Therefore this new approach to the question of how literature can be ethically significant is concerned with how literature contributes to answering the wide ethical question "How should one live?"[11]. The claim is not that all works of fiction can or should be considered as answers to this question, but that some may contribute to the inquiry of what kind of ends one should pursue, and how to realise these ends in concrete action.

One of the most significant contributions to the field of the ethical significance of narrative literature in recent years is Martha Nussbaum's literary ethical theory. Her focus on narrativity, characters and implicit value arguments in novels captures an important aspect of why we find literature not only entertaining and interesting, but even important in an existential sense. A literary work can, however, affect the reader in ways that is difficult to explain within Nussbaum's cognitive approach. Reading works like Beckett's *Molloy* or Joseph Conrad's *Heart of Darkness* and Franz Kafka's *The Trial*, is rewarding not only due to their exciting narratives, rich character descriptions or their implicit arguments concerning what is of value in human life. This is part of the reason for appreciating these works, together with the intriguing complexity of the moral choices the reader participates in by (more or less) identifying with the protagonists. But more important than these cognitive and ethical aspects is the strangeness of these works. One basic quality of these and other novels is not found in what the reader grasps or understands about them, but in something that is not readily accessible to understanding.

The common feature of these works is that their strongest impact, in my opinion, lies in their sublimity. One could say that these works point beyond both

---

9 I have chosen not to settle for either 'she' and 'her' or 'he' and 'his' when referring to the subject. By changing arbitrarily between the gender forms I may confuse the reader, but the intention is only to avoid taking side in a particular political question.

10 M. Nussbaum, *The fragility of goodness*, 364.

11 Among those who take this as their point of departure, we find R. Eldridge, *On Moral Personhood*, 1, M. Nussbaum, *Love's Knowledge*, 25 f., and, indirectly, W. Booth, *The Company We Keep*, 14 f.

their own fictive universes and the real world, as we know it. Their main impact lies in this feeling of transcendence. This experience is clearly one that many, if not all, people share. The novels in question are commonly accepted as great works of literature, and my assumption is that this evaluation has something to do with the sublime quality I have described above. But can a purely aesthetic experience influence our moral lives in any significant way?

The reasons commonly given for the alleged moral importance of works breaking with traditional structure and resisting interpretation are several. One reason is that they exhibit the meaninglessness of human existence and the grandeur of man facing this emptiness, another that they are expressions of some power underlying the appearances of things, be it the Freudian subconscious or God. More often than not do interpretations of this kind get entangled in contradictions or contain easily refuted hypotheses concerning the meaning of the text, because of the resistance of these works to the construction of meaningful totalities. We should neither attempt to avoid interpreting such works, nor reject reading them as answers to the question "How should one live?" Many of these works obviously are concerned with this problem in some way or another. But I will attempt to supplement these ethical interpretations by developing a Kantian theory of the ethical significance of the aesthetic judgement of the sublime.

Problem: The ethics of Beckett's *Molloy*

The point of departure in this book is Samuel Beckett's novel *Molloy*. Like so much of Beckett's writings from the post-war years, the novel has been subject to a wide array of interpretations, including ethical ones. The first reason for selecting this work is that *Molloy* often has been ascribed a positive moral function despite its amoral, even nihilistic stories and characters. The explanation of this experience of *Molloy* as morally significant suggested here is that this novel is a sublime work of art, and that the feeling of the sublime is of moral significance. Many literary works have sublime qualities[12], but the sublime appears to be the core feature of Beckett's work, and this is the second reason for

12 Bloom selected works for "their sublimity and their representative nature" when putting together his canon, and he draws the lines of this literary sublime back to the Yahwist, the original author of *Genesis*, *Exodus*, and *Numbers*. H. Bloom, *The Western Canon*, 2 ff. The sublime is not a new phenomenon in literature, nor particularly connected to the writings of our time, although its expression is different in literature from different epochs.

using *Molloy* as background for the theory developed in this book. A third reason is that the anti-moral character of the two stories of *Molloy* sharpens the contrast between the content of the novel and the experienced ethical value of it, as expressed by several commentators. The question concerning how to explain the moral qualities ascribed the novel by these commentators becomes more pressing when the work clearly negates many basic precepts of everyday morality. A fourth reason is that Nussbaum also discusses *Molloy* in her project of including literature as part of the general field of moral philosophy. Thus I can contrast my approach with one of the more carefully argued approaches to literature and ethics, and show that the Kantian theory of the sublime provides a valuable supplement to the more cognitive interpretative strategy advocated by Nussbaum.

The central problem of this book is raised by the presentation of some major ethical interpretative approaches to *Molloy*. I concentrate in particular on Nussbaum's reading of this novel as an argument against the value of emotions and narratives in the creation of ethical meaning in our lives[13]. Although this and related interpretations of the work are illuminating as regards the impact of this novel on our lives, there are significant emotional responses to this work left out in Nussbaum's account. We have to go beyond Nussbaum's cognitive approach and regard the aesthetic effect of the work, i.e. how it affects us independently of our cognitive evaluation of this self-negating narrative.

In *Molloy* and other works, Beckett uses techniques of immediate contradiction and doubt of statements. When a sentence or a statement is immediately denied in some way or other, the result is not the same as if nothing has been said. The reader gets confused as to what has been told. This confusion is not merely causing frustration, because the reader knows something has occurred, something meaningful, but this something is incomprehensible for the reader. The reader expects the narrative to be a comprehensive whole, and interprets it in that way, but he is unable to grasp this whole. Since we experience narratives by imagining a world or creating a fictitious universe, the failure is not primarily one of understanding. Each and every element is as such accessible to understanding. It is our imaginative capacity that is incapable of grasping the whole. Still this failure is not merely a source of disappointment. Many readers clearly experience such works as meaningful on a deeper level, as can be seen both from the critical response and from the relative popular success of Beckett's work.

---

13 Nussbaum, *Love's Knowledge*, 286 ff.

Approach: Interpretation of Kant's aesthetic and ethical theories

Kant's theory is just one among many accounts of the sublime. So why choose his theory? The reason can partly be explained by historical circumstances. The sublime has a long tradition in which it has been understood in a variety of different ways, but the interest seemed to disappear completely. But since the mid-eighties the sublime has had a renaissance as a fashionable term within the field of aesthetics. The discussion of the term has been of very varying quality, and not all of it has been easy to understand. In philosophy, as in some other research fields, it is not always the case that the latest theory is the best point of departure for further discussion. One should be particularly careful when choosing theoretical framework for a phenomenon that has not been subject to continuous research, and even has been written off as belonging to particular historical contexts and concerns[14]. When a philosophical problem or position resurfaces after a longer period of relative obscurity, one may have to return to earlier theories to find the adequate basis for discussion[15]. This is even more necessary when the contemporary discussion is not clearly focused.

Since the sublime is not an ordinary object we determine according to a concept, but is a kind of object that defies such determination, it is difficult to give a clear analysis of it. The word invites unclear presentations, which is evident in several contemporary accounts of it:

> Das Erhabene läßt sich nur mit Gewalt zu einem einheitlichen und eindeutigen Gefühl vereinfachen. Dadurch wird es – eher als das einheitliche Schöne – der grundlegende Pluralität und Komplexität der heutigen Zeit gerecht. Ja, es fordert diese Pluralität durch seine interne Inkommensurabilität sogar ausdrücklich ein. Nur indem man den "Widerstreit" von Einbildungskraft und Vernunft im Erhabenen berücksichtigt, trifft man den Kern dieses Gefühls. Pluralität und Kritik hängen eng zusammen. Das Erhabene ist auch von daher ein zutiefst kritisches Gefühl.[16]

---

[14] The sublime has both been considered to be passé (P. Guyer, Kant *and the Claims of Taste* [First edition, 1979], 399 f. note) and as connected to unacceptable political ideals (C. Pries, *Übergänge ohne Brücken*, 30 f. and 37).

[15] An example of this return to earlier theories to provide a acceptable basis for the research is the revival of virtue ethics, where especially Aristotle's ethical theory provided the foundation. Examples are A. MacIntyre, *After Virtue*, Williams, *Ethics and the Limits*, and Nussbaum, *Fragility*.

[16] C. Pries, 'Einleitung', 25. It is not clear what a "*kritisches Gefühl*" may be; critique is usually connected to rationality, not feeling. The claim that an ambiguous or complex feeling is better suited to a situation of plurality is not presented in a way that makes agreement or disagreement possible.

There are of course obscurities in Kant's account of the sublime, too, but he provides a phenomenological description of the judgement of these objects, he suggests an epistemological basis for the judgement, and argues for its connection with morality. Unlike some influential contemporary accounts, Kant's theory does not connect this judgement with contingent cultural phenomena and his theory establishes a link between the sublime and morality, a connection severed in many contemporary accounts of the sublime[17]. Kant also says that the sublime is overwhelming for our sensibility, not for our understanding, as other modern thinkers suggest[18].

Thus the choice of Kant's theory of the sublime as basis for my discussion is not arbitrary. His theory is the only one that in an adequate way explains the sublime as an aesthetic judgement with a moral significance. My investigation is restricted to Kant's theory, without comparing it with other accounts of the sublime. I relate Kant's account of the sublime to his general theory of aesthetics, to his general theory of reflective judgement, and to his moral philosophy. The framework for this interpretation of Kant is interpretations of Beckett's *Molloy* and theoretical works on the ethics of literature. Although what I present here is primarily an interpretation of Kant, this interpretation, and the application of it, can contribute to show that Kant's theory of the sublime presents a plausible account of this aesthetic phenomenon. So this is not merely a contribution to the history of philosophy, but a work that is relevant for the current concerns of aesthetics, in particular for the question of the moral significance of literature.

Presenting Kant's theory of the sublime is impossible without relating it to Kant's general theory of aesthetics, which primarily concerns the beauty of objects of nature. And his theory of aesthetics is part of his theory of reflective judgement. Therefore the framework of my interpretation of the sublime is Kant's theory of reflective judgement. This means that also Kant's theory of cognition is included in the research, but without involving in any significant degree the theory of determinative judgements as presented in the first Critique. The background for my discussion of the epistemological foundation of the aesthetic reflective judgement is Kant's third Critique. Readers who are not particularly interested in the claim to universal validity of judgements of taste and the link between the two parts of the Critique of Judgement should not spend too much time on chapter 2.3.

The discussion of the sublime is largely based on the third Critique account, although I also refer to some passages from Kant's pre-Critical work on aesthetics:

---

17 As is done in J.-F. Lyotard, *The Postmodern condition*, 76 ff.
18 A. Wellmer, 'Adorno, die Moderne und das Erhabene', 166.

Beobachtungen über das Gefühl des Schönen und Erhabenen. In discussing the basis of the judgement of sublimity in man's power of reason, I draw on Kant's second Critique, *Grundlegung*, the Dialectic of the first Critique, as well as the third Critique account. The discussion of how we are morally affected by the feeling of the sublime draws on all of Kant's published works in moral theory, with main focus on his later moral writings in *Die Religion innerhalb der Grenzen der bloßen Vernunft* and *Metaphysik der Sitten.* The theory I develop therefore involves both Kant's aesthetics, ethics, and some aspects of his theoretical philosophy with the analysis of the sublime as a focal point.

Outline of contents

The first chapter starts out with a short interpretation of *Molloy* and the *Trilogy* of which it is a part. The conventional conception of this work takes it to be concerned with the problem of meaninglessness. I discuss some ethical interpretations, with a focus on Nussbaum's approach to the work as part of her project of ethical literary theory. She interprets Beckett's voices as saying that emotions are taught through stories, and this is a cause of human suffering. By discussing this and other interpretations, I try to show one neglected morally significant feature of this novel. This is the feeling associated with the meaninglessness of these stories, which I determine as the feeling of the sublime. I argue that this feeling affects the reader morally. To develop a theory of this moral import, I have to turn to Kant's aesthetic theory.

The second chapter presents an interpretation of Kant's theory of judgements of taste. Judgements about the beauty, non-beauty, or ugliness of objects of nature are based on a feeling of the subject's mental state in representing an object. The mental state is that of a free play between imagination and understanding, Kant says. These feelings are disinterested and the judgement issues a claim to subjective universal validity, i.e. a demand that everybody should share the mental state and feeling of the subject when cognising this object. Kant claims that this judgement is the subjective condition of cognition in general. He also says that the judgement is based on the form of purposiveness of the representation of an object. I interpret these claims to mean that the mental state underlying the judgement of taste is the subjective aspect of a teleological judgement under the principle of the purposiveness of nature. We claim universal validity for this state and for our feeling of it because unless we presuppose the intersubjectivity of this representational state, the teleological judgement would be nothing more than a private assumption. It could not be part of cognition, as we take it to be.

The subject of the third chapter is the judgement about sublime objects in nature. This judgement is also based on a feeling, albeit a complex, ambivalent one. Kant says that this judgement involves the faculty of reason instead of understanding in the free relation with the imagination. The judgement is a sign of man's supersensible vocation [*Bestimmung*]. The judgement of the sublime can be regarded as an aspect change from nature to man's reason. The feeling of the sublime is not one kind of feeling, but a family of feelings, bound together by their connection to ideas of reason and by their complexity. Kant's discussion of the sublimity of human affects has generally been neglected, but it plays an important role in understanding the sublime qualities of narrative works. There are two modes of the sublime because the feeling is either connected to the greatness of the object, the mathematically sublime, or to its might, the dynamically sublime. In the first case the sublime involves theoretical reason, and appears to have no connection with morality, which belongs to practical reason. I argue that even theoretical reason is connected to the moral ideas of spontaneity and autonomy.

The judgement of the sublime, like the judgement of taste, issues a claim to subjective universal validity, under a principle of the purposive use of nature for reason. This demand, unlike the demand in judgements of taste, has an additional presupposition of the knowledge of moral ideas in others. Kant claims that this judgement can serve the purpose of man's reason, i.e. of morality, but fails to provide an explanation of how this works. In his account the experience of the sublime remains a purely aesthetic judgement with a moral basis. An account of this moral import must be reconstructed on the basis of Kant's theory of ethics.

The first part of the fourth chapter is a presentation of the real sublime, the autonomy of man's practical reason. Kant says that some people do not experience the sublime due to a lack of moral ideas which seems to contradict his repeated claim that everybody posses knowledge of the moral law. Kant should have said that the preoccupation with and awareness of moral ideas make people more susceptible to the experience of an object as sublime. The main question of this chapter concerns how the sublime affects us in a way that influences the way we act: how are we morally affected by the sublime? Recent interpretations of Kant's moral theory emphasise its concern with the character of the agent. The feeling of sublimity can influence the development of character in two ways. It can give impulses to moral conversion and it can contribute to character development. One reason for this is the phenomenological similarity between the feeling of the sublime and the moral feeling of respect. Additionally the sublime is a way we can admire the source of this feeling of respect. I also argue that although beauty can be morally significant as a symbol of morality, this provides us only with an indirect connection between aesthetics and ethics. The sublime provides a direct influence on our disposition for moral action, and has therefore a special moral significance.

The argument of the chapters on the sublime and its moral import is based on Kant's analytic of the sublime, which is basically concerned with the sublime in nature. To make this argument relevant for literature, Kant's analysis must be shown to be valid for the sublime in art in general too, and in particular for fictional literature. The first problem here is that aesthetic reflective judgements in general display purposiveness without purpose of the objects of nature, whereas objects of art have determinate purposes. The solution to this is that fine art according to Kant is a product of the talent of genius, which is not intentionally controlled and is still rule giving, and this talent accounts for the purposiveness without purpose in art. I argue against the common assumption that Kant says that art cannot be sublime. The crucial passages can be understood differently, an interpretation that is supported by examples of sublime art discussed in the third Critique. Kant does not include novels in his list of fine arts, but he does include poetry and narrative art forms. It is reasonable to assume that his argument is relevant for narrative fiction in general, too. If fine art in general can be sublime, so can novels.

The final chapter returns to Beckett's *Molloy* to see whether the sublime as analysed by Kant can be found in this novel. The basic assumption is that the sublime must be found in the reader's imaginative creation of the work of art on the basis of the text, rather than in the text itself. Three forms of sublimity are found in *Molloy*: (1) The self-negating form is mathematically sublime. (2) The character's stoic adherence by principles contrary to their desires and interests is dynamically sublime. (3) Some poetical passages connected to the recurrent theme of the sound of murmur underlying everything display a combination of the dynamical and mathematical modes of the sublime. It is emphasised that this Kantian analysis is a supplement and not an alternative to the ethical literary theory of Nussbaum. Finally I argue that although the sublime often is connected to descriptions of amoral and immoral acts this does not mean that we should not take pleasure in it, as long as we simultaneously feel the appropriate repulsion of evil and sympathy for the people who suffer.

1. Beckett's *Molloy* and the ethics of literature

Molloy[1] consists of two first-person narratives, the first being Molloy's story of his attempted journey to his mother's home, while in the other agent Jacques Moran is telling of his assignment to find Molloy. Molloy is incessantly doubting his own memory and constantly contradicting himself, with the result that his story is negated as he tells it. He claims to have "forgotten how to spell too, and half the words" (M 8) although the story presented as his contains no misspelled words and has a rich vocabulary. That could be a warning not to trust the narrator, or it could mean that this is not Molloy writing[2]. Another explanation of this contradiction is that his papers are being corrected; we are told that they are collected and returned with marks Molloy does not understand (M 7).

Although it is possible to give a description of the general outline of Molloy's story and read it as a traditional narrative with beginning, middle and end[3], the self-negating story defies such presentations. Still, there is some kind of story of an "unreal journey" (M 17) with no purpose, a story we may call meaningless. The story, as told by Molloy, is of a life that appears to be deprived of goal and meaning, but the self-negating style makes even such claims inadequate, because they imply that the narrative in itself can be ascribed unambiguous meaning.

Moran's story starts out in a traditional style, but gradually develops towards Molloy's self-refuting style, as Moran disintegrates (see M 158). Already in the scene where he is reflecting on his inner Molloy, this confused style is evident (M 112 ff). Finally, the end of Moran's narrative negates the whole story. And Moran's life prior to his journey is in a way even more meaningless than Molloy's

---

1 *Molloy* [M] is the first part of Beckett's *Trilogy*; the other two are *Malone Dies* [MD] and *The Unnameable*[U]. I have mainly discussed *Molloy*, but my argument is based on the *Trilogy*.

2 There are several passages in the *Trilogy* suggesting that all of it (together with earlier Beckett novels) is told by the same narrator (see M 138 and U 305).

3 Following the definition of tragedy as being a whole in Aristotle, *Poetics*, 1450b25-30. In *Molloy* the beginning would be Molloy's decision to reach his mother, the middle the journey towards this goal, and the end sitting in his mother's room writing the story of his journey. A similar outline would fit even better on Moran's story. In the two following books of the *Trilogy*, there are several stories interspersed between reflections on the state of the narrator (or the subject) and problematisations of narration. The text "as a kind of commentary on itself" (R. Scruton, *The Aesthetic Understanding*, 196) is more prominent in these novels, destroying the apparent similarity with traditional narrative found in the first part of the *Trilogy*.

when it comes to purposes, filled as it is with pedantic concern about details and adherence to senseless duties. I will argue that these stories display meaninglessness in 1) actions, 2) human lives, and 3) literary form.

Can such a novel have any moral significance? If so, what significance, and how does it come about? Obviously, any story that presents a picture of human life as meaningless (if that is what *Molloy* does) may give support to arguments against moral imperatives as such. Morality is a system of meaningful statements presupposing some kind of meaning to human life, and a denial of such meaning implies a denial of the meaning of ethical statements as well. Interpretations of Beckett's work along these lines are not uncommon, and appear to gain support from some of the author's statements about his own work. This is not to say that there are anti-ethical arguments in this novel, however. I think we can safely suppose that his works are not to be read as coded philosophical arguments[4] because such interpretations always seem inadequate and are ridiculed by the text itself [5]. Still, it does not follow that we cannot develop philosophically significant arguments on the basis of Beckett's works. It can be argued that *Molloy* tells stories of meaningless lives on the fringes of what we would call human existence, lives that may be basis for questioning what we take to be the meaning of our own lives.

A systematic ethical interpretation of the *Trilogy* is developed by Martha Nussbaum in 'Narrative Emotions: Beckett's Genealogy of Love'[6]. She finds arguments in the *Trilogy* claiming emotions to be social constructs "taught, above all, through stories."[7] But unlike Nussbaum herself who considers this to be a valuable aspect of narratives in human life, Beckett's voices see this as a negative, meaningless inheritance of pain, and argue for an undoing, unwriting, of this practice. She also claims that their arguments suggest some kind of freedom in a life beyond the stories. I will discuss this interpretation on the basis of Nussbaum's general theory of the moral significance of literature, and argue that her interpretation of *Molloy* can be extended to include a radical rejection not only of emotions and religion, but also of all production of meaning, but not as a universal claim about the human condition.

---

4 This is the case despite all references to philosophical works in Beckett's fiction, as discussed among others by P.J. Murphy, 'Beckett and the philosophers', 222 ff. The philosophical allusions are presented within narratives, not in a discursive setting, and subvert more than support the positions alluded to.

5 S. Critchley, *Very Little ... Almost Nothing*, 142 f.

6 In Nussbaum, *Love's Knowledge*, 286-313.

7 Ibid. 287.

Regardless of the plausibility of Nussbaum's interpretation, Beckett's work may have a different kind of ethical significance based not on arguments, but on the emotional effect of the text. This might appear somewhat obscure, but the basic intuition is well known; the idea that art in a way challenges our given conception of the world, altering the basis of our moral beliefs. I will argue that the incoherence and lack of meaning to the human lives we find depicted in Beckett's *Molloy* give rise to a feeling in the reader (not necessarily *every* reader[8]) that has this kind of ethical function. The void that is felt by reading this self-negating and in a sense meaningless text indicates something beyond or above the socially constructed norms that are rendered meaningless according to Nussbaum's interpretation. This kind of aesthetic experience has traditionally been classified as an experience of the sublime. My claim is that *Molloy*'s main characteristic is sublimity, and that this sublime is morally significant.

Before embarking on a short paraphrase of the stories of Molloy and Moran, it is necessary to stress the restricted scope of my interpretation. Making sense of a literary text requires interpretation, and interpretation involves the reader and her knowledge, personal experiences, and feelings. Iser says that the reader constitutes the text as aesthetic object by filling in indeterminate "blanks" in the text[9]. On this assumption, interpretations must be partially subjective. Furthermore it must be noted that the complexity of this work, including techniques of negation, irony, use and misuse of clichés[10], hidden literary and philosophical references, invites a rich variety of different perspectives. Thus my interpretation is just one of many, and deals with just a few aspects of this many-faceted novel.

Admittedly subjective and restricted, my reading belongs to a well-established interpretative tradition, one concerned with the question of meaning and negation of meaning. It is also worth noticing that since my main concern is to explore how this work is morally significant, my main focus is the question of how the reader is affected.

---

8 At this point in the argument I take for granted that my subjective experience of the story is generally relevant in the discussion of this work. Later on I will discuss those elements of the text that gives rise to this reaction, and cite evidence for this being a common experience in reading this novel. The claim to universal validity for aesthetic judgements is discussed in the presentation of Kant's theory of the sublime, see chapter. 3.5.

9 W. Iser, *The Act of Reading*, 182 ff.

10 See Scruton, *Aesthetic Understanding*, 200 ff. for a discussion of Beckett's use of clichés.

1. 1 Meaninglessness and ethics

Searching for no reason

There are two journeys in *Molloy*: one is Molloy's attempt to find his mother and "settle things between them", the other is Moran's search for Molloy, an assignment from his employer Youdi, transmitted by Gaber, the messenger. Moran does not know what to do when he finds Molloy, and is not even sure whether that was specified in the assignment. Although he spends rather much time thinking over that problem, it does not really worry him. He will be told (M 136 ff.). Apparently his journey has a clear end point, but it lacks a purpose. It is his duty to go through with it, but he is given no reason for doing it. The arbitrary nature of the assignment is also evident from a sudden change of direction and mission delivered by Gaber without explanation (M 164).

Molloy himself is likewise travelling towards a determined goal, his mother, but he seems to have a purpose, too, in that he wants to settle things between them and establish their relations on a "less precarious footing" (M 87). However, he does not appear to know what the problem or the matter between him and his mother is and negates the need: "I must have needed my mother, otherwise why this frenzy of wanting to get to her? ... Need of my mother! No, there were no words for the want of need in which I was perishing." (M 34) This conclusion is supported by the fact that he had visited her on several earlier occasions, and relates how she is virtually deaf and has a seriously deficient memory, making it improbable that it is possible to settle anything at all with her.

> I got into communication with her by knocking on her skull. One knock meant yes, two no, three I don't know, four money, five goodbye. ... For she seemed to have lost, if not absolutely all notion of mensuration, at least the faculty of counting beyond two. It was too far for her, yes, the distance was too great, from one to four. (M 18)

Molloy has a goal but no understandable reason for seeking this goal, and during the description of his travels we find that he does not even try very hard to reach this goal. Maybe Molloy's wish to get to his mother has the same character as the wait in *Waiting for Godot* as Robbe-Grillet understood it: "The wait in Waiting for Godot represents neither hope nor longing nor even despair. It is merely an excuse."[11] When Molloy, after having deteriorated to the state of

---

[11] A. Robbe-Grillet, 'Samuel Beckett or "Presence" in the Theatre', 111. These claims can be contested both for the play and the *Trilogy*, and that is how it must be when taking into account the form of these works. I will argue that just the fact that it is impossible

dragging himself forwards by his hands, at last ends up in his mother's rooM it is not due to his own efforts. He is transported there in some vehicle by someone (probably Youdi's people) and told to write the story of his journey (M 7).

Much has been written about how Jacques Moran develops from being a pedantic bourgeois practising Catholic to becoming a mirror image of the disintegrated Molloy he is hunting (to the extent of ending up using crutches because of a stiff, painful knee)[12]. More interesting are the apparent differences between the two parts, e.g. how Moran's narrative does not seem as contradictory and self doubting as Molloy's. Moran's story is told by a man who has been travelling through a country he knows and can find his way about[13], and who usually is quite certain of what happened, although he admits that he has been putting lies in the narrative (M 128), which undermines the reader's confidence in his story. He also recognises the impossibility of the whole project of writing stories:

> Oh the stories I could tell you if I were easy. What a rabble in my head, what a gallery of moribunds. Murphy, Watt, Yerk, Mercier and all the others. I would never have believed that - yes, I believe it willingly. Stories, stories. I have not been able to tell them. I shall not be able to tell this one. (M 138)

Moran appears to be heeding the conventions of story-telling when describing the preparations for, and the unsuccessful execution of, an unusual kind of work. But that is really not the case, because the whole story ends up in the repetition of the opening sentences, and their denial:

> Then I went back into the house and wrote, It is midnight. The rain is beating on the windows. It was not midnight. It was not raining. (M 176)

Although Moran's story exhibits the conventional structure of narratives, stating a story as something that happened, the end of the story undermines this adherence to the conventions. This ending mirrors Molloy's way of contradicting and doubting the events he relates, making the form of the story fit the content. As

---

to decide beyond doubt whether or not Molloy's journey and life is plain meaningless represents a further obstacle to the wish to ascribe meaning to the work as a whole, supporting my overall claim that the problem of meaning and understanding is a fundamental theme in these works. I will return to the problems raised by such claims.

12 See for example R. Cohn, *Back to Beckett*, 88 ff.

13 The extent of the difference between the description of the same landscape in the two parts is emphasised and explained in J.Fletcher, *The Novels of Samuel Beckett*, 126: "the place which Molloy describes as a fairly large region of hills, forest, plain, sea and distant islands, exists for Moran merely as a small area of copse, pasture, bog, creek and muddy sands. ... Molloy is a figure of myth moving in a mythical country whereas Moran is a fairly prosaic wage-earner inhabiting a world of suburban villas and farms."

Moran disintegrates into a creature hardly distinguishable from Molloy, his style of narration changes from a pedantic way of relating events and thoughts as given facts, to the self-contradictions and doubt similar to the ones dominating the first story. This ends up in the negation of the start of Moran's story, and, thus, his story as such[14].

Another seemingly significant difference between the two parts of the novel is found in their respective hopes for the end of the life of story-writing. Both wish their story to end, but what expectations do they have for what comes afterwards? Molloy would like to "speak of the things that are left, say [his] goodbyes, finish dying" (M 7), whereas Moran writes about clearing out and ceasing to be a man (M 176) which allows for continuing life although not a human life. His hope is connected to his supposed understanding of the languages both of birds and of a voice inside him (which we must suppose is speaking some non-human language, too):

> But in the end I understood this language. I understood it, I understand it, all wrong perhaps. That is not what matters. (M 176)

If Moran understands it correctly (and I understand Moran correctly), the voice inside indicates a way out of the human condition to some other kind of existence associated with living in the garden and with animal life. Unlike Molloy, Moran is not finished with existence, although he finishes off human life; i.e. the life as a social, rational and communicating being. He seems to aim for some kind of *nirvana* like the one the hero of Beckett's first published short-story, *Assumption*, ended up in[15], although not the transcendent *nirvana* of that story. Moran's new life is to take place within this physical world. That is the kind of life he is aiming for.

Can we believe such a life to be possible? Or is Moran losing his grip on reality? When Moran does not believe the truth of his own story, and doubts his understanding of the inner voice, why should we believe his account of the message? This is not the only reason for doubting the possibility of Moran's alternative, non-human life: The source of Moran's belief in a life beyond language is his inner voice. But the same voice is commanding him to write the report, a report associated with the bidding of Youdi, Moran's employer. The messages of Moran's inner voice are Youdi's commandments, and Youdi

---

14 In M. Nadeau, 'Humor and the Void', 35, *Molloy* is called a non-work because of the self-destructing narrative. The consequence of this is that in every interpretation "we must ignore a great deal else we have been told; or in other words misrepresent the book."

15 Fletcher, *The Novels*, 14.

represents control, not liberation. Besides, the freedom that is indicated seems to be clothed in references to former dreams of the freedom in casting off the cloak of civilisation, as Nussbaum points out[16], and these references may be ironic.

In a way Molloy and Moran's respective goals for life after narration are not that different after all, in that both wish to finish their stories and their human lives. It is possible that Moran's voice is pointing to a real alternative to human life, but it is more likely that the state Moran desires will turn out to be death. Such an alternative life would, just like death, not be a communicable kind of existence, and viewed from the narrative, it would be as inaccessible as death. This wish to end life as we know it, and in particular life as producer of words, dominates the whole *Trilogy*, especially the last novel:

> Ah if only this voice could stop, this meaningless voice which prevents you from being nothing, just barely prevents you from being nothing and nowhere … . (U 374)

> [H]ow to understand, ... if it's I who speak, that I speak without ceasing, that I long to cease, that I can't cease … . (U 393)

The aim is primarily to stop this kind of life, not to gain any other life but the life of silence or emptiness. The only way to express the wish for a life outside of words is through words like 'silence', 'emptiness', and 'void'. The desire is for something we do not know, something that is neither imaginable nor understandable, since we have no experience of it. These words are associated with the feeling of the sublime, at least in Kant's conception of it[17].

Molloy consists of two stories; both narrated by some man sitting in a room desiring to end a story he has to write. Their aim is more to end the pain of existence, the pain of speaking or writing, than to achieve something in particular within this existence. The desire of the narrators to end the life of writing is as bereft of any positive aim as are the journeys described in their stories. Both Molloy and Moran has a goal for the journey, but their stories provide us with no understandable reason for seeking these particular goals rather than some other. Both feel obligated to pursue their goals; Molloy due to a never clearly defined

---

16 See p. 41 f.

17 In a lengthy footnote to his pre-critical *Beobachtungen über das Gefühl des Schönen und Erhabenen*, Kant cites example of the sublime from a dream in a story he found in Bremen magazine: "Als ich mich dem äußersten Ende der Natur näherte, merkte ich, daß die Schatten des grenzenlosen Leeren sich in die Tiefe vor mich herabsenkten. Ein fürchterliches Reich von ewiger Stille, Einsamkeit und Finsterniß!" (B 209 f).

(and negated) need, and Moran by orders from his employer, but that does not explain the *reason* for seeking out this or that particular goal[18].

When they reach their respective destinations, they do not know what to do there. They might as well not reach their goals, which in fact neither of them do (although Molloy believes he has reached his mother's room - but he can be any other place, neither he nor his reader would know the difference). Both stories deal with a man writing a story about a quest lacking any coherent, stated reason, and both narrators just aim to finish off the writing, i.e. ending the story. What all the four goals described in *Molloy* have in common, is that they appear meaningless.

Three forms of meaninglessness

Calling an action or a whole life meaningless is based on a wide sense of the word 'meaning'. In relation to this novel three different ways of using the word can be distinguished:

1) If we assume that human action is not mere happening, physical or mental, but that it is intentional, i.e. a movement or an utterance with a purpose, then Molloy's story consists of a series of meaningless acts. There is no answer to the questions of why he did this rather than something else.

2) In the same way a whole human life or a larger portion of it can be said to have meaning in that it is directed at some general purpose or that there are some higher-order goals or ideals giving purpose to that person's actions, thoughts, and utterances. This sense of the word is related to what Williams calls having a ground project:

> [M]y present projects are the condition of my existence, in the sense that unless I am propelled forward by the conatus of desire, project and interest, it is unclear why I should go on at all … . A man may have, for a lot of his life or even just for some part of it, a *ground* project or set of projects which are closely related to his existence and which to a significant degree give meaning to his life.[19]

Molloy and Moran lead lives that are in this sense meaningless.

3) Underlying these two forms of meaninglessness in this novel, there is also the loss of semantic meaning. The narrators and characters of the *Trilogy* in many

---

18 Professional duties require no additional reason beyond being duties, one may argue. But Moran's story leaves the reasons of his employer meaningless when his assignment is annulled after his transformation into a Molloy-like figure.

19 B. Williams, *Moral Luck*, 12.

cases seem to fail to understand both the words they and other people utter, the feelings they have, and sometimes even their own perceptions. When words lose meaning, there can be no meaningful actions or ground projects giving life meaning either.

Meaninglessness and ethics

It used to be common to read Beckett's prose as making a general claim of the meaninglessness of all human existence:

> The absurdity of the world and the meaninglessness of our condition are conveyed in an absurd and deliberately insignificant fashion: never did anybody dare so openly to insult everything which man holds as certain, up to and including this language which he could at least lean upon to scream his doubt and despair.[20]

Even those who emphasise that "Beckett does not concern himself with abstract and general verities" and that "no universal lessons, no meanings, no philosophical truths could possibly be derived from the work", find his stories to constitute an exploration "into the nature of human existence itself"[21]. There is a certain existentialist ring to such statements, but although the *Trilogy*, along with other central works by Beckett, was written in a Paris dominated by existentialist thought, there are problems with this, once popular, labelling[22]. There are affinities between this perspective on *Molloy* and the philosophy espoused by the Paris existentialists in viewing human existence as devoid of essential meaning, but this is merely a superficial similarity.

The existentialism of Sartre, as presented in *Existentialism & Humanism*, finds in man's abandonment through the non-existence of God, not merely meaninglessness, but a demand to create meaning and values, i.e. an elevated responsibility for his own actions[23]. Because there are no ready-made values anywhere, we are obligated to create values and, thus, give meaning to our lives. This is expressed in the slogan: "Existence before essence". In describing particular humans struggling with a personal void of meaninglessness, Beckett

---

20 M. Nadeau, 'Critique in "Combat"', 53.
21 M. Esslin, 'Introduction', 4.
22 Ibid. 4 ff.
23 J.-P. Sartre, *Existentialism & Humanism,* 32 ff.

avoids the general claims found in this version of existentialism[24]. In his interpretation of *Endgame*, Adorno rejects the relevance of existentialist philosophy for Beckett's work:

> Waren bei Kafka die Bedeutungen geköpft oder verwirrt, so ruft Beckett der schlechten Unendlichkeit der Intentionen Halt zu: ihr Sinn sei Sinnlosigkeit. Das ist objektiv, ohne alle polemische Absicht, sein Bescheid an die Existentialphilosophie, welche Sinnlosigkeit selber, unterm Namen von Geworfenheit und später Absurdität, im Schutz der Äquivokationen des Sinnbegriffs zum Sinn verklärt. Beckett setzt ihm keine Weltanschauung entgegen, sondern nimmt ihn beim Wort.[25]

Sartre finds a demand to create values and meaning when confronted with existence as not meaningful, whereas we find no such obligation to, nor any attempt at giving meaning to life in *Molloy*. There is a felt obligation to finish writing, but is that conceived to be a meaningful occupation? It is as meaningless as the other activities the characters of the novel engage in.

Moran's life prior to the journey is admittedly not a life experienced as meaningless, but the description of his hypocritical religion, how he uses 'principles' for subduing his son and his house maid, and his pedantic obsession with detail, reveal a life arguably as devoid of meaning as the one led by Molloy in his aimless wanderings. That is due to the discrepancy between his words and his deeds. And this appears to be Moran's conclusion, too, as he lets himself disintegrate and refuses to return to his former way of life. Beckett's characters experience the lack of meaning that was proclaimed by the existentialists to be the basic human experience, but they do not conclude that there is any obligation to create meaning. They do not even come up with a consistent set of values, which was an important consequence of the acceptance of 'abandonment' in Sartre's view. On the contrary; Moran murders a man without reason (M 151 f) and Molloy attempts the same (M 84), and they certainly see nothing wrong in their acts[26].

Molloy cannot be read as a successful application of existentialist philosophy both because the stories negate the obligation to create meaning, and because it is difficult to justify the claim that the narrators and characters of the novel represent

---

24 The literature written by existentialists as Sartre and Camus is closer to the kind of meaninglessness explored by Beckett. My main aim in this discussion is not to attack this philosophy, but merely point out that Beckett's characters and the style in his novels contradicts reading his novels as expressing an existentialist point of view.

25 T. W. Adorno, *Noten zur Literatur*, 293.

26 The description of meaningless lives can have a moral function, though, in creating in the reader a reflection on the meaning of his own life. This is probably the way Beckett was read by those who found his works to be existentialist. I return to that possibility below.

humans as such. We are not warranted in claiming general validity for the experiences of life suffered by these people. This is made even clearer by the kind of persons Beckett deals with. Neither Molloy nor Moran in the later part of the story can be regarded as representatives of humanity as such. Their experiences, their choices, their relationships with others are not familiar for most of us. Unlike the heroes of Sartre and Camus, it is difficult to identify with the main characters of Beckett's novel, although we certainly recognise them as humans living conceivable lives[27]. We might even think that we have seen or talked to one of Molloy's spiritual brothers in one of the tramps living on the outskirts of society. But the fact that he exists on the border of society only serves to emphasise that he cannot be representative of everyman. We need not take Beckett to describe human life as meaningless; he is only exploring a particular kind of human experience. I do not say that Beckett by that claims 'normal' human life to be meaningful as opposed to the life on the edge of society; the description of Moran's pre-journey life leaves little room for such claims. Still it can be claimed that one main reason for the attraction of this novel (as well as of other works by Beckett) lies in these characters; familiar and alien at the same time.

But a story about existence on the border of what is considered human life can still be relevant to human life as such. The narrated experiences of Molloy and Moran can give the background for an argument to the extent that normal human life has no meaning or, at least, that conventional moral claims are illusory. Moran represents a perverted picture of common hypocritical morality, and his falling apart could be seen as a change from an inauthentic conventionalism to an existence facing the truth of human life as devoid of values and meaning. Likewise, Molloy encounters the accepted morality on his journey in encounters with the law (M 20 ff), with a mob after running over a dog (M 32 f), and during his stay at Lousse's house (M 34 ff). Seen from the outside of society, Molloy's nihilism appears healthier and more in keeping with the life he leads than the reactions of the authorities and citizens.

Seeing society through Molloy's eyes give us an outsider perspective enabling us to assess the conventions we live by[28]. We find this view ironically expressed in one of Molloy's reflections on his own role in society:

---

27 The act of reading narrative probably requires *some* identification with the narrator, regardless of his unfamiliarity. But Molloy is not familiar as we find Roquetin in Sartre's *The Nausea* to be.

28 This view is related to Bataille's argument, see p. 48 f., but Bataille is more concerned with the sublime attraction we feel to Molloy. His argument is primarily concerned with the aesthetics of *Molloy*, whereas the position suggested here is ethical.

> And if I have always behaved like a pig, the fault lies not with me but with my superiors, who corrected me only on points of detail instead of showing me the essence of the system, after the manner of the great English schools, and the guiding principles of good manners, and how to proceed, without going wrong, from the former to the latter, and how to trace back to its ultimate source a given comportment. (M 25)

This perspective that can be read out of the stories of Moran and Molloy, does not claim meaninglessness to human life as such, nor does it point out an alternative way of life to the conventional life of adhering to the established norms of society. It merely presents normal life as absurd by viewing it from an outside we do not know by experience, but one we can accept as a possible human life. Thus, there are no general arguments to be found, only a questioning of the accepted meaning as to how one should lead life. Through the stories of two meaningless journeys, narrated by the travellers themselves, the question is posed to the reader whether the lives we are familiar with are any more meaningful than the ones put forward in these two fables.

This is one possible ethical argument to be extracted from *Molloy*, and I believe it can be developed into an interesting position on the problem of nihilism. As such, it is in the tradition of Dostoevsky's literary treatment of this challenge to established morality. Beckett's story is set in a world abandoned by the God that was Dostoevsky's answer to nihilism[29], and religion is only part of the conventions rendered meaningless by Moran's irony over his abandoned religious belief ("How much longer are we to hang about waiting for the antechrist [*sic*]?" (M 167)). Although the problem of facing the apparent meaninglessness of human life is one significant line of interpretation of this novel, there are several other ways this work can be morally significant. Before closing in on how this work evokes the feeling of the sublime, I will discuss Nussbaum's interpretation of the work in connection with her project of incorporating literature into discussions of ethical problems.

1.2 Molloy *and ethical literary theory*

Nussbaum's project

Nussbaum argues for an Aristotelian conception of ethics, where the basic question is: "How should one live?" rather than more restricted ones such as

[29] F. Dostoevsky, The Karamazov Brothers.

"What is my duty towards myself and others?" The answer to the wider question will be informed by our conception of the good life for human beings, which will be one of many conceptions put forward in public discourse. We can draw on several kinds of sources in the open-ended search that is ethical discourse, and Nussbaum claims that some works of literature are important sources. Her point of departure in arguing for the ethical significance of fictional literature is the statement "Literary form is not separable from philosophical content, but is, itself, a part of content ..."[30]. When one is expressing a view of life, this view is, according to Nussbaum, not always independent of the way it is presented:

> Life is never simply *presented*; it is always *represented as* something. This "as" can, and must, be seen not only in the paraphrasable content, but also in the style, which itself expresses choices and selections, and sets up, in the reader, certain activities and transactions rather than others.[31]

Thus, an essay written in the abstract style typical of analytic philosophy will necessarily express something different from a literary text (including at least all fictional or semi-fictional texts) even if the aim of the essay is to reproduce the content of this text in the most accurate way. But what does that difference amount to, and why is there such a difference? The basis for this alleged difference is, according to Nussbaum, found in some claims as to what is important in human life.

The first of these claims holds that emotions are not senseless, immediate and uncontrollable responses, but have an unique cognitive function, and what we learn through our emotional response to phenomena cannot be translated into pure conceptual thought without loss[32]. Emotions are especially important as sources of ethical knowledge, because they give us a way to understand what is valued in life. If I tell myself that my parents do not matter more to me than any other person I meet, my emotions in relating to my parents will show me to be wrong (or, as is the case for some people, right).

It does not, however, follow from Nussbaum's argument that in my presentation of her position on the role of emotions in acquiring ethical knowledge, the message is negated by the abstract discursive style I am using. A text claiming emotions to be of inescapable value in understanding human life need not support that argument through its form[33], because that claim can be a

---

30 Nussbaum, *Love's Knowledge*, 3.

31 Ibid. 5.

32 Ibid. 41 f.

33 Nussbaum seems to claim just that, though: "An article, for example argues that the emotions are essential and central in our efforts to gain understanding of any ethical

statement primarily directed at intellectual understanding in the strict sense. But the argument would be in need of specification in the form of concrete examples to be understood as a proposition valid for me and other readers, and not as an empty claim. In such examples, using the same abstract language would be to let the form carry a different message from the content. The same would be the case if one were discussing any particular ethical problem, given that one ascribed such ethical significance to emotions. A suitable form for such an exemplification or discussion would, as Nussbaum claims, probably involve a presentation usually associated with fictional literature rather than philosophy. Several places during her argument, Nussbaum utilises a narrative style, which demonstrates her point about the importance of form in discussing ethical subjects[34].

The statement that emotions have a cognitive function does not imply the claim that they are infallible sources of knowledge[35]; it merely means that they, together with our conceptual beliefs, contribute to our overall conception of life. Nussbaum is not the only contemporary philosopher making this claim[36], and the argumentative support for the assertion is convincing. More important is her claim that drawing on fictional literature is one way these emotional aspects of our knowledge can be involved in philosophical discussions because the form of such works can express emotions.

There are different genres within literature; each having more or less particular formal requirements, which means that not all literature is of relevance. We cannot claim all literature to be a perfect marriage between form and paraphrasable content, either. How do we pick out the works relevant for some particular problem? Nussbaum holds that the choice depends on our interests or preoccupations. We choose particular texts that we find to deal with the questions we are trying to answer, and that do it in a way we think contributes to this attempt[37]. In this respect our choice of literature does not differ from the way we choose relevant philosophical literature for discussion. If we can read an interesting argument out of a novel, or it describes a complex situation dealing with the problem under discussion, it is relevant.

---

matter; and yet it is written in a style that expresses only intellectual activity and strongly suggests that only this activity matters for the reader in his or her attempts to understand." (Ibid. 21) But the style of ethical writing is not so much an ethical matter as a literary matter, and it is not obvious that arguments on style should be presented in an emotional form.

34 E.g. ibid. 11 f.

35 Ibid. 41.

36 See R. Nozick, *The Examined Life*, 87 ff.

37 Nussbaum, *Love's Knowledge*, 45 f.

Another important reason for using literary work in philosophical investigations is found in the claim that in ethical questions, moral perception is of greater importance than application of abstract principles. By perception, Nussbaum means "the ability to discern, acutely and responsively the salient features of one's particular situation"[38]. She argues that since ethical choices are made in concrete situations, general principles are insufficient due to the complexities of the context, containing morally relevant features particular to that situation. The particular situations often contain features that are new and not anticipated in general rules. What is called for is practical wisdom, what Aristotle calls *phronesis*, which, of course, requires education in general rules, but even more practice and learning by example from persons who are wise, who have developed moral perception.

This Aristotelian emphasis on the particular in moral judgement represents no rejection of the principle of universal validity of moral decisions, according to Nussbaum. But as the contexts of moral decisions seldom are exactly similar, the judgement on the right action in one situation can only contribute 'rules of thumb'. These principles can become part of the basis for reasoning from analogy as in casuistry[39], rather than supplying general principles directly applicable in later circumstances. Nussbaum also argues that the traditional Kantian or utilitarian moral philosophies will have problems in dealing adequately with this aspect of the ethical in their discussion due to the preoccupation with rules and principles within these traditions. What is needed to supply the general principles found in rules of thumb and paradigmatic cases is the development of moral perception. But that is done through learning by experience, which requires

> the cultivation of perception and responsiveness: the ability to read a situation, singling out what is relevant for thought and action. This active task is not a technique; one learns it by guidance rather than by formula. [Henry] James plausibly suggests that novels exemplify and offer such learning: exemplify it in the efforts of the characters and the author, engender it in the reader by setting up a similarly complex activity.[40]

Novels (and other literary texts) are more suitable than constructed examples (which is the common way of illustrating moral problems in philosophy), because they bring forth the complexities of situations, and make room for emotions as an

---

38 Ibid. 37.

39 A discussion of the Aristotelian basis of the casuistic tradition of the Catholic Church and an argument for the revitalisation of a reconstructed casuistry can be found in A. Jonsen and S. Toulmin, *The Abuse of Casuistry*. See in particular pp. 24-74 for the Aristotelian connection.

40 Nussbaum, *Love's Knowledge*, 44.

integrated part of understanding and deliberation. Many novels are in some ways more informative and valuable than observing real life because they are "giving the reader experience that is deeper, sharper, and more precise than much of what takes place in life"[41]. Suitable literature at its best can function both 'educational' and be good examples just because of its refined complexity of form.

Nussbaum, Kant, and the separation of aesthetics and ethics

Harpham says that Nussbaum's project joins ethical and aesthetic perspectives on literature[42]. That may be correct, depending on what one takes 'aesthetic' to mean. Nussbaum's aim is first and foremost the "literary-ethical inquiry"[43] which means an ethical approach to literary texts, without reducing this approach to a question of finding a moral content regardless of formal aspects of the work. In developing her project, Nussbaum reaches back to the ancient Greeks by fusing aesthetics and ethics as integrated parts of the pursuit of the question about how humans should live:

> The idea that art existed only for art's sake, and that literature should be approached with a detached aesthetic attitude, pure of practical interest, was an idea unknown in the Greek world, at least until the Hellenistic age. Art was thought to be practical, aesthetic interest a practical interest - an interest in the good life and in communal self-understanding.[44]

In reviving that project, she is at the same time rejecting the strict division between ethics and aesthetics[45] as regards this project. She envisions a future where "literary theory (while not forgetting its many other pursuits) will also join with ethical theory in pursuit of the question 'How should one live?'"[46] If the 'aesthetic perspective' is the same as the perspective of literary theory, then Nussbaum does join these perspectives.

Nussbaum's main concern is with literature as part of moral philosophy, and she relates to literature from that specific angle. She does not, however, argue that literary theory in general should be subordinated to ethical theory, since she says

---

41 Ibid. 48.
42 G. Galt Harpham, *Getting It Right*, 159.
43 Nussbaum, *Love's Knowledge*, 173.
44 Ibid. 16.
45 Even epistemology must in some way be included in her project as we can see from her position on realism, ibid. 223 ff.
46 Ibid. 168.

that literary theory has other pursuits. Nussbaum does not give examples of these pursuits, beyond the following general description:

> We do approach literature for play and delight, for the exhilaration of following the dance of form and unraveling webs of textual connection. (Though even here I would not be quick to grant that there is any coherence to an account of aesthetic pleasure that abstracts altogether from our practical human interests and desires.)[47]

There is room for taking pleasure in the text without seeing this pleasure as part of the ethical appreciation of the work. It should be added that taking pleasure in formal features as described here, is not the same as the disinterested pleasure of beauty that Kant held to be a subjective condition of cognition in general (KU§9, 217).

In the parenthesis in the quote above, Nussbaum questions the coherence of an account of a disinterested aesthetic pleasure in art. The notion of aesthetic judgement as based on a disinterested pleasure is one of the central ideas in Kant's third Critique (KU§2, 204 f), and plays a key role in the approach I am developing in the following chapters. I will argue that the aesthetic judgement of the sublime is an important aspect of the ethical significance of a work such as *Molloy*, and a presupposition of this ethical import is that the feeling of the sublime is disinterested. My interpretation of the Kantian account attempts to show that it is coherent. At this point I will only point out that despite Nussbaum's questioning of the coherence of a disinterested aesthetic pleasure, her approach does not rule out the possibility of a disinterested appreciation of art. Since my aim is to show that the ethical import of the sublime is a supplement to the ethical interpretation developed by Nussbaum, it is important that there is room for a supplement of this kind.

Nussbaum's application of literature to ethics faces a problem following from her acceptance of the legitimacy of non-ethical literary theory, and the fact that these non-ethical ways of judging the text are value-judgements, namely how to deal with conflicts between interpretations based on ethical and non-ethical values. If there is room for reading books or watching movies just for the pleasure we take in their formal qualities, can we do so even if the work is ethically questionable, i.e. that its answer to the ethical question is one that the reader finds unacceptable? Supposing that the moral question is the same in both literature and film, Quentin Tarantino's movie *Pulp Fiction* is a suitable example. In this movie, torture and accidental murders are presented in a way that makes the audience laugh rather

---

[47] Ibid. 171.

than experience these acts as ethically wrong. Still a number of critics praised the movie for its formal and aesthetic qualities. Can this positive assessment of the movie be legitimate; disregarding as it does the ethical influence it has by making these scenes merely entertaining?

If we accept that evaluation of works of art is not necessarily subordinated to ethical concerns, there must be room for this kind of assessment. The main reason for praising this movie probably lies in "the exhilaration of following the dance of form and unraveling webs of textual connections" as Nussbaum puts it. How can these two kinds of assessments be combined when the one is not subordinated to the other? The pleasure in the formal aspects of the art work becomes a value on par with the ethical value of the work.

This is a case of what Nussbaum calls noncommensurable values[48]. Her Aristotelian view admits that the ethical life involves choices between goods that cannot be measured in a common value, and that choosing one good can mean rejecting some other good worth pursuing in its own right. But when we choose between these goods they still all fall under the common pursuit of the good life for human beings. All these goods are parts in a conception of how to live life, and as such the choice we undertake is between elements belonging to the same supreme goal.

Evaluating the formal features of a work of art cannot be classified as looking for an answer to the question "How should one live?", although arguing for this value is an answer to this question. Thus deciding to disregard the ethical world view of the art work and how this affects the audience is in itself an ethical choice, as is argued by Mooji[49]. The consequence is that deciding to spend time on art is an answer to the ethical question, deciding to focus on its ethical significance is an answer to the same question, and the ethical significance of the art work itself is brought out by regarding it as an answer to this same ethical question.

Still, one may get the impression that there is another "primacy of ethics" in Nussbaum's project, namely that the ethical literary theory should trump the non-ethical when there is a conflict. In W. Booth's related ethical criticism this is an implicit claim. He claims that the sexist views of Rabelais made him reevaluate his judgement of him as a great novelist[50]. This prior judgement was based on a formal assessment, so the ethical criticism affected his formal appreciation of the work. In her discussion of Booth's book, Nussbaum cites this reevaluation of

48 Ibid. 56 ff.
49 J. J. Mooji, 'Literature and Morality', 105 f.
50 Booth, *Company*, 403 ff.

Rabelais, apparently with approval[51]. Thus aesthetic (in a wide sense) and ethical approaches are not on an equal footing as assessments of literature. Studying aesthetic features independently of the ethical question is not an equal (or even primary) source of appreciation of the work, and it thus loses the force of being a genuine alternative to the ethical interpretation.

I believe Booth and Nussbaum to be right in their more or less implicit argument for the primacy of ethical (in this wide, Aristotelian sense of the word) criticism. Fiction affects us in one way or another, and being aware of these effects is the only way to avoid being influenced without being aware of it. Since their respective approaches to literature are sophisticated enough to avoid moralising, this is not problematic. One can still enjoy the humour and formal mastery of Rabelais, but be aware of how these features contribute to a denigration of women.

Another problem concerning the combination of Kant's theory of the moral significance of pure aesthetic judgements with Nussbaum's project can be raised on the ethical side. Kant holds that a disinterested sublime pleasure in nature or a work of art affects our view of the world as well, and can be ethically significant. This ethical aspect in a work of art cannot be brought out in a Nussbaumian ethical interpretation, because it is part of the aesthetic appreciation of the work of art, and cannot be read as answer to the ethical question. Moreover, it is not an aspect of the text as narrative, but as a work of art. The Kantian analysis of aesthetics becomes one of the other pursuits of literary theory, and cannot become part of Nussbaum's ethical inquiry, regardless of any ethical significance that can be claimed for this approach to literature.

The possibility that aesthetic judgements have ethical import is based both in Kant's aesthetic and his ethical theory. Nussbaum is critical of Kant's position on ethics, on the grounds that the Kantian theory separates moral duties from other human pursuits. She claims her approach to include the possibility of non-Aristotelian answers to her questions, including Kantian ones, but her description of the Kantian position, through an interpretation of H. James' *The Ambassadors*, leaves it unattractive:

> To the noble and autonomous agent, nature has, and should have, no power to jolt or surprise, and also no power to inspire delight or passionate wonder. ... What seems like insensibility in the women of Woollett is, from their point of view, the high determination to treat each other person as an autonomous moral will, relating to them through the moral faculties and judging them with a stringency that shows respect for their freedom. Any note of tenderness would compromise this moral relation. ... Mrs. Newsome is no mere caricature, but a

---

51 Nussbaum, *Love's Knowledge*, 235.

> brilliantly comic rendering of some of the deepest and most appealing features of Kantian morality … .[52]

Contrary to Nussbaum I think there are good reasons not to claim this to be the "most appealing features of Kantian morality"; it gives an uncharitable picture of his theory. In Kant's third Critique, nature certainly both jolts and surprises the agent, and is the prime source of the feeling of beauty as will be shown in the second chapter of this thesis. Likewise, believing that respect and tenderness contradict each other also is contrary to the Kantian position, a position that accepts love as a natural attraction between people without making it part of morality in the strict sense (MS 406 f), and discusses sympathy both as a natural feeling and a conditional duty (MS 456 f).

Contradicting Nussbaum's version is also Kant's discussion of friendship as being concerned with finding the balance between involvement and distance, showing an awareness of the need for close ties as well as the problems involved in blind trust (MS 469 ff). Nussbaum's rejection of the Kantian position on morality is not based on arguments against Kant's theory, but on arguments against a simplified and prejudiced presentation of a "Kantian" character in a novel. One does not do justice to Kant's moral theory by creating a hero obsessed with morality, who dislikes and avoids emotions[53], and cannot be marked by life[54]. This misrepresentation of Kant is of course only Nussbaum's responsibility, and not due to James' novel. Nussbaum is the one associating this coldness, detachment and moralism depicted in the novel with Kant[55].

Nussbaum states there are other valid ways to approach literature besides regarding it to be an answer to the ethical question. We can conclude that a one-sided view of literature should be avoided, on behalf of an acceptance of the complex character of fictional narratives as: i) works of art, i.e. objects for disinterested aesthetic judgement ii) formal structures, i.e. objects of formal criticism like structuralism and related approaches, iii) sources of influence on how we judge characters and actions, i.e. objects of ethical criticism, iv) paradigmatic stories of action and events similar to the ones we perform or encounter in our

52 Ibid. 178.

53 Language is treacherous; like and dislike are emotional reactions, which shows the inconsistency of this misunderstood Kantianism.

54 Ibid. 177.

55 The assumption that a rigid, rule-following literary character is a good example of a Kantian personality is not uncommon. See Baron's criticism of Julia Annas' use of literature in M. Baron, 'Was Effie Briest a Victim of Kantian Morality?'. Baron argues that what Annas takes to be a person acting on Kantian principles is better seen as a judgmental person acting on the wrong kind of principles.

lives, i.e. models for moral perception, v) concealed philosophical arguments; ethical, political, or epistemological, vi) entertainment, and vii) sources of imaginative escape from everyday life and its demands (including moral demands). The points ii) - v) are drawn from the books of Nussbaum and Booth, and I have added perspectives suggested by Kant (i) and Rushdie[56] (vii). There probably are other perspectives worth applying to narratives as well, so this is an open-ended list. One can choose one or more of these lines of interpretation, but must bear in mind other possible interpretative keys as well. If not, one risks advancing an interpretation of the text that is shown to be inadequate when regarded in a more comprehensive view. Although Nussbaum's interpretation of *Molloy* discloses interesting philosophical arguments, I believe her account shows the necessity of reflection on other perspectives as well.

Guilt, shame and love in *Molloy*

Nussbaum's integration of literature in ethical discourse is not limited to works that support and expand on her basic views of human life. When discussing Beckett's *Trilogy*, she does it in order to introduce serious objections to her own view on the relation between moral knowledge and stories. As referred above, the stories in Beckett's *Molloy* are first-person narratives, and also in *Malone Dies* and *The Unnamable* we encounter stories and reflections in the first person, but with growing doubt throughout the *Trilogy* as to whether the voice belongs to the "I" speaking or there are some others ("they") speaking through the narrator (U 389)[57]. Even the existence of the narrator gets more uncertain during the last novel, fittingly named *The Unnamable*: "if only I knew if I've lived, if I live, if I'll live, that would simplify everything." (U 417) At the same time this narrator identifies himself both as Molloy and as Malone, giving the impression that their stories are told by him, the one who doubts his existence and possession of the voice. Thus we are presented with the possibility of an infinite regress of narrators of increasingly uneventful and minimal stories, ending in murmurs and, finally, silence. Putting an end to the speech and terminating the existence of stories and words is the professed goal of all the narrators of the *Trilogy*.

---

[56] S. Rushdie, *Is Nothing Sacred*, The Herbert Read Memorial Lecture, February 6, 1990. My source is Mooji, 'Literature and Morality', 104 f.

[57] This problem of the "I"can be read psychoanalytically, as Nussbaum does, or it can be regarded a part of the post-Cartesian discussion concerning the status of the subject, as is done in Adorno, *Noten*, 293 f.

This doubt as to the existence and identity of the narrators is the basis for Nussbaum's claim that the voices in the *Trilogy* all hold the position that

> emotions are not feelings that well up in some natural and untutored way from our natural selves, that they are, in fact, not personal or natural at all, that they are, instead, contrivances, social constructs. ... We learn emotions in the same way that we learn our beliefs - from our society.[58]

And the way we learn them is, first and foremost, through stories. That is in keeping with the view of Nussbaum (as well as many other contemporary philosophers involved in revitalising Aristotelian ethics) on the relationship between narratives, the shaping of character, and emotions. Unlike the basically positive assessment of emotions in the Aristotelian approach, the feelings that dominate the stories of Beckett's narrators are negative ones like guilt, fear and disgust. This is the reason that the narrators want to end the story-telling life. The wish to end the narratives is, according to Nussbaum, based on the assumption that stories teach us emotions that cause suffering, and that there is a positive hope in breaking off the chain of stories that form human existence as we know it:

> If stories are learned, they can be unlearned. If emotions are constructs, they can be dismantled. And perhaps the silence onto which this deconstructive project opens is an opening or clearing in which human beings and animals can recognize one another without and apart from the stories and their guilt. And perhaps, too, the longing for that silence is itself an emotion of and inside the stories. Perhaps the negative project is a happy-ending story trapped, itself, inside the very thing it opposes.[59]

Opposing the Aristotelian moderate optimism concerning our lives, emotions, and narrative texts, Beckett's voices present a bleak picture in which these stories are the main sources of human suffering, and the aim is writing oneself out of this narrative-guided guilt and pain.

Nussbaum regards this to be a basic challenge to her project of incorporating literature into the search for the good life. If story-telling as such teaches us a life of constructed emotions, sources only of suffering and pain, these stories must be excised from human life, and the life we strive for must be one purged of such influences. One can ask whether that is possible, given that it is taken for granted that self-understanding has a narrative structure[60]. If stories are constitutive of human understanding, then it appears as if any meaningful claim affirms this narrative basis. If we accept Nussbaum's reading of the claims underlying these

---

58 Nussbaum, *Love's Knowledge*, 287.
59 Ibid. 288.
60 An extended argument for this view is found in MacIntyre, *After Virtue*, 216 ff.

narratives, we see that the wish to end the life of story-telling is, and perhaps must be, expressed within a narrative. Nussbaum's interpretation may appear weakened by the fact that the arguments against narratives she reads into *Molloy* are themselves presented narratively, and, hence, seem to affirm the form they oppose.

On the other hand, there is a more sophisticated argument saying that a dominant way of perceiving the world can only be shown inadequate through its own form, and I believe that this is Nussbaum's position. Her use of the words "deconstructive project" in describing the argument of the Beckettian voices supports this interpretation of her argument, in that deconstruction is associated with the idea of showing the inadequacy of a way of thinking through its own language and argumentation[61].

Nussbaum points to a tradition of accepting emotions as connected to value beliefs, but regarding these beliefs as "both false and in other ways pernicious" and causing only suffering[62]. She places the Beckettian argument within this tradition associated primarily with Stoicism, adding that the voices of Beckett regard stories as the most important source for education about these emotions. And the fact that stories do not deliver emotions one by one, categorised and separated, but rather intermingled with each other, showing their interdependence and immersion in particular lives, makes stories particularly useful in arguments concerning the role of emotions in human life. This is clearly expressed in a sentence in *Molloy*, crucial to Nussbaum's interpretation:

> It is in the tranquility of decomposition that I recall the long confused emotion which was my life, and that I judge it, as it is said that God will judge me, and with no less impertinence. (M 25)

Molloy here equates his life with one emotion, not even a cluster of emotions, showing how emotion and story, for him, are inseparable. According to Nussbaum, Beckett's voices are presenting arguments concerning both the close relations between stories and constructing emotions, and the ultimate destructiveness of these emotions.

She also finds support for her interpretation in Moran's reflections on the Molloy he carries an inner picture of, because she claims Moran's search to be one "for and through his own insides", making it "more than usually apparent that the story of this novel is the story of emotions"[63]. Now, exactly where Moran makes

---

61 "The goal of deconstruction, therefore, is to locate a point of otherness within philosophical or logocentric conceptuality and then to deconstruct this conceptuality from that position of alterity." S. Critchley, *The Ethics of Deconstruction*, 26.

62 Nussbaum, *Love's Knowledge*, 293.

63 Ibid. 297.

this alleged claim about his search is difficult to discover; on the page referred to, he reflects on his knowledge of Molloy prior to the assignment, not the actual search for him. *This* reflection is an inner search (in some sense), but he emphasises that between this inner Molloy and the Molloy he was trying to hunt down, "the resemblance cannot have been great" (M 115), thus separating the reflection on his inner images from the actual search. Besides, the inner images Moran is reflecting on are not cognitive emotions, but uncontrolled outbursts, foreign to Moran's conception of the world. He describes it as if he were possessed:

> This was how he came to me, at long intervals. Then I was nothing but uproar, bulk, rage, suffocation, effort unceasing, frenzied, and vain. Just the opposite of myself, in fact. It was a change. (M 114)

And the Molloy we know from the first narrative, certainly differs from Moran's inner picture of him, making his description of several Molloys, one of which is the real one, to the point. The inner search and the search "over hill and dale" (M 115) are not the same.

Thus, Nussbaum contradicts the text in one of its least ambiguous passages, making her subsequent argument weak due to this failing in establishing the premises. Her interpretation of the text as an inner journey of a geography of emotions draws further support from the obscenities in the names given to Molloy's country and towns: Turdy, Hole, and Bally, making the emotions shame and guilt due to the filthiness of life the central theme. Now these names might as well be seen as ironic jokes or even provocations, especially when combined with religious images as when Moran invents the Turdy Madonna as a pilgrimage goal (M 174). The names do not add to the shame, they diminish and ridicule it by humour[64]. Disregarding this use of ironic form weakens Nussbaum's interpretation.

Molloy's reflections on love and conception, and his search for his mother's room, combined with religious imagery of the absent, commanding, and perhaps

---

[64] Critchley, *Very Little*, 202, note 49 says that Nussbaum is "swallowing Beckett's psychoanalytic red herrings whole and with some sauce". The implication is that the author is deliberately confusing the reader by providing misleading interpretational signals. I am arguing for a different understanding of Beckett's psychoanalytic references. If the main focus of this work is the question of meaning, then these psychoanalytic references serve a function similar to the philosophical and religious references, in being patterns of meaning undermined by the narrative. They do not mislead the reader.

forgiving chief of Moran's organisation (Youdi[65]), inspire Nussbaum's overall interpretation of the work:

> We could summarize the emotion story that is Molloy's life by saying that it is the story of original sin, of the fear of God's judgement, and of the vain longing for salvation.[66]

The voices of Molloy and Moran tell stories of a Christian set of emotions concerning the literally filthy sin of sex, filthy because the genitalia are covered in excrements and the act of love is a dirty union of partly disabled and ugly persons. This picture is of course reinforced by the hypocritical religious life of Moran, humiliating and terrorising his son, teaching him "horror of the body and its functions" (M 118).

Nussbaum sometimes moves too fast when gathering support for her reading of the novel:

> Molloy feels always, in this world, that he dwells in an "atmosphere of finality without end" (p. 111) and that he is a "contrivance" of this world, a role-player "playing my parts through the bitter end" (p. 114, 122). The substitution of "through the bitter end" for the expected "through to the bitter end" expresses his sense that all social parts are played out through filth.[67]

The first, and least, mistake Nussbaum makes in this passage is not acknowledging that these are Moran's feelings and reflections, not Molloy's. It is not *in* this world, but withdrawn from the "spray of phenomena" (M 110), i.e. the empirical world, he can feel the "finality without end". This sequence of the novel is, as we can see, rich in references to theoretical philosophy. "Finality without end" is of course Kant's famous description of the aesthetic judgement (KU§10, 220), a description connected to its disinterested character. And this is exactly the point of Moran's subsequent argument. Just because he is removed from the real

---

65 When Nussbaum equates Youdi's name with the judgement "You die", it is striking how that suggestion diverges from the actual narratives. Both Molloy and Moran are brought in by Youdi's men to write, not to die. There is no reasonable way to conceive of that assignment as punishment for original sin, and it certainly is not death. More plausible is the suggestion in R. Cohn, *The Comic Gamut*, 131 of "you" and "id", indicating the Freudian associations scattered throughout the novel. Nussbaum's interpretation is related to a psychoanalytical understanding of the *Trilogy*, but it is not sensitive to the possibility of these elements being parodistic, like the moral, philosophical, and religious elements. N. Frye, 'The Nightmare Life in Death', 21, suggests that "Youdi" invokes Yahweh and points to Moran's reference to his longing for "the Obidil" (M 162), anagram for the libido. Thus, Beckett hands us both the religious and psychoanalytical clues for symbolic interpretation. Given his irony, these clues might as well ridicule all such meaningful interpretations.

66 Nussbaum, *Love's Knowledge*, 298.

67 Ibid. 299.

world, he can get access to Molloy. “For where Molloy could not be, nor Moran either for that matter, there Moran could bend over Molloy” (M 112). He goes on to state that this inner examination most probably would be of no use for the actual search, further stressing the disinterested character of his withdrawn reflection. It is unclear how this passage supports Nussbaum’s interpretation, but it points to an important aspect of the *Trilogy* that could supplement or modify her psychological reading, namely its mockery of philosophical arguments and positions[68].

The philosophical and, in general, conceptual constraints on human existence are as important keys to the (self-undermining) argument of Beckett’s voices as the inherited emotional structures. If we overlook the philosophical connotations of this passage, we miss an important part of the message contained in the novel. My objections do not amount to a rejection of Nussbaum’s overall interpretation, but I will argue that not only the meaning conveyed through stories and emotions, but their own lives conceived as a constant production of meaning must be included as the target of these voices. In that connection, stories, religious practices and cognitive emotions are just parts adding to the wholesale rejection of the project of finding or creating meaning. I will return to this later.

When Moran describes himself as a contrivance, this can, admittedly, be read as a comment on how we are created through stories and inherited emotions. An interesting and probable alternative, however, is to take Moran at his word, and regard him as a construct, i.e. as a character in a novel rather than as a real life person. E. P. Levy argues that the narrator rather than the story is the focus of Beckett’s prose, and that this narrator turns out to be the same in all of the novels:

> [E]ach work is told by the same narrator whose reason for telling or trying to tell stories never varies. Finding this single narrator in the works preceding *The Unnamable* is not always easy for often, as in *Molloy* and *Malone Dies*, he hides behind the named personae through whom he seeks to express who he is.[69]

Support for this is found in the reference to characters and narrators of earlier Beckett-stories in *The Unnamable* where the narrator laments wasting time on these earlier characters instead of speaking of himself “in order to stop speaking” (U 305). When Moran calls himself a contrivance, his observation is a statement of the narrative reality. He is invented by the narrator to tell a story of a search for another contrivance, Molloy. The whole trilogy is told by one single narrator

68 “Beckett’s *ouevre* echoes and reechoes of the inconsistencies [of] western philosophical traditions from Zeno and Pythagoras to Wittgenstein and Sartre.” S. E. Gontarski, ‘Literary Allusions in Happy Days’, 309.

69 E. P. Levy, *Beckett & the Voice of Species*, 5.

inventing several narrators as his voices. These narrators occasionally comment on their stories, breaking the illusion of reality[70]. Thus it is reasonable to regard Moran's comment in this light rather than as a reference to a social constructionist view of identity.

The last passage cited from Nussbaum illustrates the problems concerning her interpretation of this work. She claims that the narrator combines the socially constructed emotions of love and guilt with excrement, and finds support for that interpretation when "to" is missing in an expected "through to the bitter end". But this absence is merely due to a misprint in the American Grove Press edition of the trilogy. In the British 1994 reprint of the 1959 J. Calder edition we find the conventional "through to the bitter end", rather than the sentence inviting Nussbaum's "All utterance, like birth, is anal."[71] The version found in the British edition apparently conforms best to the original French: "*J'allais assez volontiers jusqu'au bout de mes rôles*"[72], weakening Nussbaum's reading of it. In any case, she should have questioned her reading when regarding the sentence as a whole, since Moran says he "quite enjoyed playing his parts through ..." which is unlikely if those parts he is referring to are so repulsive. Moran is, after all, at that point in the story still the defender of conventional morality, and nowhere in his story do we find sexuality associated with excrement; that is one of Molloy's themes.

Nussbaum is not alone in her interpretation of the *Trilogy*, although P. Davies' related account connects these aspects of Beckett's story to Cartesian philosophy and Jungian psychology:

> There are two cycles, or to be more precise, one process seen in two different ways [in the *Trilogy*]. The first is the negative one which Beckett's people are in as they narrate: from sexuality arises the sin and pain of birth, and then during life the fear of engagement with further generative sexuality. ... Birth, relationships and language being felt as sinful or futile, the only refuge is death, oblivion, never having been. The second cycle is the one which the characters dimly remember and sometimes long for, the non-Cartesian one. Here they recall and glimpse now and then, a state where the circle was positive instead of negative and consisted of the primordial identity of I and not-I.[73]

---

70 Nussbaum acknowledges this one narrator speaking through his contraptions but without letting this acceptance influence her interpretation's focus on social construction of identity through stories. Nussbaum, *Love's Knowledge*, 308.

71 Ibid. 299.

72 I would like to thank Knut Stene Johansen for help in comparing the English and French versions of this part of *Molloy*.

73 P.Davies, 'Giving up the ghost to be born at last', 47 f.

Thus far we have seen Nussbaum's version of what Davies calls the first cycle. On the second one she is more restrained than Davies in giving it a positive expression, and I believe she is right in doing that. In affirming too strongly the possible (Jungian) esoteric content hinted at in the novels, Davies goes beyond what is stated in the text. As has been described many times in commentaries, Beckett's work is preoccupied with an experience of something inexpressible, but it is not altogether clear that this can be called "primordial Ipseity"[74] or any other mystical name. This problem is discussed below as belonging to the experience of the sublime.

There are parts of *Molloy* and the two later novels inviting a reading along the lines suggested by Nussbaum, but what is absent in her analysis (except for a small parenthesis) is an account of the black humour[75] involved in these descriptions. When Molloy suspects that his only sexual experience was anal, he is worried that it would not count as "true love" (M 57). Thus the author mocks the discrepancy between our concepts and the reality of everyday life. The relationship between Molloy and his unattractive lover is a parody of love; they meet in a rubbish dump, he gets paid for the love making which is described as troublesome and tiring, and the parody ends with his praise of this love:

> I never sought to repeat the experience, having I suppose the intuition that it had been unique and perfect, of its kind, achieved and inimitable, and that it behoved me to preserve it in my memory, pure of all pastiche, in my heart … . (M 58)

This parody of love is repeated and made even more extreme in the story of Macmann and Moll (MD 259 ff) where the discrepancy between the language of romantic love and the disgusting relationship is emphasised in the lovers' traditional love letters.

Considering this use of humour, I believe we are warranted in seeing the same kind of black and perhaps tragic humour in Molloy's confused relation to women and sexuality. The physical fact of the proximity between vagina and anus is the reason for Molloy's insecurity as to what hole children are born through, and his question whether the sexual act can be considered "true love" if it is not vaginal. This is but one aspect of Molloy's general confusion throughout the story in almost any situation, including the question of his own name and previous experiences, most clearly expressed through his habit of contradicting himself.

---

74 Ibid. 63.

75 Black humour is, according to Nadeau, 'Humor and the Void', 33-36, central in Beckett's project of producing "non-work".

One element in the confusion is his problem with understanding metaphorical language[76] and social conventions, exemplified in the absurd confrontation with the police sergeant (M 20 ff.). Molloy is responding to the literal meaning of the questions, missing the intended meaning: "So it always is when I am reduced to confabulation, I honestly believe I have answered the question I am asked and in reality I do nothing of the kind." The result of these misunderstandings is humorous in its tragic manner.

The problem for Molloy, then, is not the guilt associated with the dirtiness of being born from filthy sex, but his lack of comprehension of the meaning of the vocabulary he has learned. He is uncertain of the meaning of notions like "true love", "good manners", "values", "duty", and "fundamentals", and all such notions:

> Oh, they weren't notions like yours, they were notions like mine, all spasm, sweat and trembling, without an atom of common sense or lucidity. But they were the best I had. (M 68)

He does not have the necessary grasp of a conceptual apparatus to understand guilt in the received sense connected to moral and religious notions. He uses these terms, but confesses he does not understand them and shows his lack of understanding in immediately denying his own statements or using them in wrong contexts. His problems are not only, as Nussbaum claims, due to a vulgar Christian teaching (transmitted through stories) that sex and birth are filthy, and love associated with guilt, but also due to a vocabulary he does not understand because he is unable to grasp the meaning of it. And that vocabulary includes the concepts of birth, life, death, emotions, the human body and its functions, human relations, philosophy, and religion. The result is a story of black humour and tragic emptiness of life, questioning the whole idea of finding meaning in life, at least in Molloy's life[77]. Whether there is a claim that human life as such is meaningless, I will discuss after presenting Nussbaum's interpretation of the ending of Moran's story and the argument that can be drawn from it.

---

[76] Compare this to the discussion of the "hidden literality" of *Endgame* in S. Cavell, *Must We Mean What We Say*, 119 ff.

[77] Molloy not only admits having difficulty understanding words, both his own and others', but even finds the information presented by his senses to be beyond his understanding (M 50).

Ending the production of words

Moran's disintegration is at the same time liberation from his religious beliefs, his oppression of son and servant, and his bourgeois life with its rules and attachments. Nussbaum points to an "even more radical collapsing of the emotional structure itself"[78], that indicates a life beyond the one constructed through stories. She associates this with the Epicurean tradition of antireligious salvation through a life free of emotions, attachments and, thus, risk; but she cautions the reader: "Beckett's antinarrative is too many-sided, too ironic to leave us with any comfort."[79] The story to end stories of emotions results in the emotion of disgust inscribed in yet another story. Even if there appears to be a life beyond the human suffering we know, that is just another illusion transmitted to us from others. Nussbaum goes along with the narrator(s) in doubting the possibility of a life beyond the emotions and stories, but claims his bleak picture of human life is due to neglect both of the diversity of human ways of life, and of the self-creating force of the individual, creating himself on the basis of a plurality of stories in a setting of open arguments. She blames this on Beckett's religious world view; obsessed with mortality as punishment and unable to maintain a distance from the life he condemns[80].

It is certainly true that Beckett's voices express a view of human life as suffering, a view accentuated by a form ridiculing everything that is held to be valuable both in religious *and* secular conventions within our culture. But the reason for this negative view is not merely that life consists in emotions constructed through stories linking life, sex and love with filth and guilt, nor are these claims invalidated by stories of human life free from this combination of elements. Beckett's voices are concerned with the role of language as such, with the compulsiveness of writing and speaking, with the production of meaning; seeing silence as the only conceivable form of freedom for these characters.

Nussbaum does recognise the problem of writing (or expression in general) as an important challenge to her project. She asks how this challenge could be raised as a question within the writing of stories and treatises that is her project[81]. This recognition invites a question of why she narrows her discussion of *Molloy* to the role of emotions within narratives, which I will argue cannot be seen in isolation from the novel's comprehensive questioning of the production and construction of

---

78 Nussbaum, *Love's Knowledge*, 301.
79 Ibid. 305.
80 Ibid. 308 f.
81 Ibid. 311.

meaning in all language. Nussbaum's narrowing of the scope results, as shown above, in an ascription of arguments to the novel that is hardly supported by the text, and that is implausible when considering the *Trilogy* as a whole.

If we consider the argument of *Molloy* to be this more radical challenge to human life as production of meaning, a production in which we identify this illusory meaning with reality, and this identification is the real cause of suffering, the escape from pain probably would lie in ending the production of meaning, that is in ceasing to speak and write. There is some support for this interpretation. Sometimes Molloy has mystical experiences that hint at a state beyond the desire to understand:

> And there was another noise, that of my life become the life of this garden as it rode the earth of deeps and wildernesses. Yes, there were times when I forgot not only who I was, but that I was, forgot to be. (M 49)

This has a striking similarity to central themes in Buddhist thought[82] where the goal is a state liberated from all desires, including the desire to know. I will not, however, claim this to be Beckett's position, only that reading Beckett in that perspective would pose an even more basic challenge to Nussbaum's project than the Epicurean could and that a Buddhist interpretation might better succeed in doing justice to form and content of the *Trilogy*.

Particular stories and universal statements

There is, however, one problem with interpretations that claim *Molloy* to be making statements about human existence as such; they are contradicted by the most prominent formal feature of the novel. When a story is told by a narrator inventing narrators to tell his own story of how *he* experiences the world as incomprehensible and wishes to escape the whole process of compulsive writing and speaking, it is not reasonable to regard that as a statement about human life as such without further argument. Nussbaum supplies one argument, based on the *Trilogy* being told by one voice only:

> And the sclipsism of this voice's sense of life is so total that we get no sense of the distinctive shape of any other lives in this world. An implicit claim is made

---

[82] J. Wetlesen, *Selverkjennelse og frigjøring*, 12 ff. discusses the Buddhist view that one basic reason for human suffering is that we take our beliefs about the world to be reality, not realising the illusory character of these beliefs. For a Buddhist interpretation of Beckett, see P. Foster, *The Beckettian Impasse*.

> by these voices to be the whole world, to be telling the way the world is as they tell about themselves.[83]

I cannot see what support there is for finding the novel to claim to be telling how the whole world is. Even the almost solipsistic narrator of *The Unnamable* supposes there to be others somewhere although he does not experience them directly, and both Molloy and Moran encounter other people viewing the world differently from them.

There is, on the contrary, good reason to believe the *Trilogy* and the rest of Beckett's work to be aiming at something different from giving a description of how the world really is and from presenting a claim about the real nature of human life. Molloy and Moran tell their stories relating to the society surrounding them, and Molloy emphasises how he is unable to understand and live the ordinary life with its conventions and regulations. This ordinary life is admittedly ridiculed and parodied, but it is more plausible to ascribe that to the narrator's peculiar situation rather than to any absolute claim about the value of this life. Moran's apparently normal life prior to the journey is a parody of bourgeois life, not a precise description of that life, something that is emphasised by the distance Moran keeps from his fellow citizens and his claim not to like either men or animals (M 106). These voices do not make universal claims; they tell stories differing from the commonly accepted view of the world without claiming this view to be invalid.

The striking feature of this work of Beckett's is its particularity; the way both story, characters and form resist universal claims[84]. If it did aim at universality, why portray a main character (narrator) so far removed from normal human life? Since Molloy is a confused tramp living on the margins of society, almost unable to understand both human and natural laws[85], he would be a strange portrait of man as such. He is portrayed as a complete outsider in that he does not understand others and they do not understand him, and that must be taken as a clear warning not to interpret his description of the world as more than an expression of his experiences told from his point of view. It would be more plausible to take the

---

83 Nussbaum, *Love's Knowledge*, 308.

84 It has been pointed out that the name Macmann from Malone Dies means 'son of man', and Mahood from The Unnamable only lack an 'n' to be named Manhood, which seems to make them representatives for all humanity (or at least the male part of it). I find this implausible, given that Christ called himself Son of Man, suggesting another irony aimed at conventional religion, and Mahood may refer to motherhood, as suggested in Scruton, Aesthetic Understanding, 211 f.

85 It must be admitted, though, that he has an impressive amount of fragmented academic knowledge and his mastery of mathematics is good, which is shown by his calculation of farts per minute (M 30) and creation of a system of sucking-stones (M 69 ff.). Petter Aaslestad pointed out this as a problem for my interpretation.

portrait of Moran as a description of how we really are, but that will not work either, because of his seclusion from all the social interaction typical of ordinary human life. He is an outsider even before his disintegration, and neither his life nor his development can be regarded as exemplary in any way. These voices are counter-voices, showing a view of the world we are unfamiliar with but still can recognise.

Bataille describes the character Molloy as a well-known figure to us all:

> in the grip of a timorous craving, we have met him at street corners, an anonymous figure consisting of the ineluctable beauty of rags, apathy, and an indifferent gaze, the age-old swarm of ordure; at a loss, to be sure, as regards being, and, like us, a derelict as regards doing.[86]

We recognise him as the outsider, as someone we have seen but cannot identify with in the way we can with most other human beings. It is true that we can see him as object for our concern and treat him with the charitable gesture against which Molloy sees no defence (M 24), but there is no identification involved in that. Bataille describes the impossibility of communication with the Molloy-figure and calls attention to our fascination with the absence of humanity experienced when encountering these persons[87]. *Molloy* is not a description of human life in general, but a description of a limit case of human life.

Does this rejection of the *Trilogy* as a representation of human life in general invalidate Nussbaum's ethical reading of the *Trilogy*, and is it a first step toward dismissing her project of introducing fictional narratives into philosophical discourse? I have argued against several aspects of her interpretation, on the basis that it ascribes arguments to the novel that are not supported by the text when considered in the context of the *Trilogy* as a whole. I believe Nussbaum herself reveals a problematic aspect of her reading when stating that "Beckett's antinarrative is too many-sided, too ironic to leave us with any comfort"[88], since she finds a clear line of argument in this antinarrative. I have tried to show how the irony and many-sidedness of Beckett's work undermines her interpretation. This does not invalidate her main point about these stories as a challenge to her project. In a way she does not go far enough in using the many aspects and ironies as support for her claim that Beckett's fiction presents a basic challenge to her project. Her project is based on the value of the examined life, to invoke the Socratic phrase, whereas Beckett's self-negating narrative ridicules this value.

---

86 G. Bataille, 'Molloy's Silence', 131.
87 Ibid. 132.
88 Nussbaum, *Love's Knowledge*, 305.

Aristotle, Nussbaum's professed hero, takes as self-evident that "all men by nature desire to understand"[89] and considers that to be good in itself, whereas Beckett's voices in the *Trilogy* consider this desire to be the cause of their pain. Thus the Aristotelian vision appears to be challenged at its basis. It is not challenged in the sense of making a claim about the human condition, though. The denial of the desire to know cannot be made into a claim about man as such without getting involved in the following kind of self-refuting statements: The meaning of life is to rid oneself of the quest for meaning. Thus we are only presented with a stream of self-contradictory phrases by characters and narrators stripped of most normal human traits, preventing any claim to universal validity. The *Trilogy* presents lives where even the least specified and most comprehensive ethical question: "How should one live?" is rejected. The whole project of ethics is refused together with the search for meaning in general, but only for these characters in their particular lives.

These stories may still express something universal by *showing* it rather than arguing for it[90]. When the narrators refute or doubt their own statements and misuse philosophical, religious, and psychological tenets, this may be a way to show that seeking knowledge and making sense of human life is impossible. If this is Beckett's project, then his voices do not present implicit arguments about the meaninglessness of meaning, but the stories show this meaninglessness. The reader experiences this meaninglessness in his own life, although it cannot be presented discursively. I will leave open the possibility of this kind of universal message in the *Trilogy*. This message does not alter my main claim that these novels do not make claims about meaning. Experiencing this potential message is not a precondition for appreciating the work of Beckett, either.

Molloy does not state any position and thus resists being translated into philosophical discourse, even within a project sensitive to the philosophical content of form. That creates a further challenge to Nussbaum's project. It is one of several works that cannot be translated into argument without doing violence to its form. These novels do not readily lend themselves to

> a type of philosophical commentary that will point out explicitly the contributions of the works to the pursuit of our question about human beings and human life, and their relation to our intuitions and our sense of life.[91]

---

89 Aristotle, *Metaphysics*, 980a21.

90 Thomas Pogge pointed out this possible interpretation to me. The distinction between saying and showing is presented in L. Wittgenstein, *Tractatus Logico-Philosophicus*, 4.121-4.1213.

91 Nussbaum, *Love's Knowledge*, 49.

This squares well with Nussbaum's statement that not all texts are appropriate for her project, and that the decision as to what texts are applicable, and to what extent they are relevant, must be performed in the same way as we relate to relevant philosophical texts. But even if *Molloy* cannot contribute arguments to the project, it is valuable for this project both because it presents human beings who reject the ethical question that is the basis for her project, and because the form of the work prevents the construction of any definite meaning with general validity, thus exemplifying one kind of literature that cannot be enrolled in the project. I have shown how Nussbaum touches on both these points without developing them in her discussion of the *Trilogy*, making it one positive contribution of her reading of *Molloy*; another being that she points out Beckett's place within, and destruction of, the Epicurean tradition of non-religious salvation.

Her project of incorporating literature into moral philosophy is not affected by my objections to her use of *Molloy* in a way that goes beyond my previous comments on the relation between her ethical project and other aims of literary theory. Nussbaum does not test her ethical reading against other possible lines of interpretation, scarcely remarking on the role of humour in the novel, and totally ignoring how the text would appear if regarded as an object of aesthetic pleasure (or displeasure). That is a consequence of regarding the text as a potential answer to the ethical question rather than giving room for a wider range of questions or concerns.

Focusing on one aspect of the text and excluding others is not wrong. We always read a text from a certain perspective, having some preconceptions, vague or specific, about its content that become part of the basis for our understanding of the work[92]. These preconceptions will be determined by the tradition we belong to, our experiences and education, and will bring ethical, aesthetic, epistemological and other concerns into play when reading the text. Thus, we cannot avoid bringing in both ethical and aesthetic perspectives when appreciating a literary work. But when we systematise the reading in an interpretation, the question(s) we choose will place some constraints on the inquiry. What is important, if one thinks that the goal of interpretation is to make sense of the literary text (rather than use it for some purpose independent of it), is to start with an open mind so that the range of interpretative possibilities is not narrowed prior to the actual systematic interpretation. One such limitation is what Nussbaum describes as an "absence of

92 This horizon of preconceptions (or literally pre-judgements, *Vorurteile*) as a necessary condition for understanding is discussed at length in H.-G. Gadamer's major work, *Wahrheit und Methode*, e.g. 307 ff.

moral philosophy"[93] in recent literary theory, but in redressing the balance she sometimes, as in her *Molloy*-interpretation, seems to limit her approach too much in the opposite direction, creating an absence of aesthetics.

My objection to interpreting *Molloy* as moral philosophy takes in not only Nussbaum's interpretation, but also existential, religious, and other similar ways of reading positive general claims into the novel. Attempts at finding hidden epistemological and ontological arguments in the novel are ruled out, if my claim about the particularistic nature of the work is valid. At most, there is an argument that questions the self-evidence of the claim that searching for meaning is an essential human trait, but without offering anything as an alternative. Still I will support Nussbaum's initial claim that this work is ethically significant, not only because it poses a challenge to hers and similar projects. To establish a different approach to the ethical significance of these antinarratives, I will turn to some descriptions of the aesthetic effect it has on the reader.

1.3 The sublime in Molloy

The experience of nothing

I have described the *Trilogy* as being about men existing on the outskirts of society, telling their stories about their respective unsuccessful journeys, constantly negating what they relate. I have further argued that these characters seem to seek a way out of the desire to understand and create meaning, thus opposing what is regarded to be an essential trait in human nature. But the effect of this anti-desire is to create just another meaningful structure, unless one uses Beckett's device of contradicting the elements that contribute to this meaningfulness.

In the *Trilogy* Beckett is close to achieving the effect he himself called for within the field of painting:

> The expression that there is nothing to express, nothing with which to express, nothing from which to express, no power to express, no desire to express, together with the obligation to express.[94]

This is not an ordinary program of aesthetics or philosophy of art, because it represents a refusal to treat art and literature as expressive of something, even be it meaninglessness. Duhuit calls Beckett's position "a violently extreme and personal

---

[93] Nussbaum, *Love's Knowledge*, 170.
[94] S. Beckett and G. Duthuit, 'Three Dialogues', 17.

point of view"[95] showing how works of art produced according to such a principle are unable to communicate anything of general interest. Why bother with reading and discussing a personal point of view expressing nothing, unless it is of some interest? The answer is found in the reaction when reading this work, a reaction not based on understanding, but on the experience of failing to understand.

To clarify this obscure formulation, I will discuss some reviews and articles on *Molloy* concerned with this emotional experience more than with the content of the work. Levy argues that Beckett is presenting a human experience not intentional in the Husserlian sense, i.e. "directed toward objects or structures whose natures are open for exploration, but an awareness of Nothing"[96], which points at the essence of this work. I believe, however, Levy is overtaxing this experience in claiming it to be "for our age the meaning of man"[97]. I have argued that such universalistic claims are undercut by the structure of Beckett's narrative, leaving the awareness of Nothing as an exceptional experience the main contribution of this work. Esslin's description of the early critical response points to another aspect of this experience: "…there can be no doubt that these critics are, above all, responding to an overwhelming emotional, almost a mystical, experience."[98] The philosophical, ethical and formal features of the *Trilogy* are all interesting points of discussion for understanding the impact of this work, but the impact itself is characterised as dominated by an emotional experience.

Many writers on Beckett note this emotional experience, although not all: "That 'Molloy' is almost unendurably boring to read would not be denied, I imagine, by its keenest admirers"[99]. Which goes to show that when dealing in the emotional responses to art (or any event whatsoever) one cannot count on unanimity. If we proceed to the majority of the early critics, who find this to be a valuable literary work, we discover that they see the work as pointing beyond words to an absence, or showing a void, or being about silence or about Nothing. Nothing with a capital N certainly must be something different from nothing, indicating that what is aimed at is something inexpressible, something beyond understanding.

Bataille speaks of a "*formless* configuration of *absence*" in a "speech disheveled by the wind and pitted with holes, but with the kind of authority that a

95 Ibid. 17.
96 Levy, *Voice of Species*, 126.
97 Ibid. 128.
98 Esslin, 'Introduction', 14.
99 P. Toynbee, 'Critique in "Observer"', 75.

ruin cannot help but have" leading "to the unsoundable depths of *Molloy*"[100]. The metaphor of the ruin hits the mark since *Molloy* on the surface appears to be a normal narrative satisfying the conventions in the tradition from Aristotle's *Poetics*, and is analogous to the structure of the building that has deteriorated into a ruin. But since the story is negated, the actions are without purpose, and the characters are disintegrating together with their dwindling thoughts, the apparent construction is really "pitted with holes" as a ruin. The question is (to remain in the metaphor): What is seen through these holes making this novel attractive far beyond the fashion of "the absurd"?

If we return to Esslin's description of the emotional impact of Beckett's work, he describes it as an exhilarating experience, and strives to explain why such a depressing tale can yield positive emotions:

> To see a lone figure, without hope or comfort, facing the great emptiness of space and time without the possibility of miraculous rescue or salvation, in dignity, resolved to fulfill its obligation to express its own predicament - to partake of such courage and noble stoicism, however remotely, cannot but evoke a feeling of emotional excitement, exhilaration.[101]

The description of the despair and loss of hope combined with exhilaration seems to cover the mixed feelings experienced in reading the work, but this presentation of the Beckettian hero as dignified, and courageous in his intent to fulfill his obligation, does not fit any of the narrators of the *Trilogy*[102]. They are not intentionally acting, but are driven by inner voices or external demands, only wishing to end their meaningless tasks, rather than resist the emptiness they are facing. There is no "courage and noble stoicism" to get exited about, so what is the ground for the attraction and pleasure in this repulsive scenario?

Bataille argues, in his discussion of *Molloy*, that "the two domains - of terror and pleasure - are more contiguous with one another than we might have supposed"[103], also claiming that death and inhumanity are the limiting cases of the life we lead, and, thus, its backcloth and ultimate reality[104]. The pleasure we take in the terror we feel is, on his account, the pleasure in aesthetically confronting the void which is outside of the conventions of society. We take pleasure in seeing a

---

[100] Bataille, 'Molloy's Silence', 133.
[101] Esslin, 'Introduction', 14.
[102] I think that the description fits other of Beckett's characters, for example Winnie in *Happy Days*.
[103] Bataille, 'Molloy's Silence', 139.
[104] Ibid. 138.

real danger that could threaten us without having to face it. We find delight in confronting the horror of Molloy because we could be like him, but we are not.

Bataille does not state directly that this is a morally significant experience, but at least it serves a function in preserving society. When we experience the void surrounding our socially constrained lives, we are thrown back into the life of conventions and moral rules, but with a different perspective on these norms[105]. As an expansion on this argument, taking the risk of turning it into something more or less contradictory to Bataille's aesthetic theory, I will suggest that this experience may present us with tools for a basic criticism of the conventions and traditional moral position we usually practice without reflecting on them. When we have seen the norms virtually from an outside position, this alternative life not only makes us affirm the conventions that prevent us from becoming like Molloy, but also gives us the opportunity to affirm some and reject others. Experiencing the possibility of a meaningless life beyond conventions, a life that could be mine, makes me choose to adhere to conventions giving meaning to my life, and thus discard those that I find to be mere outward forms.

Bataille's reading, perhaps unintentionally, opens an understanding of the novel as not carrying any implicit universal moral argument, but still being of moral significance due to the emotional experience it produces. This experience may result in reflection on the life and social relations of the reader. The problem is that this is still an experience based on a particular understanding and interpretation of the text. Esslin and Bataille agree on the attraction of the inscrutability of the novel, but their explanations for the attractiveness of this incomprehension, or experience of meaninglessness do, in fact, contradict each other. Esslin sees a moral superiority in the protagonist, whereas Bataille claims him to be the antithesis of morality, beyond the border of what we consider human. I find, on account of my interpretation of the *Trilogy*, Bataille's account to be the plausible one, but Esslin's view, regarding the Beckettian hero as representative of humanity, or at least "modern man", seems to be the way the majority of the early critics read the novel (and Beckett's work in general).

This leads to a problem: If the reasons given by Esslin to explain his emotional response to the novel are correct, and the same is the case for Bataille, then the identity of their emotional responses is only apparent because their explanations exclude each other. If there is one common reason for the feelings described by

---

105 Bataille has a somewhat more sophisticated account of this experience of the limit to human life and its normative function in other works. In this context, however, I choose to relate the argument as presented in his article on *Molloy*.

Bataille and Esslin, which means they write about the same kind of feeling, both explanations must be rejected.

We cannot accept Bataille's explanation of the feeling described by Esslin and others, because Bataille's explanation is based on the reader experiencing Molloy as an outsider, as the true limit to what is humanly possible, as the extreme which gives meaning to our social mores. If we do not see him as this way, our emotions cannot be explained as a response to such a view. A similar argument would work the other way around as well. There are two possible solutions to this; either the emotional responses described just happen to *appear* similar, or these responses have a common source, but one different from the ones suggested by Esslin and Bataille.

The phenomenological similarities between the emotions described do not necessarily lead to the conclusion that there is a common source, but I find this conclusion to be the most plausible. The feeling of terror combined with pleasure in the experience of something overwhelming our comprehension is a well-known phenomenon having its own place in the history of aesthetics and rhetoric. It is called the experience of the sublime. The sublime is usually contrasted with the beautiful, because both can be described as emotional responses to different kinds of phenomena. Traditionally the beautiful is connected to pleasure, whereas the sublime is connected to terror and pain, but not exclusively, since we find it attractive as well.

In the rhetorical treatise on the sublime from about 100 AD wrongly ascribed to Longinus, the author states that the effect of the sublime, as presented by the greatest authors, "is not to persuade the audience but rather to transport them out of themselves". The reason for this effect is that sublime objects "exercise an irresistible power and mastery, and get the better of every listener."[106] The feeling is beyond the persuasive; thus it is not connected to the comprehensible in an argumentative sense. But according to Pseudo-Longinus, the feeling of the sublime is a feeling of elevation and grandeur, often containing an element of terror as in the references to the Battle of the Gods and descriptions of divine nature in the *Iliad*[107], all explained through human nature seeking beyond its own limits as well as those of nature:

> [Nature] has called us into life, into the whole universe, there to be spectators of her games and eager competitions; and she therefore from the first breathed into our hearts an unconquerable passion for whatever is great and more divine than ourselves. Thus the whole universe is not enough to satisfy the speculative

[106] Longinus, *On the Sublime*, 1, 4.
[107] Ibid. 9, 5-9.

> intelligence of human thought; our ideas often pass beyond the limits that confine us.[108]

We can connect this to what Burke says of the beautiful as associated with the small, smooth, well-formed, and delicate[109]. The beautiful creates positive feelings within the limits of our perception and understanding, whereas the sublime transcends these limits of the recognisable towards that which exceeds the world we know. It has something divine to it, without necessarily being divine.

But how can Beckett's *Trilogy* with its miserable characters be sublime if this sublimity concerns something great, divine, and elevating? The explanation is that the sublime is not necessarily something elevated; it is the word for any experience characterised by this particular kind of feeling arising in the encounter with something incomprehensible. When we have an experience of something that we cannot fully grasp or cope with, resulting in a feeling simultaneously positive and negative, we have an experience of the sublime. That is a precise description of the experience related by so many readers of Beckett. I find the sublime to be the key to understanding one of the crucial impacts of this work.

Harold Bloom recognises Beckett as a writer of the sublime, although in a minimalist and negative version of it, exploring the same world as Kafka:

> The "beyond" is where Beckett's later fictions and plays reside. Call it the silence, or the abyss, or the reality beyond the pleasure principle, or the metaphysical or spiritual reality of our existence at last exposed, beyond further illusion. Beckett cannot or will not name it, but he has worked through to the art of representing it more persuasively than anyone else.[110]

The sublime is an experience of something not part of our daily lives and concerns, indicating something beyond the world of ordinary human experiences. For Pseudo-Longinus it is clearly connected to the divine in many ways, thus it is associated with power and physical greatness.

The sublime of Beckett moves the other way, exploring the agony and pain of the powerless. Still there is a parallel to the preoccupation with the greatness of the gods in the Greek conception of the sublime, because the Christian God is depicted as powerless and pitiful in the most crucial moment in the Bible; the crucifixion. Thus, the Christian image of God is not solely one of greatness, but also one of the

---

108 Ibid. 35, 2-3.

109 E. Burke, *Ideas of the Sublime and Beautiful*, 102 ff.

110 H. Bloom, 'Introduction', 5. When Bloom refers to "later fiction and plays" he probably means those after 1960, but I will argue that the description also covers the period after World War II, although the exploration of this "abyss" is even more clearly represented in the later works.

greatness in the despicable and powerless. The preoccupation of the Christian faith with God as the antithesis of what is commonly held to be valuable, opens for a recognition of the sublime in suffering, agony, and abandonment, not only in the *megalopsuchia*[111] of heroes like Ajax who in abandonment prays for the light that will enable him to go down fighting[112]. The miserable, hunted Molloy is as far as it is possible to come from this picture of the hero; he does not stand up to the overwhelming challenge, just drifts along negating all ideas of honour and purpose. This negative sublime is probably made possible through Christianity's revolution of values. It is difficult to conceive of Molloy as a Greek hero, because the Greeks would not see Molloy's life as anything but despicable and it would just create a feeling of repulsion.

I am not claiming that the experience of sublimity by necessity is religious in nature, but that the images leading to this experience have to be recognisable as not just empty in a plain sense. These images must be seen as containing something, because plain meaninglessness cannot be regarded as attractive in itself[113]. The Greeks lacked the context enabling them to regard Molloy to be more than a degenerated human because he is without *ethos*. There would be no void of incomprehension because his life would be the life of a man turned animal. His role could at best be that of the natural slave, living without human flourishing [*eudaimonia*] and incapable of decision[114]. No Greek would find anything sublime in the life of a natural slave. Because they were able to categorise and understand the life of Molloy, there could be no sublimity to that life. For us, who are living under the influence of Christian images, the life of Molloy, abandoned and miserable, is not the life of animals or slaves, but a kind of human life. Thus our eyes are opened to an incomprehension not accessible to the Greek self-consciousness nourished on the *Iliad* and *Odyssey*.

This expansion of the sublime of Pseudo-Longinus following the images of Christianity, results in two different kinds of sublimity; one pointing towards lofty ideals and power, the other towards the despicable and powerless. But the nature of this aesthetic experience is such that these recognisable descriptions do not take part in the experience itself; they merely present the context for the experience. That is emphasised in Burke's association of the sublime with whatever is

111 Greatness of soul, which is described by Aristotle to be characteristic of the ethically best of men; *Nicomachean Ethics*, 1123b26-31.

112 Longinus, *Sublime*, 9, 10.

113 Sentences like: "Colourless green ideas sleep furiously" and "Quadruplicity drinks procrastination" are meaningless, but certainly not sublime. These are classical examples in philosophy of language, cited from J. Lyons, *Semantics*, 386.

114 Aristotle, *Politica*, 1280a31-34.

regarded as terrible, "whether this cause of terror, be endued with greatness of dimensions or not."[115] Burke also accounts for the element of incomprehension:

> To make anything very terrible, obscurity seems in general to be necessary. When we know the full extent of any danger, when we can accustom our eye to it, a great deal of the apprehension vanishes.[116]

In chapter three I discuss Kant's argument against Burke's empirical explanation of the sublime, but in this context, my aim is a description of the main elements of the sublime, and his work is valuable for that purpose. Using Burke's description, we realise that the vacuity of *Molloy*'s hell is a source of the experience of the sublime like the power of the Old Testament God, the vastness of the ocean, and the infinity of the universe.[117] There is no difference between a high and a low kind of sublimity, because what matters is the simultaneous feelings of attraction and repulsion when encountering something incomprehensible.

The moral significance of the sublime

I have claimed that the feeling of the sublime is a major component in the experience recounted in the reception of Beckett's *Molloy*, and I have tried to point out some of the general reasons for this. But what is the moral element in this sublime? We have seen that the sublime traditionally has been associated with religious experiences, but not exclusively, and not always with the moral aspect of religion, either. There seems to be something profoundly amoral about many stories considered sublime by Pseudo-Longinus, Burke, and other writers on this subject. This is of course the case with *Molloy*, too. Maybe we are not facing a real problem here, since the moral significance is associated with the feeling of sublimity only, not with the object of this feeling. It is not arguments, sense of life, or a moral universe communicated in the words that make a particular story sublime and give it moral significance, but the feeling induced by the way this particular story is told.

In *Molloy* this emotional effect is brought about by constant negations combined with indirect indications of something present but indescribable. When Molloy reflects on freedom he admits that he doesn't know what the word means or what the use of it is and concludes that

---

[115] Burke, *Sublime and Beautiful*, 53.
[116] Ibid. 54.
[117] Ibid. 59-70.

> you would do better, at least no worse, to obliterate than to blacken margins, to fill in the hole of words till all is blank and flat and the whole ghastly business looks what it is, senseless speechless issueless misery. (M 13)

But that is not exactly what is revealed in the process of continuous destruction, because there seems to be something left, "a whisper of that final music or that silence that underlies All."[118] That is not a hope for the truth underneath all deceptions or a perfect life beyond the conventions of society, but a description of an experience of the sublime. It is merely a description of the experience of seeing beyond the understandable world of images and concepts. Beckett's way of doing this is through notes that "annihilate all they purport to record." (MD 261)

Beckett is not always just pointing to the void by means of a text destroying itself; sometimes he records obscure experiences, which are not presented with irony. Molloy claims that all his nights are moonless (M 15, 41), but still he describes waking up in the middle of the night in the house of Lousse (or was her name Loy?), shaven, cleaned and washed, deprived of his dirty clothes, watching the moon through the window. He reflects on his former interest in different sciences, including astronomy, physics, and anthropology, but realises now that he is a ruin understanding nothing, or, rather, he is "the indestructible chaos of timeless things" at a place devoid of the "familiar mysteries" and he describes this experience:

> I listen and the voice is of a world collapsing endlessly, a frozen world, under a faint untroubled sky, enough to see by, yes, and frozen too. And I hear it murmur that all wilts and yields, as if loaded down, but here there are no loads, and the ground, too, unfit for loads, and the light, too, down towards an end it seems can never come. For what possible end to these wastes where true light never was, nor any upright thing, nor any true foundation, but only these leaning things, forever lapsing and crumbling away, beneath a sky without memory of morning or hope of night. ... And I too am at an end when I am there, my eyes close, my sufferings cease and I end, I wither as the living can not. ... But I will not listen no longer, for the time being, to that far whisper, for I do not like it, I fear it. (M 40)

Molloy is unable to enter or leave this place at will, and despite his fear of the place, he describes it as less displeasurable to be there than at familiar places where he is free to leave when he chooses to. What is peculiar about this passage is that it adds to the self-negating story an almost positive description of the

---

[118] Beckett commenting on *Watt* and the difference between his and Joyce's writings, cited from Bloom, 'Introduction', 3.

existence beyond the world of concepts. As we can see, absence or emptiness is still the theme, but here it is not presented through negation of the ordinary conventional phrases, philosophical or religious systems, or emotions learned in a life structured on narratives, but through poetic images of ceaseless destruction.

These images evoke feelings of the sublime, being simultaneously threatening and attractive, and seem, together with Molloy's experience another night in Lousse's garden and Moran's attempt to break out of human life, to be the underlying theme of these narratives. This other (moonless) night, Molloy listens to a sound usually covered by other noises and he forgets to be:

> Then I was no longer that sealed jar to which I owe my being so well preserved, but a wall gave way and I filled with roots and tame stems for example, stakes long since dead and ready for burning, the recess of night and the imminence of dawn, and then the labour of the planet rolling eager into winter, winter would rid it of these contemptible scabs. (M 49)

This is not romanticising nature as the true life compared with our socially constructed everyday lives, but an image evoking feelings of something incomprehensible, but real, beyond the meanings affirmed and denied in everyday life.

Beckett is not alone in having the sublime as a major preoccupation. Bloom situates him in the great modernist tradition concerned with the sublime including Kafka, Proust and Joyce[119]. Lyotard suggests that the sublime is the artistic sensibility characteristic of modernity[120] because the main theme of artistic reflection of this period is the ambiguous emotion connected to the indeterminate. He also writes that Montaigne, Proust and Beckett all have the same concern, striving to express something essential without having the means to express it[121]. The result is the feeling of reaching beyond the known world to something exceeding it, but without being able to say what this is. The feeling in itself is significant because it is the experience of a presence that is not part of our well-known reality. This presence does not, however, have to be real; our feelings can delude us. Feeling the presence of something exceeding our cognitive faculties, is no proof that there exists something beyond what we can comprehend. And these artists striving to give form to this experience[122] are not involved in ontological

---

[119] Bloom, 'Introduction', 5.

[120] J.-F. Lyotard, *Om det sublime*, 52.

[121] C. Pries and J.-F. Lyotard, 'Das Undarstellbare - wider das Vergessen', 323.

[122] If they are, in fact, trying to express any such experience at all. It is quite possible for a work of art to be sublime, without the artist attempting to express something of the kind. Since the sublime is a feeling in the reader or spectator, the feeling is not causally dependent on the intentions of the author.

claims in the way a philosopher would be; they do not claim that the phenomenon apparently creating the feelings of sublimity exists. All these authors do is create a work of art concerned not with the beautiful, which is connected to what Molloy calls "the familiar mysteries", but with the sublime, the feeling of the unknown.

How can this feeling have anything to do with morality? There is a tradition for combining the sublime with morality beginning with Pseudo-Longinus' thesis on the subject. However, the sublime is one among many feelings having a moral significance. *On the Sublime* is a rhetorical treatise, and rhetoric in the Greek tradition is an offshoot of ethics and politics[123], in that it discusses the arguments and techniques used in speeches aimed at ethical purposes. The sublime is one of the techniques convincing the audience of the orator's point of view, and although it has no part in *logos* (argument)[124], it has a role to play in the two other sources of persuasion; *ethos* (character of the orator) and *pathos* (feelings in the audience)[125]. Seen in this context, the experience of the sublime functions as motivation for acting in a certain way. The feeling itself is amoral, just as the arguments used in persuasion, but the effect is ethical in that it leads a to deliberate choice of action, whether right or wrong. On the other hand, the feeling is connected to the sublime even if it occurs in situations not aimed at persuasion and subsequent action. The audience of the Homeric epics did experience the sublime, but not in situations demanding action, even though the sublime in epics is important in depicting ideals for the shaping of character.

This effect of the sublime is part of a general effect connected to all feelings in rhetorical contexts, and an analysis of it belongs to the larger discussion of the ethical function of feelings in general. But my claim here is that the sublime is experienced by a special kind of feeling, having a particular role to play in our moral understanding. When we encounter the sublime, we get a glimpse of something that is not part of our everyday life, and cannot be fitted into our existing structures of understanding. This feeling of transcendence indicates a reality beyond the constraints of this physical world and our moral conventions. Thus the feeling we have when reading a work like *Molloy*, is one of freedom: we feel that reality is not restricted to the world as we normally experience it, constrained by physical phenomena and social institutions. One effect of such an

---

[123] Aristotle, *Rhetoric*, I,ii,7.

[124] Longinus, *Sublime*, 1, 4 states that the effect of the sublime is not persuasion, but it is reasonable to read that as meaning argumentative persuasion as opposed to being brought over to the orator's point of view through emotional effects and the perceived character of the orator. The latter is the rhetorical effect of emotions such as the feeling of the sublime.

[125] Aristotle, *Rhetoric*, I,ii,4-6.

experience is at least the possibility of regarding the known and accepted moral systems as not necessary, giving an opportunity for criticising these systems from an outside position.

The moral function of this feeling is different from the function of feelings like compassion, anger, empathy, joy, because these feelings all have a function connected to reality as we understand it, as is argued by Nussbaum. Thus these other feelings can all contribute to the affirmation or rejection of particular actions, institutions and conventions, but only from within a given moral conception of the world. They are first and foremost taking part in a revision of our moral understanding, which is why feelings are so important in Nussbaum's project of literature and philosophy. Her Aristotelian theory indicates that our basic moral conceptions are determined by the notion of man as a rational and social animal, which restricts our morality with biological and established social norms.[126] There is no outside perspective on morality, because the good is always understood as the *human* good, even though we can seek some kind of internal transcendence[127] in striving for excellence.

The sublime, however, gives us a feeling of transcending these limits, indicating some other reality. The sublime is experienced as powerful, overwhelming, diminishing the everyday reality. We are presented with something that appears greater than we are and, thus, to be a challenge to the ethics of everyday life. The sublime as described here is related to the religious experience of the holy, but not connected to any religious dogmas or ideas of the divine. Like religious experience, it presents us with something that appears to be greater than the social mores we live by, thus giving a position from which to reevaluate these rules and norms. But in a strict sense, the experience is cognitively empty since it is beyond comprehension and is merely a feeling of a presence of something.

When there are no religious dogmas or moral ideas in this experience, how can it be a moral experience? A feeling of freedom gives no reasons for a moral reexamination so long as the feeling is disconnected from any determinate alternative to the norms and values one lives by. If we state that total freedom in itself demands moral reflection and choosing responsibility, we return to the existentialist position briefly discussed above. This is hardly a sustainable position, because it does not answer its own nihilistic problem; if I am free, I can act without taking responsibility for my actions. This is what Molloy does when he kicks the

---

[126] M. Nussbaum, 'Non-relative virtues', 48 ff. This does not imply that these norms cannot be corrected and improved, but that human biology and rationality determine their basic foundation.

[127] Nussbaum, *Love's Knowledge*, 379 f.

defenceless charcoal-burner in the forest and leaves him unconscious (M 83 ff.). There is no morality involved in that, just plain absence of morality. Thus, freedom in itself does not lead to morality, unless one can argue that this freedom is inescapably connected to responsibility or obligation in some way.

The claim I want to make is the following: the sublime is experienced by a feeling connected to a 'reality' beyond the empirical world. This feeling indicates human freedom from the regularity of causal laws and social norms because as rational beings we are able to give ourselves rules to live by; we are self-legislating, as Kant says. If Kant is right, the experience of something beyond the comprehensible phenomena is no mere illusion but an indication of man's freedom as morally obligated. Whether this position is sustainable and can be applied to the sublime in *Molloy*, can only be discovered through an interpretation and discussion of Kant's analysis of the sublime.

2. Kant's theory of aesthetic reflective judgement

I have claimed that one ethically significant aspect of Beckett's Molloy may be found in the reader's feeling of emptiness or nothingness, or of opening a void. This is the feeling of the sublime as described in Kant's aesthetic theory. My aim is to show (1) that Kant's theory of the sublime is relevant for literature of the kind written by Beckett, and (2) that an interesting theory of the ethical or moral significance of the sublime can be developed on the basis of Kant's ethical and aesthetic theories. To do that, I have to start with Kant's general theory of aesthetic reflective judgement.

The judgement of the sublime is one of the two kinds of aesthetic judgements of reflection, the other being the judgement of taste, which declares an object to be beautiful, non-beautiful[1], or ugly. Both kinds of judgement are based on a disinterested feeling and claim subjective universal validity, which means that we demand from everyone agreement with the judgement. The paradigmatic aesthetic reflective judgement concerns beautiful objects of nature. To apply Kant's theory of the sublime to literature, we must first understand his theory of judgement about beautiful objects of nature, and then discuss how the judgements about *sublime* objects of nature differ from these. Finally, on the basis of this interpretation, I will attempt to make sense of Kant's theory of aesthetic reflective judgements about objects of art, in particular about sublime literature.

This chapter deals with the first part of this project: presenting an interpretation of relevant aspects of Kant's theory of judgements of taste. There are several problems concerning this theory I will not discuss, such as the form of his presentation, including how to understand the four moments of the analytic of the beautiful[2], and where to find the deduction of the judgement of taste[3]. The

---

1 I have borrowed this term from C. Fricke, *Kants Theorie des reinen Geschmacksurteil*, 7. The statement "This is non-beautiful" expresses a neutral mental state, whereas claiming something to be beautiful expresses a state of pleasure, and the statement that something is ugly expresses a state of displeasure. Regrettably, Henry Allison's *Kant's Theory of Taste: A Reading of the* Critique of Aesthetic Judgment, Cambridge: Cambridge University Press, 2001, appeared to late to be integrated in my discussion of Kant's aesthetic theory. Allison discusses in an illuminating way both the problem of non-beautiful objects and many of the other interpretative problems encountered in this and the following chapter.

2 For a discussion of the moments, see S. Kemal, *Kant's Aesthetic Theory*, 23 ff.

3 See D. Crawford, *Kant's Aesthetic Theory*, 66 ff. and Guyer, *Claims of Taste*, 248 ff.

distinction between free and accessory beauty [*anhängende Schönheit*] (KU§16, 229 f), the ideal of beauty (KU§17, 231 f), and the empirical and intellectual interest in the beautiful (KU§41-42, 296 ff) are also interpretative challenges that I will leave untouched. Although I do try to make sense of some passages from the Dialectic, the systematic significance of this part of the Critique is not discussed.

Judgement is, according to Kant, the capacity [*Vermögen*] to subsume under concepts not derived from this capacity itself but given from elsewhere, either understanding or reason. Despite this dependent status, the capacity does have its own principle (EE II, 202 f). It follows that the power of judgement [*Urteilskraft*][4] is always activated in conjunction with other capacities: understanding, reason, and imagination. This is the case even for aesthetic reflective judgements that do not involve determinate concepts[5] in that these judgements are not based on concepts nor directed to them as purposes (KU§5, 209). Instead, these judgements are based on a 'free play' of cognitive powers. In judgements of taste, imagination and understanding are involved, whereas in the judgement of the sublime, imagination and reason are at play (KU§26, 256) (although the metaphor of play is less suitable in this case, since the relationship is more solemn (KU§23, 244 f)). An account of the capacities involved is necessary to make sense of this theory of aesthetic reflective judgement. Therefore, this chapter starts with a discussion of how to understand this vocabulary of capacities or faculties.

The next step is to try to interpret some central claims in the Analytic of the Beautiful. Every judgement of taste involves a representation[6], a free relation between imagination and understanding, a mental state, a feeling, and a claim to subjective universal validity. Basing my account on interpretations by Hannah Ginsborg and others, I suggest that the judging [*Beurteilung*] of the object is a feeling that is the subject's awareness of this mental state of free play in the representation of an object. This feeling is disinterested, and one we hold that everybody should share. Some places Kant seems to think that there is a distinction

---

4 "The *Urteilskraft* which Kant describes in the Analytic of Principles and *The Critique of Judgment* (*Kritik der Urteilskraft*) is the actualization of the *Vermögen zu urteilen* under sensory stimulation." B. Longuenesse, *Kant and the Capacity to Judge*, 7.

5 Kant both say that it is indeterminate which concept is referred to in aesthetic reflective judgements (KU§23, 244) and that the judgement of taste is based on an indeterminate concept (the supersensible substrate of appearances) (KU§57, 340 f).

6 'Representation' refers "to such objects of our direct awareness as sensations, intuitions, perceptions, concepts cognitions, ideas, and schemata." (Pluhar's translation of *Critique of Judgment*, 44, note 4). Pluhar uses 'presentation' to translate *Vorstellung* on the ground that Kant's theory is not representational. Although I agree with him on that, the disadvantages of breaking with an established term in Anglo-American Kant scholarship appear greater.

between the judging and the judgement [*Urteil*], so that we must distinguish between the awareness of this mental state, and the proposition "This is beautiful". It is unclear whether he holds that the feeling *is* the judgement or merely the main component in this judgement.

This is followed by a presentation of Kant's distinction between this disinterested, universally shareable feeling, and other interested feelings such as the liking for the agreeable and for the good. In this section I seek to establish only the plausibility of the assumption that we do experience such disinterested feelings against the background of Nussbaum's doubt about the coherence of such an account. Many Kant interpreters has discussed whether pure judgement of taste includes only judgements about beautiful objects, or whether there also can be judgements about non-beautiful and ugly objects. According to my interpretation, Kant must hold that all objects of nature can be judged aesthetically, but he is not thereby forced to claim that everything is beautiful.

The last part of the second section is an attempt to determine the nature of the object of aesthetic judgements. Kant says it is the *form* of the object, but at the same time he also says that the judgement is concerned with the mental state of the judging subject. I propose to understand the form of the object as the structuring activity performed by the cognitive powers imagination and understanding.

The third section consists in an attempt to disentangle the problems surrounding Kant's assertion that we are justified in requiring everybody to share the feeling we have. There are two reasons for the significance of this section, the first being that Kant's observation that we actually do demand agreement for our aesthetic judgements (KU§56, 338) is plausible, even in this relativistic age. The other reason is that this assertion makes sense of the fact that we do make these seemingly superfluous judgements, regardless of the status of their claim to subjective universal validity. Several commentators[7], have argued that the section called Deduction of Judgements of Taste (KU§38, 289 f) does not provide any convincing justification of the claim to universal assent for the judgement. Kant's main point in this section seems to be that the intersubjective validity of the judgement of taste rests on the subjective condition of the power of judgement, a condition for the possibility of judgement or cognition in general. But cognition as the subsumption of an intuition under a concept should not need any subjective condition for ensuring universal validity. The *Probierstein* of truth, Kant says, is not found in introspection but in the object, which is the common ground for

---

7 For example Guyer, *Claims of Taste*, 277.

agreement in judgements (KrV A820f/B848 f). So why introduce a subjective condition of validity, one we judge in aesthetic reflective judgements?

I suggest that this problem can be solved if we read the deduction (and the so-called first deduction in §21)[8] in connection with the account in the two introductions, where aesthetic and teleological judgements of reflection are said to be united under the principle of the purposiveness of nature (EE XI, 243 f). This principle, when applied to objects, results in a teleological determination of the object that is valid for judgement, but does not result in an objectively valid judgement of nature. Unless we assume that the mental state we are in when making these teleological judgements is valid for everybody, the determination based on this state has merely private validity. Since all of nature is subject to teleological judgements (KU§75, 398), every act of cognition of nature must, at least potentially, include these judgements. If we do not assume that the mental state of free play (which is the basis of judgements of taste) is valid for everybody, neither can we assume that this teleological determination is valid for everybody. This assumption of intersubjective validity is necessary if our teleological judgements are to have more than private validity, i.e. are to count as cognition. And since determinative judgements are not sufficient for cognition of nature (EE IV, 208 ff), we must always supplement them with judgements under the principle of purposiveness, i.e. teleological judgements. This is the basis for the claim to subjective universal validity for judgements of taste.

Since I propose a new and presumably controversial interpretation of this problem, section 2.3 is fairly long and detailed. I base my analysis of the judgement of sublimity on this interpretation, so it is important to go into some depth in this discussion. Still, this section is not required for understanding the following chapters. Those who have less interest in this kind of exegesis may go directly from section 2.2 to chapter 3.

---

8 Crawford, *Aesthetic Theory*, 66 ff., argues that the deduction does not consist only of the passages under that heading in §38. The justification of the universal communicability of the feeling (§9, 217), the harmony of the faculties (KU §38, 290), the *sensus communis* (KU §40, 293 f), the subjective purposiveness of nature for our cognition (KU §11, 221), and the idea of a supersensible substrate of phenomena (KU§57, 339 ff) are all parts of the transcendental deduction. In section 2.3 I attempt to interpret Kant's claims as regards the deduction of aesthetic reflective judgements.

2.1 The faculties involved in judgement

Understanding and imagination

A faculty or capacity [*Vermögen*] is the potential for achieving some specific end. As we shall see, the basis for aesthetic reflective judgement is a free play between the faculties or cognitive powers. Making sense of this metaphor requires first and foremost that the faculties be not conceived as independently existing entities in the human mind (which also is no entity). A faculty is a potential for a certain activity, and has no reality independent of this activity. In Kant's analysis of human reason, the aim is to disclose which rational capacities have to be assumed to explain human cognition and action. The faculties of the human mind are the means we employ to shape the world into graspable units related to one another.

If I am to think the world as shaped by my way of conceiving it, but without assuming myself to be the sole creator of the world, I have to think that which is shaped by me as a manifold given in intuition. The act of cognition as performed by understanding [*Verstand*] must be thought as the act of organising this manifold according to rules, and subsuming the manifold under concepts does that:

> Wir haben den *Verstand* oben auf mancherlei Weise erklärt: durch eine Spontaneität der Erkenntnis, (im Gegensatze der Rezeptivität der Sinnlichkeit) durch ein Vermögen zu denken, oder auch ein Vermögen der Begriffe, oder auch der Urteile, welche Erklärungen, wenn man sie bei Lichte besieht, auf eins hinauslaufen. Jetzt können wir ihn als *Vermögen der Regeln* charakterisieren. ... Sinnlichkeit gibt uns Formen, (der Anschauung) der Verstand aber Regeln. (KrV A126)

Understanding is the capacity to provide a system of rules, under which the appearances of sensibility are placed. This system of rules must be based on some rules independent of the appearances presented in intuition, and these rules Kant calls categories, the most important of which are the categories of substance and causality.

The manifold, which is subsumed under categories, must itself be formed, and thus there is a productive aspect to our sensibility. This is our capacity for imagination [*Einbildungskraft*]:

> Die Einbildungskraft (*facultatis imaginandi*) als ein Vermögen der Anschauungen auch ohne Gegenwart des Gegenstandes, ist entweder *produktiv*, d.i. ein Vermögen der ursprünglichen Darstellung des letzteren

> (*exhibitio originaria*), welche also vor der Erfahrung vorhergeht; oder *reproduktiv* ... . (A 167)

Productive imagination is required for the figurative synthesis (KrV B151 f), which is the affection of sensibility by understanding. Thus, in determinative judgements, productive imagination is bound by the rules of understanding. The sensible manifold is formed according to laws derived from the categories. In judgements of taste, however, imagination is considered, paradoxically, as free from the rules of understanding, yet as lawful (KU§22, 240 f). I will return to this in the last section of this chapter.

Practical reason

Now if we think the world as organised in accordance with such necessary rules (laws of nature), action becomes a problem, because when we act we have to conceive of ourselves as making a choice between several possible options. But this world we live and act in is regulated by necessary laws which are the condition of its intelligibility, and which govern our own actions as worldly events. When we act we cannot conceive of ourselves as under the regulation of understanding, but as being free from the necessity implied by these rules.

The first Critique established the *possibility* of freedom from natural causation, but not that there in fact is such a freedom (KpV 15). This fact is established by our consciousness of a moral law:

> Freiheit und unbedingtes praktisches Gesetz weisen also wechselweise auf einander zurück. ... Also ist es das *moralische Gesetz*, dessen wir uns unmittelbar bewußt werden (so bald wir uns Maximen des Willens entwerfen), welches sich uns *zuerst* darbietet, und, indem die Vernunft jenes als einen durch keine sinnliche Bedingungen zu überwiegende, ja davon gänzlich unabhängigen Bestimmungsgrund darstellt, gerade auf den Begriff der Freiheit führt. (KpV 29 f)

Man must be able to prescribe a different set of rules to himself independent of theoretical understanding, rules that apply to the practical aspect of rationality. These are rules of freedom, and presuppose the capacity of reason, i.e. the ability to give rules independent of the world of sense.

This results in the problematic idea that man is simultaneously under two different kinds of legislation, one theoretical and one practical, but both concerning the same empirical world. Kant talks of this as belonging to two different realms: the theoretical and the practical, a position regarded by many to be indefensible. In chapter 4, I present the now common line of interpretation of this claim, seeing the theoretical and the practical realms as two perspectives we must adopt on the world to explain the way we understand and relate to it[9]. Thus, the faculties of imagination and understanding (together with theoretical reason) are necessary for explaining cognition, and the faculty of practical reason is necessary for action. Kant wrote the two first Critiques to analyse and show the necessity of these human capacities.

Judgement - determinative and merely reflective

This short, superficial account presents the capacities discussed in the first two Critiques. One would expect that these works covered all the a priori principles of the field of philosophy, and accordingly accounted for all the capacities we must presuppose to explain human knowledge. That is at least an assumption Kant found reasonable (EE II, 202), but rejected. Understanding is just the faculty of rules in general, which means that we also need a capacity for subsuming the particulars, i.e. the objects we experience, under these rules, and this is called the capacity to judge [*Urteilsvermögen*]. In the first Critique, this is described as a special talent that cannot be exercised according to rule (because it would lead to a regress of rules), and can only be learned through examples and practice (KrV A132f/B171 f). In this context judgement is determining the particular and has no a priori principle apart from understanding. Kant did, however, change his view, concluding that judgement was not merely a talent; it was a capacity based on a priori principles, connected to feeling and to teleology[10]. Judgement depends on other cognitive capacities since its function is to relate the particular to the universal. Thus it is the capacity to apply concepts acquired from other human capacities.

This change of view does not have to be seen as a revolution in Kant's theory of judgement; the main difference between the two accounts of judgement is that in the third Critique judgement is not only an ability to subsume under an already given universal, but it is also the capacity for finding the universal for a given particular (KU IV, 179), i.e. judgement is not only determinative, it also reflects independently of the rules provided by understanding. This must not be misunderstood as meaning that as soon as the reflective judgement finds a

9 See L. W. Beck, *A Commentary on Kant's Critique of Pure Reason*, 192 ff.
10 Zammito, *Genesis*, 46 f.

universal for the given particular, this universal concept can be used in determinative judgement as the rule under which new particulars can be subsumed. Determinative judgement is only judgement under the universal transcendental laws of understanding (KU IV, 179 f). Even though we find a concept by merely reflective judgement, and subsume other representations under this concept, this determination is still a merely reflective, and not a determinative judgement. Thus the distinction between determinative and reflective judgement does not concern whether the judgement starts with the universal or the particular, but what kind of principle the judgement is performed under.

Reflection is a necessary component of every judgement (KrV A260/B316 f), and is characterised as an act of comparison:

> *Reflektieren* (Überlegen) aber ist: gegebene Vorstellungen entweder mit andern, oder mit seinem Erkenntnisvermögen, in Beziehung auf einen dadurch möglichen Begriff, zu vergleichen und zusammenhalten. Die reflektierende Urteilskraft ist diejenige, welche man auch das Beurteilungsvermögen (facultas diiudicandi) nennt. (EE V, 211).

In the determinative use of judgement, understanding is the principle of judgement, providing it with rules (EE V, 212)[11], but in the merely reflective use of judgement no concept is given, and judgement requires its own principle. This is the principle of purposiveness of nature as regards our cognition of it (EE V, 214 ff). I will come back to the role of this principle in the last section of this chapter.

Although there are two distinct kinds of judgement, they are aspects of the same capacity in that both kinds concern the relationship between the universal and the particular and both reflect, i.e. compare given representations [*Vorstellungen*] with other representations or with the subject's cognitive faculties. And since both judgements involve universals, they must be conceptual in some way. This is, as we shall see, a problem when it comes to aesthetic reflective judgements, which involves no concept of the object.

Judgement differs from reason and understanding in that these latter faculties represent two independent ways of relating to the world of appearances, whereas

---

[11] As is pointed out by B. Longuenesse in *Capacity to Judge*, 163 ff, judgement is reflective also in its determinative function. She suggests that we should, as Kant sometimes does (e.g. KU IV, 179), call those judgements that do not subsume under concepts provided by understanding, but find the universal by comparison, *merely* reflective. I think this distinction between reflective and merely reflective is more important when the main concern of the discussion is determinative judgements (as it is in her book), so I will adhere to the established practice of calling these judgements reflective and contrast them with determinative judgements.

judgement is integral to both these perspectives on the world (KU III, 177). Determinative judgement is essential in subsuming given representations under concepts in theoretical knowledge, and plays a similar role in judging whether a maxim falls under the categorical imperative. Reflective judgement has two theoretical functions: one (the aesthetic) deals with judgements on beauty and sublimity, and one (the teleological) finds empirical laws for given phenomena (EE VII, 219 ff). But reflective judgement might even play a role in moral assessment (even though Kant apparently says nothing about it) when we seek to decide which subjective rule of action an agent, be it myself or some other agent, has been acting on. The particular action is given, and what is required is the rule, i.e. the universal[12].

In Kant's architectonic discussions at the end of the introductions, he relates the higher cognitive capacities to the capacities of the mind in general (KU IX, 196ff and EE XI, 245 f). In this context, too, judgement differs from the other two cognitive capacities. The capacity of mind corresponding to judgement is the feeling of pleasure and displeasure (KU III, 177 ff). Remembering that a capacity is a potential for performing some kind of function or activity, it is difficult to see how feeling can be defined as a capacity at all. Usually we think of a feeling as a bodily or mental state (cf. KU§29, 277 f and §9, 217), and not the capacity for an activity, at least when the feeling is regarded in isolation and not related to other faculties. On the other hand, by calling feeling a faculty of the soul Kant at least shows that feeling is not a passive receptivity, but an activity contributing to our experience of the world in some way or another. This is evident from his definition of pleasure and displeasure:

> Das Bewußtsein der Kausalität einer Vorstellung in Absicht auf den Zustand des Subjekts, es in demselben zu *erhalten*, kann hier im Allgemeinen das bezeichnen, was man Lust nennt; wogegen Unlust diejenige Vorstellung ist, die den Zustand der Vorstellungen zu ihrem eigenen Gegenteil zu bestimmen (sie abzuhalten oder wegzuschaffen) den Grund enthält. (KU§10, 220)

These states are defined by their self-conserving or self-discontinuing nature, which must be described as an active contribution to our shaping of the world. By connecting judgement directly with feelings, he also indicates the key role of the aesthetic in judgement.

---

12 Suggested by Larry Krasnoff on the discussion list kant-l@bucknell.edu, 24.05.97. I do not claim that Kant ascribed a moral function to reflective judgements, but the proposal is in keeping with his theories on ethics and judgement, and seems to be a reasonable supplement.

Judgement has a crucial role to play in gaining knowledge of the world, because it links the conceptual and the intuitive with each other, but also because Kant claims judgement to be the bridge between the realms of theoretical and practical legislation (KU IX, 195 ff).

2.2 Judgements of taste - feelings claiming intersubjective validity

Feeling and judgement

An aesthetic reflective judgement is not a judgement based on concepts; its determining ground is feeling:

> D.i. weil eben darin, daß die Einbildungskraft ohne Begriff schematisiert, die Freiheit derselben besteht, so muß das Geschmacksurteil auf einer bloßen Empfindung der sich wechselseitig belebenden Einbildungskraft in ihrer *Freiheit*, und des Verstandes mit seiner *Gesetzmäßigkeit*, also auf einem Gefühle beruhen ... . (KU§35, 287)

Not just any feeling can be the ground of an aesthetic reflective judgement; the feeling must be an expression of a particular cognitive relation between imagination and understanding. The feeling is the way we experience the relationship between these two faculties, to which relationship we have no other access[13]. How do I know that the feeling I have is expressing this relationship of the faculties, and not expressing some other state, e.g. a pleasure in a good wine or the pain at seeing a loved one suffer? At least we know that the feeling is not connected to the private circumstances of the subject in this way, because it is a disinterested feeling, which means that the feeling is not based on my interest in the existence of the object (KU§2, 204 f). The point of this distinction seems to be first and foremost to distinguish a *pure* aesthetic judgement from judgements based on other feelings. Kant says that this inquiry is concerned with pure aesthetic judgements based on a disinterested feeling.

Following the discussion of the disinterested character of judgements of taste, is an inference that the judgement is valid for everyone:

> Folglich muß dem Geschmacksurteile, mit dem Bewußtsein der Absonderung in demselben von allem Interesse, ein Anspruch an Gültigkeit für jedermann,

[13] "Also kann jene subjektive Einheit des Verhältnisses sich nur durch Empfindung kenntlich machen." (KU§9, 219)

> ohne auf Objekte gestellte Allgemeinheit anhängen, d.i. es muß damit ein Anspruch auf subjektive Allgemeinheit verbunden sein. (KU§6, 212)

The judgement involves a claim to subjective universal validity[14], presumably because it is based on a disinterested, and hence not merely private, feeling. This is not a very convincing argument: why is a disinterested, but merely private feeling impossible? Kant does not say so, but I assume there is an implicit assumption that any feeling (or any other human capacity, for that matter) must serve a function. Feelings must either be expressive of our inclinations or our practical interests, or serve a function in cognition. In the latter case, everybody must share the feeling. Still I do not think anything depends on Kant's claim that since the feeling is disinterested, the judgement must also be valid for everyone. He can claim that it is disinterested *and* intersubjectively valid, because he has a separate justification of the latter claim. Nothing depends on this inference in §6. Actually, the inference seems to be more in keeping with Kant's exposition if turned around: since this feeling serves a cognitive function, it is valid for everyone, and must be disinterested.

When I claim subjective universal validity for a judgement, I claim that everybody should judge the object the same way as I do, not by referring to the properties of the object as in an objective, universally valid judgement, but because I hold the feeling to be a common, i.e. not private, feeling. A judgement of taste includes the claim that everybody else should make the same judgement because we must presuppose a common sense underlying the feeling that is the ground of the judgement (KU§20, 237 f). Thus the judgement is also subjectively necessary; we cannot prove the judgement by arguments, but we still require everybody to share it.

What is the judgement of taste? As we saw in the preceding presentation of the faculties, judgements combine the universal and the singular and that is done by subsuming a representation under a concept: 'This is a rose', and by combining concepts in further predications like 'This rose is yellow'. But in a judgement of taste the representation is not combined with a predicate but with a feeling:

---

[14] Universal validity is objective when it is based on concepts of the object. This judgement is valid for everything contained under the concept and for everyone who represents an object by this concept, which means that this universal validity is also subjective. An aesthetic judgement does not involve concepts, nor does it judge the object itself, but the state of the judging person. It is universally valid in the sense that it is valid for all judging persons, and this is what is meant by its being subjectively universally valid (KU§8, 215). Likewise, it is a subjectively necessary judgement (KU§22, 239 f). This is what we today would call intersubjective validity or necessity.

> Das Befremdende und Abweichende liegt nur darin: daß es nicht ein empirischer Begriff, sondern ein Gefühl der Lust (folglich gar kein Begriff) ist, welches doch durch das Geschmacksurteil, gleich als ob es ein mit dem Erkenntnisse des Objekts verbundendes Prädikat wäre, jedermann zugemutet und mit der Vorstellung desselben verknüpft werden soll. (KU VII, 191)

When we make an aesthetic reflective judgement the representation is accompanied by a disinterested feeling that we require everybody to share. This is expressed in statements like: 'This is beautiful' or 'This is ugly', which is the same as saying 'This (object) is accompanied by a feeling of pleasure/displeasure that I require everybody to share'. Since Kant often says that we judge by the feeling, or says that the feeling is the determining ground of the judgement, it makes sense to draw the conclusion that the judgement of taste is the proposition 'This is beautiful'.

'This is beautiful' is, as Fricke points out, not an objective statement since 'beauty' and 'beautiful' are not objective concepts, and the relation between subject and predicate is not one of subsumption of a representation under a concept[15]. I think this misleading nature of the sentence 'This is beautiful' should make us cautious about saying that aesthetic reflective judgements are these kinds of quasi-propositions. We should say that such statements are ways of expressing the judgements and are the conventional shorthand for saying something like: 'I feel a pleasure connected to the representation of this object that I demand everybody else to have at the representation of the same object'. Or as Kant puts it:

> Sagen: diese Blume ist schön, heißt ebensoviel, als ihren eigenen Anspruch auf jedermanns Wohlgefallen ihr nur nachsagen. ... Man sollte aber denken daß ein Urteil a priori einen Begriff vom Objekt enthalten müsse, zu dessen Erkenntnis es das Prinzip enthält; das Geschmackurteil aber gründet sich gar nicht auf Begriffe, und ist überall nicht Erkenntnis, sondern nur ein ästhetisches Urteil. (KU§32, 281 f)

To say that something is beautiful is not to make a proposition, because then the judgement of taste would be the ascription of the property 'beauty' to something given in intuition. Then the judgement would not be aesthetic, i.e. based on feeling.

In the section called "The Key to the Critique of Taste" Kant's frequently repeated claim that the basis of the judgement of taste is the feeling is apparently questioned:

---

[15] Fricke, *Kants Theorie*, 11f.

> Diese bloß subjektive (ästhetische) Beurteilung des Gegenstandes, oder der Vorstellung wodurch er gegeben wird, geht nun vor der Lust an demselben vorher und ist der Grund dieser Lust an der Harmonie der Erkenntnisvermögen .... (KU§9, 218)

There is a judging (or estimation, as Guyer calls it) which is the basis of the pleasure elsewhere said to be the basis of the pleasure of taste. To avoid circularity, Guyer suggests that we distinguish two separate acts of judgement, the first estimating the representation, and the second claiming intersubjective validity for the feeling resulting from the first estimation:

> We might thus distinguish between "estimating" an object and "judging" a pleasure as the two stages of reflection leading to a judgement of taste. ... The necessity of distinguishing two acts of judgement might be most simply demonstrated by pointing to the fact that Kant describes the feeling of pleasure as both the product of judgement and the ground for determination for judgement; yet if aesthetic judgement resulted from a single act, this would be to say that the same feeling of pleasure both succeeded, as its product, and yet preceded, as its evidence or ground, a single judgement. This is clearly absurd.[16]

Another absurdity Guyer finds in this key section is that the ground for a judgement of taste is said to be the universal communicability of the *Beurteilung* with the pleasure as its consequence (KU§9, 217)[17]. Thus the intersubjective validity is not established in the judgement of the feeling, but is constitutive of it. Guyer argues that this aspect of the theory must be rejected, especially because the judgement's "possible intersubjective validity simply plays no role in Kant's explanation of how reflective judgment can produce pleasure … ."[18]

Other interpreters have argued that these absurdities only arise from Guyer's own presuppositions that the relation between *Beurteilung*, feeling, and *Geschmacksurteil* must be a causal relation[19]. Ginsborg argues that the key is rather to regard the feeling as being self-referential in the sense that it is an awareness of the mental state of the subject:

> Kant does mean to say that the pleasure is consequent on the act of judging that the pleasure is universally valid. For he wants to claim that the feeling of pleasure is a self-referential state of awareness. To feel pleasure in the beautiful, he wants to indicate, is to be in a self-referential state of mind which

---

[16] Guyer, *Claims of Taste*, 98 f.

[17] Ibid. 137 f.

[18] Ibid.138. Guyer explains Kant's "mistake" as being due to an earlier, rejected theory, which influenced Kant in these passages.

[19] For a careful and detailed discussion and rejection of Guyer's reconstruction, see H. Ginsborg, *The Role of Taste in Kant's Theory of Cognition*, 6-19.

> constitutes awareness of its own appropriateness and hence of its own universal validity.[20]

Without yet going into other, and perhaps more problematic aspects of Ginsborg's account, we can see the merit of this interpretation as compared with Guyer's. Her interpretation makes sense of the apparent circularity that leads to the two-acts interpretation. The feeling is not caused by the judging, but is our awareness of this mental state, which is the feeling itself[21]. Thus we avoid the division of the act of judging into two separate acts of judgement, one about the subject's apprehension of the object, the other about the feeling resulting from this initial judging. Ginsborg's account also avoids the counterintuitive notion of an estimation of which we are not aware. One should assume that a minimal requirement of a *Beurteilung* is that the subject is aware of it.

Although Kant says that the *Beurteilung* precedes the pleasure, he also says that the mental state of free play of the cognitive powers in a representation is something the subject becomes aware of by feeling, and he even equates the free cognitive activity with the feeling:

> Also muß der Gemützustand in dieser Vorstellung der eines Gefühls des freien Spiels der Vorstellungskräfte an einer gegebenen Vorstellung zu einem Erkenntnisse überhaupt sein. (KU§9, 217)

> Die Belebung beider Vermögen (der Einbildungskraft und des Verstandes) zu unbestimmter, aber doch, vermittelst des Anlasses der gegebenen Vorstellung, einhelliger Tätigkeit, derjenigen nämlich, die zu einem Erkenntnis überhaupt gehört, ist die Empfindung, deren allgemeine Mitteilbarkeit das Geschmacksurteil postuliert. (KU§9, 219)

What is judged about in the aesthetic reflective judgement is the mental state of the subject. But this state is exactly the feeling that makes the judgement, thus making this reflective judgement a feeling feeling itself, as Lyotard expresses it. Due to this double status of being object as well as law, Lyotard calls the aesthetic reflective judgement "tautegorical"[22]. We can see a possible Kantian expression of this self-referentiality in the statement that the aesthetic judgement is both object to itself and law to itself:

---

[20] H. Ginsborg, 'Kant on the Subjectivity of Taste', 464.

[21] Other interpretations related to Ginsborg's in this respect include R. Aquila, 'A New Look on Kant's Aesthetic Judgments', 107, and J.-F. Lyotard, *Lessons in the Analytic*, 9 ff.

[22] Lyotard, *Lessons*, 12 f.

> Hierauf gründet sich nun die Aufgabe, mit der wir uns jetzt beschäftigen: Wie sind Geschmacksurteile möglich? welche Aufgabe also die Prinzipien a priori der reinen Urteilskraft in *ästhetischen* Urteilen betrifft, d.i. in solchen, wo sie nicht (wie in den theoretischen) unter objektiven Verstandsbegriffen bloß zu subsumieren hat und unter einem Gesetze steht, sondern wo sie sich selbst, subjektiv, Gegenstand sowohl als Gesetz ist. (KU§36, 288)

This passage says that the power of judgement is the object of the judgement, which means that neither the statement 'This is beautiful' nor the free play of imagination and understanding disregarding our awareness of this relation can be the judgement referred to. The statement is not object to itself; its object is the mental state, and the relation between the faculties regarded in isolation from the feeling of this relation is not a judgement in the sense of being a conscious act. The two-acts view cannot account for this passage.

I do not believe that this passage proves beyond doubt that Kant holds the judgement to be the feeling itself; it could be an unfortunate mistake due to the haste in producing the Critique. After all, the passage is not perfectly lucid. On the other hand, there are other passages supporting this interpretation. Aquila cites three passages suggesting that the judgement is the feeling itself; two from the introduction[23] and one from the first section:

> Ein regelmäßiges, zweckmäßiges Gebäude mit seinem Erkenntnisvermögen (es sei in deutlicher oder verworrener Vorstellungsart) zu befassen, ist ganz etwas anderes, als sich dieser Vorstellung mit der Empfindung des Wohlgefallens bewußt zu sein. (KU§1, 204)

We are conscious of the representation (with a sensation of pleasure), and it is difficult to see what more than consciousness of a judgement is required to make a judgement. A judgement is, after all, not something that *has* to be presented to other people in a propositional form such as 'This is beautiful'. It can certainly be only the consciousness of the content of this proposition. And Kant says that this consciousness is the sensation of pleasure.

If we return to §9 and its initial question whether the feeling or the judging comes first, Kant's answer seems to be that the judging [*die Beurteilung*] comes

---

23 Aquila, 'A New Look', 107 f. The two passages are the following: "Der Gegenstand heißt alsdann schön; und das Vermögen, *durch* eine solche Lust (folglich auch allgemeingültig) zu urteilen, der Geschmack." (KU VII, 190, my emphasis) "Eben so macht derjenige, welcher in der bloßen Reflexion über die Form eines Gegenstandes, ohne Rücksicht auf einen Begriff, Lust empfindet, ob zwar dieses Urteil empirisch und einzelnes Urteil ist, mit Recht anspruch auf jedermanns Beistimmung." (KU VII, 191) One can of course argue that '*dieses Urteil*' refers to the reflection and that the pleasure is only a consequence of this reflection, but then one is forced to hold the strange view that we are making a judgement of which we are not conscious.

first (KU§9, 218). This conclusion is based on an initial argument stating that the pleasure cannot come first because it would then be the pleasure of the merely agreeable and could not be connected with a claim to intersubjective validity. After stating that the feeling cannot be first, Kant does not immediately draw the conclusion that the judgement is first; he introduces a condition that underlies both judgement and feeling:

> Also ist es die allgemeine Mitteilungsfähigkeit des Gemütszustandes in der gegebenen Vorstellung, welche, als subjektive Bedingung des Geschmacksurteils, demselben zum Grunde liegen, und die Lust an dem Gegenstande zur Folge haben muß. (KU§9, 217)

The basis is neither the judgement, nor the feeling, but rather the universal communicability[24] of the mental state as regards the given representation. This mental state is the one we find in the relation between the representational powers insofar as they relate a given representation to cognition in general [*sofern sie eine gegebene Vorstellung auf Erkenntnis überhaupt beziehen*] (KU§9, 217). We experience this mental state by feeling, and we cannot separate this judging from what is judged, a fact that makes it reasonable to call this feeling, that is both the judging and object of this judging, a self-referring feeling. A serious draw-back of this interpretation is that it appears to embroil Kant in a vicious circle, as discussed by Guyer: the ground for this feeling is the universal communicability of that same feeling; i.e. the feeling is the consequence of an aspect of this same feeling. Ginsborg avoids this circularity by rejecting that this as a causal relation and by holding that this feeling is expressing a demand to universal validity for itself:

> But how can a pleasure be consequent on its own universal communicability? Clearly the relation of consequence here cannot be construed in the way that Guyer does, as a causal relation. Instead, I want to suggest the relation is an intentional one: the pleasure constitutes awareness of (consciousness of, sensitivity to) its own universal communicability.[25]

We do not only feel a particular pleasure; we feel this pleasure as a pleasure that everybody ought to feel when having the same representation. Thus the aesthetic reflective judgement concerns a feeling containing a claim to subjective

---

24 Kulenkampff argues that Kant by *mitteilen* refers to the older meaning 'share with others' or 'allowing others to take part in' rather than the modern 'communicate', see J. Kulenkampff, *Kants Logik des ästhetischen Urteils*, 191, n.15. By *allgemeine Mitteilbarkeit* we should understand 'universal shareability' rather than the common 'universal communicability'. Due to its central position in the commentary literature I will use the traditional, if misleading, translation.

25 Ginsborg, *Role of Taste*, 23.

universal validity. Furthermore, it is not about an object as such, but about the way the subject feels when apprehending an object[26]. This feeling is determined by the subject's representation of the object, so the judgement tells us something about the object. Still, the representing subject, not the represented object, becomes the focus of interest in aesthetics. This mental state we feel is, according to Kant, our way of being aware of the free play between the different parts of the mind; imagination and understanding in judgements of taste, and imagination and reason in judgements of sublimity.

Although I have rejected Guyer's two-acts view, nevertheless the feeling of a universally communicable mental state is not the same as the thought or utterance 'This is beautiful'. There remains the distinct possibility that the judgement is a sentence based on an awareness of the mental state. Kant's often repeated statement that the *basis* of the judgement of taste is a feeling (e.g. KU VII, 191) supports this view. Still this is not a two-acts view in Guyer's sense, because the claim on universal agreement is contained in the feeling. Thus the content of the feeling and the judgement is identical. I doubt that the sentence serves any function beyond communicating our judgement to others, but given the intersubjective nature of aesthetic reflective judgements, this function has some importance. Maybe we should, on these grounds, avoid asserting that the aesthetic reflective judgement is the feeling.

On the other hand, saying that the judgement is the sentence is problematic, too. What is added to the intuition is not a concept, which appears to be the case in the statement 'This is beautiful'. The judgement adds a *feeling* to the intuition, Kant says (KU§36, 288)[27], and a feeling cannot be expressed in words. It can only be felt. The impression is that Kant is wavering between two ways of understanding aesthetic reflective judgement; either as disinterested feeling or as a quasi-proposition based on a feeling. Anyway, the important aspects of the judgement: disinterestedness, universality, subjective purposiveness, and necessity are all aspects of the feeling. Hence the sentence adds nothing to the feeling. The

---

26 It is the apprehension of some particular object that gives rise to the feeling, and it is the object that is called beautiful. But this beauty is not an attribute of the object, but a feeling in the subject only. That makes it impossible to use objective criteria to decide questions of taste. One has to settle for the claim that the object is beautiful, and demand agreement of others without argument. Kant argues for the legitimacy of such demands.

27 "Daß Geschmacksurteile synthetische sind, ist leicht einzusehen, weil sie über den Begriff, und selbst die Anschauung des Objekts, hinausgehen, und etwas, das gar nicht einmal Erkenntnis ist, nämlich Gefühl der Lust (oder Unlust) zu jener als Prädikat hinzutun."

cognitive function of the judgement is, as I will argue, only connected to the judging, i.e. to the feeling of the free play of the cognitive powers.

Thus the judgement of taste is expressed in a sentence such as 'This is beautiful', which is based on a feeling of a mental state of free play of imagination and understanding in the representation of an object. This feeling issues a claim to subjective universal validity for itself. Saying that we are aware of this self-referential feeling in the *Beurteilung*, does not amount to a claim that we *have to* be aware of this mental state. I will argue that every act of cognition involves the free play of the cognitive powers without claiming that we always judge the object aesthetically in the sense of being aware of this play. Therefore my claim is that every act of cognition presupposes a mental state that can be subject to aesthetic judgement. I will return to this in the last section of this chapter.

Disinterested aesthetic reflective judgements and other feelings

Since the aesthetic experience does not involve theoretical knowledge, it follows that our understanding, the categories, and thus, all concepts, cannot be relevant for the experience (KU§31, 280 f). This does not mean that knowledge of the objects in question is excluded, in which case statements such as Kant's 'This flower is beautiful' would be impossible (KU§32 281). We can make determinative judgements of the same object that we judge aesthetically, but the concept of this determination is not involved in the aesthetic reflective judgement. Thus we have no cognitive 'interest' in the existence of the object. Furthermore, we do not desire the object directly (KU§3, 206), nor do we think of it in terms of a purpose, either on a prudential or a moral basis (KU§4, 208 f). Desires and purposes are connected to the power of desire (KU§5, 209), and Kant defines these as feelings connected (directly or indirectly) with an interest in the existence of an object (KU§2, 204 f).

When Kant defines the feeling in aesthetic reflective judgements as disinterested, he does not mean that we do not take any interest at all in aesthetic objects[28], but merely that this interest is not connected to desire in any of the aforementioned senses. And only in this context can we make sense of his statement that even the existence of object is irrelevant for the judgement of taste (KU§5, 209). There must be a *representation* of an object, but the object itself is

[28] On the contrary; we both take an empirical interest in beauty on a social basis (KU§41,296 ff) and an intellectual interest in beauty on a moral basis (KU§42, 298 ff).

not of interest because (in this particular judgement) we do not relate to it as object of desire or part of our purposes. I will take it for granted that this way of defining disinterestedness not only is meaningful, but that it refers to feelings that are recognisable as part of the human repertoire of feeling. We have seen that Nussbaum, as many other commentators, has expressed doubts as regards the coherence of this account[29]. I do however believe Kant's view is one that at least does not contradict common beliefs about the aesthetic appreciation of nature and art.

Pleasure in beauty seems to be an irreducible part of the experience of nature, at least in modern times. Most people will agree that there are areas and objects of nature that we call beautiful, an agreement reflected in the "growing institutionalization of natural appreciation" and "widespread public agreement concerning the beauty of certain landscapes"[30]. It is also agreed that feeling plays an important role in the appreciation of natural beauty, although we also seek criteria for beauty, such as symmetry, proportion and so forth. That this feeling is directly connected to an interest in the existence of the object, in the sense discussed by Kant, is not plausible. The pleasure we take in the beauty of nature is not connected to the good or the desirable, unless we take the fact of pleasure to be proof of an interest by itself. Thus, by mere exclusion, the pleasure of beauty in nature is not interested.

I am not arguing that the pleasure in beautiful objects and landscapes must be disinterested in any strong sense. One can never rule out the possibility that a pleasure really expresses a repressed desire, or that we take pleasure in an object because it is the kind of object that is appreciated within the group we desire to belong to. My aim is to argue that the kind of feeling Kant is talking about is recognisable, and the assumption that this feeling is disinterested in the weak sense suggested by Kant is not by itself incoherent. Disinterestedness in this sense is, however, no indication that this feeling carries a justified claim to universal validity.

A pure, disinterested feeling does not exclude the possibility of having feelings connected with interest at the same time. A farmer looking at his wheat fields at the end of summer probably would take as much pleasure in the prospects for a good harvest as in the natural beauty of the scenery, and it would be difficult for him to decide where one kind of pleasure ends and the other starts. The same would be the case for someone reading a well-written novel with a good moral.

---

29 See p. 28.
30 T. J. Diffey, 'Natural Beauty without Metaphysics', 45.

The pleasure induced by the virtuous story would be mixed up with the pure aesthetic pleasure created by the aesthetic ideas expressed in the form of the novel[31]. To make certain that a pleasure is the basis of a *pure* judgement of taste, all such moral and theoretical interests must be purged from the experience:

> Daß der, welcher ein Geschmacksurteil zu fällen glaubt, in der Tat dieser Idee gemäß urteile, kann ungewiß sein; aber daß er es doch darauf beziehe, mithin daß es ein Geschmacksurteil sein solle, kündigt er durch den Ausdruck der Schönheit an. Für sich selbst aber kann er durch das bloße Bewußtsein der Absonderung alles dessen, was zum Angenehmen und Guten gehört, von dem Wohlgefallen, was ihm noch übrig bleibt, davon gewiß werden ... . (KU§8, 216)

This act of abstraction is an essential part of making a pure judgement of taste, and it also includes abstracting from the pleasure of accessory beauty, i.e. pleasure dependent on a concept of the purpose of the object (KU§16, 231).

An object of nature can, according to what Kant says here, give rise simultaneously to qualitatively different kinds of feelings with different sources. Judging the object by a disinterested feeling does not mean that this is the only way we apprehend the object. We can have a concept of what the object is (an apple), we can judge it purposively, teleologically (intrinsic: colour and taste make birds and animals eat it and ensure the spreading of the seed; extrinsic: nourishing food for human beings and animals (EE XII, 250)), we can judge it by an aesthetic judgement of sense (tasty, desirable (EE VIII, 224)), we can judge its accessory beauty (perfect colour and shape in relation to the purposes of the apple (KU§16, 230)), and we can judge it by pure aesthetic judgement (beautiful). Moral feeling is presumably not part of the apprehension of an apple, although it may be for other objects or events.

The disinterested feeling in the judgement of taste is just one of several aspects of our experience of an object, and in many cases it is 'covered up' by these other feelings. Thus we are not aware of it. That we are not always making judgements of taste does not preclude that the mental state and the feeling underlying aesthetic judgements are always present. But we do not always feel this mental state because these other judgements and feelings require our attention. Or we feel it only in

31 'Form' can have at least two meanings in this context. What I call the form of a novel refers to the way the plot is presented, to the way the content is presented, but what Kant calls the form is defined only negatively, as the object considered apart from the material content. But when we speak of the form as a literary tool, it is conceptualised and loses the connection to the Kantian notion of form in aesthetic reflective judgement. I will return to how 'form' can be understood in judgements of taste.

combination with these other feelings. At least this is how I propose that we understand Kant's theory.

Beauty and ugliness

Thus far I have mainly discussed the pleasure in the judgement of beauty. What feeling does the subject have if the object of judgement is ugly? Given the logic of the statement above, we would have an experience of displeasure presumably due to a free[32], but *dis*harmonious play between imagination and understanding. But is that the case in Kant's account? He does not seem too concerned with clarifying the differences between the beautiful and the ugly, nor does he specify how lack of harmony between the faculties in their free play differs from the harmonious play of beauty[33]. The only places where this negative aesthetic judgement is touched upon are in the numerous passages where the feeling is said to be either a pleasure or a displeasure (e.g. KU VII, 189 and §5, 209 f) and in a short discussion of how fine art describes beautifully ugly objects of nature:

> Die schöne Kunst zeigt darin eben ihre Vorzüglichkeit, daß sie Dinge, die in der Natur häßlich oder mißfällig sein würden, schön beschreibt. Die Furien, Krankheiten, Verwüstungen des Krieges, u.d.gl. können, als Schädlichkeiten, sehr schön beschrieben, ja sogar im Gemälde vorgestellt werden ... . (KU§48, 312)

Hudson takes this to be evidence for the assumption that Kant held that nature can be judged to be ugly[34]. It is not clear, however, that Kant is referring to a *pure* aesthetic judgement of ugliness here. These examples are of objects and events are that harmful to human beings, not disinterestedly displeasureable. These objects or events appear to be examples of accessory ugliness, which means that the displeasure depends on a concept of the purpose of the object or the event[35] (KU§16, 229 f).

---

[32] It cannot be unfree, because the freedom of imagination is necessary for there to be any play at all, be it harmonious or disharmonious.

[33] A pre-critical reflection shows that Kant thought that almost all natural objects are beautiful, see Zammito, *Genesis*, 100. This can explain his lack of interest in judgements of ugliness, but it does not prove that judgements of beauty are the only kind of judgement of taste. Since Kant thought that it is possible that some, albeit few, objects are ugly, this has to be explained within the framework established in his theory of aesthetic judgements.

[34] H. Hudson, 'The Significance of an Analytic of the Ugly in Kant's Deduction of Pure Judgements of Taste', 88 f.

[35] Hannah Ginsborg pointed this out to me.

In the Deduction (KU§38, 289 f) as well as other central passages the impression is that pleasure is the only feeling containing a claim to universal validity for itself. This is underscored by the title of the first book being 'Analytic of the Beautiful', not of taste. This equation of taste with the beautiful is not strange when considering that Kant repeatedly states that *harmony* in the free relation (KU§22, 240 f) or the proportioned attunement[36] of the faculties is the condition of cognition:

> Eine Vorstellung, die, als einzeln und ohne Vergleichung mit andern dennoch eine Zusammenstimmung zu den Bedingungen der Allgemeinheit hat, welche das Geschäft des Verstandes überhaupt ausmacht, bringt die Erkenntnisvermögen in die proportionierte Stimmung, die wir zu allem Erkenntnisse fordern, und daher auch für jedermann, der durch Verstand und Sinne in Verbindung zu urteilen bestimmt ist (*für* jeden Menschen), gültig halten. (KU§9, 219)

Kant expresses the relationship between the faculties mainly in musical and vocal metaphors, such as *Harmonie*, *proportionierte Stimmung*, and *einhellig* activity. These passages suggest that only the relation experienced as pleasurable is a condition for cognition, which would mean that only judgements of beauty can be considered as necessary judgements[37]. The unhappy consequence would be that the field of a priori judgements of taste is restricted to judgements of beauty (and of the sublime), and that objects cannot be ugly, or, at best, that the judgement of ugliness is a subjective, private judgement like the aesthetic judgement of sense which we cannot demand others to share. This is contrary to common usage of the terms 'beautiful' and 'ugly', which both seem to claim some kind of intersubjective validity. If judgements of ugliness have merely private subjective validity, then Kant must either reject the common view that beauty and ugliness have same epistemological status, or accept that also judgements of beauty have merely private subjective validity.

---

[36] Meredith uses 'accord' whereas Pluhar prefers 'attunement' as translation of *Stimmung*. *Stimmung* can both refer to a mood or atmosphere in the psychological sense, as well as to the tuning of a musical instrument, but here the musical or vocal sense selected by the translators seems to be most appropriate. The German usage of the word *Stimmung* includes more or less good or bad tuning, mood, or atmosphere, whereas both English translations are words equivalent to 'harmony' in suggesting that an optimal relation is already established. My reconstruction aims at saving Kant from having an 'either beauty or nothing'-theory, and since 'accord' appears closest to 'harmony' in this respect, I prefer Pluhar's choice.

[37] This is a variant of the 'everything is beautiful'-paradox as formulated in R. Meerbote, 'Reflection on Beauty', 81. Harmony of the faculties is required for cognition, and such harmony is experienced as pleasurable. This means that every act of cognition is pleasurable and, thus, every object that can be cognised is beautiful.

Kant says that the proportionate attunement of the cognitive powers is required for cognition in general (KU§21, 238), and I take this to mean that every act of cognition must presuppose this attunement. It follows that if there is no such attunement, no cognition can arise[38]. The consequence would be that we could only have knowledge of beautiful objects, because ugliness is a feeling of a lack of this attunement. Then every object is beautiful, and every object is judged to have the same aesthetic value, which makes them cognitively superfluous. If every object we cognise is accompanied by the same feeling, then this feeling carries no information. For Kant's conception of *judgements* of taste to be meaningful, not all objects can be judged to be beautiful. Some objects must be judged to be not beautiful. How is that possible, if a particular proportionate attunement is required for all cognition?

Not only must the theory account for judgement on ugly objects, it must also account for objects that are judged neither beautiful nor ugly. Perhaps most objects are considered neither ugly nor beautiful. We can follow Fricke in calling these aesthetically neutral objects 'non-beautiful' [*nicht schön*][39]. Allison has found evidence that Kant did have such a three-fold classification of judgements of taste:

> Kant distinguishes between these two species of negative judgements of taste in *Logik Philippi* 24: 364 and *Logik Pölitz* 24: 520. In the former he claims that ugliness is something positive, not merely the absence of beauty (which he seems to equate with dullness [*Trockenheit*]), but the existence of that which is contrary to beauty.[40]

If we assume that there are these three kinds of judgement of taste, the question is how to explain these non-beautiful judgements in terms of the attunement of the cognitive powers.

The fact that Kant held that there were judgements of non-beauty and of ugliness does not show how to find room for these judgements in his theory. One possible solution to this problem is to differentiate between 'harmonious' and 'proportionate' in Kant's text. The mental state which is a condition for cognition is the proportionate attunement between imagination and understanding, while

---

38 This is based on the most plausible understanding of how judgements of taste are necessary for any cognition. I will, however, in reconstructing the deduction suggest another way of understanding this claim by taking judgements of taste to be a condition of teleological judgements as a necessary part of cognition. The present argument is based on the common interpretation, but the logic would be the same on the basis of my suggested interpretation. Claiming that we could only ascribe empirical laws of teleology to beautiful objects, whereas ugly objects could only be judged according to universal laws of nature would sound even more absurd.

39 Fricke, *Kants Theorie*, 7.

40 H. Allison, 'Pleasure and Harmony in Kant's Theory of Taste', 478, note 15.

what makes this proportionate attunement pleasurable, is this attunement's play being harmonious. It would then follow that in the experience of something ugly there still is an attunement of some particular proportion but this is of a disharmonious kind. There is a continuum of proportions in *Stimmung* from optimal harmony via neutral proportion to disharmony. The obvious problem here is how something proportionate can be disharmonious, because a proportionate attunement in itself seems to be harmonious. Usually being proportionate means that two elements stand in a certain regular relationship; that they fit together. This is not Kant's view, though:

> Die Beurteilung eines Gegenstandes durch Geschmack ist ein Urteil über die Einstimmung oder den Widerstreit der Freiheit im Spiele der Einbildungskraft und der Gesetzmäßigkeit des Verstandes .... (A 241)

Proportionate *Stimmung* does not have to be *Einstimmung*.

The key passage decisive for how to understand Kant on this account is found in §21 where Kant describes an optimal relationship between understanding and imagination giving the best conditions for cognition, and that the experience of this relationship is the experience of beauty.

> Aber diese Stimmung der Erkenntniskräfte hat, nach Verschiedenheit der Objekte, die gegeben werden, eine verschiedene Proportion. Gleichwohl aber muß es eine geben, in welcher dieses innere Verhältnis zur Belebung (einer durch die andere) die zuträglichste für beide Gemütskräfte in Absicht auf Erkenntnis (gegebener Gegenstände) überhaupt ist. (KU §21, 238 f)

Here Kant explicitly says that the proportion varies according to the differences in the objects, which means that there is not only one proportion leading to cognition. If only the optimal proportion referred to in the second sentence led to cognition, then the different objects mentioned in the first sentence could not have been cognised. And then they would not be objects. Thus a less than optimal proportion in the attunement of the faculties can be experienced by a neutral or a negative feeling, depending on the proportion[41].

Bernstein rejects this answer because it implies "that those [objects] that were beautiful were better in the sense of more knowable, which is counter-intuitive in

[41] This interpretation is related to the one suggested in K. Ameriks, 'How to Save Kant's Deduction of Taste'. But in Ameriks' account, only harmony of the faculties results in aesthetic reflective judgements. The other proportions lead to cognition but only a range of harmonious relations are resulting in aesthetic judgements, see 299 f. Thus he avoids the claim that everything is beautiful, but he lacks an account of judgements of ugliness. I will discuss the solution proposed in Allison,'Pleasure and Harmony', 478 ff. below.

the extreme"[42]. One can only agree with Bernstein in his claim that assuming beautiful objects to be more knowable is counterintuitive. This is not the only alternative to an 'everything is beautiful'-thesis, though. Kant defines pleasure and displeasure as self-preserving and self-terminating states:

> Das Bewußtsein der Kausalität einer Vorstellung in Absicht auf den Zustand des Subjekts, es im demselben zu *erhalten*, kann hier im allgemeinen das bezeichnen, was man Lust nennt; wogegen Unlust diejenige Vorstellung ist die den Zustand der Vorstellungen zu ihrem eigenen Gegenteile zu bestimmen (sie abzuhalten oder wegzuschaffen) den Grund enthält. (KU§10, 220)

What we can say is that beautiful objects are more attractive objects of contemplation, due to this self-preserving character of pleasure. Kant says we linger in our contemplation of the beautiful (KU§12, 222). In this way beauty is more conducive to knowledge, because we spend more time contemplating beautiful objects than ugly ones. This harmony does not make beautiful objects more knowable. They are just the kind of objects we spend time contemplating. Thus the conditions for cognising them are optimal.

Ugly objects are less attractive, and do not evoke a positive mood, to draw on another meaning of the word *Stimmung*. Although we experience such phenomena as not pleasurable, they are not less knowable. The lack of pleasure itself signifies an attunement between the faculties of the mind, namely a disharmonious one. The faculties are brought into play with each other, and this is an indication of some sort of proportionate relationship between them. The feeling, positive or negative, shows that the faculties are interacting, 'playing' with each other. But we do not linger over them, and the conditions for cognition are not as good as for the objects we take pleasure in merely by watching them.

My interpretation of the attunement of the cognitive power has two steps: (1) The proportionate attunement is just the fact that the faculties are capable of coordinated play, which gives rise to a more or less pleasurable feeling, and this is the necessary condition for any cognition. (2) That attunement, however, is more or less harmonious, making some objects appear beautiful, some non-beautiful, and some ugly[43]. The first point would be part of the transcendental conditions of

---

[42] J. Bernstein, *The Fate of Art*, 22.

[43] There are several passages in the third Critique that suggests that Kant held judgements of taste not to include judgements of ugliness, and that do not fit with this interpretation (e.g. EE VIII, 224 f). One reason might be that Kant (as Bernstein and others suggest) really meant that pleasure is part of the transcendental conditions of judgement, and thought that all objects are beautiful. Another reason might be that it is just in some cases the relation between the cognitive powers is such that a judgement of taste can arise, and that is at the representation of beautiful objects, as Ameriks suggests. A third

aesthetic reflective judgements, whereas the other would be empirically dependent on the appearances that are judged aesthetically. If accepted, this solves one aspect of the problem related to the possibility of judgements of non-beautiful and ugly objects, namely the one connected to the harmony of the faculties as a condition of cognition.

There is another problem left for Kant's aesthetic theory as regards non-beautiful and ugly objects. This is the central claim that the basis of judgements of taste is the subjective purposiveness or form of purposiveness in the representation of the object, which is directly linked with the feeling of pleasure (KU§11, 221). This problem I will discuss in connection with the problem of understanding the justification of the subjective universal validity of the judgements of taste.

Judging the form of the object

Another difficulty facing my interpretation is the claim that the aesthetic judgement deals with the form of the object (KU§14, 224 f.). I have insisted that it is the mental state of the subject in the act of cognising the object that is judged. How can that be reconciled with the claim that it is the form of the object that is judged? Now the notion of form or shape of an object is possible to understand merely negatively as that which is not material. The crucial question must be what we can say positively; i.e. what is that which is left when we regard the process of cognition purged of the material content of intuition?

The few positive clues Kant provides in the third Critique are words such as 'outline' [*Abriß*], 'shape' [*Gestalt*], 'play' [*Spiel*] (KU§14, 225), and 'boundedness' [*Begrenzung*], which mean that the object has some kind of limits (KU§23, 244). Although 'play' indicates something different from the other terms, this still seems to place Kant solidly within the Aristotelian tradition of aesthetic theory. Form within this tradition is a structure, a way of presenting some material[44], e.g. the design in pictorial arts or the composition in music (KU§14, 225). This concept of form is convincing in a theory of art, but not in a theory of how we judge nature by feeling. These formal elements of art are based on a

---

reason why Kant does not express this difference between beauty and ugliness more clearly might be that he is primarily concerned with the beautiful, and, thus, with pleasure. As Hudson puts it: "Kant's *Critiques* emphasize the accounts of cognitive truth, moral goodness, and aesthetic judgments of beauty. And do not tend to dwell on their counterparts, cognitive error, moral evil, and aesthetic judgments of ugliness." Hudson, 'The Significance', 89.

44 Aristotle, *Poetics*, 1449b ff.

conceptual framework within a tradition of creating objects of art, whereas aesthetic judgements are supposed to be a way we must respond to nature, independently of which concepts we subsume the object under. Besides, these formal concepts seem to be part of the material of cognition. What is presented in intuition, according to the first Critique, is a manifold that is bounded by the productive imagination according to the rules of understanding, and it is difficult to see what the form or the boundedness of the object independent of this determination can mean.

R. Meerbote suggests that the form consists in some invariant features that the manifold must possess for it to be conformable to the laws of the understanding:

> what Kant appears to have in mind are at least the general requirements of orderliness or orderability and lawfulness of elements of any manifold.[45]

This certainly is a tempting way to solve the problem. The object's form is the fact that the manifold satisfies requirements that must be present for it to be subsumed under the concepts of understanding. This solution allows for a hypothetical division between intuitions that satisfy these requirements and intuitions that do not, and this division conforms to the division between what can be cognised and what cannot. The problem is, as Meerbote points out, how to make room for forms of different objects leading to more or less harmony, and thus, more or less pleasure. It seems as if the form of the object on this construal either is or is not orderly and lawful in keeping with the invariant features of concepts. The consequence is that all cognisable objects are beautiful. This problem can be solved by assuming that the objects are more or less in accordance with these general requirements, and thus, more or less beautiful. Another difficulty is that the requirement of orderability is an unnecessary addition to the act of cognition, because it only says that those objects that are ordered according to the rules of understanding must be represented in intuition as an orderable manifold. It is odd that feeling this orderability should be a condition of cognition, because the act of synthesising the manifold shows this orderability.My solution is to say that what is left of the object of cognition when the content is abstracted away is merely the activity of our cognitive capacities. This is in keeping with Kant's general view on form and content, where the form is our capacity for ordering the manifold in time and space and subsuming it under concepts of understanding. But the faculties or capacities of cognition are more than mere potentiality. To have certain abilities means that one is capable of performing a

---

45 Meerbote, 'Reflection on Beauty', 79.

certain act. And the form of the object is the same as our cognitive capacities in the act of cognition.

This seems too obvious. Is that not the basis for all cognition, and another way of stating Meerbote's suggestion of invariant features? Doesn't it lead us right back into the 'everything is beautiful'-trap? No, because Meerbote's suggestion is that all cognisable objects share some features prior to the act of cognition, whereas I claim that what the objects share independently of cognition is just that they are structured by human judgement. Since the manifold is different in each and every act of cognition, it is also likely that the structuring activities of imagination and understanding differs accordingly. The form of the object is the activity of the cognitive powers in structuring the manifold so that it gives rise to a concept of the object. The only way we can judge this cognitive activity in isolation from the matter of the judgement, is in the way it affects the subject, i.e. the way we feel this activity. This makes the judging of the form of the object identical with judging the mental state of the subject.

There is a passage in the Anthropology that shows that this is what Kant means:

> Im *Geschmack* (der Auswahl) aber, d.i. in der ästhetischen Urteilskraft, ist es nicht unmittelbar die *Empfindung* (das Materiale der Vorstellung des Gegenstandes), sondern wie es die freie (produktive) Einbildungskraft durch Dichtung zusammenpaart, d.i. die *Form*, was das Wohlgefallen an demselben hervorbringt: denn nur die Form ist es, was des Anspruchs auf eine allgemeine Regel für das Gefühl der Lust fähig ist. (A 240 f)

In this account it is only the activity of the imagination that is called the form of the object, but I think Kant has to include the understanding as well, because there cannot be a cognition without the discursive element of understanding. Human cognition must combine the sensible and the discursive elements in one way or another, and the form of the object is the combined activity of these two aspects. This means that the estimation of the form of the object is the disinterested feeling of this mental state in representing the object.

2.3 Universal validity of judgements of taste

The subjective condition of cognition

A judgement of taste is based on a feeling of pleasure or displeasure that is our experience of a proportionate attunement of the cognitive powers imagination and understanding in the representation of an object. In this relation, the faculties are in free play, which means that the productive imagination is considered in its freedom, despite the paradoxical nature of this claim:

> Der Verstand allein gibt das Gesetz. Wenn aber die Einbildungskraft nach einem bestimmten Gesetze zu verfahren genötigt wird, so wird ihr Produkt, der Form nach, durch Begriffe bestimmt, wie es sein soll; aber alsdann ist das Wohlgefallen, wie oben gezeigt, nicht das am Schönen, sondern am Guten (…), und das Urteil ist kein Urteil durch Geschmack. Es wird also eine Gesetzmäßigkeit ohne Gesetz, und eine subjektive Übereinstimmung der Einbildungskraft zum Verstande, ohne eine objektive, da die Vorstellung auf einen bestimmten Begriff von einem Gegenstande bezogen wird, mit der freien Gesetzmäßigkeit des Verstandes (welche auch Zweckmäßigkeit ohne Zweck genannt worden) und mit der Eigentümlichkeit eines Geschmacksurteils allein zusammen bestehen können. (KU§22, 241)

In cognition, as described in the first Critique, imagination operates according to the rules of understanding, but in the relation underlying judgements of taste imagination is not under this restriction. Still imagination displays lawfulness, and this is not the empirical, associative laws of reproductive imagination (KU§22, 240). Kant's view is that lawfulness is required if imagination is to enter into a relation with understanding, which is presupposed to operate according to laws. I will add that since imagination is said to perform the apprehension of the manifold in intuition (EE VII, 220), i.e. the synthesis by going through and bringing together the manifold (KrV A99), lawfulness is required even regardless of this harmonisation with understanding. Any synthesis must display some kind of lawfulness. The first problem we can note is: what kind of lawfulness is imagination displaying in this free play, and why is there any such free relation at all[46]?

Kant says that the feeling in the proportionate attunement of the faculties is universally valid in the sense that we can demand the same feeling from others experiencing the same object[47]. The basis for this demand is that the proportionate attunement of the cognitive powers is a condition for cognition in general. Now every act of cognition must involve a relation between imagination and

---

46 Several commentators have noticed the further difficulties posed by the metaphorical language Kant employs to describe this relation. See E. Schaper, *Studies in Kant's Aesthetics*, 66 f., and D. Henrich, *Aesthetic Judgement and the Moral Image of the World*, 40.

47 This includes that agreement is demanded of the subject's own self, now and in the future, as is pointed out in Ginsborg, *Role of Taste*, 86 ff., where the claim to universal communicability is connected to the self-perpetuating character of pleasure. I return to a discussion of this later on.

understanding determined by the latter (KrV B162), but in that case the relation is not free, and is not one that requires an intersubjective agreement on the mental state in question. Then a claim to subjective universal validity will be a consequence of the objective universal validity in applying the concept to an object (KU§8, 215), and no separate demand for agreement is required. Thus it is not this *determinate* relation between the cognitive powers that is at stake in the third Critique. Guyer suggests that the free relation is a preparatory stage preceding this determination in object, and identifies it with the two first steps of the three-fold synthesis (KrV, A98 ff):

> The first step would be to distinguish between psychological and epistemological elements in Kant's analysis of knowledge: a theory of syntheses as mental processes by which mental states of cognition are *produced*, and a theory of the categories as rules by which the *verification* of claims to cognition may proceed.[48]

As Guyer himself notices, this contradicts Kant's view that synthesis is subject to the categories[49], and there is no evidence that Kant changed this basic aspect of his theory of cognition from the first to the third Critique, at least not as regards determinative judgement. On the contrary, he affirms it several places (see e.g. KU IV, 179 f). Distinguishing between empirical production and verification under transcendental conditions also seems rather un-Kantian. The question is, then: where do we fit the free relation between imagination and understanding into Kant's theory of cognition?

In the so-called First Deduction[50], KU§21, Kant says about the attunement of the cognitive powers that it is the subjective condition of cognition,

> weil ohne diese [Stimmung der Erkenntniskräfte] als subjektive Bedingung des Erkennens, das Erkenntnis als Wirkung nicht entspringen könnte. Dieses geschieht auch wirklich jederzeit, wenn ein gegebener Gegenstand vermittelst der Sinne die Einbildungskraft zur Zusammensetzung des Mannigfalten, diese aber den Verstand zur Einheit desselben in Begriffen, in Tätigkeit bringt. (KU§21, 238)

Here Kant explicitly says that without the attunement of the cognitive powers cognition could not arise, and that this attunement has a role every time an object induces imagination and understanding to act. The implication must be that underlying every act of cognition is a free relation between the cognitive powers that gives rise to a feeling.

---

48 Guyer, *Claims of Taste*, 86.
49 Ibid. 85.
50 Ibid. 252 f. and Ameriks 'How to Save', 295 f.

It is reasonable, then, to see aesthetic reflective judgement as concerning the activity in every act of cognition when regarded from a subjective point of view. Evidence for this interpretation is found in the First Introduction:

> Denn in der Urteilskraft werden Verstand und Einbildungskraft im Verhältnisse gegen einander betrachtet, und dieses kann zwar erstlich objektiv, als zum Erkenntnis gehörig, in Betracht gezogen werden (wie in dem transzendentalen Schematism der Urteilskraft geschah); aber man kann eben dieses Verhältnis zweier Erkenntnisvermögen doch auch bloß subjektiv betrachten, so fern eins das andere in eben derselben Vorstellung befördert oder hindert und dadurch den *Gemütszustand* affiziert und also ein Verhältnis, welches *empfindbar* ist (ein Fall, der bei dem abgesonderten Gebrauch keines andern Erkenntnisvermögens statt findet). (EE VIII, 223, see also KU VII, 188 f)

The judgement of taste is no separate act of judgement occurring prior to cognition, but a judgement of how the subject is affected in the act of cognition. It is the same representation by which an object is given, but instead of referring it to the cognition of the object, we judge how the feeling of the subject is affected by this representation. Thus, this subjective aspect of cognition has its own 'jurisdiction' in aesthetic reflective judgement as a separate capacity. Claiming that the mental state is an aspect of every judgement, with the implication that every object can be judged aesthetically, is compatible with common use of aesthetic language. We can assess the aesthetic qualities of *any* object, although we seldom do so for commonplace phenomena. Although my neighbourhood mainly consists of dull buildings and gardens that are neither beautiful nor ugly, it still makes sense to discuss whether these objects are beautiful, and compare their respective aesthetic qualities.

Kant repeatedly claims that the aesthetic judgement does not result in cognition (e.g. EE VII, 222, KU VII, 189, and KU§15, 228), although it involves an exhibition of a concept in general [*Darstellung eines Begriffs überhaupt*] (EE VIII, 223.) This has been taken to mean that although the aesthetic reflective judgement rests on the same kind of attunement of the cognitive powers as in cognition, in this case the attunement does not result in cognition, but merely in a feeling:

> The free play of the faculties does not take place in every or, indeed, in any act of cognition. It is only when I take my imaginative activity in the perception of some particular object to exemplify how I ought to be with respect to that object that my faculties may be said to be in free play. And that does not happen in perceptual cognition, but only in the special case of aesthetic experience: for it is only in aesthetic experience that I take my imaginative

> activity to be as it ought to be without having in mind any determinate rule to which is conforms.[51]

There are at least two good reasons for interpreting Kant as saying that the judgement of taste is based on a cognitive activity distinct from cognition. First, if one believes Kant to be saying that every judgement of taste is pleasurable, this is a way to avoid the 'everything is beautiful' implication. Second, Kant's theory of determinate judgement leaves no room for a free play of the cognitive powers, so it is better to find room for this as an activity separate from this cognitive act. Despite the immediate plausibility of the thesis, assuming aesthetic judgement to be based on a separate activity of the cognitive powers not leading to cognition is not convincing, since there is no reason to require this activity to be shared by everybody in the same situation. The aesthetic judgement becomes superfluous and the claim to university validity implausible. Therefore I will search for another way to understand these basic claims of the third Critique.

I will, for the time being, merely assume that the free play of the faculties is involved in every act of cognition, and that aesthetic reflective judgements are based on the feeling of this mental state. My assumption is that this mental state, which we become conscious of through feeling, be it pleasurable, neutral or displeasurable, is the subjective aspect of every cognitive act. Kant's claim on behalf of this subjective judgement, however, is even stronger in that he calls it a subjective *condition* of cognition (KU§39, 292). He also connects the free play to the claim to universal validity of our way of representing in this judgement of taste:

> Die subjektive allgemeine Mitteilbarkeit der Vorstellungsart in einem Geschmacksurteile, da sie, ohne einen bestimmten Begriff vorauszusetzen, stattfinden soll, kann nicht anders als der Gemützustand in dem freien Spiele der Einbildungskraft und des Verstandes (sofern sie unter einander, wie es zu einem *Erkenntnisse überhaupt* erforderlich ist, zusammenstimmen) sein indem wir uns bewußt sind, das dieses zum Erkenntnis überhaupt schickliche subjektive Verhältnis ebensowohl für jedermann gelten und folglich allgemein mitteilbar sein müsse, als es eine jede bestimmte Erkenntnis ist, die doch immer auf jenem Verhältnis als subjektiver Bedingung beruht. (KU§9, 217 f)

This argument can be rearranged as follows: (1) the subjective condition of every determinate cognition is a relation between imagination and understanding as they 'attune' to each other in free play. (2) This is a condition of cognition, and

---

[51] H. Ginsborg, 'Lawfulness without a Law', 74. Compare also Fricke, *Kants Theorie*, 70 f., where she contrasts the synthesis of aesthetic judgement with the synthesis involved in cognition.

we are conscious that it must hold for everyone. (3) Therefore we require that everyone should share this relation in free play. (4) This relation is a mental state which is identical with the subjective universal communicability of the way of representing, without presupposing a determinate concept, in a judgement of taste.

The attunement of the cognitive powers is a condition of cognition because unless imagination and understanding do enter such a relation, the representation could not give rise to a concept. But cognition, understood as an act of determinative judgement, presupposes the concept:

> Der Begriff vom Hunde bedeutet eine Regel, nach welcher meine Einbildungskraft die Gestalt eines vierfüßigen Tieres allgemein verzeichnen kann, ohne auf irgendeine einzige besondere Gestalt, die mir die Erfahrung darbietet, oder ein jedes mögliche Bild, was ich in concreto darstellen kann, eingeschränkt zu sein. (KrV A141/B180)

The concept guides the imaginative structuring of the manifold. Acquisition of new concepts can be thought of as dependent on more general empirical concepts we already possess in a reflection on the representation guided by this more general empirical concept[52]. In this judgement the imagination is not free in regard to understanding, so the claim to universal communicability cannot be based on the relation we find in cognition as determinative judgement. It can be argued that the cognitive powers do relate harmoniously in determinative judgement, too, but this relation is not one of free play.

Besides, determinative judgements assert objective validity, which means that the intersubjective validity of these judgements rests on objective grounds (KrV A820/B848 f, KU§8, 215) and need no subjective condition of a claim to validity for everyone for a mental state on which the judgement must be based. When I cognise an object, my judgement is not only valid for every instance of this concept, it also carries subjective universal validity, because I share a common ground with other people for my judgement: the object. Thus it is more than clear that we must assume either that (1) Kant changed his theory of cognition, or that (2) the judgement of taste is not concerned with the subjective aspect of the relation of the cognitive powers in an actual act of cognition, or that (3) he is using 'cognition' in another sense than the one suggested above. It is this third solution I will argue for.

---

[52] See Pluhar, 'Translator's Introduction' in Kant, *Critique of Judgement*, xxxiii ff. For a more complex version on Kant's view of concept formation, see Longuenesse, *Capacity to Judge*, 115 ff.

Subjective and objective reflective judgements

To develop this interpretation, I follow Ginsborg's lead by discussing how aesthetic reflective judgement is related to objective reflective judgement, although my view turns out to be quite different from hers[53]. This approach is justified, since Kant unites these two kinds of reflective judgements under the same a priori principle:

> Es wird also die *Ästhetik* der reflektierenden Urteilskraft einen Teil der Kritk dieses Vermögens beschäftigen, so wie die *Logik* ebendesselben Vermögens, unter dem Namen der *Teleologie*, den andern Teil derselben ausmacht. Bei beiden aber wird die Natur selbst als technisch, d.i. als zweckmäßig in ihren Produkten betrachtet, einmal subjektiv, in Absicht auf die bloße Vorstellungsart des Subjekts, in dem zweiten Falle aber als objektiv zweckmäßig in Beziehung auf die Möglichkeit des Gegenstandes selbst. (EE XII, 249)

Not only are the aesthetic and the objective employment of the power of judgement aspects of the same capacity. Kant even sometimes says that the mental state in aesthetic judgement is the subjective condition of the objective use of the power of judgement:

> Ein bloß *reflektierendes* Urteil aber über einen gegebenen einzelnen Gegenstand *kann ästhetisch sein*, wenn ... die Urteilskraft, die keinen Begriff für die gegebene Anschauung bereit hat, die Einbildungskraft (bloß in der Auffassung desselben) mit dem Verstande (in Darstellung eines Begriffs überhaupt) zusammenhält und ein Verhältnis beider Erkenntnisvermögen wahrnimmt, welches die subjektive bloß empfindbare Bedingung des objektiven Gebrauchs der Urteilskraft (nämlich die Zusammenstimmung jener beiden Vermögen untereinander) überhaupt ausmacht. (EE VIII, 223 f)

The question is what kind of judgmental activity "*des objektiven Gebrauchs der Urteilskraft überhaupt*" refers to. Both Guyer and Ginsborg take it to mean judgements that claim objective validity, i.e. determinative judgements[54], which is a reasonable assumption when considering the immediate context of the passage.

---

[53] Ginsborg, *Role of Taste*, 192 ff. Ginsborg takes 'harmony of the faculties' to be merely a metaphor for the universally communicable state of mind (ibid. 73 f), although she has later modified her view of that account in 'Lawfulness'. She also holds that every judgement of taste involves the feeling of pleasure (ibid. 25 ff) and she argues that all empirical conceptualisations are objective (merely) reflective judgements (ibid. 182). As will become clear, I disagree with her on all these accounts, but I will still emphasise the importance of her interpretation of Kant's theory of aesthetic judgement, in pointing out several new ways of understanding key passages of this work.

[54] Guyer, *Claims of Taste*, 85, and Ginsborg, *Role of Taste*, 58 ff.

Still, another interpretation is possible on the basis of the distinction between subjective and objective *reflective* judgements, which is the same as the distinction between aesthetic and teleological reflective judgements (EE VII, 221). This is a distinction between judgements of feeling and cognitive judgements, which share status as reflective judgements, which, among other things, means that they do not claim objective validity. Both kinds of reflective judgement contain a claim to intersubjective validity only. My suggestion is that the claim to universal agreement for the attunement underlying a judgement of taste is the subjective condition of the objective employment of reflective judgement only, and has no direct role to play in determinative judgements[55].

In the published Introduction, there is another passage pointing towards the same kind of interpretation. First Kant says that someone who makes a single judgement of experience rightly requires that everybody else must judge the object to be the same way, because the judgement was made in accordance with the universal conditions of determinative judgements, under the laws of a possible experience in general. This supports my claim that the universal communicability of the subject's mental state is not a subjective condition of determinative judgements. No such condition is needed. Kant then says that someone who finds pleasure in a mere reflection on the form of an object rightly demands agreement from everyone,

> weil der Grund zu dieser Lust in der allgemeinen obzwar subjektiven Bedingung der reflektierende Urteile, nähmlich der zweckmäßigen Übereinstimmung eines Gegenstandes (er sei Produkt der Natur oder der Kunst) mit dem Verhältnis der Erkenntnisvermögen unter sich, die zu jedem empirischen Erkenntnis erfordert wird (der Einbildungskraft und des Verstandes), angetroffen wird. (KU VII, 191)

A peculiarity of this passage is that this state is said both to be a subjective condition of reflective judgement and to be required for every empirical cognition. This can mean that every empirical cognition is a merely reflective judgement, as Ginsborg argues[56], but I will rather suggest that it implies that every empirical cognition *also* is a merely reflective judgement. Since the passage in discussion follows immediately after a contrasting description of an empirical judgement that

---

[55] I do not, however, argue that Kant's repeated statements that the claim to universal agreement for the feeling is a subjective condition for cognition in general should be disregarded. I will in the following argue that objective reflective judgement is a necessary part of cognition, and that a subjective condition of a necessary element in cognition, is also a condition of cognition in general.

[56] Ginsborg, *Role of Taste*, 182.

is determinative and, therefore stands under the laws of understanding, it is unlikely that empirical judgements are identical with merely reflective judgements.

The free play relation of the cognitive powers is usually not said to be a *condition* of aesthetic reflective judgements, but to be the basis for these judgements. I will therefore assume that when Kant in this passage says that the basis of the pleasure is a condition for reflective judgements, he means that it is a condition for objective reflective judgements, not for aesthetic reflective judgements. Another reason for assuming this is that Kant usually says that the free play of the cognitive powers is the condition of cognition in general, and it is reasonable to think of teleological judgement as part of cognition in general since it provides a concept and a law for the object. Aesthetic judgement, on the other hand, provides no cognition (KU§15, 228) and there is no good reason to assume that the free play of imagination and understanding is a condition for these judgements.

Purposiveness and teleology

If the basis of the aesthetic reflective judgement is the subjective condition of objective reflective judgement, then the unity of the whole Critique comes into focus, especially as it is described in the two introductions. Kant connects the central problem of his critique of the power of judgement with the first Critique's transcendental requirement that nature be regarded as a systematic unity, which means that experience must constitute a system of empirical cognition in universal and particular laws (EE IV, 208f). He continues by pointing out that even though nature must be such a system, it does not follow that the system of natural laws is such that we can grasp it. These empirical laws may be heterogeneous and dissimilar to a degree that makes it impossible for us to think them as united in a system. To be able to cognise these laws, we must presuppose that nature is not heterogeneous to this degree. But, Kant says, for us there is no difference between the unity of nature and the unity of possible experience, so we must not only presuppose this conceivable unity, but also that we possess the ability to grasp these laws:

> Also ist es eine subjektiv-notwendige transzendentale *Voraussetzung*, daß jene besorgliche grenzenlose Ungleichartigkeit empirischer Gesetze und Heterogenität der Naturformen der Natur nicht zukomme, vielmehr sie sich, durch die Affinität der besonderen Gesetze unter allgemeinere, zu einer

> Erfahrung, als einem empirischen System, qualifiziere. Diese ist nun das tranzendentale Prinzip der Urteilskraft. (EE IV, 209)

Judgement has its own principle since it is not merely the capacity for subsuming intuitions under already given concepts, but is also the capacity for finding laws for the given, particular intuition. As stated here, this principle does not provide much guidance for judgement. Presupposing that nature is not too heterogeneous for us to subsume it under a system of laws, does not tell us what kind of system this is, and how we arrive at these laws.

To provide a content for this principle which the power of judgement gives as a law to itself, Kant says that we must think the empirical laws of nature as given by another understanding, functioning the same way as our own (KU IV, 180). This leads to the principle of purposiveness:

> Weil nun der Begriff von einem Objekt, sofern er zugleich den Grund der Wirklichkeit dieses Objekts enthält, der *Zweck,* und die Übereinstimmung eines Dinges mit derjenigen Beschaffenheit der Dinge die nur nach Zwecken möglich ist, die *Zweckmäßigkeit* derselben heißt: so ist das Prinzip der Urteilskraft, in Ansehung der Form der Dinge der Natur unter empirische Gesetzen überhaupt, die *Zweckmäßigkeit der Natur* in ihrer Mannigfaltigkeit. D.i. die Natur wird durch diesen Begriff so vorgestellt, als ob ein Verstand den Grund der Einheit des Mannigfaltigen ihrer empirischen Gesetze enthalte. (KU IV, 180 f)

Zweck is usually translated 'end' in Kant's moral works, and is, according to Pogge, what we usually call goal or aim, i.e. "states of affairs or events that one has in mind while acting and tries to attain through one's conduct"[57]. The word is used by analogy in the third Critique, in that we think the world *as if* it were created by an understanding similar to our own, i.e. one that has created the world and the objects in it with a particular end in mind. *Zweckmäßigkeit* can mean either the character of an object or action understood in relation to being someone's end or purpose, or the relative perfection of an object, or the usefulness of an object. To retain the connection between *Zweck* and *Zweckmäßigkeit*, I will follow Pluhar's use of 'purpose' and 'purposiveness', but keep in mind that the same word is translated 'end' in the moral works.

The principle of formal (KU V, 181) or logical (EE V, 216) purposiveness is not a basis for ascribing laws to nature, but merely to the subject's *judgement* of nature, which judges nature on analogy with art. This Kant calls the technic of nature in contrast to the mechanism of nature found in non-purposive causality (EE VII, 219). In reality it is judgement that is technical, and nature is called so insofar

---

[57] T. W. Pogge, 'Kant on Ends and the Meaning of Life', 361.

as it harmonises [*zusammenstimmt*] with judgement (EE VII, 220). This harmony, which is displayed in the attunement of the cognitive powers, is judged by aesthetic reflective judgement (EE VII, 221). Thus we presuppose that nature is purposively arranged according to a principle that is only valid for judgement, but which we ascribe to an object of nature insofar as the representation of this object gives rise to a proportionate attunement of imagination and understanding in free play. The principle is expressed in several propositions concerning general organisation: that nature is organised as a graspable hierarchy of genera and species, and that all the different kinds of effects in nature, can be ascribed just to a small number of principles and so forth (KU V, 185).

Judgement has a principle of formal, subjective purposiveness and we find a formal, subjective purposiveness in the form of an object if the representation is accompanied by a feeling expressing an attunement of the cognitive powers. But why should the principle of judgement contain a presupposition about a logical arrangement of nature? The obvious explanation is that this principle is also the basis for judging nature according to concepts, concepts not derived from the transcendental laws of understanding. Therefore Kant says that there are two ways in which we can represent purposiveness in an object of nature, either on a subjective basis as in the basis of the aesthetic judging,

> oder aus einem objektiven, als Übereinstimmung seiner Form mit der Möglichkeit der Dinge selbst, nach einem Begriffe von ihm, der vorhergeht und den Grund dieser Form enthält. (KU VIII, 192)

Kant calls this an objective, or real, purposiveness, but that does not mean that these judgements claim objective validity; teleological judgement is only reflective judgement proceeding according to concepts (KU VIII, 194) and it too presupposes the principle of the purposiveness or technic of nature.

Thus, when we bring an object under an empirical concept of a purpose, we presuppose this object to belong to a class of objects belonging to a system of genera and species, and both the properties of the object itself as well as the connection between the objects must be regarded under the principle of purposiveness. It is reasonable to assume that the principle is called a principle of logical purposiveness in the First Introduction because it is a principle for the logical use of judgement (EE V, 214), and the logical use of judgement is judgement proceeding according to concepts. If this assumption is correct, then the principle of the organisation of nature must be specified in the conceptual, albeit merely reflective, teleological judgement of the object. We must presuppose the principle of purposiveness in our judgement of the contingent aspects of the object, to be warranted in seeing the relation between the properties of the particular object as part of a systematic totality. The principle is also required for our understanding of the connection between these objects to be part of a systematic totality[58]. Without this presupposition, these connections would not be more than contingent aggregates. We would lack the principle by which we orient ourselves in the world. Our cognition of these objects would be blind, since it would be performed without any guiding principle (EE V, 212).

Teleological judgements are concerned with finding concepts of objects (EE V, 211), and, presupposing this concept, judge the object according to an empirical law (EE IX, 234). Teleological judgements may seem to be concerned with organic nature only, since these judgements are necessary for objects as purposive forms, i.e. objects internally arranged according to a concept of a purpose. That is not the case. Kant mentions not only the shapes of flowers and the inner structure of plants and animals as objects that we must take to be systematically arranged according to a purpose, but also crystal formations (EE VI, 217). These organised (and self-organising) beings are both cause and effect of themselves because the concept of the purpose of the object must be thought as cause of the elements that together produce the object (KU§65, 372). Organised beings also display the same final causality as species, through reproduction:

> Ein Baum zeugt erstlich einen anderen Baum nach einem bekannten Naturgesetze. Der Baum aber, den er erzeugt, ist von derselben Gattung; und so erzeugt er sich selbst der *Gattung* nach, in der er einerseits als Wirkung, andererseits als Ursache von sich selbst unaufhörlich hervorgebracht und ebenso sich selbst oft hervorbringend, sich als Gattung beständig erhält. (KU§64, 371).

Organised beings display intrinsic purposiveness. There are also objects or events that are not organised according to this principle, but still serve as beneficial for other creatures. In this case the purposiveness is extrinsic or relative (KU§63, 367) and seems to encompass most natural phenomena. Examples are wind, rain (KU§68, 384), rivers, soil, sand, sea (KU§63, 367 ff).

Still, the paradigmatic example of teleological judgement is the explanation of the organisation of a living organism:

---

[58] Obviously, the principle of purposiveness also guides the systematic classification of empirical concepts determined by understanding. Still it has a particular function in relation to teleological judgements, because here both the 'determination' of the objects as well as the hierarchical classifications of the objects proceed according to the idea of nature organised by an understanding similar to human understanding.

> Organisierte Wesen sind also die einzigen in der Natur, welche, wenn man sie auch für sich und ohne ein Verhältnis auf andere Dinge betrachtet, doch nur als Zwecke derselben möglich gedacht werden müssen, und die also zuerst dem Begriffe eines *Zwecks*, der nicht ein praktischer sondern Zweck *der Natur* ist, objektiv Realität, und dadurch für die Naturwissenschaft den Grund zu einer Teleologie, d.i. einer Beurteilungsart ihrer Objekte nach einem besondern Prinzip, verschaffen .... (KU§65, 375 f).

Teleology has its primary scientific use in the biological sciences (KU§66, 376 f) and in understanding living nature we are forced to resort to the principle of the purposiveness of nature, according to Kant. Even today, despite the causal explanations of evolutionary biology and molecular biology, this principle is held by many philosophers of biology to be indispensable[59]. It is even claimed that nature as a system is so complex that it is impossible for us ever to gain complete insight in the lawfulness of the interplay within ecosystems[60]. Even if we did fully understand the mechanism underlying the functions of live organism, and how an organism adapts to its environment, biology would not gain the kind of theoretical insight on the basis of mechanical causality found in physical science. This claim echoes Kant's claim that we will never be able to gain insight in the totality of empirical laws of nature, because our understanding functions discursively, i.e. deduces from the universal to the particular (KU§77, 406).

Even if the science of biology one day is advanced to a stage where all of organic nature can be completely understood causally, this may not be sufficient to dispense with teleology. As Ginsborg argues, Kant must hold that teleological judgement is not required merely for scientific explanations[61], although he says that it is a principle inherent in natural science (KU§68, 381 ff). I will not go into the details of how teleological judgement is considered necessary for experience in general, but some suggestions can be made. For the farmer the principle that there is regularity determining when the crop is ripe is necessary for his livelihood. He cannot find out when to harvest unless he assumes that every plant ripens according to the same laws, which are inherent in the plant. It would even be a risk to eat its fruit without a lawful connection between the way our body react to the fruit and the way fruits appear to us. We would never know if the fruit would be nourishing or poisonous.

---

59 F. J. Ayala, 'The Distinctness of Biology', 268 ff. See also the critical discussion of some philosopher's claims about the need for teleological explanations in biology in N. Roll-Hansen, 'The Meaning of Reduction in Biology', 125 ff.

60 J. Lemons et al., ' The Precautionary Principle: Scientific Uncertainty and Type I and Type II Errors', 216 ff.

61 Ginsborg, *Role of Taste*, 180 f.

Similarly the fisherman would not have any basis for discovering the regularities in the movements of fish, and the best ways to catch them. Although these facts are established a posteriori, our reliance on them, and the way we discover them are based on assumptions of regularity (a condition of knowledge as such), and the idea of purposiveness; the assumption that this regularity has a cause we can grasp. If we did not assume this idea, the regularity that we expect could be one that we were unable to fathom. But since we conceive of the regularities under the principle of the purposiveness of nature, we are warranted in claiming that we have discovered a lawfulness[62], although it is not objectively valid, but merely valid for our cognitive capacities[63]. Thus we do not have a principle of purposiveness of nature as such, but of purposiveness of nature for our cognition only. And this kind of purposive explanation is an ingrained aspect of our everyday orientation in the world.

Although organic nature, and some objects within inorganic nature must be judged as purposive intrinsically, and many phenomena, both organic and inorganic, must be judged as purposive extrinsically, this does not justify my claim that every act of cognition involves objective reflective judgements under the principle of purposiveness. Kant does, however, say that every object must be judged according to this idea, because nature must be considered a system of purposes (as a subjective maxim):

> Alles in der Welt ist irgendwozu gut; nichts ist in ihr umsonst; und man ist durch das Beispiel, das die Natur an ihren organischen Produkten gibt, berechtigt, ja, berufen, von ihr und ihren Gestzen nichts, als was im Ganzen zweckmäßig ist, zu erwarten. (KU§67, 379)

Even if an object does not display intrinsic purposiveness, which is the case for most of inorganic nature, it still should be judged reflectively as displaying extrinsic purposiveness, because nature must be thought as a purposive system. When something is judged as purposive in relation to something else, this extrinsic purposiveness depends on the intrinsic purposiveness of the object it benefits (KU§82, 425). Pogge interprets Kant's argument for this claim to be

---

62 The primary use of teleological judgements is in discovering lawfulness, but assuming the lawfulness to hold requires not only empirical observations, but also the continued assumption of the basis for this regularity, i.e. the purpose. So teleological judgement is needed even for the assumption that the lawfulness holds.

63 These examples are from the primary industries, but the same general ideas can for example be found in practical medicine (as well as in medical science), navigation, and furthermore in the way we trust a number of the experiences on which we base the calculations of everyday life.

> that viewing A as having the purpose to bring about or sustain B means thinking of A *as if* intentionally produced so as to bring about or sustain B. But this thought requires more than the mere fact that A brings about or sustains B. It also requires the idea that B is intended. And there is no ground for this thought when B is a simple inorganic substance or process, such as the rhythm of the tides, for example, sustained by the moon's revolutions. In such a case, an explanation in terms of mechanical causation alone seems fully satisfactory. To be an extrinsic purpose, something must then, directly or indirectly, contribute to bringing about or sustaining a natural end, something that has a purpose in itself.[64]

This system of intrinsic and extrinsic purposes, which we must think as intentionally produced without assuming the reality of this intention, leads to the question of the final purpose of nature (KU§67, 378):

> *Endzweck* ist derjenige Zweck, der keines andern als Bedingung seiner Möglichkeit bedarf. ... Nun haben wir nur eine einzige Art Wesen in der Welt, deren Kausalität teleologisch, d.i. auf Zwecke gerichtet und doch zugleich so beschaffen ist, daß das Gesetz, nach welchem sie sich Zwecke zu bestimmen haben, von ihnen selbst als unbedingt und von Naturbedingungen unabhängig, an sich aber als notwendig vorgestellt wird. Das Wesen dieser Art ist der Mensch, aber als Noumenon betrachtet .... (KU§84, 434 f)

The final purpose or end of nature is unconditioned, but every purpose in nature, extrinsic or intrinsic, is conditioned, except for man considered as noumenon, i.e. as a moral being. In this respect is man self-legislating, and his existence is an end in itself (KU§84, 435, compare G 428). Thus if we think the world as teleological system of purposes, the final purpose justifying this unity is man as a self-legislating moral being (KU§86, 442 ff).[65]

Kant holds that nature must be thought as a systematic unity of purposes, so that every object must be judged by teleological reflective judgement. No act of cognition is complete without teleological judgements, since determinative judgements always leave something undetermined in the object of cognition. For example, determinative judgement cannot explain growth, regeneration, the internal connection and reciprocal dependence of organisms. Thus, human cognition is not adequately explained by determinative judgement only, because there will always be some aspect of the object or connection within it that is intuited but not subsumable under causal laws, i.e., something appearing contingent in this perspective (KU§77, 405 f). This does not mean that we always

64 Pogge, 'Kant on Ends', 369.

65 For a more detailed discussion of Kant's argument on the final purpose of nature, see ibid. 370 ff.

must supplement determinative judgement with teleological judgement. We do not always have to cognise every aspect of an object, and a determinative judgement may be sufficient for our interest at the moment. But every act of determinative judgement leaves some material undetermined. This material can be judged reflectively under the principle of the purposiveness of nature, so that every act of cognition is *potentially* also a teleological judgement.

The subjective condition of teleological judgements

Teleological judgement provides the contingent elements of an act of cognition with a concept, and thus ascribes an empirical law to the object (KU§76, 404). The concept is not derived from the objectively valid laws of understanding, but has a merely heuristic function. When I explain the function of an organ by referring to a purpose, such as saying of the lens in the eye that it serves to reunite light rays in one point (EE IX, 236), my claim is not objectively valid. The judgement that the light rays do unite in one point due to the lens is objectively valid, but explaining the position, material and variable shape of the lens with reference to this purpose is not a statement about the actual organisation of the world. What is the status of this claim, then? Is it merely my private judgement about the world as I personally see it, with the implicit assumption that other people may arrive at completely different judgements, based on different perceptions? It is clear that different properties may be ascribed to the represented object, but still we do not think that this difference in conceptualisation is due to these judgements being merely private. The underlying assumption in any judgement of this kind is that we share the way we intuit the world.

If we think of the act of teleological judgement as one in which imagination and understanding are relating freely, and we find a concept on the basis of this free play, as we may call it, then the way my cognitive powers relate in the representation may be completely different from the way the cognitive powers of everybody else relate. If this is the case, then the empirical laws I propose for this object are valid merely for myself. The further implication is that teleological judgements have the same cognitive status as my liking for green olives. Then these judgements are merely private. This is at odds with the way we understand these judgements. We take the hypotheses of the teleological power of judgement to say something about the world as a human being must experience it, not merely about the world as I happen to see it.

To avoid this conclusion, I must presuppose that the *basis* on which I find the concept for the object, is a basis that would be found in everybody else judging this object. Or as Kant puts it in the footnote to the Deduction:

> Um berechtigt zu sein, auf allgemeine Beistimmung zu einem bloß auf subjektiven Gründen beruhenden Urteile der ästhetischen Urteilskraft Anspruch zu machen, ist genug, daß man einräume: 1) Bei allen Menschen seien die subjektiven Bedingungen dieses Vermögens, was das Verhältnis der darin in Tätigkeit gesetzten Erkenntniskräfte zu einem Erkenntnis überhaupt betrifft, einerlei; welches wahr sein muß, weil sich sonst Menschen ihre Vorstellungen und selbst das Erkenntnis mitteilen könnten. (KU§38, 290, note)

Remembering that *mitteilen* just means 'share with', rather than 'communicate', we see that the assumption that everybody share the same relation of the cognitive powers when activated for cognition in general is a condition for shared cognition. Unless this relation is the same in everybody, the representation and judgement I make will carry merely private status. But this assumption cannot concern determinative judgements. It is only in the cognitive activity of teleological reflective judgement that it makes sense that imagination has to schematise without a concept (KU§35, 287). Thus, when Kant talks about the cognitive powers being engaged in a relation that is a condition of *Erkenntnis überhaupt* I suggest that the cognition he refers to is the act of teleological reflective judgement, because in this judgement, the cognitive powers must be relating freely since the activity concerns finding a concept, rather than conforming to one.

In objective reflective judgement, the imagination structures the manifold freely as regards the rules of understanding; still it must conform to understanding so that a concept can arise. We cannot rely on the concept to guarantee objectivity, since the concept is not determined by necessary conditions, and the threat of relativism lies close at hand. Unless I presuppose the structuring activity in the representation of the object to be the same in everybody, the concept is merely an arbitrary rule, not one I can suppose to say anything about how I must take the world. Thus I demand that everybody share the same cognitive activity. Without this shared cognitive relation we cannot share cognition, understood as objective reflective judgement, either:

> Erkenntnisse und Urteile müssen sich, samt der Überzeugung, die sie begleitet, allgemein mitteilen lassen; denn sonst käme ihnen keine Übereinstimmung mit dem Objekt zu: sie wären insgesamt ein bloß subjektives Spiel der Vorstellungskräfte, gerade so wie es der Skeptizism verlangt. Sollen sich aber Erkenntnisse mitteilen lassen, so muß sich auch der Gemützustand, d.i. die Stimmung der Erkenntniskräfte zu einer Erkenntnis überhaupt, und zwar

> diejenige Proportion, welche sich für eine Vorstellung (...) gebührt, um daraus Erkenntnis zu machen, allgemein mitteilen lassen: weil ohne diese, als subjektive Bedingung des Erkennens, das Erkenntnis, als Wirkung, nicht entspringen könnte. ... diese Stimmung kann nicht anders als durch das Gefühl (nicht nach Begriffen) bestimmt werden. (KU§21, 238)

We cannot claim the judgement to be in harmony with the object rather than being a mere personal fantasy, unless we presuppose that the attunement of the cognitive powers on which the objective reflective judgement is based, is the same in everybody. As we have seen above, this mental state is not something we can cognise in any other way than by feeling it. We cannot know that the relation is the same in other people, since we cannot feel their mental state, nor are we in a position to predict that it will be the same. What we do is *require* that it is the same in everybody, which brings out the cognitive normativity involved in the claim to subjective universal validity.

On this basis the 'free play'-metaphor makes sense too. In objective reflective judgement imagination is structuring the manifold and relates to understanding's activity of providing concepts for this structuring activity. We get some idea of how Kant thinks of this activity in the section dealing with judgement about art. Kant says that beauty in art *and in nature* is the expression[66] of aesthetic ideas (KU§51, 320). An aesthetic idea is

> diejenige Vorstellung der Einbildungskraft, die viel zu denken veranlaßt, ohne daß ihr irgend ein bestimmter Gedanke, d.i. Begriff adäquat sein kann, die folglich keine Sprache völlig erreicht und verständlich machen kann. (KU§49, 314)

What is worth noticing here is that the imagination represents the object in a way that leads to a lot of thinking, which is another way to describe a free play between imagination and understanding. This free play describes an activity of imagination where it represents the object in ways that lead understanding to many concepts, without fastening on one particular as adequate to the representation. That no concept is adequate for the representation may mean that we are unable to provide the object with a concept, or that no concept can be considered a final

[66] 'Expression' may sound strange in connection with non-intentional nature. This shows that according to Kant is the ability to express aesthetic ideas nothing but the tendency of a representation to produce a rich array of thoughts in the cognising subject. It is not so much something put into an object by the artist as a characterising feature of any object that induces aesthetic pleasure (or displeasure) in those who experience it. This indicates that Kant should not be linked to closely with 'expressionist' theories of art, as expressionism is described for example in Danto, *Philosophical Disenfranchisement*, 101 ff.

determination of the object. If we accept the latter alternative, then the activity of reflection without a determinate concept may be as follows: The object is represented in a free play consisting in the imagination's structuring activity and the understanding's attempt to produce concepts for this intuited material. The subjective or aesthetic reflective judgement is based on the feeling of this activity, and the objective or teleological reflective judgement of this representation consists in the determination of one concept as more adequate than others. This concept does not represent a perfect fit with the representation, so one may later find a more adequate concept. The inadequacy of the concept can be understood as another way of expressing that the concepts found in reflective judgements are not, and cannot become, objectively valid. All concepts and laws of reflective judgements are heuristic devices for interpreting the world, which means that they may always be replaced by other, more adequate concepts and laws.

Now, imagination cannot be free in the sense of being without guidance. If that were the case, any attunement with understanding would be highly unlikely, which is why Kant uses terms as 'free lawfulness' and 'lawfulness without a law' (KU§22, 240 f) to describe this particular kind of freedom that is capable of being attuned to the conceptual regularity of understanding. On my interpretation, this lawfulness in the activity of imagination is explained by Kant's statement that the aesthetic power of judgement contains the principle of the purposiveness of nature:

> In einer Kritik der Urteilskraft ist der Teil, welcher die ästhetische Urteilskraft enthält, ihr wesentlich angehörig, weil diese allein ein Prinzip enthält, welches die Urteilskraft völlig a priori ihrer Reflexion über die Natur zum Grunde legt, nämlich das einer formalen Zweckmäßigkeit der Natur nach ihren besonderen (empirischen) Gesetzen für unser Erkenntnisvermögen, ohne welche sich der Verstand in sie nicht finden könnte. (KU VIII, 193)

Since the principle is contained in the aesthetic judgement, it is also reasonable that this principle is what provides imagination with the lawfulness that enables it to conform to understanding. Imagination is not synthesising blindly, but according to a principle of purposiveness, and in this way, it provides forms that can be subsumed under concepts. The principle of purposiveness is, as we remember, the principle that nature is structured as if created by an understanding functioning the same way as our own. Still, imagination is free as regards determination by understanding. The lawfulness of imagination is not a lawfulness determining the synthesis of the representation, as is the case in determinative judgement. Imagination's freedom as regards understanding is underscored by Kant's statement that the concepts provided by understanding are not wholly adequate to the representation. They can only be wholly adequate in the case where the concept is providing the rule for the representation of the manifold, as in determinative judgement.

If we understand reflective judgement this way, we also understand why the free play of the representational powers does not end when a concept is found. The concept and the empirical law found in objective reflective judgement are heuristic devices, never completely adequate, and may always be replaced by a new one. Therefore the free cognitive activity continues, although we have reached the goal of judgement, which is finding a concept and ascribing a law to the object. This law can, in principle, always be improved. In this way the aesthetic reflective judgement can be a separate act of judgement while its 'object' is the same judgmental activity that results in a concept of the object. As Kant says, what we judge is the mental state as it is expressed in a feeling, but this mental state is the activity of the cognitive powers in the representation of an object. Thus reflective judgement consists in two ways of relating to the same representational activity, one objective, resulting in a concept of the object, the other subjective, judging the feeling of the subject.

So, any teleological judgement is based on the claim that we share a mental state when representing an object, because it is primarily for this state that we claim universal agreement, not for the cognitive claims regarding the object's properties as purposively arranged. If the reflective judgement of the object made on the basis of a certain representation is to be valid for everybody, everybody must share our mental state. That is the basic assumption of reflective judgement. But we experience the mental state when cognising an object as a disinterested feeling. If we are warranted in claiming that our cognition of objects include teleological judgements which we must claim to be intersubjectively valid, a subjective condition of this claim is that the feeling of our state of mind is intersubjectively valid as well, because the validity claim of teleological judgement is not related to the object as such, but to the way we human beings take the object to be, given our cognitive apparatus.

Judgements of taste hold a special position as a foundation for man's reflection on nature, as we saw above, because it is only the aesthetic aspect of reflective judgement that contains the principle of formal purposiveness without which "the understanding could not find its way about in nature" as Pluhar translates it[67]. Thus

---

[67] "...weil [die ästhetische Urteilskraft] allein ein Prinzip enthält, welches die Urteilakraft völlig a priori ihrer Reflexion über die Natur zum Grunde legt, nämlich das einer formalen Zweckmäßigkeit der Natur nach ihren besonderen (empirischen) Gesetzen für unser Erkenntnisvermögen, ohne welche sich der Verstand in sie nicht finden könnte ..."(KU VIII, 193)

reflective judgement is necessary for orienting ourselves in nature. This indicates a more holistic, interpretative perspective applied by reflective judgement to nature[68], by contrast with the subsumption under categories in determinative judgement. Orientation in, or making sense of, nature is dependent on reflective judgement, and the only essential principle, i.e. the only principle that we must presuppose for the possibility of this kind of judgement, is the principle of formal purposiveness, which is contained in aesthetic reflective judgement. Kant goes on to say that understanding requires this principle of formal purposiveness as a preparation for postulating objective purposes of nature, since we have no basis for claiming objective purposiveness in the concept of nature as an object of experience (KU VIII, 193 f).

An act of empirical cognition must be understood under two transcendental principles: the constitutive principles of the unity of apperception, and the regulative principle of purposiveness. These are both necessary for understanding cognition in its entirety. The subjective universal validity of the relation of the cognitive powers is the subjective condition of reflective judgements, a condition that is not required for determinative judgement because this subsumes under universal laws (KU§69, 385), which ensure its objective validity. The universally sharability of the mental state underlying judgements of taste is a condition of this reflective aspect of cognition, and has at the same time autonomy in the aesthetic judgement independent of the determinate concept found for the object.

Form of purposiveness

Kant says that the basis determining the judgement of taste is the form of purposiveness or, in the famous phrase, purposiveness without a purpose[69] in the representation of an object:

> Also kann nichts anders als die subjektive Zweckmäßigkeit in der Vorstellung eines Gegenstandes, ohne allen (weder objektiven noch subjektiven) Zweck,

---

68 The holistic, orientational character of reflective judgements is discussed in R. A. Makkreel, *Imagination and Interpretation*, see e.g. 154.

69 Fricke, *Kants Theorie*, 82, points out that when Kant introduces the expression *Zweckmäßigkeit ohne Zweck* in §10 he uses it in a wide sense including all objects, mental states, or acts where we have to assume them to be based on a causality according to purposes, without assuming the reality of a will behind these purposes. Thus also objective judgements under the principle of purposiveness are included in this definition. In the passage above, he calls it a *subjective* purposiveness without a purpose, which refers to judgements on purposiveness without a purpose where even no concept of a purpose is involved, i.e. aesthetic reflective judgements.

> folglich die bloße Form der Zweckmäßigkeit in der Vorstellung, wodurch uns ein Gegenstand *gegeben* wird, sofern wir uns ihrer bewußt sind, das Wohlgefallen, welches wir, ohne Begriff, als allgemein mitteilbar beurteilen, mithin den Bestimmungsgrund des Geschmacksurteils, ausmachen. (KU§11, 221).

A generally accepted line of interpretation links the form of purposiveness with the pleasure in judgements of beauty, and there is convincing evidence for such interpretations in Kant's own writing. He says that the consciousness of the formal purposiveness[70] is the pleasure (KU§12, 221 f), and even that the pleasure *is* the subjective purposiveness (KU§38, 289 f). We become conscious of the subjective purposiveness of the form of the object by this disinterested pleasure. On my interpretation, which takes the mental state underlying the judgement of taste to be the subjective aspect of every act of cognition, this should be avoided because it leads to an 'everything-is-beautiful'-problem, and leaves no room for the intersubjectively valid judgements of objects that are not beautiful.

There are reasons for linking the form of purposiveness with the feeling of pleasure. Guyer suggests that a "representation which causes aesthetic response may be called final because it is in fact related to a general objective - not a specific interest, but the general aim of cognition itself."[71] Thus we feel pleasure in the attainment of this goal, as we do in any other goal-fulfilment. This is problematic because then there is a purpose and an interest involved in the formal purposiveness, although a merely general one. It is also difficult to see in what way the feeling is informative, because each and every act of cognition is a fulfilment of the general aim of cognition, and then such a feeling is superfluous.

Ginsborg has a different explanation for the connection between the form of purposiveness and the pleasure in beauty. Her point of departure is Kant's definition of pleasure as the consciousness of the causality of the representation to keep the subject in the state it already is in (KU§10, 220) which means that pleasure is a self-preserving mental state. Thus, the pleasure not only issues a claim on myself to remain in the state I am in, but also demands that everybody else ought to share this mental state. Since this pleasure is disinterested, and thus, not connected to any particular purpose, it exhibits a mere form of purposiveness[72]. I believe the function Ginsborg assigns the pleasure is

[70] Formal purposiveness is the same as subjective purposiveness, see e.g. KU VIII, 193. Thus formal purposiveness, subjective purposiveness, purposiveness without a purpose, and form of purposiveness all refer to the same. They still point to different aspects of this phenomenon.

[71] Guyer, *Claims of Taste*, 193 f.

[72] Ginsborg, *Role of Taste*, 86 f. and 26 f.

unnecessary. If the mental state underlying a judgement of taste contains a claim to subjective universal communicability for itself, it can issue this claim whether it is a pleasure or displeasure. We experience the feeling as one everybody ought to share, regardless of it being a pleasure or displeasure, because it is a feeling of our mental state of representation. Taking the pleasure to express the universal communicability of the feeling because pleasure is a self-sustaining state is an unnecessary doubling of the claim to subjective universality.

To say that the universally communicable pleasure is the expression of *subjective* purposiveness might mean that the object "stands in a certain relation to the subject who perceives and enjoys it"[73], namely a relation producing the harmony of the cognitive powers. Another possibility, which is in line with my general interpretation, is that this indicates that the universal communicability of the mental state is the necessary subjective aspect of an objective reflective judgement of purposiveness, and thus the awareness of this state expresses the subjective purposiveness of the representation. On the same interpretation, purposiveness without a purpose means that the concern is with a judgement according to purposes without regard to the objective aspect of the judgement, i.e. the concept of the purpose. In these subjective judgements we abstract from what the object is as purpose, and look only at how the subject is affected in this cognitive activity:

> Das Formale in der Vorstellung eines Dinges, d.i. die Zusammenstimmung des Mannigfalten zu Einem (unbestimmt was es sein solle) gibt, für sich ganz und gar keine objektive Zweckmäßigkeit zu erkennen; weil da von diesem Einem, als *Zweck* (was das Ding sein solle) abstrahiert wird, nichts als die subjektive Zweckmäßigkeit der Vorstellungen im Gemüte des Anschauenden übrig bleibt. (KU§15, 227)

This again means that the judgement concerns only the form of purposiveness, as opposed to the matter of purposiveness, which is the purpose we ascribe to the object.

The law or the concept found for the object or relation is the matter of the judgement of purposiveness. To get the form of the judgement, i.e. the form of purposiveness, we have to abstract from this matter. What remains after this abstraction, is the factor that is common for all judgements of purposiveness, which is not pleasure, but the subjective universal validity of the feeling expressive of the mental state when judging the object. Kant says, in the discussion leading up to the Deduction, that what is presented a priori as a universal rule for the power of

---

[73] Guyer, *Claims of Taste*, 192.

judgement is not pleasure, but the universal validity of this pleasure (KU§37, 289). This makes it likely that the form of purposiveness is the universal communicability rather than the particular quality of the feeling. So the form of purposiveness of a representation is the universal communicability of the mental state we feel when judging the object according to purposes[74]. Since we abstract from the concept of the purpose in the judgement of taste, the judgement displays purposiveness without a purpose, and since it concerns merely how the subject is affected when making the judgement, it is called a subjective purposiveness. The judgement concerns only formal purposiveness, since it concerns only the formal aspects of the judgement according to purposes, i.e. that these judgements claim universal assent for the feeling of the mental state in representing the object.

On my interpretation, beautiful, non-beautiful, and ugly objects display the form of purposiveness, since the judgements of all these objects involve a claim to subjective universal validity for the mental state underlying the judgement. Also Hudson and Allison hold that Kant's theory has room for pure judgements of ugly objects. They both take the Third Moment in the Analytic of the Beautiful to connect consciousness of the form of purposiveness to the feeling of pleasure, implying that only beautiful objects display form of purposiveness. According to them, the displeasure in the judgement on ugly objects thus display form of counterpurposiveness[75].

These interpretations encounter problems when we consider Kant's own use of the term counterpurposiveness. He says that sublime objects display counterpurposiveness, and that is because they cannot be contained in any sensible form (KU§23, 245). Sublime objects are such as a powerful waterfall, the endless sea, or an abyss, objects that are formless because they cannot be delineated. Ugly objects have form, and are not counterpurposive in the sense that they have no delineated form. The displeasure in the sublime is connected to this failure to contain the object within a form (KU§27, 259), whereas the displeasure of ugliness reveals something about the relation *between* imagination and understanding, since they do not further, but hinder each other (EE VIII, 223). If this is counterpurposiveness for cognition, it is of a different kind from the one in the sublime, which altogether prevents cognition of the object under the principle of

---

[74] One may object that the form of purposiveness is an aspect of the object, not the judgement; in the judgement we become conscious of this form of purposiveness. But an object is something that is constituted by our judgement, which makes form of purposiveness a function of the object *and* of the judgement. The object display purposiveness because we judge it under the principle of the purposiveness of nature

[75] Hudson, 'The Significance', 91 ff., and Allison, 'Pleasure and Harmony', 479 f.

the purposiveness of nature. It is strange that 'counterpurposive' can mean both something that cannot be adequately judged, as the sublime, and something that can, as the ugly. Still it is possible that we can cognise objects that are 'counterpurposive', if we assume these two very different meanings of the same expression[76].

The main problem concerning this interpretation is that if we do suppose that these objects can be cognised, the term 'counterpurposive for cognition' suggests at least that these objects do not lend themselves as easily to cognition. Then we return to Bernstein's problem that ugly objects are less cognisable than the beautiful ones, since the former are counterpurposive for cognition and the latter purposive. It is difficult to find any way out of that problem for this reconstruction.

On my suggested interpretation, this is not a problem, since also ugly objects display form of purposiveness. This means that form of purposiveness should not be connected with pleasure, but with the claim to subjective universal validity for the feeling. When I find something to be ugly it means that this is the kind of object I find it unpleasant to contemplate, a displeasure I claim others should share, because this feeling expresses how my cognitive powers relate in the representation of this object. I claim subjective universal validity for my feeling regardless of the empirical qualities of this feeling, and any feeling containing this claim to intersubjective validity displays form of purposiveness. The particular degree of pleasure in the feeling is an empirical fact that must be left out of the account, although it tells something about the object in our empirical assessment of it.

All disinterested feelings we claim universal assent for, are feelings we ascribe to the attunement of the cognitive power, which means that they must contain the principle of the formal purposiveness of nature. Every such feeling thus displays the form of purposiveness, just because it is a feeling of the cognitive basis that enables us to determine the object according to a concept of a purpose. Therefore pure judgements of ugly objects must display form of purposiveness, since also

---

[76] Hudson gives as evidence for his suggestion a passage where Kant discusses a counterpurposive attunement gradually making the object disgusting (KU§52, 325 f). What Hudson fails to see is that Kant talks about a pleasure in the matter of sensation [*der Materie der Empfindung (dem Reize oder der Rührung)*], not in the form of the object. Thus this passage does not deal with a pure judgement of taste. And even if it did it would not help Hudson's reconstruction, because Kant describes the feeling as an enjoyment gradually turning into disgust, and that is not a description of a judgement of ugliness, which should be displeasurable all the way through. Hudson, 'The Significance', 93.

these objects can be judged according to a purpose under the formal purposiveness of nature.

Intersubjective and objective validity

We can never prove that we actually share this feeling of the mental state in the free play of the cognitive powers, but we have to require that we do if not our claims about what the world is like (i.e. those claims that extend beyond the claims about the object derived from the universal laws of understanding) are to be discounted as mere subjective opinions. Kant is not arguing that the position of the sceptic[77] is problematic in itself, but merely that the subject, in her conception of the world, distinguishes between what is merely private and what she takes to be necessary ways of seeing the world. If this distinction is to be justified, then she must, as a condition of cognition, demand that everybody else represent the object the same way as she does.

These subjective conditions must be thought of as parts of the cognitive process, meaning that there is no *necessary* temporal difference between these subjective aspects of cognition, and objective cognition. Furthermore it is necessary that we regard teleological and determinative cognition to be two aspects of the same cognitive process, which together is cognition in general [*Erkenntnis überhaupt*]. It is not as if we determine the object as something in particular, and then proceed to judge the remaining contingent aspects according to the principle of purposiveness. Cognition is one process including several aspects with their separate transcendental requirements. The task of both the first and the third Critique is to analyse and prove the necessity of these conditions. On my reading, then, the third Critique is a necessary addition to the first Critique, without changing any central aspects of that work. The most important adjustment is the realisation that objectivity and intersubjectivity are not interchangeable terms [*Wechselbegriffe*], as is claimed in Prolegomena (P 298)[78]. The field of intersubjectively valid cognition encompasses much more than objectively valid cognition, and the judgements claiming objective validity are parts of a potentially complete cognitive whole under the principle of purposiveness presupposed in intersubjectively valid judgements.

---

77 See quote from KU§21, 238, p. 103 f.

78 For a discussion of the significance of this claim to intersubjectivity in regard to what is called Kant's methodological solipsism, see my 'Intersubjectivity in Kant's Third Critique'.

3. The judgement of the sublime in nature

According to Kant, there are two kinds of aesthetic reflective judgement: the judgement of taste and the judgement of sublimity. The latter is relevant for the assessment of Beckett's *Molloy*. Both kinds of aesthetic reflective judgements are singular and based on a disinterested feeling for which we claim subjective universal validity. In chapter five, I will specify the conditions under which aesthetic reflective judgements can be applied to art, but here, in order to grasp the main characteristics of the sublime, I will follow Kant and start with a discussion of how the sublime appears in nature.

The sublime object is an object of nature that is represented as overwhelmingly great or mighty and involves imagination in a free representational play with reason rather than understanding. Since reason can be either theoretical or practical, there are two modes of the sublime[1]. The former Kant calls the mathematically sublime, whereas the latter is called the dynamically sublime. Kant says that the sublime also can be found in formless object in the sense that the object is represented as unbounded. I argue that Kant must hold that the sublime objects are of three kinds, those that must be represented as unbounded, such as the starry night (KU§29, 270), or those that are represented as limitless from a certain viewpoint, such as the pyramids (KU§26, 252), or those that are represented as bounded, such as the absence of affects [*Affektlosigkeit*] in one who pursues immutable principles (KU§29, 272).

The sublime object does not necessarily appear to our senses as different from the objects that are subject to judgement of taste. Since we cannot use the appearance to distinguish between these judgements, a more likely criterion of difference is the quality of the feeling involved. Kant says that the feeling of the sublime is a complex feeling involving a simultaneous displeasure and pleasure, and apparently connects these two aspects to humiliation of imagination and a subsequent triumph of reason respectively. This turns out to be problematic. Kant's description of this phenomenology varies, and he does not provide a clear, coherent account of the basis for the complexity of the feeling. A closer look

---

[1] Kant says that imagination refers the mental agitation of the sublime either to the cognitive faculty or to the faculty of desire (KU§24, 247). In the Introduction the cognitive faculty is defined as theoretical reason and the faculty of desire as practical reason (KU III, 176 ff).

shows that there is a great variety of feelings of the sublime, such as respect, amazement, admiration, melancholy, and grief. I suggest that there are qualitative similarities between these feelings, but that feelings in judgements of taste and of the sublime may be almost indistinguishable, since both judgements are based on a family of feelings with some common characteristics. The paradigmatic feelings of the sublime are the complex and agitated feelings that move the subject, because these are the ones we find more attractive. These may even be of greater moral significance than the more dampened varieties, because of their powerful effect.

I suggest that the judgement of the sublime can be seen as what Wittgenstein calls a change of aspects from perceiving the physical world to experiencing the unconditioned basis of this world. The judgement can also be regarded as an aspect change from the theoretical to the practical perspective on the world. This change involves a turn from the object towards the judging subject: the real sublime is not the overwhelming object, but our own supersensible vocation. I discuss how the two modes of the sublime can be regarded as such aspect change, in that both display the superiority of reason to nature, even at its greatest or mightiest. Although Kant claims this feeling to show our supersensible vocation, which is connected to our moral freedom, I argue that Kant does not show how the mathematically sublime is an exhibition of this practical aspect of man's nature. I therefore turn to the account of the ideas of reason in the first Critique, to show how even the ideas of theoretical reason are related to the practical ideas of spontaneity and autonomy.

A part of Kant's exposition that is seldom discussed, but which is important in relation to the sublime in narrative literature is his notion of sublime affects. Human affects can be sublime in two ways, either as evoking fearfulness without actual fear, as in the dynamically sublime, or as evoking admiration, which the pre-Critical Kant called the noble sublime. These affects are sublime since man here is acting without concern for his own interests. Some of these affects may be morally commendable, but some may even be contrary to morality and still be regarded sublime because they awake the awareness in us of an ability to resist the forces of nature as moral beings.

I hold that it is difficult to discover exactly how Kant thinks we are morally affected by the sublime, although it has a basis in our capacity for self-determination. Other commentators have taken the opposite position and argued that the judgement of sublimity in Kant's account appears to be a moral, not an aesthetic judgement. One reason for this claim is that Kant calls the feeling of the sublime respect, the same term he uses for the proper attitude. I compare these feelings, and argue that they differ both in phenomenology and context, although both describe a relation between reason and sensibility. An argument often raised against Kant is that there must be a cognitive judgement of the superiority of reason underlying the judgement of sublimity, and thus it is not an aesthetic judgement in the same way as the judgement of taste is. I defend Kant and argue that if this claim were true, his exposition of the sublime would suffer from a grave inconsistency. My suggestion is that we read the passages where Kant seems to suggest a conceptual judgement underlying the feeling, as analogies used to describe the feeling involved in the judgement.

Finally, I attempt to retrace Kant's argument for the subjective universal validity of the judgement of the sublime. I suggest that the principle of the purposiveness of nature guiding the judgement of taste is replaced by a principle of the purposive use of nature for our supersensible vocation. In this judgement, nature is used to display our vocation, and this vocation is connected to our freedom to choose purposes for ourselves. This ability is unique for rational beings, and makes every rational being an end or a purpose in itself. Thus objective reflective judgement, for which the judgement of sublimity is a subjective condition, is a judgement about man as an end in itself. Just like the judgement of taste, the judgement of sublimity contains a claim to subjective universal validity for the cognitive relation, which is the basis for the objective reflective judgement according to purposes. Unlike judgements of taste, the judgement of the sublime involves an additional demand besides the required intersubjective assent, namely that everybody should have moral feeling and a developed knowledge of moral ideas. This demand is a moral demand, which we must presuppose to be satisfied if we are to claim universal validity for the feeling of the sublime. If not we cannot assume others to share our judgement of the sublime.

3.1 The feeling of the sublime in nature

The formlessness of the sublime

Like the judgement of taste, the judgement of sublimity [*das Erhabene*] is a singular judgement based on a disinterested feeling expressing the mental state found in a relation of cognitive powers in the representation of an object. These judgements also assert subjective universal validity for the underlying feeling (KU§23, 244) and display subjective purposiveness (KU§24, 247). But both the object, the quality of the feeling, and the cognitive basis of the judgement is different from the one connected to judgements of beauty, non-beauty or ugliness.

> Das Schöne der Natur betrifft die Form des Gegenstandes, die in der Begrenzung besteht; das Erhabene ist dagegen auch an einem formlosen Gegenstande zu finden, sofern *Unbegrenztheit* an ihm, oder durch dessen Veranlassung, vorgestellt und doch Totalität derselben hinzugedacht wird: so daß das Schöne für die Darstellung eines unbestimmten Verstandesbegriffs, das Erhabene aber eines dergleichen Vernunftbegriffs genommen zu werden scheint. (KU§23, 244)

Although imagination relates to a capacity for concept formation in both kinds of aesthetic reflective judgements, in the judgement of sublimity this capacity is not understanding, but reason. And this is because unboundedness is represented in the object (or induced by the object[2]) of judgement. As Lazaroff has pointed out[3], Kant says that *also* formless objects can be represented by unboundedness and thus be sublime, which must mean that objects with form can be sublime, too. This is confirmed by a passage in the Introduction:

> Die Empfänglichkeit einer Lust aus der Reflexion über die Formen der Sachen (der Natur sowohl als der Kunst) bezeichnet aber nicht allein eine Zweckmäßigkeit der Objekte in Verhältnis auf die reflektierende Urteilskraft, gemäß dem Naturbegriffe, am Subjekt, sondern auch umgekehrt des Subjekts in Ansehung der Gegenstände ihrer Form, ja selbst ihrer Unform nach, zufolge dem Freiheitsbegriffe … . (KU VII, 192)

These objects that show purposiveness of the subject with regard to freedom can either have form or lack form. This gives rise to two questions: (1) What is it for an object to be represented as formless? (2) Must an object with form be represented as formless to give rise to the feeling of the sublime?

I have argued that the form of the object is the structuring activity of the cognitive powers imagination and understanding in the representation of an object. Imagination displays lawfulness by synthesis of the manifold according to the principle of the purposiveness of nature, and thereby attunes itself to the rules of understanding. I will suggest that a formless object is an object in the representation of which this activity is not successfully accomplished. The object is such that it cannot be structured according to the principle of purposiveness of

---

2 I take Kant's distinction between unboundedness either as represented in the object or as induced by the object to mean that some objects are such that they must be represented as unbounded, whereas others are such that they can, under the proper circumstances, be represented as unbounded. Kant discusses the pyramids and St. Peter's Basilica as belonging to the latter kind (KU§26, 252).

3 A. Lazaroff, 'The Kantian Sublime: Aesthetic Judgment and Religious Feeling', 206.

nature, and no attunement between imagination and understanding can arise. The paradigmatic example of a formless object is the starry sky which we must see as a vast vault that encompasses everything [*ein weites Gewölbe das alles befaßt*] (KU§29, 270). The sheer size of this 'object' prevents any imaginative structuring because all the elements of the object cannot be intuited simultaneously.

To forestall objections: there are very many objects that contain elements that cannot be intuited simultaneously, but which nonetheless have form. I am, for example, unable to comprehend a tree in one intuition. I must walk around it to see all its elements. This does not make it sublime. I cannot take in all of *Molloy* in one intuition, either, and have to spend some hours to read it and have to represent the content in a series of subsequent intuitions. But this is not why I call it sublime. In that case, even *Sesame Street* would be sublime. When I intuit the tree, I comprehend it as one single limited object, although I know that to familiarise myself with all its elements I would have to do some further investigation. The starry sky is not like that. I cannot walk around it, nor can I move immediately to the end, as I can when reading a novel. It is represented in intuition as one object and still not limited. Our imaginative capacity is unable to structure the intuited manifold into a unity under the principle of the purposiveness of nature. This prevents any proportionate attunement of imagination with understanding, and the mental state we feel is not one that can give rise to a judgement of taste.

Kant's claim that the sublime object is formless, which means that it cannot be represented as a structured unity under the principle of the purposiveness of nature, seems to imply that formlessness is one condition of an object being judged as sublime. The statement that also the form of an object can be judged, indicates something else. I will suggest that we take Kant literally and suppose that both kinds of objects can be judged sublime. The first kind can be nothing but sublime, the second can be judged both by taste and as sublime. There are two ways we can represent this object for the aesthetic power of judgement; with form or as formless. If I stand at the edge of Lake Geneva one misty winter morning and see the lake as a never-ending expanse of water, the feeling of the sublime is induced in me. But on a clear autumn day viewed from above, it is seen merely as a beautiful lake, lying at the foot of the Alps[4].

A third possibility not usually discussed in commentaries is that the sublime also can be experienced in objects with form, even without the object being represented as formless. Crowther mentions the possibility[5], but dismisses it and

4 This example is comparable to Kant's example of the pyramid as sublime when regarded from the correct distance. See p. 138 f.

5 P. Crowther, *The Kantian Sublime*, 79.

ends up stating that it is "only formless objects which can make us aware of this moral sublimity in a way that has positive consequences for sensibility."[6] There are numerous passages in Kant's discussion supporting Crowther's view, for example the discussion of the difference between the beautiful and the sublime as regards the purposiveness of nature. Kant says that sublime ideas represent no form in nature, but merely a purposive use of the representation of nature (KU§24, 246). But, as we shall see, Kant also mentions as examples of the sublime fearless persons, warriors (KU§28, 262), and the absence of feeling [*Affektlosigkeit*] in someone who pursues his immutable principles (KU§29, 272). It is not obvious that these are examples of something that defies imagination any more than for example fearful persons and cowards. 'Objects' like these cannot be called formless, whether one understands the form of an object as the structuring activity of imagination and understanding, as I have suggested, or as invariant features, or as a delineation of the object.

The passages where Kant insists on the formlessness of the sublime object can be regarded as dealing with cases in which the sublime is most clearly distinguished from the beautiful. This does not mean that every sublime object has to be represented as formless. Also, objects that are represented in a free play of imagination and understanding can be sublime, as long as the imagination also engages reason. Thus a formless object, an object with form represented as formless, or an object with form can be sublime. If this is right, then the object's lack of form cannot be a criterion for classifying the object as sublime. Besides, aesthetic reflective judgements are based on feelings, and we must assume that the quality of the feeling is the basis for determining the object as sublime, not our perception of the form or formlessness of the object.

The quality of the feeling of the sublime

I have argued that there is a continuum of feelings from the pleasure of beauty to the displeasure of ugliness, with a neutral middle point. When Kant introduces another kind of disinterested aesthetic feeling transcending the range of simple feelings from pleasure through 'dull' to displeasure, a feeling also claiming universal validity independent of concepts, a few problems arise: In what way do we distinguish this judgement from the judgements of taste, keeping in mind that these judgements are made merely on the basis of feeling? Or to put the question

6 Ibid. 133. Compare P. Guyer, *Kant and the Experience of Freedom*, 217.

differently: What is the qualitative distinction between the pleasure of beauty and the pleasure of the sublime?

Beck and Guyer both argue that Kant holds that there exist only two qualitatively different kinds of feeling, pleasure and displeasure. According to Guyer, it follows that the difference between feelings within these two groups is merely a question of contexts or objects[7]. And this assumption is reasonable when considering the definition of pleasure as a self-preserving state[8], which is echoed in the definition of the disagreeable and the agreeable in the Anthropology:

> Was unmittelbar (durch den Sinn) mich antreibt meinen Zustand zu *verlassen* (aus ihm herauszugehen): ist mir *unangenehm* - es schmerzt mich; was ebenso mich antreibt, ihn zu *erhalten* (in ihm zu bleiben): ist mir *angenehm* es vergnügt mich (A 231)

If feelings are nothing but such self-preserving or self-terminating states, then the claim to qualitative differences between them certainly seems unfounded, and no qualitative difference between the beautiful and the sublime is warranted. Both are self-preserving states. An alternative reading, avoiding this conclusion, would regard these identical definitions used both for aesthetic feelings and for feelings of gratification to give the common features of all feelings, leaving room for qualitative differences among different sub-classes such as feelings of the agreeable, the good, the beautiful, and the sublime.

This can be countered by the standard passage that seems to prove Kant thought the only difference between feelings is in their particular degrees of self-preservation and strength:

> Die Vorstellungen der Gegenstände mögen noch so ungleichartig, sie mögen Verstandes-, selbst Vernunftvorstellungen im Gegensatze der Vorstellungen der Sinne sein, so ist doch das Gefühl der Lust, wodurch jene doch eigentlich nur den Bestimmungsgrund des Willens ausmachen (die Annehmlichkeit, das Vergnügen, das man davon erwartet, welches die Tätigkeit zur Hervorbringung des Objekts antreibt), nicht allein so fern von einerlei Art, daß es jederzeit bloß empirisch erkannt werden kann, sondern auch so fern, als es eine und dieselbe Lebenskraft, die sich im Begehrungsvermögen äußert, affiziert und in dieser Beziehung von jedem anderen Bestimmungsgrunde in nichts als dem Grade verschieden sein kann. (KpV 23)

This appears to be an explicit statement of the qualitative identity of all feelings, supporting Guyer's interpretation, but Allison has provided an alternative reading of this passage:

---

7 Beck, *A Commentary*, 93 f. and Guyer, *Claims of Taste*, 103 f.
8 See p. 68.

> What is crucial here is that Kant is not talking about pleasure *per se*, but rather about pleasure as a motivating factor (determining ground of the will). In other words, the claim is merely that any qualitative difference between pleasures is irrelevant in this regard, since what matters is merely the effect of the pleasure on the faculty of desire.[9]

Allison continues by showing how Kant, in the First Introduction, repeatedly identifies the consciousness of subjective purposiveness with pleasure (EE VIII, 227 ff), which means that the feeling is qualitatively different from other feelings by having this particular quasi-cognitive feature[10]. Although there is solid evidence for this interpretation, I have in the previous chapter argued that Kant in fact claims that consciousness of subjective purposiveness is identical with a feeling claiming universal validity for itself, whether the feeling is pleasurable or displeasurable. This does not alter Allison's point that there is a distinct qualitatively difference between these feelings and other feelings of pleasure and displeasure. Another qualitative aspect of aesthetic reflective feelings not mentioned by Allison is their disinterested character.

One problem still remains: given that there are these qualitative differences between groups of feelings as inclinations, moral feelings, and reflective feelings, it is not obvious that there are such differences within these groups as well. Consequently, a potential problem is that the disinterested, subjectively purposive feelings demanding universal assent for themselves differ only in degree, not in kind. Then there would be no criteria for distinguishing the feelings in the judgement of sublimity from the feelings in judgements of taste. After all, the pleasure in the sublime is repeatedly said to be subjectively purposive, just as it is disinterested and claims intersubjective validity (e.g. KU§26, 253). Perhaps, as Guyer suggests, the only qualitative difference between these two kinds of aesthetic reflective feelings is the complexity of the sublime[11]. The feeling of the sublime is described as a mixture between pleasure and displeasure, or a combination of simultaneous attraction and repulsion, related to admiration and respect, and thus called negative pleasure (KU§23, 245). If this complexity is the only difference between the feelings in judgement of taste and those involved in judgement of the sublime, we have a problem. The feeling of the sublime may be nothing but a combination of the feelings in the judgements of beauty and ugliness, respectively. Then there would be no difference between a sublime object and one that is simultaneously beautiful and ugly.

---

9 Allison, 'Pleasure and Harmony', 475.
10 Ibid. 476 f.
11 Guyer, *Experience of Freedom*, 203 ff.

There are several answers to this problem. First and foremost, Kant says that the difference between the beautiful and the sublime is not only connected to the complexity of the latter. He connects the judgement of sublimity to ideas of reason rather than to concepts of understanding, and explicitly says that the sublime is subjectively *counterpurposive* for cognition (KU§23, 245 ff). This is not too helpful, though, in pinpointing the qualitative distinction between the feeling of the sublime, and a combination of feelings of beauty and ugliness. And a discussion of the relation between the two components of the feeling of the sublime does not bring us as far as we should hope, either.

The relationship between attraction and repulsion

Kant is not very precise in his descriptions of the dual nature of the feeling of the sublime. In some places he adds a temporal factor to the feeling, making it a displeasure followed by a pleasure (KU§23, 245), other places he describes it as a rapid alternation between attraction and repulsion (KU§27, 258), and other places again the components are presented as simultaneous aspects of one feeling (KU§27, 257). This variety of descriptions is hardly acceptable, if the quality of the feeling is to serve as a criterion for determining an object as sublime.

The initial impression is that unlike the feeling of beauty, which is produced by the play between two cognitive powers, the feeling of the sublime consists of one feeling connected to the failing abilities of imagination and another feeling due to the triumph of reason. It seems to be two separate feelings with separate causes occurring more or less simultaneously. But then the similarity with the judgement of taste is reduced more than acceptable, because in one case the reason for the feeling is the play *between* the powers, whereas in the other the powers produce the feelings on their own. Although supported by some parts of the exposition, this interpretation contradicts central passages of the text, as in this statement of how the sources of the pleasure in the beautiful and the sublime are similar in having reference to an indeterminate concept,

> mithin das Wohlgefallen an der bloßen Darstellung oder dem Vermögen derselben geknüpft ist, wodurch das Vermögen der Darstellung, oder die Einbildungskraft, bei einer gegebenen Anschauung mit dem *Vermögen der Begriffe* des Verstandes oder der Vernunft, als Beförderung der letztern, in Einstimmung betrachtet wird. (KU§23, 244)

It is the attunement between the faculties that gives rise to the feeling, not each faculty separately.

That rules out the possibility of two separate but simultaneous feelings composing the judgement; the opposing components of the feeling must stem from the same source. There seems, however, to be some ground for holding the feeling to be one of rapid alternating pleasure and displeasure, because it is difficult to understand how it is possible to be in two different states at the same time, given that they are mutually exclusive according to Kant's definition cited above. Displeasure drives me to leave the state in which I am, whereas pleasure drives me to remain in the state. In an ambiguous feeling, I would simultaneously be driven both to remain *and* to leave the state I am in, which seems to be impossible. A solution proposed by Crowther is to think the state of the sublime as being one of rapid alternation between two such opposed states:

> Kant takes the experience of sublimity to involve a mental movement that is, temporally speaking, so rapid as to manifest itself at the explicitly conscious level only in a complex feeling where the elements of displeasure and pleasure cannot be discriminated as successive.[12]

This is an unhappy solution, since Kant says that the basis of the feeling is the harmonisation of imagination and understanding through their conflict. On Crowther's reading there is a continuous conflict without any resolution.

More promising is Makkreel's suggestion that the ambiguous feeling is possible due to the purposiveness of the feeling of the sublime:

> The two feelings would cancel each other if one of them were not felt to be purposively related to the other. Representations that are purposively related are not juxtaposed in a mere mechanical succession, but are felt to coexist. One is comprehended by virtue of the other.[13]

Makkreel says that the feelings in the judgement of the sublime are purposively related, which must mean that they serve some purpose, namely to show that we have a reason independent of sensible constraints. Although I believe feelings can have a cognitive content, I also think Kant is putting too much content into the pleasure when he claims that we *feel* the supersensible:

> Denn so wie Einbildungskraft und *Verstand* in der Beurteilung des Schönen durch ihre Einhelligkeit, so bringen Einbildungskraft und *Vernunft* hier durch ihren Widerstreit subjektive Zweckmäßigkeit der Gemütskräfte hervor: nämlich ein Gefühl, daß wir reine selbständige Vernunft haben … . (KU§27, 258)

---

12 Crowther, *Kantian Sublime*, 125. Makkreel, on the other hand, holds that since the two feelings are purposively related, they cannot be successive, Makkreel, *Imagination and Interpretation*, 79.

13 Makkreel, *Imagination and Interpretation*, 79.

There are two possibilities here; either we are able to feel a 'presence' of absolute causality merely through the combined pleasure and displeasure, as Lyotard suggests[14], or the displeasure leads to a "conscious reflection in conceptual terms" of the superiority of reason, a reflection that is pleasurable, as Guyer suggests[15]. I think the latter suggestion is the better because it avoids obscurity. The feeling of a presence of something without perceiving or thinking this something is incomprehensible, especially when this something is an abstract idea. But Guyer's proposal is not without its problems, because it means that we have to reject Kant's claim that the sublime is an aesthetic judgement in the sense of being based on feelings only. Besides, Kant's own claim is problematic because he connects subjective purposiveness to a purpose, namely displaying the superiority of reason. Thus he undermines his own theoretical framework, where he connects the aesthetic reflection to a subjective purposiveness without purpose:

> Denn da ... diese Bewegung [des Gemüts] aber als subjektiv zweckmäßig beurteilt werden soll (weil das Erhabene gefällt): so wird sie durch die Einbildungskraft entweder auf das *Erkenntnis-* oder auf das *Begehrungsvermögen* bezogen, in beiderlei Beziehung aber die Zweckmäßigkeit der gegebenen Vorstellung nur in Ansehung dieser *Vermögen* (ohne Zweck oder Interesse).

Connecting the purposiveness to exhibition of the superiority of reason wrongly introduces a purpose in the judgement.

Despite Kant's insistence on connecting the consciousness of subjective purposiveness to the feeling of pleasure, I will suggest that also his theory of the sublime makes better sense if we instead connect it to the claim to intersubjective validity for the feeling. Furthermore, we must regard the judgement of sublimity to be the subjective aspect of an objective reflective judgement of nature under the principle of the purposive use of nature for the awakening of rational ideas (KU§27, 259) or for practical reason (KU§29, 267). I will return to this later.

Since subjective purposiveness cannot be connected to a determinate purpose, such as the fulfilment of some general goal, the two aspects of the feeling of the sublime cannot be described as purposively related as Makkreel suggests. Still one can say that one feeling is comprehended by means of the other. But this does not explain why the displeasure is not cancelled out by the pleasure arising from it, as soon as the pleasure is aroused. Whichever way one attempts to explain the

---

14 Lyotard, *Lessons*, 140.

15 Guyer, *Experience of Freedom*, 212 f.

ambivalent character of the feeling of the sublime, the account encounters interpretative difficulties.

A possible solution is to accept Kant's claim that the feeling of the sublime is qualitatively different from the feelings of beauty and ugliness, but without letting the notion of complexity play the central role. We should not take the sublime to be felt in one way only, definable by this complexity. Since the feelings in judgements of taste, at least according to the interpretation I am proposing, can vary in intensity and over a range from maximum pleasure to maximum displeasure, one may suspect that also the sublime can vary in a similar way. Then there is not one feeling of the sublime, but a family of feelings presumably united in some common characteristics. And the analytic of the sublime confirms this assumption.

Feelings of the sublime

There are several passages where Kant describes the feeling of the sublime as violent to the imagination, as a feeling that arises from an inhibition of the vital forces followed by an even more powerful outpouring of them (KU§23, 245), and draws a contrast between the restful contemplation of the beautiful with the mental agitation of the sublime (KU§24, 247). But Kant has also other descriptions of the feeling of the sublime pointing towards other feelings. I will argue that Kant's view of the feeling of the sublime is too many-faceted to be conclusively captured in these terms.

I will start with a brief sketch of Burke's empirical study of the sublime, because this probably was an important frame of reference, mediated by Mendelssohn's work, for Kant's treatment of the sublime[16]. The most important points for Burke are that the sublime overwhelms us, anticipates our reasoning, and affects us with an irresistible force. He calls this feeling astonishment, in contrast to the weaker feelings admiration, reverence and respect[17]. But behind all these different modes of feeling of the sublime there is one basic feeling: "Indeed terror is in all cases whatsoever, either more openly or latently the ruling principle of the sublime."[18] But Burke's sublime is experienced with delight, i.e. the kind of feeling we experience when a pain ceases, which is not the case in real terror or

16 Zammito, *Genesis*, 32. Zammito's source is T. Gracyk, 'Kant's Shifting Debt to British Aesthetics', *British Journal of Aesthetics* 26 (1986), 204-217.

17 Burke, *Beautiful and Sublime*, 53.

18 Ibid. 54.

fear. Thus, experiencing the sublime requires that we are not in any danger, that is we have "an idea of pain and danger, without being actually in such circumstances."[19]

The sublime is, according to Burke's account, related to the feeling of relief, of escaping danger, or viewing the threat from a safe distance. This might explain the attraction human beings tend to find in the suffering of others as witnessed in the popularity of public executions and the large number of spectators to major catastrophes. It also accounts for the delight we take in watching nature at its most terrifying, usually at a distance which is safe, but not more than barely so. The distance is necessary when experiencing the sublime, because if we were the ones suffering pain or terror, our feeling would be negative only, without any delight, and we would not want to seek more, but rather try to get away immediately. If we are afraid or feel pain, we wish to escape, whereas the feeling of the sublime is delightful, and thus attractive like the pleasure we take in beauty.

Kant agrees with Burke in locating the crucial aspect of the sublime in the attraction to things normally considered repulsive, but he refuses to make self-preservation and terror the sole keys to the problem. First, he stresses the importance of beholding mighty, sublime objects from a safe position:

> *Wer* sich fürchtet, kann über das Erhabene der Natur gar nicht urteilen, so wenig als der, welcher durch Neigung und Appetit eingenommen ist, über das Schöne. *Jener* fliehet den Anblick eines Gegenstandes, der ihm Scheu einjagt; und es ist unmöglich, an einem Schrecken, der ernstlich gemeint wäre, Wohlgefallen zu finden. (KU§28, 261)

If this pleasure were one of relief due to cessation of pain or terror, one would never willingly subject oneself to the experience once more, Kant says. But the aesthetic pleasure is certainly something we would want to relive, and Kant thinks Burke is at least partly wrong.

Another problem that weakens Burke's position is that terror as the basic component in the feeling cannot properly explain the mathematical mode of the sublime. This mode leads to the experience of infinity (regardless of the object actually being infinitely great), according to Burke causing delightful horror[20]. But can terror or horror really account for the feeling aroused by the experience of infinity, especially when the threat to our self-preservation is supposed to be the cause of this feeling? It can be an acceptable description of the feeling of looking down an abyss, but seems an unlikely account of the feeling of the sublime when

---

[19] Ibid. 47.
[20] Ibid. 67.

viewing an endless plain or the ocean. There is no threat to our self-preservation in that. This does not amount to a complete rejection of Burke's claim that there is *some* connection between the feeling of terror and of the sublime; they are phenomenologically related. But this points to the weaknesses in Burke's attempts at grounding the feeling in self-preservation, and helps us to close in on one of Kant's major contributions to this subject; namely his placing the emphasis on the judgement of the sublime as being a *disinterested* aesthetic reflective judgement.

There are several feelings said by Kant to be involved in these judgements. At one place he agrees with Burke in calling the feeling astonishment or amazement bordering on terror [*die Verwunderung, die an Schreck grenzt*], and even horror and sacred thrill [*das Grausen und der heilige Schauer*] (KU §29, 269). Later he says that amazement is too closely connected to the feeling of novelty to be suitable for the judgement about the sublime cast of mind of a noble man. This feeling is better described as the related but longer-lasting admiration [*Bewunderung*] (KU §29, 272). This indicates that the sublime can be an experience of suddenness, but it can also be based on a different, more balanced feeling. Kant also calls the feeling of the sublime respect [*Achtung*] (KU§27, 257), which draws the sublime close to morality.

It seems almost impossible to give a clear-cut empirical description of the feeling the sublime that covers all the different instances of it. Not even the fact that the sublime is experienced by a feeling of ambiguity can give us a criterion for knowing when we are feeling the sublime. Ambiguous feelings of simultaneous attraction and repulsion can occur in many situations, as when I admire the cleverness of a thief and simultaneously am angry because he stole my money. Nor can we describe the feeling of the sublime as admiration, firstly because we can admire objects and affects that are not sublime, and secondly because Kant also mentions other feelings besides mere admiration to exemplify the feeling in the judgement of sublimity.

The examples of different feelings of the sublime mentioned by Kant, show a continuity between the empirical, psychological aesthetics of the pre-Critical *Beobachtungen* and the account presented in the third Critique. A comparison between some passages in these two works can be useful, because the diversity of phenomena rightfully termed sublime is often lost when the focus is on the complexity, the seriousness, and the negative pleasure of the sublime. Kant describes three different types of the sublime in his early work:

> Das Erhabene ist wiederum verschiedener Art. Das Gefühl desselben ist bisweilen mit einigem Grausen oder auch Schwermut, in einigen Fällen bloß mit ruhiger Bewunderung und in noch andern mit einer über einen erhabenen

> Plan verbreiteten Schönheit begleitet. Das erstere will ich das *Schreckhaft-Erhabene*, das zweite das *Edle*, und das dritte das *Prächtige* nennen. (B 209)

Kant does not divide the sublime into these types in the third Critique, and his main focus is certainly on the terrifying sublime. We saw above that Kant mentions horror, and we shall see later that the related feeling of fearfulness is required for the dynamically sublime (KU§28, 260). More interesting is the fact that also melancholy [*Schwermut*] belongs to the early account of the terrifying sublime, considering that he in the Critique he exemplifies the sublime also by "*tief beschatteter, zum schwermütigen Nachdenken einladender Einöden*" (KU§29, 269). This kind of feeling recurs later in the same section when Kant discusses the interesting sadness of wastelands in contrast to the insipid sadness of the Savoy mountains described by Sausurre:

> Er kannte daher auch eine *interessante* Traurigkeit, welcher der Anblick einer Einöde einflößt, in die sich Menschen wohl versetzen möchte, um von der Welt nichts weiter zu hören, noch zu erfahren, die denn doch nicht so ganz unwirtbar sein muß, daß sie nur einen höchst mühseligen Aufenthalt für Mensche darböte. (KU§29, 276)

In this description it is the landscape that exhibits sadness, but it is difficult to understand how one can experience the sadness of the landscape by any other feeling than this same sadness[21], especially when considering the related passage cited above. Thus the feeling of the terrifying sublime has a dual nature, one tending towards terror, the second towards melancholy, but they are united in the feeling of amazement.

As we shall see below, the feeling of the noble sublime is also retained in the examples in the third Critique. It concerns admirable attitudes or affects within human nature (KU§29, 276 ff), and is as such quite different from the sublime based on fearfulness. The splendid sublime is exemplified in the Observations by the beautiful ornamentations on the large and simple frame of St. Peter's in Rome (B 210). In the Critique St. Peter's is only treated as mathematically sublime, but we can find traces of the splendid sublime in Kant's discussion of art, where he says that the sublime and the beautiful can be combined in some works of art. He

[21] Lyotard, *Lessons*, 150 ff., even takes all the affects described as sublime to be feelings that can be basis for judgements of the sublime. Here these feelings are called "sublime feelings" and include both feelings such as admiration and astonishment, as well as enthusiasm, anger, and lack of feeling. This is based on a misreading of Kant's text, where the first group consists of feelings evoked in the subject by the sublime object, the other group consists in feelings that are sublime and evoke the first kind of feeling in the judging subject. The misinterpretation may be Lyotard's, but it can also be due to the translation of his book from French to English.

indicates that in *some* cases this combination heightens the beauty of the work, by doubting that this is *always* the case (KU§52, 325 f). In the post-Kantian discussion of the sublime, the splendid sublime regains a central role[22].

This analysis of the different feelings underlying the judgement of sublimity indicates that the phenomenological description of a complex feeling of pleasure and displeasure should not be given the criterial function suggested by some commentators[23]. Just as the lack of form is not decisive for the sublimity of an object, neither is the complexity of the feeling. Although the paradigmatic feeling of the sublime is the mental agitation of a serious, complex feeling of displeasure and pleasure, called negative pleasure, the sublime can also be based on the moderate feelings of admiration or melancholy. This is not surprising when we compare the judgement of the sublime with the judgement of taste as I have interpreted it, where the pleasure of beauty is the paradigmatic feeling of taste without being the only universally communicable feeling in such judgements.

The judgement of sublimity is not based on one particular feeling, although the feeling of the sublime must always contain a demand for everybody's assent, whether it is described as delightful horror, melancholy, or admiration. On the basis of a comparison with judgements of taste one can even suspect that the judgement about a sublime object can contain a neutral state of feeling, similar to the 'dullness' of judgements of non-beautiful objects. Then the qualitative distinction between the feeling in judgements of taste and judgements of the sublime may seem to disappear altogether. The fact that there may be cases in which the feelings in judgements of taste and of sublimity may appear indistinguishable does not mean that the difference between judgements of taste and of the sublime is erased. There is a difference between the feelings that is most clearly seen if one compares the paradigmatic judgement of beauty based on a simple pleasure with the paradigmatic judgement of the terrifying sublime based on the feeling of amazement or wonder. But these two types of judgements can also be based on feelings that are similar, in which case we have to take the objective reflective judgement of the object into consideration to decide whether this is a judgement of taste or of the sublime.

If the feeling of the sublime is defined as a universally communicable feeling expressing a mental state of free play between imagination and reason, the quality of this feeling may vary. But then we cannot even assume that every kind of judgement of sublimity contains a feeling we find aesthetically enjoyable. When it

---

22 For a discussion of theories that subsume the sublime under the ethical and/or the beautiful, see Pries, *Übergänge*, 11-31.

23 Guyer, *Experience of Freedom*, 205.

comes to aesthetic enjoyment, we presumably prefer the sublime described in the paradigmatic account. This is the sublime that moves by agitated feelings, and we prefer this in the same way as we choose to linger over the pleasure of beauty rather than the displeasure of ugliness. I will also argue that the agitated feeling of the sublime is of greater ethical significance, but even the more dampened feelings may be ethically significant, as long as they accompany the reflection on rational ideas based on the intuition of an object of nature.

3.2 The aspect change of the judgement of the sublime

The sublime and aspect change

The judgement of the sublime is based on a feeling that arises when we experience something that overwhelms our cognitive faculties. As in any experience of the empirical world, we presuppose the idea of the technic of nature, i.e. that nature can be made understandable under the principle of purposiveness. This expectation is not fulfilled by the incapability of imagination to unite the manifold under this principle, a unity that is necessary if understanding shall be able to find a concept for this unity. Thus there can be no relation of free play between imagination and understanding. But there is still a demand that we cognise all of nature as united in a rule-governed system. The power of judgement has to resort to a different principle to fulfill this demand in the encounter with these objects, a principle of nature as a sign of a different kind of purposiveness. He contrasts this with the principle of judgements of beauty and says that the judgement of the sublime

> auch auf ein (zwar nur subjektives) Prinzip a priori bezieht, aber nicht so wie das erstere, auf eine *Zweckmäßigkeit der Natur* in Ansehung des Subjekts, sondern nur auf einen möglichen zweckmäßigen *Gebrauch* gewisser sinnlicher Anschauungen ihrer Form nach vermittelst der bloß reflektierenden Urteilskraft. (EE XII, 250)

Kant continues by saying that this use of the representation is contingent, and does not serve to cognise the object, but serves a different feeling, "*nämlich dem der innern Zweckmäßigkeit in der Anlage der Gemütskräfte*" (EE XII, 250). When Kant says that the use of this object serves a different feeling, he probably refers to a feeling different from the feeling of the sublime[24]. This is the moral feeling (KU§29, 267).

The feeling of the sublime is an intimation of a different realm, the intelligible realm, as something standing above the sensible realm. But these realms are better seen as two points of view we can have on the same world. Each point of view is ruled by a determining legislation, through the concepts of nature and the concept of freedom, respectively (KU II, 174 f). We are able to, and do, change between these perspectives on the world, and we can regard it as some kind of changing of aspects[25]; I cannot see both perspectives at once, but can change between them.

Recki points out that the feeling of the sublime is based on an expectation of beauty[26]. When we look at nature as nature, we always regard it from the empirical point of view, unless we are using it for symbolical purposes. But the experience of the sublime constitutes a sudden aspect change, where the intelligible point of view somehow breaks into the empirical through a 'negative pleasure'. We feel the presence of the other perspective, and are made aware of the primacy of the intelligible over the empirical, which can be expressed through the idea of freedom. This neither leads to concrete actions nor gives any insight in how to deal with moral dilemmas, but has its importance in signifying our moral vocation, which is tied to our rational nature.

This aspect change is not connected to the relation between sensibility and rationality in the same way as in the moral feeling respect. The judgement of the sublime does, however, presuppose this relation: if we did not feel respect as moral motivation, we would be incapable of experiencing the sublime. But this presupposition cannot give the sublime a moral function, which is Kant's implicit claim when he says that the sublime object is purposive for the use of the moral feeling. The mathematically sublime is even further from having a moral function, because it is not evident that it can be connected with *practical* reason at all. Although Kant repeatedly says that the judgement of sublimity displays a subjective purposiveness of the object, it is not clear that there is any basis for a claim to subjective universal validity for the basis of the judgement, based on a similarity between this judgement and the judgement of taste. To establish that the judgement of sublimity is a intersubjectively valid judgement with a moral import, I will look more closely at the change in aspect from nature to freedom in this judgement.

---

24 Pluhar assumes Kant means different from the feeling of beauty, but there is nothing the context warranting this assumption.

25 L. Wittgenstein, *Pilosophical Investigations*, 193 ff.

26 B. Recki, 'Ästhetische Einstellung und moralische Haltung', 168.

The free play of imagination and reason

I have rejected both the formlessness of the sublime object and the complexity of the relevant feeling as necessary conditions for a judgement's being a judgement of the sublime. More important is the objective reflective judgement, which is accompanied by this aesthetic judgement of sublimity. In the judgement of the sublime, imagination has found a new, and more demanding playmate: reason. As Guyer describes Kant's paradigmatic account:

> What results from "free play" of reason and the imagination is not a simple feeling of harmony but a complex psychological state, including both frustration at the imagination's inability to satisfy the bidding of reason through any finite synthesis of sensibility - hence the element of displeasure in our response to the sublime - and the sense that this very frustration itself is a representation of the infinite, a sensible representation which satisfies the bidding of reason in an unexpected way and is thus the ground of our ultimate pleasure in the sublime.[27]

It is no coincidence that imagination is brought into play with reason rather than understanding[28]. In judgements of beauty, the form of the object is judged, while judgements of the sublime also relate to formless objects, i.e. objects that we perceive as limitless (KU §23, 244). These objects cannot be completely comprehended by imagination, and we are incapable of finding a concept for them under the principle of the purposiveness of nature, which means that we are unable to cognise the contingent aspects of these objects in teleological terms. The feeling of the sublime is induced by something that may appear counterpurposive [*zweckwidrig*] for judgement since we are unable to represent it in imagination, but Kant says that this makes it even more sublime (KU §23, 245).

Pries argues Kant's account of the sublime in fact undermines his own epistemological framework:

> Wenn man Kants Synthesen als den Vorgang versteht, durch den Gegebenes überhaupt erst rezipiert und ... weiterverarbeitet wird, so wird am Erhabenen deutlich, daß hier ein Gegenstand begegnet, der nach dem grundlegenden Modell der Wahrnehmung in der *Kritik der reinen Vernunft* nicht wahrgenommen werden kann und deren Zeit-Konzeption aus den Angeln hebt.

---

[27] Guyer, *Experience of Freedom*, 207.

[28] It is, to some extent, misleading to talk of play between the faculties in the sublime experience, because this is not a playful relationship like the beautiful, but is expressed in an emotion that is more serious (KU §23, 245).

> Gleichwohl läßt sich nicht bezweifeln, daß er dennoch wahrgenommen wird - sonst gäbe es kein Gefühl des Erhabenen.[29]

I do not believe this captures Kant's argument. We are able to determine these objects according to the basic model of cognition as presented in the first Critique. This is also admitted in the last sentence of the quotation. It is the basic model of objective reflective judgement of the third Critique that is insufficient. But it follows from the demand of systematicity that also these objects must be determined as regards what is left contingent by determinative judgement. Since the principle of the purposiveness is inadequate for these objects, judgement must resort to another, but related principle to find concepts for these objects. And this is the principle of the purposive use of nature for the mind's supersensible vocation (KU§29, 268).

Imagination and understanding cannot enter into a free play when perceiving these kinds of objects, but this is not due to an insufficiency of understanding. It is rather imagination that is unable to structure the manifold in accordance with the principle of the purposiveness of nature in the way it usually does. Kant says that the most important distinction between the beautiful and the sublime is that

> die Naturschönheit (die Selbstständige) eine Zweckmäßigkeit in ihrer Form, wodurch der Gegenstand für unsere Urteilskraft gleichsam vorherbestimmt zu sein scheint, bei sich führt und so an sich einen Gegenstand des Wohlgefallens ausmacht; hingegen das, was in uns, ohne zu vernünfteln, bloß in der Auffassung, das Gefühl des Erhabenen erregt, der Form nach zwar zweckwidrig für unsere Urteilskraft, unangemessen unserem Darstellungsvermögen und gleichsam gewalttätig für die Einbildungskraft erscheinen mag, aber dennoch nur um desto erhabener zu sein geurteilt wird. (KU§23, 245)

Objects, beautiful, non-beautiful, or ugly, carry purposiveness in their form, which I take to mean that these objects are structured by imagination in apprehension according to a principle of the purposiveness of nature. This again makes it possible for understanding to provide a concept of a purpose for the object. Sublime objects, Kant says, are, in their form, incommensurable with our power of exhibition, imagination. I take this to mean that these objects cannot be structured according to the principle of the purposiveness of nature. It follows that we cannot ascribe any concept of purpose to the object, since it displays no

[29] Pries, *Übergänge*, 138. Pries' interpretation of the sublime as Kant's promised connection between the theoretical and the practical realm of human experience, ibid. 193 f., also suggets she takes the theory of the sublime to be supplementing the first Critique more than undermining the epistemological framework established there.

regularity. When Kant says that the object is counterpurposive [*zweckwidrig*] for our power of judgement we should not take this only to mean that the object does not serve the purpose of judgement, which is the combination of particulars with universals. The power of merely reflective judgement is guided by the principle of nature as purposive, and the sublime object cannot be structured according to this principle. It follows that the object cannot be judged according to a concept of a purpose, either. Thus the object resists the system of purposes that we rely on in judging the world, and this makes it, for our power of judgement, counterpurposive.

Since imagination cannot structure this material according to the principle of purposiveness, these objects appear to defy the requirement of systematicity. Not everything can be understood as arranged according to laws of nature. This does not mean that we stand powerless when confronted with reason's demand for totality and the impossibility of fulfilling this demand through our cognitive powers. But this inadequacy awakens in us concepts different in kind from those concerning purposive laws of nature. We search for concepts that are not restricted by sensibility, and thus the imagination enters into a relation of free interaction with reason (KU§26, 256). We have seen that Kant hesitates to call this relation 'play' because it is more serious, either due to the lack of cognitive success, or because moral ideas are involved. What is important is that also in this relation, imagination is not determined by any concept. It is even less determined in this relation than in the one underlying judgement of taste, since the attunement does not even result in a concept of the object, but in a concept that is mistakenly ascribed the object, as we shall see.

The mathematically sublime

Reason, as the capacity for ideas, can be either theoretical or practical. In the first case it guides cognition by the principles of unity (KrV A702/B730), in the second to what Kant calls desire, i.e. to action. Imagination can relate to reason in both of these functions, if the object is such that imagination is unable to synthesise a representation according to the principle of purposiveness. Consequently, there are two different modes of the sublime, one mathematical, the other dynamical (KU§24, 247)[30]. Both modes are covered by the definition given

[30] That these are not two different kinds of experience is clear, in that the same pattern of feeling is present, the same parts of the human consciousness are involved (imagination and reason), and both are stimulated by objects defined as formless. There is a

by Kant: "*Erhaben ist, was auch nur denken zu können ein Vermögen des Gemüts beweiset, das jeden Maßstab der Sinne übertrifft.*" (KU§25, 250) Since the central question for our discussion of the Kantian sublime concerns the *ethical* significance of the sublime, one would expect that only the dynamical mode, the one referring to the faculty of desire, would be of interest. I will claim that the mathematical mode is also interesting from a moral point of view, but that this is not immediately obvious from Kant's account.

The mathematical-sublime is something that is, or is represented as, large beyond all comparison (KU§25, 248). Kant contrasts this with how we always connect some kind of subjective standard of magnitude with our judgement of objects, even in practical or aesthetic judgements. This is not the case with the sublime:

> Wenn wir aber etwas nicht allein groß, sondern schlechthin-, absolut-, in aller Absicht- (über alle Vergleichung) groß, d.i. erhaben, nennen, so sieht man bald ein: daß wir für dasselbe keinen ihm angemessenen Maßstab außer ihm, sondern bloß in ihm zu suchen verstatten. Es ist eine Größe, die bloß sich selber gleich ist. (KU§25, 250)

The way Kant introduces the analysis of aesthetic[31] estimation of sublime objects is confusing, because he says that to assess the magnitude of an object we must compare it with a measure. Thus no magnitude is absolute; it is always comparative (KU§25, 248). Several commentators have assumed that Kant's initial discussion concerning relative size and the need for an aesthetically determined unit of measure means that sublime objects too must be measured in this way. Crowther holds that it is in seeking out this measure that imagination is overtaxed:

> As I interpret him here, Kant is saying that in the case of vast formless objects reason demands that we estimate their magnitude in relation to a unit of measure provided by a single intuition. In order to satisfy this demand the imagination will at first try out easily comprehended measures such as a foot or a perch, but is then driven to find larger units as a measures for these, and so on and so on, until it arrives at infinity itself as the only appropriate measure.[32]

---

difference, but, as I will argue, that difference does not make these modes play essentially different roles in human experience.

31 Here 'aesthetic' means pertaining to the sensible intuition of an object. The word does not refer to the subject's feeling of the mental state in a representation of the object, which is the way Kant normally uses the word in the third Critique. He discusses these two meanings of the word in the introduction (KU VII, 188 f).

32 Crowther, *Kantian Sublime*, 97. See a related account in M. Budd, 'Delight in the Natural World', 236 ff.

On the basis of this interpretation, Crowther criticises Kant for unnecessarily bringing in the idea of infinity, when the impossibility of grasping "the phenomenal totality of *any* object in a single whole of intuition"[33] is sufficient to show the superiority of our rational being compared to our sensibility. This leads Crowther to introduce a distinction between a baroque thesis invoking the idea of infinity, and an austere one, just concerned with the insufficiency of the imagination's ability to represent the object as a whole.

Crowther's account is more complex than required to give a plausible interpretation of Kant's theory, but his misreading is understandable when considering how Kant structured the exposition. Matthews provides a thorough discussion and criticism of Crowther's interpretation, and shows that the two theses of the mathematically sublime described by Crowther, really are one:

> When Kant speaks of using imagination to comprehend the infinite, he is speaking of the infinite as the object in nature we are trying to measure. From a subjective point of view, this object *seems* infinite. We are not trying to measure the infinite independently of the object in nature.[34]

Although Matthews shows what is wrong in Crowther's account, even her account is not quite precise. The object we call sublime does not seem infinite. At most, it seems limitless. It is an object we are unable to grasp as one complete unity in intuition. This inability leads the reflective judgement in its objective use to an idea of reason, in this case the idea of the infinite.

This becomes somewhat clearer in the second section on the mathematically sublime where Kant contrasts apprehension [*Auffassung*] and comprehension [*Zusammenfassung*] in intuition (KU§26, 251). The first runs through the manifold, and can continue indefinitely. Comprehension brings together the manifold in a unity, and reaches a maximum it cannot overstep. Imagination is inadequate only in this function, not in the apprehension based on a measure. Thus we are unable to grasp an object as a united totality, and it appears to the subject as having no limits. This comprehension is *aesthetic*, meaning that it deals with our capacity for bringing together a perceptual manifold in one intuition (KU§26, 252). Kant states that we have the ability to proceed indefinitely with a numerical progression, but that does not help us grasp the infinity of the number series in one intuition (KU§26, 255). This unfulfilled demand gives rise to a feeling of a superior power in our mind; our reason that is able to form ideas of the infinite as a totality:

---

33 Crowther, *Kantian Sublime*, 102.
34 P. Matthews, 'Kant's Sublime: A Form of Pure Aesthetic Reflective Judgement', 173.

> Das Unendliche aber ist schlechthin (nicht bloß komparativ) groß. Mit diesem verglichen ist alles andere (von derselben Art Größen) klein. Aber, was das Vornehmste ist, es als *ein Ganzes* auch nur denken zu können, zeigt ein Vermögen des Gemüts an, welches allen Maßstab der Sinne übertrifft. (KU§26, 254)

The sublime is not the object at all, but the ability to think the infinite, or other related ideas of reason. It is this that is really immeasurable, because objects that we are unable to comprehend in intuition, we are still able to think as a totality. In this way, our inability to comprehend the object as a unity by the power of imagination directs our attention to that which is absolutely great. This transition from imagination to reason also involves a change of principle for the power of reflective judgement. The object cannot be judged objectively under the principle of the purposiveness of nature, because the object overtaxes the capacity of imagination. Still there is a demand for a totality of experience, which means that the object must be judged reflectively. Therefore this object is judged under the principle of the purposive use of nature for a non-natural end. Imagination's inability to comprehend vast objects (or objects appearing to be vast) explains the mathematically sublime aspect change.

Is this feeling of the mind's superiority a judgement with a moral content? Kant's talk about an elevation seems to point in that direction:

> Aber das Gemüt fühlt sich in seiner eigenen Beurteilung gehoben, wenn es, indem es sich in der Betrachtung derselben, ohne Rücksicht auf ihre Form, der Einbildungskraft und einer, obschon ganz ohne bestimmten Zweck damit in Verbindung gesetzten, jene bloß erweiternden Vernunft überläßt, die ganze Macht der Einbildungskraft dennoch ihre Ideen unangemessen findet. (KU§26, 256)

Still I will argue that this elevation is not an aesthetic judgement with a moral content. First, it is not our autonomy as self-legislating that is felt as elevated above nature. It is merely our ability to think the infinite or the unconditioned. Now Kant has, as I will discuss later, given an argument connecting this ability to moral freedom in the first Critique. But he does not state explicitly this connection when he claims our ability to form ideas of the infinite to be the basis for the elevation felt in the aesthetic judgement. In Kant's argument it is merely our capacity to *think* the supersensible basis of nature that makes reason superior to nature, not our capacity to *act* in a certain way. Second, even after this Kantian connection between theoretical and practical reason is established, it only shows that our moral freedom is a presupposition of the feeling of the sublime. The feeling of the sublime does not have a moral content any more than the judgement of taste has a cognitive content. We do not cognise the object by judgement of taste, and we make no moral judgement in the judgement of sublimity.

Another problem is that Kant's exposition of the mathematically sublime describes attempts to comprehend objects that result in reflection on ideas of reason. These are conceptual judgements, not aesthetic. How does his exposition relate to aesthetic reflective judgement? To explain the nature of this judgement, Kant has to start with its objective counterpart. The aesthetic reflective judgement is based on the feeling of the relation between imagination and understanding in this unsuccessful representation of the object. This feeling contains a claim to intersubjective validity, because the subject takes this way of relating to the object to be the way everybody should relate to this same object. So when Kant describes the unsuccessful comprehension of the object that leads us to the idea of the infinite, he must be describing the objective reflective judgement of which the judgement of sublimity is the subjective aspect.

What kind of natural objects are classified as mathematically sublime? Kant gives examples of mathematical sublimity when he says that these objects merely serve as reminders of the true sublime as found in the human mind:

> Man sieht hieraus auch, daß die wahre Erhabenheit nur im Gemüte des Urteilenden, nicht in dem Naturobjekte, dessen Beurteilung diese Stimmung dessélben veranlaßt, müsse gesucht werden. Wer wollte auch ungestalte Gebirgsmassen in wilder Unordnung über einander getürmt, mit ihren Eispyramiden, oder die düstre tobende See u.s.w. erhaben nennen? (KU§26, 256)

The sea, mountain masses, and, as he mentions other places, deep gorges and wastelands (KU§29, 269), are examples of objects that cannot be grasped in one intuition, and the same is the case with the infinite universe when considering how it transcends any standard of measure (KU§26, 256). It is important to notice that Kant emphasises that there is no concept involved in our intuition of the universe. It must be regarded as an all-encompassing vault (KU§29, 270). Budd doubts that we can experience the night sky as unlimited without resorting to our knowledge of the size and distance of the stars[35]. But Kant's point is maybe better illustrated in the Observations where he talks of

> die ruhige Stille eines Sommerabendes, wenn das zitternde Licht der Sterne durch die braune Schatten der Nacht hindurch bricht und der einsame Mond im Gesichtskreise steht … . (B 209)

[35] Budd, 'Delight', 248.

Here the depth of the universe is perceived as it gradually emerges. In the gradual darkening of the sky and emergence of the stars we perceive the sky as we see an abyss; without limits. No concept of infinity needs to be invoked. On the contrary, the perception of this starry sky *results* in the idea of infinity.

Mathematically sublime objects with form

Kant also illustrates the mathematically sublime by man-made objects that, viewed from particular points, appear unbounded, such as the pyramids and St. Peter's Basilica in Rome (KU§26, 252). It follows that it must be possible for such objects to be judged both by taste and by a judgement of sublimity, but that requires that we are able to regard the object from two different points of view. The object can be regarded aesthetically from different perspectives: either as beautiful, i.e. as having form, or as sublime, as formless. How is that possible?

Kant refers to the observations of a Savary who says that the proper distance is required "in order to get the full emotional effect" of the pyramids in Egypt (KU §26, 252); not too close or too distant. When a pyramid is observed from a short distance, the main objects of perception are the stones regarded as single units. The pyramid is really a number of stones piled on top of each other, and we experience them in that way, one by one. As Kant has already told us, when we add one object to another, the apprehension can go on infinitely without any problem. When standing very close to the pyramid, the focus of perception is the single stone. As new stones are perceived, the earlier ones disappear from perception, and we grasp each single stone as a unity. When the pyramid is observed from a distance, it is not seen as consisting of stones, but as one unit with a 'closed' form. It is neither overwhelming nor perceived as unbounded. In both these cases, the pyramid is judged as an object of taste, because it provides forms for the free play between imagination and understanding. When we stand at an intermediate distance, close enough to see the stones but still distant enough to feel the overwhelming quantity of stones that make up the pyramid, we experience the illusion that it is without limits. Kant states that at this distance we can feel the sheer size of the pyramid defying our cognitive ability and the pyramid is judged sublime.

Not everybody finds Kant's analysis convincing as an explanation of Savary's claim:

> Kant shows, rather, that if we view [the pyramids] from close proximity our capacity for comprehension is soon overwhelmed. It is this which leads us to the full emotional effect.[36]

Intuitively Crowther's objection appears reasonable and in keeping with Kant's general account of the mathematical-sublime where comprehending the infinite as a totality fails. But what seems to be Kant's (poorly stated) point is that when we are too close, we do not even have a challenge for comprehending the pyramid as a whole, because its single elements dominate the field of vision. In a similar way, walking in a forest normally does not challenge our cognitive faculties although the apprehension of trees can appear to go on endlessly, simply because the trees are too close to be conceived of as something infinite in number. We see just a few at a time, whereas the stars can be apprehended one by one forever, but they still challenge our comprehension because we can see them together in the sky (although not as an infinite whole). In the same way, when we are too close to the pyramid' what we primarily see is each single stone.

This tells us that an object can be experienced as sublime even though it has a form, as long as there is a point of view from which we experience it as formless. Kant's second architectural example shows the same: On entering St. Peter's in Rome for the first time, the visitor encounters his limited ability to comprehend the totality of the church, and experiences the pleasure of the sublime[37]. These buildings can of course also be judged by taste (that would be the normal case), but not from the same perspective nor at the same time.

The dynamically sublime

The dynamical mode is not based on a perceptual incapacity. It is connected to the faculty of desire, to the legislation under freedom presupposed for action (MS 385). Thus the sublimity is not connected to immeasurable size, but to might (KU§28, 260). When we, from a safe distance, experience objects of nature expressing a force that it would be futile trying to resist, we regard them as fearful even though we are not actually afraid of these objects.

> Aber ihr Anblick wird nur um desto anziehender, je furchtbarer er ist, wenn wir uns nur in Sicherheit befinden; und wir nennen diese Gegenstände gern

[36] Crowther, *Kantian Sublime*, 103.

[37] Note that in none of these cases the fact that what is experienced is man-made, nor the function these constructions serve does in any way influence on the experience. It is the perceptual effect that is of importance, not any idea of purpose for the architecture.

> erhaben, weil sie die Seelenstärke über ihr gewöhnliches Mittelmaß erhöhen und ein Vermögen zu widerstehen von ganz anderer Art in uns entdecken lassen, welches uns Mut macht, uns mit der scheinbaren Allgewalt der Natur messen zu können. (KU§28, 261)

This resistance is due to the same cognitive power that is involved in the mathematical sublime, reason. Reason is independent of nature, and therefore not subject to its dominance. Kant clearly states that it is not *any* kind of ideas, but moral ideas and moral feeling that are the ground of this independence required for our experience of an object as dynamically sublime (KU §29, 265 f). And there is no reason to question the moral aspect of this dynamical mode of the sublime, because it deals with an experience connected to possible action, which belongs to the moral domain.

The problem appears to be the opposite; is it an aesthetic judgement at all? Is it not a moral judgement in disguise, as is suggested by among others Schaper, Crowther, and Budd[38]? My answer is, as I will elaborate it later, that the *objective* reflective judgement on the object we call dynamically sublime, is a reflection on moral ideas. But the judgement of sublimity is a judgement of the mental state of the subject in the representation of the object that leads to this reflection on moral ideas, and this is a judgement based on feeling. The judgement of taste is not an objective determination of the object, nor is the judgement on a sublime object a judgement concerning moral ideas.

Kant's examples of dynamically sublime objects are described in a poetical way:

> Kühne überhangende gleichsam drohende Felsen, am Himmel sich auftürmende Donnerwolken, mit Blitzen und Krachen einherziehend, Vulkane in ihrer ganzen zerstörenden Gewalt, Orkane mit ihrer zurückgelassenen Verwüstung, der grenzenlose Ozean im Empörung gesetzt, ein hoher Wasserfall eines mächtigen Flusses u. dgl. machen unser Vermögen zu widerstehen, in Vergleichung mit ihrer Macht, zur unbedeutenden Kleinigkeit. (KU§28, 261)

It is interesting to note that the sea is mentioned as an example of both modes of the sublime, presumably because it appears both as limitless in extension and as exceedingly powerful when agitated in stormy weather[39]. Anyway it is not difficult

---

[38] E. Schaper, 'Taste, sublimity, and genius: The aesthetics of nature and art', 384, Crowther, *Kantian Sublime*, 165 f., and Budd, 'Delight', 246.

[39] We find this combination of the mathematical and the dynamical sublime also in other examples mentioned by Kant: "*himmelansteigender Gebirgsmassen, tiefer Schlünde und darin tobender Gewässer, tiefbeschatteter, zum schwermütigen Nachdenken einladender Einöden u.s.w.* (KU§29, 269)

to recognise the sublime attraction of the phenomena mentioned here. Other dynamically sublime 'objects' include earthquakes (KU§28, 263), but also God whom we fear without being afraid of him[40] (KU§28, 260 f). I will discuss Kant's example of man or his disposition as dynamically sublime below. Generally, it appears as if the emotional effect of the dynamically sublime is stronger than the similar effect of the mathematically sublime.

The source of the experience of the dynamically sublime lies in the fact that we are independent of the might of the empirical world, not because we actually can offer physical resistance to it, but because we are moral beings and as such independent of the force of the physical world. As empirical beings we are unable to conquer physical might, but as moral beings we are free to act according to laws we give ourselves, regardless of the consequences to our bodies. Our autonomy is the reason for our independence from the laws of nature, and the power of thinking independently of nature is the basis for the feeling in the representation of the sublime. This mode of the sublime represents an aspect change not only from the empirical to the intelligible, but from the theoretical to the practical as well.

3.3 The mathematically sublime and moral ideas

The supersensible vocation of man

Kant holds that the mathematically sublime is a feeling of our supersensible vocation [*Bestimmung*] (KU§27, 257 f), but it is not clear from the exposition why this is so when only theoretical reason is involved in this mode of the sublime, which means that the object leads to reflection on theoretical ideas, not moral ideas. It is even less clear why this feeling, even if it involves moral ideas, can be a feeling of our vocation. Our supersensible vocation must be to act according to the moral law and contribute to the creation of a kingdom of ends (G 434 ff), and the contemplative feeling of the mathematically sublime seems to be far removed from this. Still, Kant makes it clear that the ability to think the infinite is of practical significance:

> Selbst ein Vermögen, sich das Unendliche der übersinnlichen Anschauung, als (in seinem intelligibelen Substrat) gegeben, denken zu können, übertrifft allen Maßstab der Sinnlichkeit, und ist über alle Vergleichung selbst mit dem

[40] We can say that Kant follows his established pattern of paradoxical formulations of aesthetic phenomena, by indirectly calling the feelings of the dynamically sublime 'fearfulness without fear'.

> Vermögen der mathematischen Schätzung groß; freilich wohl nicht in theoretischer Absicht zum Behuf des Erkenntnisvermögens, aber doch als Erweiterung des Gemüts, welches die Schranken der Sinnlichkeit in anderer (der praktischen) Absicht zu überschreiten sich vermögend fühlt. (KU§26, 255)

The mathematical-sublime serves the same practical function as the dynamical mode of the sublime, since the feeling evoked by it indicates a supersensible side of our being, ensuring that we are not restricted by the constraints of the sensible world. But why is this so? My assumption is that the mathematical mode also involves moral ideas. Thus Kant's answer may be found in the first Critique, where he establishes a connection between theoretical and practical reason.

Theoretical and practical ideas of reason

On the face of it, one should believe that the theoretical ideas of totality or the unconditioned are sufficient for the feeling of the sublime to arise in the encounter with an object appearing to be unbounded. There is a connection between theoretical and moral ideas, in that both are rational ideas, but this is not enough to establish that moral ideas are required for the judgement on the mathematically sublime. In the *Critique of Judgement*, Kant speaks of rational ideas as being transcendent concepts because no intuition corresponding to them can be given (KU§57, 342). They differ from aesthetic ideas that are not concepts, and from concepts of understanding that correspond to possible experience. This similarity is not sufficient to bridge the gap between the two different areas of legislation that separates moral from theoretical ideas.

In the discussion of transcendental ideas in the first Critique, Kant initially focuses solely on the function of ideas in cognition:

> Also ist der transzendentale Vernunftbegriff kein anderer, als der von der *Totalität der Bedingungen* zu einem gegebenen Bedingten. Da nun das *Unbedingte* allein die Totalität der Bedingungen, und umgekehrt die Totalität der Bedingungen jederzeit selbst unbedingt ist; so kann ein reiner Vernunftbegriff überhaupt durch den Begriff des Unbedingten, sofern er einen Grund der Synthesis des Bedingten enthält, erklärt werden. (KrV A322/B379)

These two concepts that signify the same idea are also related to a third term, which in a particular employment means the same: the absolute. Ideas of this kind have no direct role to play in the cognition of objects, but they still prescribe a direction towards a unity of all conditions for every act of cognition (KrV A324ff/B380ff). This is a unity we have to presuppose for our cognition of nature;

it is not a unity we find in nature as we cognise it. These ideas of the unconditioned, the totality of conditions, and the absolute are ideas Kant thinks are sufficient to explain the positive aspect of the feeling of sublimity, because these ideas transcend the limits of the nature of appearances, thereby showing that the faculty of reason is not restricted by these limitations. In his discussion of transcendental ideas, Kant hints at a connection between these theoretical ideas and the practical employment of reason by discussing the possible rejection of the value of ideas in the sense that they have no reality since they cannot be given an image, only thought. Thus they become *mere* ideas.

Kant has several interconnected rebuttals to this rejection of the utility of ideas. The first one points to the effect of the practical idea, in which reason even has its own causality, bringing forth the content of its concept in reality. In this context the practical idea is "*die Idee von der notwendigen Einheit aller möglichen Zwecke*" (KrV A328/B385). Furthermore, these ideas are also necessary for understanding, although they do not partake in cognition directly, because they direct cognition, and, thus, improve it. This is of course a practical aspect of reason, as well, for even though there is no practical effect of reason in this employment, it still has an effect on cognition as a human practice (KrV A329/B385). Reason guides understanding in the exercise of cognition, which may justify calling cognition part of human action. On the other hand, this is far from calling cognition part of human action to succumbing these acts to *moral* evaluation. Even though the theoretical employment of reason in cognition must presuppose freedom in the sense of spontaneity[41], this is a kind of action that has no direct effect on the world. It influences the workings of understanding, but it initiates no new causal chain in the world of appearances, which is the main effect of exercising the will[42]. Thus, it is more reasonable to see an analogy between the spontaneity of reason in its theoretical and practical employments, rather than postulating a direct link explaining why moral ideas are required for the feeling of the sublime.

41 "In other words, reason, in its theoretical function, is spontaneous in the sense that it exhibits an inherent purposiveness. It is self-directed, self-determining." H. Allison, *Kant's Transcendental Idealism*, 275.

42 Maybe one could claim that acts of cognition lead to causal chains in the human consciousness, but they are still not practical in the sense of being subject to moral judgement. Knowledge can be the reason for action; still a separate act of spontaniety not caused by the act of cognition is required, which means a new causal chain is initiated.

The idea of spontaneity

Kant however hints at a possible connection between the theoretical and practical by way of moral ideas that could explain the problem posed by the sublime:

> Zu geschweigen, daß [die Ideen] vielleicht von den Naturbegriffen zu den praktischen einen Übergang möglich machen, und den moralischen Ideen selbst auf solche Art Haltung und Zusammenhang mit den spekulativen Erkenntnissen der Vernunft verschaffen können. (KrV A329/B386)

This discussion of the possible connection between moral ideas and theoretical reason, Kant says, will follow later (presumably within the same Critique), but the exact location of the discussion Kant is referring to, is difficult to pin down. The most obvious place to look is in the arguments for freedom in the discussion of the third antinomy, which deals with the problem of causation. The principle of causality leads to a regress of causes and the question of a first cause, i.e. a beginning of the causal chain (KrV A532/B560). But the regress is an indefinite one, thus precluding any attempt at disclosing an absolute totality of causes; and reason creates the idea of spontaneity understood as a beginning of a causal chain in the world. Kant goes on to emphasise this as the crucial point for the practical concept of freedom, which, as Allison points out, appears to give the basis for an outline of a theory of action[43]. This theory of action provides the necessary background for his moral theory in that human agency means freedom from causal necessitation. Kant argues that if the appearances are understood as things in themselves, the unchangeable laws of nature preclude freedom (KrV A536f/B564f). If the appearances are regarded as mere appearances, the possibility is opened for an event to have an intelligible cause as well as to be empirically caused according to the laws required by understanding (KrV A544/B572). As we see, the demand to imagine the totality of causality leads to a transcendental idea of freedom, which is a moral idea because it is an essential component in the moral idea of autonomy.

The idea of autonomy

The third antinomy does not solve the problem I set out with, because the only obvious way the concept of causality can be relevant to the sublime, is as a

---

[43] Allison, *Transcendental Idealism*, 310.

condition of the dynamical sublime, and only in relation to this mode of the sublime does the discussion above warrant us in claiming that moral ideas are necessary preconditions for the experience of the sublime. If we do not know the moral idea of freedom, we are unable to experience the dynamical mode of the sublime. But that much we already knew from the analytic of the sublime. The reason why we experience overwhelming might in nature as pleasurable, is that we are free through our rationality from being constrained by natural force. But why would Kant claim that the mathematical sublime also presupposes moral ideas? For the answer to this, we must turn to the solution of the first antinomy. The first antinomy is the one relevant for the experience of the mathematical sublime, because all Kant's examples of the mathematical sublime deal with greatness, although the infinitely small probably also can give rise to judgement of sublimity, which would relate to the second antinomy. I will avoid that problem in this discussion.

The first antinomy deals with the question of the world being either limited or unlimited in time and in space, given that the world exists independent of our perception of it, but is the way we perceive it to be (KrV A426ff/B455ff). This problem arises as a consequence of the assumption that the world is a thing in itself, independent of the perceiving subject, in which case the world has to be a whole consisting of all the objects existing in this world. The main line of argument in this disputed proof is that the world has to be without any limits, because if such limits are supposed, one also has to suppose an empty time and empty space prior to or beyond those limits. This is impossible because the world cannot stand in a relation to such non-existing objects. Likewise the world has to be limited, because if we regard it as unlimited in time, at any moment an eternity has passed away. But the completion of an eternity is impossible, and therefore it must have a beginning in time. What Kant actually is asserting here, is not clear. A reasonable interpretation of the passage is that an infinite series cannot have a final member, but that appears to be blatantly wrong[44].

The point cannot be that we are unable to think the final member of an infinite series or the possibility of adding to an already infinite series, both of which are possible as long as the argument is dealing with the mathematical notion of infinity. If the problem is conceived of as a cognitive problem, then the status of time must be the focus of interest. Time is no object of cognition, but the medium for the events in the world, and we can regard it as a succession of states of affairs.

---

44 P. Strawson in *The Bounds of Sense*, 176, believes that Kant models his argument on the counting process, which always has a start in time, and therefore assumes what he is claiming to prove.

Each state of affair is something we can cognise, and it is meaningful to speak of the end of a series of events. But in that case we think of the series as consisting of elements that are in principle cognisable. We can think of this series extended without knowing the limit of it, i.e. that the series has undetermined duration. But if we claim the series to be infinite, we claim something more specific: that this series of cognisable state of affairs is without end (or beginning), which is quite different from claiming that we know no end (or beginning) to it. This becomes not a question of definition, as in the mathematical concept of infinity, but a question of possible experience. We are unable to make sense of the notion of infinity as a possible experience. Thus the claim that the world is infinite is meaningless.

This attempt at saving Kant's argument can be countered with the standard objection to Kant's argument that he conflates what is possible with what we are able to understand[45], but that seems to be beside the point. After all, every epistemological argument can only relate to our understanding. If infinity is claimed to be a possible object of experience, we must understand what it means that an infinite series of events is possible, and this is exactly the point at which our capacity for understanding fails[46]. If it is illegitimate to claim the world to be infinite because we cannot make sense of what that would be, the conclusion is not necessarily that we have to adopt the antithesis. That is, unless we believe time to be an object as other objects, in which case it must be either finite or infinite. At least, that is what Kant asserts in calling thesis as well as antithesis "*einen natürlichen und unvermeidlichen Schein*" (KrV A422/B450), and the evidence from the history of speculative metaphysics certainly supports his claim. Even though it is tempting to suggest the suspension of belief on the matter as the natural implication of the thesis argument, Kant is probably right in claiming that also the antithesis has to be faced before a third position can be developed.

The antithesis attempts to show that we have to assume the world to be without beginning, because any beginning would lead to the problem that such a beginning must have been preceded by an empty time. But in an empty time there is not possible for anything to happen so as to give rise to existence (KrV A427/B455)[47].

---

45 Allison, *Transcendental Idealism*, 40 f.

46 This line of defence avoids the introduction of the idea of the world as a whole consisting of separately given parts, which is the basis for Allison's defence, ibid. 42 ff. Kant is not arguing the obvious impossibility of grasping the totality of infinity, but the impossibility of understanding that the series of events is infinite as opposed to indefinite.

47 Kant's argument resembles Parmenides' logical principle that nothing can come of nothing. Non-existence is inconceivable, and we have to assume some kind of existence to have a meaningful idea of creation. This Eleatic influence on Kant is also evident in his interpretation of Zeno's argument on the infinity of God (KrV, A502 f./B530 f.).

Strawson states that if we pose the question differently, we see what is wrong with Kant's argument. He claims the essence of Kant's position is that there is no reason for the world to begin at one particular time rather than another. But if we rephrase the question internally, so that we see the world's history as a sequence of events starting at a certain point, there is no problem in thinking "an earlier *addition* to that entire sequence of events."[48] Allison rejects Strawson's interpretation of the antithesis because 'the first event' is not a rigid designator pointing to some specific moment, but denotes the first event whenever that is[49], which leaves us back at Kant's conclusion; there can be no first beginning. The reason for this is, in Kant's opinion, the assumption of time as independent of our sensibility, which leads us to claim it to be either bounded or unbounded.

Kant's argument in the first antinomy aims to show that we have to apply the critical method to cognition if we want to understand all its aspects. The main element in this approach is to ask what conditions make our experience of the world possible. If we take appearances to be things existing independently of us, we are led to the conclusion that time and space are features of the world in itself. Then the antinomies arise. Thus the problem of the first antinomy is, according to Kant, a pseudo-problem caused by this wrong assumption about the world. The answer to the first antinomy is that we have to take the world as it appears to us not as a thing in itself, i.e. as something existing independently from our way of perceiving it. If time is not a feature of the world as it is in itself, but of our way of structuring the appearances the basis for arguments about the world being limited or not disappear. Kant believes that the antinomy proves indirectly that we do not experience a world as it is in itself, but the sum of appearances organised spatio-temporally (KrV A505ff/B533ff).

The notion of the totality of conditions is merely an idea, and cannot be applied to the world of appearances, because that would wrongly presuppose that this world could be restricted in exactly the way that is precluded by this world being subject to our spatio-temporal organisation. Kant shows that because the world consists of appearances only, the idea of totality has no referent, which means that this application is illegitimate. Our thinking ability is not limited by what is given in experience, because we are free to think beyond our sensible restrictions, although still limited by the rules of rationality itself. Thus the ideas of reason are guiding our understanding of the world analogously to the way understanding guides intuition (KrV A664/B692). This idea of reason is no moral idea, but it is

48 Strawson, *Bounds of Sense*, 179.
49 Allison, *Transcendental Idealism*, 47.

connected to moral ideas in a way different from the one disclosed through the discussion of the third antinomy.

Our capability of forming regulative ideas of reason tells us that our way of thinking is not limited by sensibility and the rules of understanding, and that rationality is following another set of rules. These rules, *qua* rational, must stem from rationality itself, which means that ideas of reason are autonomous ideas. They do not have their source in the sensible world or in any non-rational entity, but are rules of rationality, extended from the categories of understanding (KrV A409/B435). This autonomous status of reason in its theoretical employment is related to the moral idea of autonomy in that rationality is its own rule both in regulating cognition as well as in decisions on how to act[50]. Thus the feeling of the mathematical sublime is a feeling accompanying the idea of totality, which again is an idea made possible only through the autonomy of reason.

But this autonomy is related to the autonomy of action in being a capacity to follow rules prescribed by reason itself. Our cognition is not guided by the appearances received in intuition; ideas of reason guide cognition according to its own rules, just like action is not determined by sensuous impulses as an *arbitrium brutum*, but by the rules of rationality as an *arbitrium liberum* (KrV A534/B562). The core idea of the theoretical employment of reason is the regulative idea of autonomy, which is the key to practical reason as well. Thus the sublime experience of something great beyond comparison is the feeling accompanying the idea of the infinite as a totality, which not only reveals that we are able to think independently of the laws of nature. It also shows that we are following the laws provided by our own rationality. This is the same rational structure that is found in the structure of moral rules of action.

---

50 Williams in *Ethics and the Limits*, 67 ff. argues against such Kantian combinations of theoretical and practical deliberation on the grounds that practical reasoning cannot be autonomous in the impersonal way theoretical reasoning can, because it deals with desires belonging to the subject. Williams holds that this view of practical reason requires a person to eschew commitments in such a way that his desires do not matter at all for practical reason. This is, however, not the most plausible interpretation of Kant's moral theory. More in line with Kant's ethical writings is to say that desires do matter to the agent, but he must, *qua* rational, incorporate them in maxims. This rationality also enables him, as autonomous, to act contrary to these desires despite his involvement in them. Autonomy does not mean total detachment, but the ability to act according to rules that counter one's own short- or long-term desires and involvements. This also amounts to an engagement with one's situation, but an engagement founded on rationally based feelings. Actually, even theoretical autonomy requires involvement that in some sense is emotional. The drive to expand knowledge also must be felt, or else it is difficult to see how the practice of scientific exploration is motivated.

The autonomy revealed by our ability to think the totality of conditions not only shows the possibility of moral freedom (as the idea of spontaneity did), it also shows that we, *qua* rational beings, stand under a set of laws different from those governing nature. Thus it is not merely possible that we are free in the sense of not being necessitated by the laws of nature. We also realise that we are actually free in the sense that we are self-legislative. This is still no proof that we are capable of acting according to these laws, i.e. that they can be constitutive for action. In its theoretical use, reason is regulative, not constitutive as it is in the practical employment. Still, it is a revelation of our autonomy, which is one step further towards the moral ideas involved in the dynamically sublime.

This makes understandable in what sense also the mathematically sublime is based on a relation between imagination and reason that reveals our supersensible vocation. The ideas we determine by reflection on the sublime object are ideas that show reason's superiority over nature due to its purity and independence (KU§27, 258), and this superiority lies in our freedom from the laws of nature and our related capacity for self-legislation. These are ideas that show at least our capability for moral determination, although it does not show that we actually are able to act on moral laws.

When both the mathematically and dynamically sublime involves ideas related to our moral vocation, it may be objected not only that this is not an aesthetic judgement, but that it is a judgement with a clear moral function. This is not the case. The aspect change of the sublime shows that we have a supersensible side that is superior to nature, but one should not forget that the context is one of contemplation, not action. Besides, the object of contemplation is usually nature and the situation is one of non-involvement, which removes it further from morality. Thus, the moral significance Kant claims for the sublime by holding that the judgement of sublimity is purposive in relation to moral feeling (KU§29, 267) is not justified merely by establishing the involvement of moral ideas in the objective aspect of this judgement.

3.4 The sublime, affects and respect

Noble sublime affects

An often neglected, but important section of the comment on the exposition of the sublime, deals with the aesthetically sublime inner nature of man:

> Umgekehrt wird auch das, was wir in der Natur außer uns, oder auch in uns (z.B. gewisse Affekte), erhaben nennen, nur als eine Macht des Gemüts, sich über gewisse Hindernisse der Sinnlichkeit durch menschliche Grundsätze zu schwingen, vorgestellt, und dadurch interessant werden. (KU§29, 271)

When we deal with affects that show an ability of the human mind to conquer certain obstacles of sensibility, we judge these to be sublime. In this way, even the morally good, or elements that contribute to bringing that good about, can be presented as aesthetically sublime. Kant mentions several differing types of affects that can be sublime, while stressing their great difference from the related sentimental affects. These cannot serve any purpose, be it moral or amoral (KU§29, 273). But there are several other feelings that either are sublime, or can be converted into ones that are. One of the most important of these is the feeling of enthusiasm

> weil [der Enthusiasm] eine Anspannung der Kräfte durch Ideen ist, welche dem Gemüte einen Schwung geben, der weit mächtiger und dauerhafter wirkt, als der Antrieb durch Sinnenvorstellungen. (KU§29, 272)

Although enthusiasm is driven by ideas, it is far removed from respect for the moral law, since enthusiasm, like any affect, is blind and detrimental to free deliberation. Among the other feelings that are sublime when springing from the right source we find sadness or grief (KU§29, 276), anger, desperation (*Verzweiflung*), and even freedom from affection (KU§29, 272 f). This freedom from affection is the freedom of the one who acts on rational principles, and thus is also under the influence of the pleasure of pure reason. Kant goes on to say that this mental state is regarded as noble, presumably because it involves our resistance against giving in to our inclinations. We remember that the noble sublime is one of the three classifications of the sublime in the Observations, and that Kant said there that we experience it by the feeling of quiet wonder.

These affects indicate a subordination of the value of feelings to that of rational ideas which is always the basis for the judgement of the sublimity:

> Also muß das Erhabene jederzeit Beziehung auf die *Denkungsart* haben, d.i. auf Maximen, dem Intellektuellen und den Vernunftideen über die Sinnlichkeit Obermacht zu verschaffen. (KU§29, 274)

Kant finds this downgrading of sensibility to be quite similar to the prohibition against images in Judaism and Islam. The only possible representation of the holy is a negative one. The same is the case with the representation of the idea of freedom and the moral law in the judgement of the sublime as well (KU§29, 274). The feeling of sublimity is a *negative* representation, because the 'object' is represented in a form different from its own form, since it is represented by a sensible object, and not through a pure concept.

If we return to the nobly sublime affects, it is not clear where they belong in Kant's classification. Since these affects have nothing to do with physical greatness, but with resistance to the power of nature in the form of inclinations, they should be classified as dynamically sublime. But except for the feeling of anger, it is difficult to see how these affects can be perceived as fearful. We can choose to see these passages in the General Comment on the Exposition of Aesthetic Reflective Judgements as a residue from the pre-Critical work, but then we have to reject maybe the most important aspect of the sublime in the tradition from Pseudo-Longinus: "Sublimity is the echo of a noble mind [*megalophrosunes*]"[51]. Another possibility is to soften Kant's framework, and admit that the noble sublime is an aspect of the dynamically sublime that is not based on fearfulness and imagined resistance to nature, but only involves this imagined resistance. Although I experience this admirable cast of mind in other people, it is in the recognition that I too am able to resist nature within me that the feeling of the sublime arises. This self-reflection is the basic pattern in Kant's description of the sublime, and has to be present in the noble sublime as well. It is not the object that is sublime, but the ability to resist nature we find in ourselves (KU§28, 261).

Among these affects we find 'objects' that have form, yet are sublime. If the form of the object is the activity of the cognitive powers as they harmonise under the principle of the purposiveness of nature[52], then these affects can give rise to an attunement of these powers. As we saw, this attunement is only accessible to us by a feeling, and we cannot prove that the feeling we have really is grounded on the free play of imagination and understanding. But we have an indication that the feeling is based on this state from the successful teleological judgement of the object. When we are able to find a concept of a purpose of nature for this kind of representation, imagination and understanding must be in a state of attunement, because it is only on the basis of such an attunement that the merely reflective teleological judgement is possible. Such a teleological judgement would take the anger of Achilles as purposive for his status within the Greek war party, since a

---

51 Longinus, *Sublime*, 9, 2.

52 With other interpretations of 'form of object', finding sublime objects with form is hardly difficult at all. Most cases of the dynamically sublime is not formless (except in some obscure metaphorical sense) if the form of the object is understood as perceptual delineation or as invariant features of objects.

particular case of self-disregarding enthusiasm is purposive for carrying through a difficult project that in the long run will yield great benefits.

These affects are purposive, and in this respect no reference to ideas of reason is required. Still they are sublime at the same time. This shows, if we accept this Kantian account, that the aspect change from the laws of nature to the laws of reason also occurs here, although the judgement under the principle of purposiveness is sufficient to make sense of the event. These affects can be equally well be made sense of by reference to man's freedom as a rational being, and thus also reason is involved in the relation to imagination. The two possible ways of interpreting these affects are mutually exclusive, but equally valid. Thus an object with form can also be sublime as long as it can be judged both under the principle of the purposiveness of nature and under the principle of the purposive use of nature for our supersensible vocation. And that is the case of the affects of man judged to be nobly sublime.

Fearfully sublime affects

There are sublime affects that are not noble in the sense that they evoke our admiration, but are dynamically sublime based on fearfulness without fear. We have to turn to the Observations to find examples:

> Der Zorn eines Furchtbaren ist erhaben, wie Achilles' Zorn in der Iliade. Überhaupt ist der Held des Homers schrecklich erhaben, des Virgils seiner dagegen edel. Offenbare dreiste Rache nach großer Beleidigung hat etwas Großes an sich, und so unerlaubt sie auch sein mag, so rührt sie in der Erzählung gleichwohl mit Grausen und Wohlgefallen. (B 212)

This is clear evidence for the sublimity of man's enthusiastic feelings not only when they are directed towards what we find morally praiseworthy, but also if we disregard any moral judgement of the feeling. And of course this is a well-known kind of sublimity from myths, fairy-tales, and literature. The stories of Attila the Hun or Genghis Kahn, the fairy-tales of trolls and witches, and Raskolnikov's rationally motivated execution of the old lady in Dostoevsky's *Crime and Punishment*[53] all contain descriptions of such affects. Also in the third Critique Kant admits that human affects like enthusiasm can be sublime regardless of their moral acceptability:

---

[53] F. Dostoevsky, *Crime and Punishment*, 60 ff.

> Nun ist aber jeder Affekt blind, entweder in der Wahl seines Zwecks, oder, wenn dieser auch durch Vernunft gegeben worden, in der Ausführung desselben; denn er ist diejenige Bewegung des Gemüts, welche es unvermögend macht, freie Überlegungen der Grundsätze anzustellen, um sich darnach zu bestimmen. Also kann er auf keinerlei Weise ein Wohlgefallen der Vernunft verdienen. Ästhetisch gleichwohl ist der Enthusiasm erhaben, weil er eine Anspannung der Kräfte durch Ideen ist, welche dem Gemüte einen Schwung geben … . (KU§29, 272)

Thus affects do not have to be morally acceptable to be sublime since they are not tested by reason in the aesthetic judgement. But one correction to the pre-Critical account is found in a footnote where affects are distinguished from passions [*Leidenschaften*] such as hatred or vindictiveness (KU§29, 272, note). The latter are deliberate and have their basis in the power of desire, and represent an abolishment of reason. Presumably these passions call for a moral judgement which overrules the aesthetic judgement.

Kant provides some examples in the third Critique of what can be called fearfully (i.e. not noble) sublime affects, but in these cases he requires that they be tempered by moral constraints. He says that even the savage holds the fearless person who pursues his business regardless of any danger in highest esteem. Also, in a fully civilised society the warrior is accounted the same esteem, although we demand the virtues of peace from him, too. Examples of these virtues are gentleness and sympathy. Likewise, war is judged sublime on the condition that it is carried on in an orderly fashion (KU§28, 262 f). Kant seems to be departing too far from his own pure aesthetics in this section, and subordinates it to morality. It is the overwhelming might expressed by the warrior and experienced when hearing about the horrors of war that should be the focus, without any requirement of moral conduct. Actually Kant's most persistent view on this question seems to be the one presented in the Observation, which we find repeated in the description of the enthusiasm of the spectators for the French Revolution found in the Conflict of Faculties (SF 85)[54]. The Revolution or its effect on the spectators is sublime although it is filled with misery and atrocities.

---

[54] This reference may prompt at least two critical questions: What is the sublime object in Kant's description, the Revolution or the enthusiasm for the Revolution in the spectator? Is not the enthusiasm for the revolution a moral or politically induced feeling, rather than a purely disinterested one? To the first I will suggest that both the Revolution and the enthusiastic support found in non-participating spectators can be regarded as sublime. To the second I will say with Makkreel that the feeling "is at the same time aesthetic, teleological, and moral" (Makkreel, *Imagination and Interpretation*, 150). Thus the interesting job is to disentangle the diverse elements in Kant's account. An attempt at that is found below, p. 299 ff.

In relation to my leading question, concerning the sublime in *Molloy*, an even more interesting sentence is the one leading up to the example of the wrath of Achilles as sublime:

> Selbst die Laster und moralische Gebrechen führen öfters gleichwohl einige Züge des Erhabenen oder Schönen bei sich; wenigstens so wie sie unserem sinnlichen Gefühl erscheinen, ohne durch Vernunft geprüft zu sein. (B 212)

In the aesthetic judgement, as long as we keep any judgement by reason out of it, even vices and moral failings can be sublime or beautiful. On the basis of the discussion above I will claim that this does not contradict Kant's view in the Critical period, and it is important for grasping the Kantian sublime of the life of Molloy as narrated in the first part of *Molloy*. His lack of comprehension includes the rules of ethics, and this absence of morality in his thought and conduct is part of what makes the novel sublime. But how do we navigate between Kant's clearly stated requirement of moral constraints on the aesthetic appreciation of human feelings and dispositions, and his acceptance of some morally reprehensible phenomena as legitimate objects of sublime delight? This problem is discussed in relation to a Kantian interpretation of *Molloy* sketched in chapter six.

Another problem concerning the sublime affects is how they can be said to be a judgement of man as a natural and not as a moral, autonomous being. After all, it is our way of thinking that gives rise to these affects. I believe the answer to be that the blind affects are judged as merely natural phenomena. But when we try to explain them by a purely mechanistic or psychological perspective on man, we experience them as not explicable according to these perspectives, or as equally well understood according to the principle of freedom. This does not mean that they can be explained as caused by man's rational will, either. They are regarded as natural phenomena that are meaningful if we understand them as serving the aims of rational freedom. These affects represent, as all sublime objects, something that either cannot be subsumed under the principle of the purposiveness of nature and has to be judged under the principle of the purposive of nature for our supersensible vocation, or can be subsumed under both of these principles. In the first case, the free activity of imagination cannot relate to the lawfulness of understanding. Only by assuming reason to be a cause that can influence the causality of nature are we able to account for the source of this feeling. Therefore, imagination enters into a relationship with reason, and the result of the reflection is an idea of reason. In the second case, imagination can relate both to the lawfulness of imagination and to reason, and the free play may result in a concept either of understanding or of reason, but not both at the same time. For instance, one may explain Molloy's choice to seek out his mother either psychoanalytically or according to existentialist theory. In the first case his choice is determined by an Oedipal complex, in the second the freedom of man confronted with the meaninglessness of life means that his choice is an undetermined first cause. We can interpret the story according to both explanations, but we cannot hold both to be true at the same time.

The feeling of the sublime and respect

A common charge against Kant's theory of the judgement of sublimity is that it is too much of a moral judgement:

> Kant is so keen to stress the moral aspects of sublimity that he fails to offer anything convincing – apart from scattered hints – as to its credentials as an aesthetic concept. Indeed in the Deduction he takes a short cut whereby the judgement of sublimity's claim to universality is construed as a function of unwarranted assumption of a susceptibility to moral feeling in all humans. In the final analysis, the pressures exerted by his Critical ethics prove too great. Our experience of sublimity in relation to nature is reduced to indirect moral awareness.[55]

Why an indirect moral awareness in our experience of the sublime should be a reduction rather than an elevation of this feeling is not completely clear in Crowther's criticism of Kant, but the main problem is that the sublime loses its status as a disinterested aesthetic judgement. According to Crowther, this is illustrated in Kant's attempts at drawing the feeling in the judgement of the sublime close to the moral feeling of respect[56]. And one may easily get the suspicion that the feeling of the sublime is a variant of the moral feeling respect, since respect also is a feeling of reason's superiority over nature. This suspicion is reinforced by Kant's own words:

> Also ist das Gefühl des Erhabenen in der Natur Achtung für unsere eigene Bestimmung, die wir einem Objekte der Natur durch eine gewisse Subreption (Verwechselung einer Achtung für das Objekt statt für die Idee der Menschheit in unserm Subjekte) beweisen, welches uns die Überlegenheit der Vernunftbestimmung unserer Erkenntnisvermögen über das größte Vermögen der Sinnlichkeit gleichsam anschaulich macht. (KU§27, 257).

[55] Crowther, *Kantian Sublime*, 134 f.
[56] Ibid. 125.

Here the sublime is called respect and the description seems to connect these two feelings together; the main difference being the "subreption"[57] involved in the sublime.

But there are some important differences. Respect serves as an incentive for determination of the will in action (G 400 f), while the feeling of the sublime is merely part of our contemplation of nature (or art). And although the judgement of sublimity indicates our supersensible vocation it still cannot directly contribute to determination of the will in action, just like the judgement of taste in itself contributes nothing to the knowledge of the particular object although it is a subjective condition of cognition. The sublime has no direct motivational force. It is an awareness of our vocation, of our freedom to act according to the moral law we issue unto ourselves. But this awareness requires that we already possess knowledge of this human power.

This indicates further differences between this feeling and respect; respect stems from reason alone and we must assume everybody to possess it independently of culture and education (MS 399) while the feeling of the sublime is dependent on culture and the development of moral ideas (KU§29, 265). The feeling of the sublime has its source in the free play between imagination and reason, whereas respect is practical reason as it affects feeling:

> Und so ist die Achtung fürs Gesetz nicht Triebfeder zur Sittlichkeit, sondern sie ist die Sittlichkeit selbst, subjektiv als Triebfeder betrachtet, indem die reine praktische Vernunft, dadurch daß sie der Selbstliebe im Gegensatz mit ihr alle Ansprüche abschlägt, dem Gesetze, das jetzt allein Einfluß hat, Ansehen verschafft. (KpV 76)

This means that in respect, reason determines feeling, and the relation is not free. Besides, respect is directly related to the moral law, and reason, while the sublime takes a detour by way of a representation of an object. We see that although Kant claims that there is close affinity between respect and the feeling of the sublime, there are significant differences between these feelings.

The sublime object serves as a stand-in for the supersensible, a relationship expressed by the term subreption. What we experience is not nature at all, but our own rationality. The object in nature is really of no concern other than as a means to obtain this awareness of the idea of humanity in our own self. It is important to

[57] Lyotard, *Lessons*, 70 holds that there is always "a sense of abuse, of crime, of sin almost" present in Kant's use of the word subreption. And he seems to be right regarding the employment of the term in other contexts (e.g. KrV A643/B671 and EE VIII, 222). When it comes to the sublime, however, this replacement seems to serve a legitimate function in serving the demands of practical reason.

stress that in the experience of the sublime we only *feel* the relation of the cognitive faculties, without forming any ideas of reason. The judgement of sublimity requires prior knowledge of moral ideas, but it does not involve these concepts directly. As Lyotard states: "If the absolute were represented in sublime judgement by an Idea, the judgement would cease to be aesthetic and would become speculative."[58] Unlike the judgement of taste, where the judgement says something about the object (although it does so indirectly by judging the mental state of the subject), the object of nature is used in the judgement of the sublime only to be discarded with:

> Daraus sehen wir, daß der Begriff des Erhabenen ... überhaupt nichts Zweckmäßiges in der Natur selbst, sondern nur in dem möglichen *Gebrauche* ihrer Anschauungen, um eine von der Natur ganz unabhängige Zweckmäßigkeit in uns selbst fühlbar zu machen, anzeige. (KU§23, 246)

Actually, the sublime is an (illegitimate) projection into nature of what is the idea of humanity in ourselves, i.e. our moral freedom.

Now the problem concerning the subreption in the judgement of the sublime is not only that it is called *Achtung*, but also that it is presented with a reference to ideas. Thus the passage lends credence to Crowther's claim that the judgement of sublimity is not convincingly described as an aesthetic judgement, and appears to be a moral one. The judgement must apparently *involve* moral concepts, not only presuppose them, and then it is not aesthetic in the sense of being based on a feeling only. This has led Guyer to suggest a three-step structure for the feeling of the sublime starting with a displeasure followed by a concept followed by a pleasure:

> In explaining how fear of the power of nature is overcome by the revelation of practical reason, ... the context suggests that what ultimately moves us from fear to "soul-stirring delight" is not the mere feeling that practical reason exists but a fairly explicit judgement that its dominion exceeds that of mere nature and nature's deterministic power of disposing over our "worldly goods, health, and life."[59]

Guyer later adds that the fact that the feeling of the dynamically sublime can be subsumed under the "model of the harmony of the faculties ... may well reveal the ambivalence of that conception between a strictly psychological and necessarily more propositional state of mind."[60] Whichever way we understand this, it

---

[58] Lyotard, *Lessons*, 72.
[59] Guyer, *Experience of Freedom*, 213 f. Compare Budd, 'Delight', 240 and 249 f.
[60] Guyer, *Experience of Freedom*, 215.

amounts to a claim that a determinate concept in some sense underlies the judgement. And there is no doubt that Kant expresses himself in a way that warrants the interpretation of Guyer and others.

Still, there is something strange about the whole notion of subreption if the feeling of the sublime involves the thought of man's superior reason in some way or another. How can we mistakenly attribute the respect to the object if the ground for our pleasure is the thought of our independence from nature as moral beings? Only if no determinate concept of our rational superiority is involved, can we make the mistake of directing our respect towards the object rather than towards the idea of the humanity in ourselves. Kant leaves us in no doubt that the basis for the judgement is found in feeling only:

> Das Urteil selber bleibt aber hierbei immer nur ästhetisch, weil es, ohne einen bestimmten Begriff vom Objekte zum Grunde zu haben, bloß das subjektive Spiel der Gemütskräfte (Einbildungskraft und Vernunft) selbst durch ihren Kontrast als harmonisch vorstellt. (KU§27, 258)

Thus we should not take Kant to mean that determinate concepts of fear, resistance, or the superiority of reason underlies the judgement. If we take his claim seriously that also the judgement of sublimity is an aesthetic reflective judgement, we can instead try to explain why he talked *as if* a conceptual judgement of reason's superiority over nature is involved in the judgement of the sublime. Kant clearly wants to say that we feel some kind of fearfulness without fear, or a similarly ambiguous feeling, for which we demand universal assent. To make sense of this claim about the existence of such an ambiguous feeling, he has to exemplify the kind of feeling he is talking about. This can be done in three ways, and Kant uses all of them: 1) He can refer to the feeling by name (amazement, admiration, enthusiasm, melancholy and so forth). 2) He can provide a simplified and perhaps slightly misleading analysis (the feeling is an inhibition and subsequent outpouring of vital forces, it is a mental agitation, or it consists in a rapid alteration between attraction and repulsion). 3) He can describe it as if it were based on determinate concepts, and take the concepts as point of departure for the description.

Talking as if the subject pictures herself resisting the might of nature is a way to make vivid the kind of feeling Kant is talking about. Although the description involves imagined resistance and the pleasure involved in thinking that reason is superior to the power of nature, the feelings they illustrate involve no such concepts. This can account for Kant's reference to determinate concepts as the basis for judgement of the sublime despite the fact that he introduces the analytic by claiming that the judgement is aesthetic with no determinate concept involved (KU§23, 244). The claim is repeated several times throughout the analytic (KU§24, 247, §26, 256, §27, 258, and §29, 267). It is possible, but not likely, that Kant should contradict himself throughout the whole exposition of the sublime.

The examples themselves also indicate that the references to concepts perhaps should not be taken literally: we can imagine ourselves putting up resistance to God, but who would imagine herself resisting an erupting volcano or a hurricane? Still, most do recognise the delightful horror at watching these terrifying wonders of nature (from a safe distance). So my explanation is that Kant invokes the thinking of resistance and the reference to determinate ideas as an illustration of what kind of feeling he is talking about rather than as an account of the conceptual basis of this feeling.

The interpreters who accuse Kant of turning the aesthetic judgement of the sublime into a moral judgement base their argument on passages that can be interpreted differently. Still, the reference to respect is important for understanding the moral significance of this aesthetic reflective judgement, as I argue in chapter four. The awareness of a relation between sensibility and reason in the experience of sublime objects of nature is a feeling with a phenomenological similarity with the moral feeling respect. But this similarity does not depend on the presence of any determinate concept in the aesthetic judgement of sublimity.

The fundamental difference between the moral feeling of respect and the feeling of the sublime is also made clear in the second Critique:

> Achtung geht jederzeit nur auf Personen, niemals auf Sachen. Die letzeren können *Neigung*, und wenn es Tiere sind (z.B. Pferde, Hunde etc.) so gar *Liebe*, oder auch *Furcht*, wie das Meer, ein Vulkan, ein Raubtier, niemals aber *Achtung* in uns erwecken. Etwas, was diesem Gefühl schon näher tritt, ist *Bewunderung*, und diese als Affekt, das Erstaunen, kann auch auf Sachen gehen, z.B. himmelhohe Berge, die Größe, Menge und Weite der Weltkörper, die Stärke und Geschwindigkeit mancher Tiere, u.s.w. Aber alles dieses ist nicht Achtung. (KpV 76 f)

We recognise the description of objects that the third Critique singles out as inducing feelings of the sublime, both in the mathematical as well as the dynamical mode, and that these are rejected as unworthy of respect. It is only persons, due to their possession of freedom that are worthy of respect. It is clear that feelings of sublimity are not feelings of respect and cannot be transposed to respect because these feelings have different sources, different appearances, and function in different realms with different purposes.

3.5 Universal validity of judgements of the sublime

The distinction between judgements of taste and sublimity

The sublime has a minor role to play in Kant's theory of judgement. In a way Guyer was quite correct in his by now famous denouncement of the interest of Kant's analysis of the sublime when compared with the analysis of the judgement of taste[61]. One could even suspect that Kant agrees with that verdict when we see how little weight he puts on the sublime in the introductions (EE XII, 249 ff and KU VII, 192) as well as how he downplays its significance in the section concerning the transition from the beautiful to the sublime:

> Daraus sehen wir, daß der Begriff des Erhabenen der Natur bei weitem nicht so wichtig und an Folgerungen reichhaltig sei, als der des Schönen in derselben, und daß er überhaupt nichts Zweckmäßiges in der Natur selbst, sondern nur in dem möglichen *Gebrauche* ihrer Anschauungen, um eine von der Natur ganz unabhängige Zweckmäßigkeit in uns selbst fühlbar zu machen, anzeige. (KU§23, 246)

Further down the same page he calls the theory of the sublime "*einen bloßen Anhang*" to our aesthetic judging of nature, and mere appendices are seldom of great interest. Counting against this apparent insignificance is the wide range of examples Kant employs in the exposition of the sublime, the central position it is given in the Critique, as well as its alleged moral significance (KU§29, 267).

A plausible explanation of this asserted insignificance of the judgement of the sublime is the context of the third Critique as a whole. The power of judgement, which has its own subjective a priori principle, primarily deals with our cognition of nature (KU III, 179), and it is in this respect the judgement of sublimity is insignificant. The judgement of the sublime is not connected to a judgement of the object, although it does arise by the intuition of some object, and we mistakenly call the object sublime. Thus it cannot contribute in any great degree to understanding *nature*. Thus the sublime of nature is not as important and rich in consequences as the beautiful, and becomes a mere appendix in the primary function of merely reflective judgement that is the cognition of nature under the principle of purposiveness.

Seen in a different context, that of man as a moral being with an obligation to develop his moral character, the sublime takes on a greater significance, as I will

---

[61] Guyer, *Claims of Taste* [First edition, 1979], 399 f., note 2. Compare also with Guyer's reevaluation of this view in his *Experience of Freedom*, 187 ff.

discuss in the next chapter. What is more puzzling is how we are to understand this judgement as being only seemingly about objects of nature, but really about the judging subject. In this context the previously mentioned concept of subreption is central. Although subreption usually is an illegitimate substitution of one object for another, in the judgement of sublimity this substitution is to a certain extent justified, even though it leads us to mistakenly believe the object of experience to be sublime. Some have found this unacceptable:

> Phenomenologically what we admire in the ocean, mountains and wild animals is *their* dignity, majesty, presence, and exuberance, and what we take ourselves to be admiring in great as distinct from good art, is the powerful character *of the work*, and only secondarily and, derivatively, the capacities of the artist. I find it puzzling to be committed to the view that we are deceived in this.[62]

This can be seen as a Burkean objection to Kant's exposition of the sublime as morally founded, an objection gaining support from empirical descriptions of the experience of the sublime. Just as we find this particular landscape to be beautiful (i.e. when we look at it we feel disinterested pleasure), so we find this starry night sublime (when we look at it we feel amazement)[63]. The problem is Kant's claim that in judgements of sublimity the feeling can no longer have its source in the object at all but in the subject's rationality. Maybe Kant is overstating this point, because he says that the disinterested feeling, which is the basis of the judgement of sublimity, expresses a relation between imagination and reason in a representation of an object. It is here we find the key to the difference between the beautiful and the sublime, for a relation between imagination and reason is not a representational relation[64] at all:

---

62 M. McCloskey, 'Review of P. Crowther, *The Kantian Sublime*', 382. McCloskey is here arguing against Crowther rather than Kant, which explains the reference to the capacities of the artist. Kant does not hold that we admire the artist's capacities in sublime art any more than we admire a creator in sublime nature, but that is the theory put forward in Crowther's very liberal reconstruction of Kant's theory; see Crowther, *Kantian Sublime*, 158 ff. What we do admire, according to Kant, is man's superiority over nature due to his rational, moral capacities. But that does not answer McCloskey's puzzlement, either.

63 Here I assume McCloskey's objection to deal with the subreption involved in the sublime, and not with Kant's idea of aesthetic judgement as such referring only to a state of mind and not to any particular features of the object. Many would find that problematic in a way similar to that in which McCloskey finds the reference of the sublime to our own rational capacities to be.

64 This does not mean that there is no representation. The object is represented by the imagination, but the relation between the imagination and the reason is not representational like the one between the imagination and the understanding in cognition.

> Man sieht aber hieraus sofort, daß wir uns überhaupt unrichtig ausdrücken, wenn wir irgend einen Gegenstand der Natur erhaben nennen, ob wir zwar ganz richtig sehr viele derselben schön nennen können; denn wie kann das mit einem Ausdrucke des Beifalls bezeichnet werden, was an sich als zweckwidrig aufgefaßt wird? (KU§23, 245)

The so-called sublime object of nature is counterpurposive because it cannot be structured under the principle of the purposiveness of nature. I have argued that some objects called sublime can be structured under this principle, but that these may still lead the imagination into a relation with reason and, judged under this aspect, these objects too must be considered counterpurposive for judgement.

In these cases of counterpurposiveness, the representation is related to another principle, that of the purposive use of nature for our moral vocation. So when we find this kind of object displaying subjective purposiveness, the feeling concerns the object regarded as a vehicle for reflection on the real sublime, the superiority of reason:

> Erhaben ist, was auch nur denken zu können ein Vermögen des Gemüts beweiset, das jeden Maßstab der Sinne übertrifft. (KU§25, 250)

'Sublime' is an ethical concept, and when we use it about objects of nature we must use the word either metaphorically, or we cannot be referring to the object at all. It is wrong to say that we admire the dignity and majesty of objects of nature, as McCloskey does in the quotation above. Dignity is an ethical concept, and can only be used in a literal sense in relation to rational beings, although we can use it to describe the appearance of an object of nature or to communicate what kind of feeling the object evokes in us. And it is in this last sense Kant is using 'sublime' and related concepts.

Calling an object sublime is illegitimate in the sense that a physical object cannot be sublime, i.e. incomparably great or mighty. There is something about the object making me aware of something about myself that evokes a disinterested, universally communicable feeling in me. In this way it differs from the beautiful, which evokes a disinterested, universally communicable pleasure in me due to something about the object. But calling the object sublime is legitimate in the sense that the object will always be experienced with feelings of the sublime and lead to reflection on sublime ideas of reason. In this sense the mountain range is sublime just as the rose is beautiful. The object elicits feelings of the sublime in us.

The principle of the purposive use of nature

Kant explicitly states that the sublime appears counterpurposive in its form for the power of judgement (KU§23, 245). He also stresses the complete separation between the sublime and the idea of the purposiveness of nature (KU§23, 246), which implies that the judgement of the sublime cannot be based on a mental state that is the subjective aspect of a teleological judgement of nature. Such a state, according to my interpretation, plays a role in judgements of taste. But if the judgement of sublimity is still to be regarded as an aesthetic reflective judgement and belong in a critique of judgement, it must be disinterested, display form of purposiveness, and involve a claim to subjective universal validity and necessity. That it does share these characteristics of the judgement of taste is clearly stated by Kant (KU§23, 244). The justification of the claim to subjective universal validity for the feeling in a judgement of sublimity is presumably based on the feeling's relation to an objective reflective judgement according to purposes just as in judgements of taste. I have to show how the judgement of the sublime can display subjective purposiveness, or form of purposiveness, without being the subjective aspect of a teleological judgement under the principle of the purposiveness of nature. The assumption is that the objective aspect of this judgement must be under a different principle of purposiveness, and the judgement must ascribe a concept of a purpose to the object.

According to my interpretation, every merely reflective judgement involves a mental state claiming its own universal communicability. This is the case also with the judgement of sublimity, although this judgement does not accompany cognition of an object but the breakdown of cognition. The reason for this breakdown must be sought in the striving for the unconditioned, the drive towards the absolute or totality of something given. This is not a psychological assumption, but a necessary presupposition to explain man's way of acquiring knowledge. If we did not have this disposition, we would have no feeling of the sublime but would be content with the cognition of bounded objects, not striving to grasp the infinite as a whole. We would cognise the same objects as we do now, but we could not experience them as sublime. The universe or an abyss would not be experienced as awesome, but would merely be cognised as limited or as a successfully evaded threat to our personal safety (KU§29, 265).

I claimed that the subjective universal validity for the feeling underlying judgements of taste was justified by the fact that, when we make an objective reflective judgement of nature under the heuristic principle of the purposiveness of nature, this judgement must be based on a relation between the cognitive powers which we presuppose is shared by everybody. If we do not presuppose that, the judgement will have merely private validity since it is based on a representation that we take to be valid for this subject only. We have access to this relation only by feeling, which means that claiming that everybody should share the same relation of cognitive powers implies that everybody should share the feeling of this relation. Now the feeling of the sublime serves no such function since it is regarded as something that cannot be judged under this principle, so why claim universal validity for this feeling?

The reason for resorting to the principle of purposiveness in the first place, was to find empirical laws left undetermined by universal laws when we cognise an object. The aspect of an object that gives rise to the judgement of sublimity, must be aspects that are left undetermined even by reflective judgement under the principle of purposiveness[65], so the demand for a totality in cognition requires that the object is judged under a different principle. I suggest that this is a principle of the purposive use of nature for our moral vocation:

> Hierauf dient zur Antwort, daß das Erhabene der Natur nur uneigentlich so genannt werde, und eigentlich bloß der Denkungsart oder vielmehr der Grundlage zu derselben in der menschlichen Natur beigelegt werden müsse. Dieser sich bewußt zu werden, gibt die Auffassung eines sonst formlosen und unzweckmäßigen Gegenstandes bloß die Veranlassung, welcher auf solche Weise subjektiv-zweckmäßig gebraucht, aber nicht als ein solcher für sich und seiner Form wegen beurteilt wird … . (KU§30, 280, compare §23, 246)

We find a similar passage in the First Introduction where it is even clearer that the purposive use of nature for our supersensible vocation does serve the same function for the judgement of sublimity as the principle of the purposiveness of nature does for the judgement of taste. Kant says that, besides the aesthetic judgement based on the purposiveness of nature, there is another aesthetic judgement

> welches sich auch auf ein (zwar nur subjektives) Prinzip a priori bezieht, aber nicht, so wie das erstere, eine Zweckmäßigkeit der Natur in Ansehung des Subjekts, sondern nur einen möglichen zweckmäßigen Gebrauch gewisser sinnlicher Anschauungen ihrer Form nach vermittelst der bloß reflektierenden Urteilskraft. (EE XII, 249)

---

[65] There are cases that are fully determined by the universal laws of understanding in combination with laws under the principle of purposiveness, but still warrant the judgement of the sublime. But since formless (chaotic) objects are judged to be most sublime (KU§23, 246) they provide the clearest focus for the discussion.

The sublime needs its own principle of the purposive use of nature for our supersensible vocation, just as the judgement of taste presupposes the principle of the purposiveness of nature. Under these two differing principles, both judgements display the form of purposiveness, thus claiming universal validity for their respective judgements. Now Kant does not explicitly state that the judgement of sublimity is guided by a principle of the purposive use of nature, but it is difficult to avoid that interpretation of the passage above. Besides, any reflection requires a principle (EE V, 211), and there are no other possible candidates, so I assume that the principle for the aesthetic reflective judgement on sublime objects is that of their purposive use.

If we pursue the comparison with judgements of taste (according to my interpretation) the objective aspect of this judgement is a concept of the purpose of the object. In the judgement of sublimity, there is no such purpose involved, and the concepts are ideas of a higher purposiveness: "*indem das Gemüt die Sinnlichkeit zu verlassen und sich mit Ideen, die höhere Zweckmäßigkeit enthalten, zu beschäftigen angereizt wird.*" (KU§23, 245 f) This may indicate that the subjective purposiveness of the sublime is connected to these concepts of a higher purposiveness, something that is confirmed when Kant argues that the deduction of judgements on the sublime is the exposition of them:

> Daher war unsere Exposition der Urteile über das Erhabene der Natur zugleich ihre Deduktion. Denn, wenn wir die Reflexion der Urteilskraft in denselben zerlegten, so fanden wir in ihnen ein zweckmäßiges Verhältnis der Erkenntnisvermögen, welches dem Vermögen der Zwecke (dem Willen) a priori zum Grunde gelegt werden muß und daher selbst a priori zweckmäßig ist, welches denn sofort die Deduktion, d.i. die Rechtfertigung des Anspruchs eines dergleichen Urteils auf allgemein-notwendige Gültigkeit, enthält. (KU§30, 280)

This passage seems to say that the feeling of the sublime must have its source in a particular relationship between our cognitive capacities, and that this particular relationship is an a priori condition for the possibility of man's will, i.e. for his ability to form purposes independently of causal necessity and to act according to these purposes. To put it differently: the purposive relationship between our cognitive powers in judgements on the sublime is the same relation as the one we presuppose in the exercise of the will.

Morality and concepts of purpose

What are the a priori conditions for the possibility of free agency? Two obvious conditions are being rational and capable of deliberation about how to act, i.e. possessing the ability to follow rules (or laws) independently of immediate desires and wishes. In the *Grundlegung*, Kant expresses this metaphorically as man belonging to an intelligible world of freedom as well as belonging to the sensible world of causal necessity (G 454). This can better be regarded as two different points of view from which we can regard events in the world. If we are to be viewed as human beings, we have to regard ourselves as free in relation to sensuous inclinations. This gives us the picture of man as a creature with the ability to control his desires by rational deliberation, or as Kant puts it:

> Das Wesentliche aller Bestimmungen des Willens durchs sittliche Gesetz ist: Daß er als freier Wille, mithin nicht bloß ohne Mitwirkung sinnlicher Antriebe, sondern selbst mit Abweisung aller derselben, und mit Abbruch aller Neigungen, so fern sie jenem Gesetze zuwider sein könnten, bloß durchs Gesetz bestimmt werde. (KpV 129)

There is a conflict between immediate satisfaction of our sensuous drives and the demands of morality. If we are to suppose man to have a free will, we must assume that his sensuous nature, determined by natural causality, can be overruled by a different causality originating in man's power of reason. If we do not assume this relationship between sensibility and reason, the idea of the subject's freedom of will has to be rejected. Her status as being subject to the natural laws as an empirical subject is not altered by her transcendental freedom, but her freedom as a rational being makes her realise her superiority over this order of not self-imposed necessity.

Now the will is the capacity for ends or purposes[66] Kant claims in §30, and this indicates the central role this capacity plays in Kant's conception of humanity:

> Das Vermögen, sich überhaupt irgend einen Zweck zu setzen, ist das Charakteristische der Menschheit (zum Unterschiede von der Tierheit). Mit dem Zwecke der Menschheit in unser eigenen Person ist also auch der Vernunftwille, mithin die Pflicht verbunden, sich um die Menschheit durch Kultur überhaupt verdient zu machen, sich das Vermögen zu Ausführung allerlei möglicher Zwecke, sofern dieses in dem Menschen selbst anzutreffen ist, zu verschaffen oder es zu fördern … . (MS 392)

---

66 I would prefer to use 'purpose' for *Zweck* throughout this discussion, but as Pogge says, "'purpose' cannot be used to translate *Zweck* across the board, because the expression 'end in itself' is now too deeply entrenched and also because it is often much less fitting than some other word." Pogge, 'Kant on Ends', note 19, 384.

To be human is the same as to have the capacity to set oneself ends or choose one's purposes, which implies that we are not determined by the causal laws that govern man regarded as part of nature. And as Korsgaard points out, it is not only the adoption of morally acceptable purposes that Kant takes to be sublime:

> [I]t is the capacity for the rational determination of ends in general, not just the capacity for adopting morally obligatory ends, that the Formula of Humanity orders us to cherish unconditionally.[67]

To be free is to possess the ability to set oneself ends, and this is what we admire when we reflect on man's superiority over nature. It follows that reflecting on an idea of reason that partakes in this conception of man's freedom in relation to nature is *indirectly* reflecting on a concept of a purpose. It is not a purpose in the sense that we call an object of nature a purpose in a teleological judgement. It is a concept that relates to freedom, and thus to the ability to make something one's purpose or end. So when the experience of something dynamically sublime lead me to reflect on my ability to regard as small my everyday concerns, I reflect on the idea of freedom which is nothing but the ability to choose one's ends or purposes.

Now this relation between ideas of reason and the capacity to choose purposes may seem too indirect to justify calling the ideas of reason concepts of purpose. This is, however, just one aspect of the justification for this association. Not only is freedom the same as the ability to determine purposes for oneself, and thus to confer value on things, as Korsgaard says[68]. This freedom justifies calling man an end in itself:

> Nun sage ich: der Mensch und überhaupt jedes vernünftige Wesen existiert als Zweck an sich selbst, nicht bloß als Mittel zum beliebigen Gebrauche für diesen oder jenen Willen, sondern muß in allen seinen sowohl auf sich selbst als auch auf andere vernünftige Wesen gerichteten Handlungen jederzeit zugleich als Zweck betrachtet werden. (G 428)

This makes the idea of freedom as autonomy (as well as ideas related to this) a concept of a purpose or end, because this idea includes the concept of every rational being as an end in itself. So the idea of reason that is determined on the basis of the universally communicable mental state underlying the judgement of the sublime is a concept of a purpose. The ability to choose purposes, i.e. to set oneself ends, is an unconditional value that makes every rational being an end in itself. This same ability even plays a crucial role in teleological judgements. In the

---

[67] C. Korsgaard, *Creating the Kingdom of Ends*, 111.
[68] Ibid. 122.

teleological system of nature, it is this ability to set himself ends that makes man the ultimate purpose or end of nature, and Kant says that this is his vocation [*Bestimmung*] (KU§83, 431). *Bestimmung* is used repeatedly throughout the exposition of the sublime to designate what is revealed in this judgement, which adds further support to my claim that the objective reflective judgement of the sublime object is an idea of reason that determines one of the different aspects of our status as purpose in itself.

So the reason why Kant can say that the judgement of sublimity displays the subjective purposiveness of the object is that this judgement is the subjective aspect of an objective judgement according to purposes. It follows that this judgement also displays the form of purposiveness in a way parallel to the one we found in the judgement of taste. The aesthetic reflective judgement of sublimity contains a claim to universal validity for the mental state on which the objective reflective judgement according to purposes is based. We must claim that the mental state is such that everybody should share it, because it is on this basis that we determine the concept that we think everybody should share; in this case an idea of reason.

This may appear to be a parallel justification to the one given for judgements of taste, but it differs at one crucial point. The ideas of reason that are related to the purpose of man are not concepts of reflective judgement, because these ideas serve to determine the will. The relationship between reason and sensibility is a relation in which reason determines the will, not one in which the cognitive powers are regarded in their freedom (KpV 29 f). Just as the claim to subjective universal validity would be superfluous in regard to determinative judgement of nature, so it is superfluous in regard to the relation between reason and sensibility when this relationship stands under the principle of the freedom of the will. We do not need reflective judgement to find this concept of freedom, because it is an inescapable fact for any rational being. So the claim to universal validity for our mental state serves no function in this judgement, since the principles of morality are necessary and universal.

This objection can be answered, but it requires that we return to the comparison between the judgements of beauty and of sublimity. Kant says that both can be described as a liking [*Wohlgefallen*], as a connection between the capacities for representation (imagination) and for concepts (understanding or reason), and that they are singular judgements (KU§23, 244). This last point is important in explaining the necessity of the judgement of the sublime as a condition of objective reflective judgements about moral ideas extracted from the experience of natural objects. What we judge is not ideas of reason, but an object of nature. This object is such that we employ it to display an idea of reason. This is not a situation that requires determination of the will, and so the judgement is not determinative. Thus the imagination is engaged in a free play with reason in order to find a concept of reason that is adequate for how we grasp the object in intuition, or even for our failure to grasp it. As in any other reflective judgement, the imagination strives to structure the object according to the principle of the purposiveness of nature, and although this is unsuccessful, this striving continues. The imagination's striving towards totality means that although the attunement of imagination with reason results in an idea of reason, this is not a final determination of the object. We may always find an idea that is more adequate, or imagination may be even able to structure the object in a way that accords with the lawfulness of understanding.

Since the judgement of sublimity is the subjective aspect of an objective reflective judgement involving reason rather than understanding, it results in an idea of reason when we reflect according to a principle of the purposive use of nature for our supersensible vocation. This idea is not something we take to be a merely private reflection on the object, but one we hold that everybody should share, since it is the way we cognise the object. Therefore, we must claim that everybody should share the mental state which is the basis for this judgement. But the only access we have to this state is through the disinterested feeling of the state. Claiming that everybody should represent the object in the same way is expressed in the claim to universal validity for the feeling underlying the judgement, in this case a feeling of the sublime. Thus this judgement displays the form of purposiveness of the object, and that is the same as claiming subjective universal validity for this feeling. But there is one difference between the judgement of taste and the judgement of sublimity, because the latter involves the capacity for practical reason. An additional condition for experiencing the feeling of the sublime is that one possesses this capacity.

The sublime and moral ideas

The judgement of taste is a subjective condition of cognition in general, and is based on an attunement of imagination and understanding in free play. This judgement relates to our cognition of the world only, and involves cognitive powers that must be presupposed for there to be any theoretical cognition at all. We are warranted in assuming that everybody possesses these powers that are required for the judgement of taste to arise, because these powers are involved in any cognition. But the judgement of the sublime involves practical reason, which is not part of our cognition of the world, so we cannot, without further argument, assume that everybody has this capacity. To put it differently: since the judgement of sublimity involves an aspect change from the theoretical to the practical point of view, I cannot unconditionally require that others share my mental state in a representation of the object. I must add the assumption that they have the capacity required for regarding the world from this practical point of view. The ability to be moved by beauty is to have taste, and the ability to be moved by the sublime is to have feeling (KU§29, 265), and we demand both taste and feeling of every person, but with a difference:

> Beides aber fordern wir von jedem Menschen, und setzen es auch, wenn er einige Kultur hat, an ihm voraus: nur mit dem Unterschiede, daß wir das erstere, weil die Urteilskraft darin die Einbildung bloß auf den Verstand als Vermögen der Begriffe bezieht, geradezu von jedermann, das zweite aber, weil sie darin die Einbildungskraft auf Vernunft als Vermögen der Ideen bezieht, nur unter einer subjektiven Voraussetzung (die wir aber jedermann zu ansinnen zu dürfen uns berechtigt glauben) fordern, nähmlich der des moralischen Gefühls im Menschen, und hiermit auch diesem ästhetischen Urteile Notwendigkeit beilegen. (KU§29, 266)

On the face of it, this additional demand involved in the judgement of the sublime seems to be little more than demanding something that one can safely take for granted, since being a rational (moral) being means that one has moral feeling (MS 399).

This is not completely correct. Although we can presuppose moral feeling in everybody when we consider man in his freedom as a rational being, the judgement of sublimity is not a moral judgement. It is a judgement within the theoretical perspective, where man is regarded as part of nature and subject to nature's causal laws. This perspective does not justify any assumption about moral feeling in man, because that would be an unjustified intrusion of morality into theoretical cognition. It follows that the assumption of moral feeling in everybody cannot be an assumption claiming objective validity in relation to the judgement of sublimity. It can merely be a subjective presupposition. To claim subjective universal validity for this aesthetic reflective judgement of nature that involves the aspect change from one perspective to the other, we must demand as a subjective presupposition that everybody else also has the ability to be affected by the moral law. If they do not have this ability, they are unable to experience this aspect change.

But that does not seem to be sufficient for Kant. To possess moral feeling is just one aspect of what is required. The judgement about the sublime object has an objective aspect, which involves ideas of reason, and these are not invented in the judgement. We must not only be receptive to these ideas, as is demonstrated by our possession of moral feeling, we must already have developed these ideas to be able to feel the sublime:

> aber mit unserm Urteile über das Erhabene in der Natur können wir uns nicht so leicht Eingang bei andern versprechen. Denn es scheint eine bei weitem größere Kultur, nicht bloß der ästhetischen Urteilskraft, sondern auch der Erkenntnisvermögen, die ihr zum Grunde liegen, erforderlich zu sein, um über diese Vorzüglichkeit der Naturgegenstände ein Urteil fällen zu können. ... In der Tat wird ohne Entwickelung sittlicher Ideen das, was wir, durch Kultur vorbereitet, erhaben nennen, dem rohen Menschen bloß abschreckend vorkommen. (KU§29, 264 f)

We can demand assent from everyone on judgements of taste, but we are not directly warranted in doing that for judgements on the sublime. A person who has not developed moral ideas will be left without the pleasure, because she is unaware of her abilities and true vocation. She lacks the proper kind of education[69]. This does not mean that she is incapable of moral action; she possesses the moral law as all rational beings. But she lacks the grasp of moral ideas, a knowledge that seems to be necessary to avoid being stricken by the terror of the incomprehensible. It does not follow that the feeling of the sublime is something that we should not demand from everyone; we have a duty to develop our abilities, particularly the ones pertaining to moral action. These moral ideas probably can be learned in numerous ways; general education will in itself foster the idea of man's abilities and mastery of the world, not least his ability to gain lasting knowledge in a world of change. This shows in a most convincing way (at least for an Enlightenment philosopher) that man's abilities are not restricted by the fact that he belongs to the sensible realm. The basis of his knowledge and his desire to know is not restricted to satisfying bodily desires.

---

[69] Education is necessary for many experiences. What is the difference between this inability to experience the sublime due to lack of moral ideas, and an inability to enjoy a Japanese poem due to lack of education in Japanese language and culture? In the first case, the missing knowledge concerns our own nature as rational, and thus moral beings. It is not lack of particular empirical knowledge about one of many cultures and languages, as in the other case. We can expect people to have the knowledge required to experience the sublime, regardless of their language and cultural codes, but we cannot expect them to possess the knowledge necessary to appreciate the art of all different cultural groups. Thus we are warranted in demanding the first kind of development from people, and not the other.

This does not necessarily deliver a criterion for deciding who does and who does not have a grasp of moral ideas (although Kant may appear to think so). We cannot place people in front of a stormy ocean and suppose that those who feel fear are devoid of moral knowledge, whereas those filled with sublime pleasure have grasped man's moral destiny. People who claim to feel only fear and see no sublimity, might have their aesthetic reflective judgement overpowered by a conceptual judgement, e.g. through associating and identifying with shipwrecked seamen or victims of a flood. We are more justified in supposing those who claim they experience the sublime to possess moral ideas, but even in this case we might be mistaken. It is possible that they have an experience resembling judgements of sublimity, e.g. a religious experience[70], or they may want to impress their fellow men by their culture like the man who pretends to like what everybody else finds beautiful (KU§33, 284). This is an inescapable consequence of Kant's claim that we can only assert the universal validity of particular aesthetic reflective judgements; we can never prove them. But we are warranted in claiming that a condition for experiencing the sublime is possession of conceptual knowledge of moral ideas. These ideas are not involved in the experience, but represent background knowledge necessary for the experience of the sublime. This makes the sublime a more sophisticated judgement than the beautiful, because it requires some degree of maturity and insight.

In the judgement of the sublime the single demand to subjective universal validity found in the judgement of taste has an additional subjective requirement. There must be a double demand connected to the sublime; we have a moral duty to develop moral ideas and can on this basis demand the same feeling from everyone on encountering a sublime object:

> Denn das Wohlgefallen betrifft hier nur die sich in solchem Falle entdeckende Bestimmung unseres Vermögens, so wie die Anlage zu demselben in unserer Natur ist; indessen daß die Entwickelung und Übung uns überlassen und obliegend bleibt. (KU §28, 262)

Without a moral demand to develop moral ideas, there can be no aesthetic demand on everyone to experience the sublime 'object' as sublime.

---

70 In the Kantian context, a religious experience would involve a judgement of sublimity due to the moral character of the idea of God (KU§28, 263 f), but Otto's distinction between the sublime and the religious is worth considering as an appendix to the Kantian analysis of human knowledge. See R. Otto, *The Idea of the Holy*, 44 ff. The significance of this distinction for Kant's theory of the sublime is discussed in Lazaroff, 'Kantian Sublime' and W. B. Hund, 'Kant and A. Lazaroff on the Sublime'.

Still, this demand explains only the basis for this judgement, not its significance. So my claim is that, despite the fact that Kant clearly grounds the judgement of the sublime on our rational, moral nature, he nowhere in the exposition proves that it has any moral significance. Nor does he specify in what this significance should consist. Still he thinks that it has this kind of significance:

> Beide, [das Schöne und das Erhabene,] als Erklärungen ästhetischer allgemeingültiger Beurteilung, beziehen sich auf subjektive Gründe, nähmlich einerseits der Sinnlichkeit, so wie sie zugunsten des kontemplativen Verstandes, anderseits, wie sie wider dieselbe, dagegen für die Zwecke der praktischen Vernunft, und doch beide in demselben Subjekte vereinigt, in Beziehung auf das moralische Gefühl zweckmäßig sind. (KU§29, 267)

Just as the judgement of beauty benefits contemplative understanding, so does the judgement of the sublime serve the purposes of practical reason. To discover how this feeling can benefit practical reason, we have to look more closely at Kant's discussion of the real sublime: our supersensible vocation.

4. The moral import of the sublime

The judgement of the sublime has its basis in man's autonomy as a moral being. Kant claims that the sublime serves the purpose of practical reason, but he does not specify in what way. The exposition of the sublime merely shows that there is some connection between morality and sublimity, it does not show what the connection consists in. A theory about the moral import of the Kantian sublime must be constructed on the basis of remarks found scattered throughout the Critique of Judgement and his ethical works, combined with an outline of some central features of his theory of ethics.

Before embarking on that construction, I try to clarify the basic structure of the real sublime, i.e. that capacity of our mind that elevates us above nature, and without which we could not have any aesthetic reflective judgement about sublime objects of nature. Man's capacity for autonomous action according to a law arising from his own rationality is called sublime, but this capacity consists in, and is related to, several distinct notions also called sublime. Among these are negative and positive freedom, the moral law and practical reason, moral ideas, and man as legislator to himself. The question is: What is the central core of the real sublime, and what is sublime only derivatively, so to speak.

Freedom is related to the will in its two aspects; the executive will, which is the capacity for choice, and the legislative will, which is the lawgiving function of the will and identified with practical reason. For an incentive to count as motivation, Kant says it must be incorporated in a maxim, a subjective rule of action. When incorporated in a maxim that is chosen by the subject, the act is freely chosen, and in this sense every act is free. But only when acting according to the law and motivated by this law is man truly free. The law can be an incentive since we feel respect for this law, which affects us by negative checking self-oriented inclinations and positive recognition of the sublimity of the law. This leads to a discussion of the two-aspect interpretation of Kant's doctrine of the distinction between the empirical and the intelligible. I argue that as long as we cannot help but think of human beings as acting on their own choice, rather than as causally determined, the idea of man as free is a reality for us. I conclude this section by stating that the real sublime is the reciprocally related ideas of freedom and pure practical reason.

Then I return to the problem of people who lack the moral sensibility necessary for experiencing the sublime. How can we understand that? Kant claims elsewhere that everybody possesses moral feeling and consciousness of the moral law, and one should suppose that even children start to grasp basic moral ideas at fairly young age. My suggestion is that the crucial issue is not moral education, but concern about morality. The awareness of these ideas is necessary for the occurrence of this judgement, and it is also such ideas that are determined in the objective aspect of the judgement. This does not mean that we learn nothing new concerning these ideas, relating ideas to new circumstances may always bring out new aspects of them. But the major impact of the sublime is not cognitive but affective. This means that the moral effect of the sublime is connected to the cultivation of character.

On the basis of the analysis of the feeling of the sublime, I suggest that it can affect character in two ways; as cultivation of feeling and in conduction with moral conversion. The feeling stimulates our tendency to act on respect for the moral law by being a reminder of the pleasure of respect through its phenomenological similarity with this feeling. Furthermore, it is a way to admire the source of the moral feeling and in that way stimulate our predisposition to do good. In this way the sublime contributes to the cultivation of a character already disposed to act morally. But the feeling of the sublime can also contribute to a conversion from an evil to a good disposition. To develop this Kantian account, I take a closer look at his theory of character development.

Maxims are important in connection with character because they can be understood as the underlying principles we act on. Still maxims can have different degrees of generality from the action-specific to the most general, arranged hierarchically. Even very specific principles must be understood as expressive of an aspect of the agent's character. A maxim has moral worth if the incentives of self-love are subordinated to respect for the moral law. In this case, the basic disposition is good, in the opposite case it is evil. This disposition must be thought of as arising from a free choice, since we consider ourselves to be free. By testing the maxim against the categorical imperative we can find it to be obligatory, forbidden, or permitted. But only when the action is not only constrained by the categorical imperative, but motivated by it, do we ascribe the maxim moral worth.

Kant's conception of character is wider than this may suggest. We have a duty to develop the habit to act according to the law by cultivating natural inclinations to conform to the demands of the moral law and strive for moral perfection. Likewise we have a duty to contribute to the happiness of others. Both our natural talents and the situations we encounter vary, and how to realise this development of character is left to judgement. But the basis of such development is that we have a good disposition. I argue that although moral conversion is understood as a timeless act, and as such must be a principle underlying any morally worthy maxim, it must also have an empirical effect. The implication is that the agent also can experience moral conversion as an event in time; as the moment she decided to change her way of thinking. This discussion of Kant's theory of character confirms my assumption that the sublime can contribute to conversion as well as to cultivation of character.

Finally, I compare the moral import of the sublime with the way beauty can be morally significant. This is as a symbol of morality, which means that its moral effect is not in the judgement itself, but in our cognitive reflection on that judgement. We cannot say that this establishes a necessary relation between beauty and morality, either. The judgement of the sublime, on the other hand, is a direct experience of our moral capacity, and can be one of several elements contributing to moral conversion and the cultivation of character.

4. 1 The real sublime

Morality as the real sublime

By the term 'the real sublime', I mean that which the object of nature replaces in the judgement on the sublime. Kant uses the word subreption for this replacement, indicating that the object is in a sense arbitrary, and can be any object inducing this kind of feeling in us. But what is not arbitrary is that there is something that is really sublime, something that is the reason for our having this kind of experience at all. If there were no real sublime, the judgement on the sublime could not be caused by a subreption, but would be a case of an illusion. It would be a product of the imagination alone, and no claim to universal validity would be warranted. We cannot be certain that these claims to universal validity are warranted unless Kant's moral philosophy is proven to be true. Although many interpreters have contributed to making sense of Kant's analysis of human nature as simultaneously governed by and free from the laws of nature, there has not been given any proof of the truth of his theory. His critical approach leaves room for doubts. Therefore I will not attempt any more than a repetition of the general outline of his view as understood by some of the leading interpreters. That should be sufficient to demonstrate that Kant's theory of freedom provides at least a plausible account of human action.

Kant says that the object experienced as sublime is merely a substitution for a real sublime. The real sublime is the rational side of our being, our abilities to form concepts for something that exceeds both imagination and understanding, and to determine our will by rules we prescribe ourselves. The exposition of the sublime gave some clear indications of the nature of this sublime, and why it earns its name. In Kant's ethical works we find similar expressions of the sublimity of human morality. In the *Grundlegung*, Kant connects sublimity and worth, and he continues to state the reason for calling a person sublime:

> Denn sofern ist zwar keine Erhabenheit an ihr, als sie dem moralischen Gesetze *unterworfen* ist, wohl aber sofern sie in Ansehung ebendesselben zugleich *gesetzgebend* und nur darum ihm untergeordnet ist. (G 440)

It is not the obedience to the moral law that makes humans and other rational beings sublime, but the fact that they themselves issue the law that they act on. It is man's autonomy from all motivational sources other than those that stem from himself that is the point. If man had obeyed the will of God, it would be God to whom respect would be due, not man, since God would be the source of the law, and the principle of moral action would come from another source than the agent; it would be a case of heteronomy. Autonomous action is in itself truly free action, because it is independent of all external influences. It is the agent himself issuing the law that is obeyed. Freedom means tying oneself to the mast of the moral law to avoid following one's sensuous impulses, the inclinations, like a slave.

Kant explicitly connects the sublimity of the notion of freedom to practical reason:

> Der Begriff der Freiheit ist der Stein des Anstoßes für alle *Empiristen*, aber auch der Schlüssel zu den erhabensten praktischen Grundsätzen für *kritische* Moralisten, die dadurch einsehen, dass sie notwendig *rational* verfahren müssen. (KpV 7)

The real threat to autonomy is of course not the law of God, but our natural inclinations, which bind us to the causal necessity of the phenomenal world. What is termed sublime here, is that which lifts us above the empirical world, and that is our free will. The Kantian sublime is not, as Crowther claims, "wills determined by the moral law, that is wills that have transcended determination by any natural impulse"[1] (although this is an aspect of it and there is evidence for this interpretation, KpV 117), but the radical freedom which consists in being an autonomous legislator for oneself. In that case the will has, in fact, overcome the

[1] Crowther, *Kantian Sublime*, 20. Crowther expresses a different view on p. 28.

influence of the natural impulses, but this is a consequence of the sublime autonomy of man.

But in a way the real sublime is not only the freedom of will or autonomy, but the moral law itself, a fact expressed when Kant wants to avoid conceiving respect as merely a feeling of displeasure:

> Gleichwohl ist darin doch auch wiederum so *wenig Unlust*: daß, wenn man einmal den Eigendünkel abgelegt, und jener Achtung praktischen Einfluß verstattet hat, man sich wiederum an der Herrlichkeit dieses Gesetzes nicht satt sehen kann, und die Seele sich in dem Maße selbst zu erheben glaubt, als sie das heilige Gesetz über sich und ihre gebrechliche Natur erhaben sieht. (KpV 77)

Besides the religious rhetoric, what is most noteworthy in this passage, is the way the moral law is conceived as something elevated above man, not something he himself legislates. It seems to contradict the definition of autonomy as self-legislation. The explanation for this apparent contradiction is probably that in this passage the moral law is regarded from the perspective of the empirical self that is humiliated by respect. Due to this the empirical self sees the moral requirements of practical reason as something not part of itself. In the famous words of the last section of the second Critique, we find the connection restored:

> Zwei Dinge erfüllen das Gemüt mit immer neuer und zunehmenden Bewunderung und Erfurcht, je öfter und anhaltender sich das Nachdenken damit beschäftigt: *Der bestirnte Himmel über mir, und das moralische Gesetz in mir.* ... ich sehe sie vor mir und verknüpfe sie unmittelbar mit dem Bewußtsein meiner Existenz. (KpV 161 f)

As empirical beings we are dominated by our sensuous inclinations and the moral law is regarded as above us in an almost religious sense of the word. At the same time we realise that the moral law is in us, as part of our transcendental personality. Because of that we are incapable of getting any empirical knowledge of the moral law. It is a regulative idea for our action, and thus, it retains its character of being sublime, i.e. as something due respect or awe.

But what is still unclear after taking a closer look at the real sublime in Kant's account is which of these elements are sublime, and which are just called sublime by association. Kant said that the feeling of the sublime involves a substitution of the object of nature for the humanity in ourselves. Thus the real sublime must be that which really is worthy of respect. But it is not clear from a superficial reading of Kant's ethical works what this is. Moral ideas, the moral law, the legislator of the moral law, the person as subject to the moral law, freedom of will, freedom from determination by causality, practical reason and autonomy are all candidates for being the real sublime. Obviously these concepts are interconnected and overlapping, but which is (are) the central concept(s) from which the others are derived, and what exactly is the relationship between these concepts? To answer that, I will take a closer look at some crucial aspects of Kant's theory of man's freedom of will.

Freedom and the two concepts of will

Kant operates with different conceptions of freedom in his moral theory, and I will not discuss all of them. My concern is with the connection between Kant's concept of will and freedom of action. The human will has, according to Kant, two aspects with different functions. What is common for these two notions of will[2] is that they both refer to spontaneous initiation of action, i.e. action not explained through empirical causation. *Wille*, which is identical with practical reason (MS 213), is will as lawgiving, whereas *Willkür* is the capacity for choice. In Allison's interpretation this means that *Wille* is source of the laws given to *Willkür* as categorical or as hypothetical imperatives, and this is the basis for the maxims that one chooses to act on[3]. In the following I will take advantage of Allison's definition, and use 'legislative will' for *Wille*, 'executive will' for *Willkür*, and 'will' for the combination of the two functions, which Kant also calls *Wille*.

The executive will is connected to freedom in the sense that it is the ability to exercise a choice between real alternatives. When one chooses to follow the desire of one's sensuous nature, one does not follow impulses in a mechanical way, but acts on a reflective choice. *Choosing* to satisfy inclinations is following a hypothetical imperative, and one's action is governed by maxims. If we are following inclination automatically and acting without a maxim, i.e. a principle that guides what we are doing, there exists no action. The 'act' is merely an event in a causal chain. For there to be an action, we must consider the agent to be acting according to some motivation he is conscious of. Although he is not actually conscious of acting according to a principle, he is able to formulate such a principle if asked. This leads us to the notion of a maxim and to the notion of the executive will.

---

2 It is important to notice that this distinction is developing throughout Kant's ethical writings, and is not completely clarified until his later works. Both senses are present in the second Critique, although not clearly separated from each other because of imprecise terminology. See Beck, *A Commentary*, 176 f.

3 H. Allison, *Kant's Theory of Freedom*, 130.

This conception of rational agency is what Allison has called Kant's Incorporation Thesis, which

> makes it clear that for Kant an inclination or desire does not *of itself* constitute a reason for acting. It can become one only with reference to a rule or principle of action, which dictates that we ought to pursue the satisfaction of that inclination or desire. Moreover, ... the adoption of such a rule cannot itself be regarded as the causal consequence of the desire or, more properly, of being in a state of desire. On the contrary, it must be conceived as an act of spontaneity on the part of the agent.[4]

When we say that someone is acting, we do not only mean that there are movements of a body, but that these movements are done from reasons, and that these reasons can be formulated as some kind of principles, i.e. as maxims. What is more, we hold people responsible for the action and suppose that they could have chosen to act differently. There is no causal necessity to this relation between the motivation (understood as incentive [*Triebfeder*]) for action and the action, and this requires freedom understood as spontaneity. The agent is the source of the action, and thereby initiates a new causal series in the world.

It is not uncommon to interpret Kant as claiming that the only kind of free action is moral action, with the implication that all action motivated by inclination is determined and, thus, not free. What the Incorporation Thesis shows is that for Kant, freedom as spontaneity is a necessary prerequisite for all human action, even the kind of action motivated by inclinations. If that were not the case, man would be an animal or a machine when acting on hypothetical imperatives, which clearly is not in keeping with Kant's position. This is evident in his example of a criminal whom we hold responsible for his deeds even though he has been corrupted from early childhood and appears to have been born a villain:

> Dieses würde nicht geschehen können, wenn wir nicht voraussetzten, daß alles, was aus seiner Willkür entspringt (wie ohne Zweifel jede vorsätzlich verübte Handlung), eine freie Kausalität zum Grunde habe … . (KpV 100)

We cannot ascribe freedom as spontaneity only to actions following the categorical imperative, without losing the idea that freedom is a condition for moral responsibility.

Still, the claim that Kant holds only moral action to be free action is not unfounded, because when we act on inclinations our action is connected to the (material or psychological) causal chain, and is thereby 'pathologically affected' (KrV A534/B562). We can imagine not being motivationally influenced by any

---

4 Ibid. 140.

empirical motivation at all, but solely by human reason. That leads us to the concept of freedom as autonomy or self-legislation. Even the spontaneity of the executive will can be regarded as a kind of autonomy because here reason itself is making a rule for its own action. We are not facing a heteronomy of the religious kind where one is following a set of rules given by divine command, but making a rule incorporating an already existing incentive. But since this motivation is incorporated into the maxim, the will must still be regarded as affected by a foreign force. Is it meaningful to claim that the will can be autonomous in a stronger sense, totally independent of any influences both from God and the empirical desires?

For Kant this question is closely connected to the possibility of morality at all, because he conceives moral action in its pure form to be action motivated by respect for the law, not by any other interest. Thus, the categorical imperative, "*handle nur nach derjenigen Maxime, durch die du zugleich wollen kannst, daß sie ein allgemeines Gesetz werde*" (G 421), is only possible if the will is autonomous in this absolute sense (G 444). If the will is not autonomous, morality in the categorical sense disappears as a mere illusion, and we are left with a prudential, eudaimonistic morality in some broad sense. Then the imperative 'should' must always be followed by an 'if you want'. But since Kant holds that the categorical imperative expresses the moral law and the essence of morality, he is also committed to autonomy in the strong sense. Autonomy must involve the whole will, both in its lawgiving and in its executive functions, since autonomy means issuing a law to oneself. The lawgiving will, practical reason, gives a law to the executive will, and that is autonomy since these are two functionally different aspects of the same will.

This Kantian theory of action and morality brings out what is unique about human beings. We are empirical beings like all animals, but our capacity for rational deliberation sets us apart from the rest of creation. Rationality is connected to the mastery of rules in a broad sense, and, in this context, specifically to rules of action[5]. This capacity presupposes freedom as spontaneity, and is connected to the possibility of holding ourselves responsible for our actions. Rationality is, however, expressed in its supreme form in the principle to act in accordance with a rule that is free from all interest derived from non-rational sources, which is what we see expressed in the categorical imperative. The purely rational elements in a rule, is that which can be shared by all rational beings. Kant

---

5 T. Wyller, *Etikkens historie*, 143.

says that this can only be the form of the principle I am acting on, because the matter is tied up with my personal empirical desires:

> Also kann ein vernünftiges Wesen sich *seine* subjektiv-praktischen Prinzipien d.i. Maximen entweder gar nicht zugleich als allgemeine Gesetze denken, oder es muß annehmen, daß die bloße Form derselben, nach der jene *sich zur allgemeinen Gesetzgebung schicken*, sie für sich allein zum praktischen Gesetze machen. (KpV 27)

It is in this purely rational ability to make the legislative form of the principle a ground of determination we find man's complete freedom from the physical world, however mighty or great it may be.

Pure practical reason and feeling

Since human beings are both rational and empirical finite beings, we lack a 'holy will', which is a will that is wholly rational, and therefore always acts in accordance with the moral law (KpV 81 ff). Such a will is never tempted to act according to other incentives, because it has none. Human beings are always tempted in this way, so what stands in need of an explanation is how we are able to be motivated to act according to the moral law at all. I have already mentioned that the incentive is the feeling of respect [*Achtung*] for the moral law, which according to Kant is the same as the moral law itself considered as incentive (KpV 72). Beck argues that Kant cannot hold that the law itself is the incentive: "In spite of what Kant says, the law *itself* is not the incentive. A law is just not the sort of thing that can be an incentive. At most consciousness of the law can be an incentive."[6] Beck continues by pointing out a passage in *Metaphysik der Sitten* where moral feeling is called the subjective aspect of respect, and identified with consciousness of duty (MS 464). Since the moral feeling is the subjective aspect, we must assume that there is an objective aspect of respect, too. This must, as Allison argues, be a cognitive awareness of the moral law as commandment:

> In short, respect for the law consists simply in the recognition of its supremely authoritative character, which is to be taken to mean that it provides a reason for action that outweighs or overrides all other reasons, particularly those stemming from one's desires.[7]

---

6 Beck, *A Commentary*, 221.
7 Allison, *Theory of Freedom*, 123.

So how does this awareness affect my feeling? Kant describes first a negative component to the feeling which consists in a rejection of all sensible impulses and a checking of all inclinations that contradicts the moral law. This is a humiliation of self-conceit [*Eigendünkel*], and a checking of selfishness so that it conforms to the moral law. Such a negation of the inclinations is also a feeling, which Kant equates with pain (KpV 72 f). But this pain brings with it a positive feeling:

> Da dieses Gesetz aber doch etwas an sich Positives ist, nämlich die Form einer intellektuellen Kausalität, d.i. der Freiheit, so ist es, indem es im Gegensatze mit dem subjektiven Widerspiele, den Neigungen in uns, den Eigendünkel *schwächt*, zugleich ein Gegenstand der *Achtung*, und indem es ihn sogar *niederschlägt*, d.i. demütigt, ein Gegenstand der größten *Achtung*, mithin auch Grund eines positiven Gefühls, das nicht empirischen Ursprungs ist und a priori erkannt wird. (KpV 73)

Kant goes on to say that respect is a feeling arising from an intellectual ground, and can be known a priori. This feeling consists of a pleasure arising out of a displeasure or pain, where both displeasure and pleasure are due to a cognitive recognition of the demands of the moral law and the sublimity of freedom as autonomy (KpV 78 f).

As has been pointed out earlier, there are phenomenological similarities between the feeling of respect and the feeling of the aesthetic sublime, but this similarity cannot make respect contemplative nor the feeling of the sublime an incentive for action. The recognition of the worth of ourselves as autonomous, expressed in the feeling of respect for the moral law, is far removed from a merely aesthetic feeling.

The divided self and the two realms

A common argument against Kant's moral philosophy is that it divides the self into an empirical and an intelligible self which belongs to two separate worlds or realms. This division is the basis for the aspect change of the sublime, and a necessary presupposition of this part of Kant's aesthetic theory. Talking about a physical and an intelligible world may seem overly metaphysical, but as hinted at earlier, these realms can be regarded as two aspects or point of views on reality[8]. This is in keeping with Kant's own words (e.g. G 458). Then we can say that there are two legitimate ways of viewing human actions; either as occurrences

[8] As they are, for example, by Beck, *A Commentary*, 192 and Allison, *Theory of Freedom*, 4 f.

determined by empirical causes (which clearly includes psychological states that are inaccessible for external observation), or as freely chosen acts, initiated by the acting subject. There are not two worlds, but one world in which human action can be seen from two incompatible points of view. The division of the human self has also generally been regarded as unacceptable, and this problem is solved in a similar fashion: it is the same self regarded either as empirically bound or as free. It is worthwhile to note that this division is not the same as the division between man as rational and man as animal, because empirical man is understood in terms of his wishes and thoughts, as well as his desires. But these rational components in man as empirical are integrated in the causal chain of nature, which means that his reflections and decisions all can be explained as necessary consequences of a limited set of conditions (although it might be practically impossible to gain knowledge of the complete set of conditions which necessarily lead to the actual action). Viewed from this perspective, man can perhaps still be called free, but that sort of freedom is neither autonomy nor spontaneity.

The intelligible self is man regarded as free because he is able to spontaneously initiate a causal chain. But this ability presupposes the idea of freedom, which, unlike the occurrences in the physical world, cannot be observed. When we observe empirical man we can explain all his actions without making use of regulative ideas. We have a Humean conception of human action. Why is not that sufficient? Because it is a matter of fact that we understand ourselves as free when we act, and we do the same with other people. Unless we are studying them scientifically from anatomical, physiological, or psychological points of view, wish to excuse them, or perhaps to denigrate them[9]. And even scientists conducting scientific experiments on a person would blame the object of the study morally if she suddenly started attacking the scientist physically for no reason, even though they could (theoretically) give an account for the causal history of the event. They would not regard the act as the outcome of a necessary chain of events, but as a freely chosen act by a rational person who was capable of refraining from the attack. Man is unique because of his rationality, a rationality including the ability to choose one's line of action independently of desires and impulses. Even if we were able to explain all actions without presupposing freedom in the Kantian

---

9 Which way we choose to understand the acts of other human beings also has a moral dimension. If we interpret their acts only as causally necessitated and not free, we do not treat them as ends but merely as means. This is also the case when we use empirical explanations to excuse other people, as may be done in a murder trial where the accused is relieved of responsibility due to neglect and physical abuse in childhood or some similar cause.

sense, it is still a fact that we understand human action as free in this sense. If we stop regarding man as free, we will at the same time change our conception of what it is to be human.

The obvious objection to this line of argument is that if our conception of human agency is based on an illusory freedom, we would be better off getting rid of it by changing our conception of what it is to be a person. But that will not work because changing our conception of personhood in such a radical way would put an end to the concept of a person, as long as a person *is* a rational being with the ability to choose his line of action. If we remove the idea of freedom from our understanding of what it is to be a human being, there would be no humanity left. And it is difficult to imagine how we would behave towards another if we stopped regarding each other as free, responsible agents. It would certainly mean the end of human society as we know it. Unless we continued behaving and thinking as now, that is, holding each other responsible and thinking of ourselves as free, but at the same time claiming this to be an illusion. That is hardly a satisfactory solution compared to the Kantian suggestion, because we have to treat our actual conception of ourselves as false and illusory without being able to get rid of it. In this connection Taylor's discussion of what is to count as real, is relevant:

> What is real is what you have to deal with, what won't go away just because it doesn't fit with your prejudices. By this token, what you can't help to recourse to in life is real, or as near to reality as you can get a grasp at present.[10]

If we as a matter of fact think, speak, and treat ourselves and others as free, just denying this freedom because it does not fit in a deterministic world view cannot help us to escape this idea. Then it is the best available account of human life, and we should not trade that account for one that force us to deny some essential aspect of our perception of the world. Kant's solution is to accept the world as being the way we conceive it to be, and that includes that we have to regard human action from two different, but equally valid points of view.

There is of course a difference between these two points of view, as Beck points out: the empirical view is based on the categories as constitutive principles, whereas the intelligible view requires freedom which has status as regulative principle[11]. This can give the impression that the empirical view is the basic, 'most real' perspective because it is given in experience and is difficult to escape. We take the physical world for granted in a stronger way than we do the intelligible,

---

[10] C. Taylor, *Sources of the Self*, 59.

[11] Beck, *A Commentary*, 193. Freedom is regulative in regard to theoretical reason, but is also constitutive for practical reason (KpV 48 ff).

since the last one does not force itself on us in the way the physical world does. But that does not give the empirical point of view primacy over the other, because this last one, although not inescapable like the first, constitutes our conception of what it is to be a human being.

Autonomy and the moral law

What has been argued this far only supports (without proving) a claim about the reality of freedom as spontaneity, but to establish morality, we have seen that freedom as autonomy is necessary. But spontaneity brings with it autonomy:

> But if [the *Willkür*] is to be determined necessarily, i.e. irrespective of the desires which are the material cause of its willing, as it is if there is duty, it must be determined not by the content but by the form of the law. The form of law is universality, fitness for universal legislation. In giving such a law, reason is not responding to the promptings of nature. It is therefore a spontaneous legislator and is free.[12]

If human freedom consists in the ability to make rules of action into which motives of all kinds can be incorporated, then freedom is spontaneity. But rules or principles are universal in form, so universality is the hallmark of all free acts, be they good or evil. If an act is done not by some empirical impulse, but because acting on universal principle in itself is good or desirable (in a broad sense of the term), the act is not only free because incorporated in one's own maxim, but also because it is motivated solely by the rational principle of law. This is what gives man his dignity: his ability to act on principle. Only then is the choice of action wholly rational, not governed by any other influence but rationality itself.

Why is freedom as autonomy moral? Simply because "*Freiheit und unbedingtes praktisches Gesetz weisen also wechselsweise aufeinander zurück.*" (KpV 29) This constitutes what Allison calls Kant's Reciprocity Thesis because it claims a reciprocal relationship to exist between freedom and the moral law. Allison says it is supported by arguments of the following kind:

> (1) As a "kind of causality" the will must, in some sense, be law governed or, in the language of the second *Critique*, "determinable" according to some law (a lawless will is an absurdity); (2) as free it cannot be governed by laws of

---

12 Ibid. 198.

nature; (3) it must therefore be governed by laws of a different sort, namely, self-imposed ones; and (4) the moral law is the required self-imposed one.[13]

If we are free in the absolute sense of autonomy, the law we prescribe ourselves is the moral law, expressed in the categorical imperative. An autonomous agent is a rational agent; he acts rationally, that is according to law because it is the law. He not only acts in keeping with a universal law, but also because he wills this law, and this is what is expressed in the first and the last formulas of the categorical imperative.

The conclusion of this discussion of Kant's moral concepts shows that the central core of man as a rational, moral being is the idea of freedom as autonomy, i.e. self-legislation, which stands in a reciprocal relationship with the moral law, or pure practical reason. From these concepts we can derive spontaneity, freedom from empirical causation and man as subject to his own law. Furthermore, ideas about immortality and God are presupposed by this lawfulness. But the real sublime is the freedom of man that is expressed in his autonomous practical reason.

4. 2 Culture and moral ideas

Cultural development and the experience of the sublime

Kant claims that not everybody does experience the sublime in all circumstances when we would demand this feeling from everybody. In a way this is the case for all aesthetic reflective judgements; we demand everybody's agreement but do not postulate it. The reason for this is that we cannot know whether we have separated from the feeling all the elements belonging to the agreeable or the good. Even if we had this kind of knowledge, we certainly could not count on others to have isolated the disinterested feeling from other feelings (KU§8, 216). This is not what Kant means when he says that we cannot expect others to agree with our judgement of the sublime, because he contrasts this with the frequent fulfilment of our expectations of agreement in the judgement of beauty (KU§29, 264). The reason for this difference is that the feeling of the

---

13 Allison, *Theory of Freedom*, 203.

sublime requires culture and the development of moral ideas, and he thinks that not everybody possesses this knowledge in the degree demanded[14].

Clearly this kind of knowledge is a requirement for the possible experience of both modes of the sublime:

> Die Stimmung des Gemüts zum Gefühl des Erhabenen erfordert eine Empfänglichkeit desselben für Ideen; denn eben in der Unangemessenheit der Natur zu den letzteren, mithin nur unter der Voraussetzung derselben, und der Anspannung der Einbildungskraft, die Natur als ein Schema für die letzteren zu behandeln, besteht das Abschreckende für die Sinnlichkeit, welches doch zugleich anziehend ist: weil es eine Gewalt ist, welche die Vernunft auf jene ausübt, nur um sie ihrem eigentlichen Gebiete (dem praktischen) angemessen zu erweitern und sie auf das Unendliche hinaussehen zu lassen, welches für jene ein Abgrund ist. In der Tat wird ohne Entwickelung sittlicher Ideen das, was wir, durch Kultur vorbereitet, erhaben nennen, dem rohen Menschen bloß abschreckend vorkommen. Er wird an den Beweistümern der Gewalt der Natur in ihrer Zerstörung und dem großen Maßstabe ihrer Macht, wogegen die seinige in nichts verschwindet, lauter Mühseligkeit, Gefahr und Not sehen, die den Menschen umgeben würden, der dahin gebannt wäre. (KU§29, 265)

The infinite, which a cultured person judges mathematically sublime, becomes a threatening abyss for those who lack this fundamental moral insight. Such people take no pleasure in the violent power of nature of the dynamically sublime because they see it as cause of danger and misery only. But what are these people lacking? There are several more or less explicit answers to this question in the text. Kant claims that the feeling of the sublime requires receptivity to ideas, which should mean that (1) these people lack this kind of receptivity to (moral) ideas. Then he says that (2) they are uncultured, and (3) lacking in the development of moral ideas. Finally, he says further down on the same page that the basis for culture is the predisposition to moral feeling that we presuppose in all of mankind; which opens for (4) that the moral feeling of respect is lacking. We can be sure that if these people lack moral feeling, then they would not be cultured, have developed moral ideas, or be receptive to such ideas. But Kant probably did not mean that those who are insensitive to sublimity lack moral feeling altogether, because he says, as we have seen, that we have to assume moral feelings in all human beings. Furthermore, he explicitly says that the Savoyard peasant whom he uses as an example of those who do not experience the sublime, was both good and otherwise sensible (KU§29, 265). We can readily assume that a good man cannot lack moral

[14] I have argued that this does not undermine the claim to intersubjective validity for the judgement on the sublime, since there is a moral demand to develop moral ideas that are required to experience the sublime. See p. 170 ff.

feeling, and it would also be strange if he did not have culture and developed moral ideas. Development of moral ideas, cultivation of moral feeling, and the possession of culture are closely connected (KU§60, 356), so if one of these elements is underdeveloped, so are the others.

If we look at the second to last sentence in the passage cited above, the development of moral ideas is accorded the decisive role for the possibility of feeling the sublime, and the implication is that in this context being cultured means having developed, or rather, being in the process of developing this kind of knowledge. If this is right it is also reasonable to assume that development of moral ideas increases the receptivity to these ideas. Kant clearly does not adhere to a theory that the less we have moral ideas, the more we crave for them. It seems to be the other way around, which makes sense on the basis of his theory of the predisposition to good and the propensity for evil (R 26ff). Being concerned with moral principles enhances our awareness of these principles. We should also assume that the awareness of moral ideas increases our awareness of the demands of the moral law. The more we are aware of the demands of morality, the more likely are we to experience the world according to the principles of morality. The affinity between moral feeling and the feeling of the sublime explains why these principles are relevant for the judgement of the sublime, too: if we have a clear idea of freedom and morality, the short-comings of imagination engage reason in a search for adequate rational ideas, and the less we are aware of these ideas and their importance, the less likely are we to be led to moral ideas by the humiliation of imagination, and furthermore to experience a pleasure at this humiliation.

This interpretation is not very attractive, though, since it forces us to the conclusion that there is a direct connection between education and the ability to experience the sublime. I do not find this very plausible. To prevent misunderstandings: the problem here is not the same as the one discussed above concerning whether the absence of feelings of the sublime can be used as criterion for judging the moral development of the person. I concluded that it cannot. The present problem concerns what connection there is between the development of moral ideas and the potential for judging some object sublime. It is clear that I cannot assume that I, if I do not judge the unlimited or mighty nature to be sublime, have a moral deficiency, or that I am evil. These questions concern my disposition for action, not my capacity for aesthetic judgements.

A way to approach the solution of this problem, is to ask what kind of people Kant thinks lack the necessary foundation for this judgement. Since his example of such people is a peasant from the mountain region of France, it is reasonable to suppose he was thinking of uneducated people living on the outskirts of what was then considered civilisation. Probably also children and the mentally disabled would be included. On the other hand, the development of ideas of freedom and moral responsibility start at an early age so it must be fairly young children in that case. Likewise most cultures have a godhead representing freedom and the unconditioned, showing that these ideas are present, however 'primitive' a form. And this was of course something Kant knew very well. Besides, the peasant he is referring to in his example probably was a devout, God-fearing Christian, and it is difficult to imagine Kant arguing that people of that kind lacked basic insight into moral ideas.

It seems as if a plain lack of the basic ideas connected to morality is not what Kant was aiming at in this passage. I have to find an alternative account for explaining why the good and sensible Savoyard peasant did not grasp the sublimity of glaciered mountains. Kant furnishes the obvious one: He was too immersed in the everyday toil, and could only regard these mountains from an interested point of view. The feelings connected to his interest in the survival of himself and the ones he cared about covered up, so to say, the disinterested feeling of the sublime. It is much easier to feel this way for someone who has no direct personal interest in the area. And even more so for someone who is there with a particular concern for moral matters as Sausurre was:

> So war aber seine Absicht Belehrung des Menschen; und die seelenerhebende Empfindung hatte und gab der vortreffliche Mann den Lesern seiner Reisen in ihren Kauf oben ein. (KU§29, 265)

Herr v. Sausurre had the objective of enlightenment at heart, and therefore he was concerned with the cultivation of moral ideas. And being concerned with moral ideas, his receptivity for moral ideas was enhanced, as well as his receptivity for the feeling of the sublime The peasant could only view the mountains as threatening, and it was not necessarily his lack of culture or moral ideas that prevented him from taking in the full sublime delight, but his lack of direct concern with those ideas in this situation.

I believe there are good reasons to assume that everyone from a certain age has the necessary grasp of moral ideas to be able to experience the sublime. We do not have to take Kant to assume this grasp to be insufficiently developed in some. The passage can mean that some have a less developed sense of these ideas, increasing the possibility that the feeling of the sublime will be overpowered by feelings and concerns connected to interest. This interpretation enables us both to retain the assumption that everybody has the grasp of moral ideas necessary for feelings of the sublime to arise in them, and at the same time to differentiate between more or less developed knowledge of these ideas in different people. Having a better grasp of these ideas entails being more susceptible to experiences of the sublime, even in situations where others just feel the influence of their daily worries and concerns. But this grasp of the ideas reflects actual awareness and concern with them, rather than abstract education. Furthermore, the claim that the receptivity to the sublime depends on the awareness of moral ideas tells nothing about the moral quality of the person. There is no *direct* correlation between the knowledge of moral ideas and moral disposition, not to mention good conduct, although there must be some connection. Maybe we could say that people who are concerned with moral ideas, usually are more aware of the demands of the moral law, as well? They do not necessarily act according to law, though.

One could easily get the impression by Kant's argument that educated people who spend their time studying philosophy, theology, or physics are most susceptible to feelings of sublimity. I do not think this is the best interpretation. If this were correct, Kant would be at odds with everyday experience, because very often young people seem to be more open to experiencing the sublime in nature than mature, sophisticated men of learning. The contemplation of the infinity of the starry heavens or the power of the ocean during a storm probably is more common among teenagers than among the cultural elite (or moral philosophers, for that matter)[15].

Assuming this, we still do not have to modify Kant's argument to fit the empirical reality, because, at least in our culture, youth is a period in life devoted to reflection on moral matters. There may be many reasons for this, but the main ones include that there is sufficient time for contemplation of moral questions as well as of the wonders of nature. Furthermore, it is a time dedicated to choice of occupation and what kind of life to pursue (and these are as much moral as prudential questions), and, finally, at this time of life one is not yet seriously concerned with the practical matters of everyday, which leaves more room for aesthetic response. Having culture and developed moral ideas is not the same as being educated, if that education does not further the contemplation of moral ideas. Being cultured means spending time being exposed to these ideas in a wide variety of ways. The conclusion is that there is no necessary disagreement between Kant's statement that culture and developed moral ideas are necessary for experiencing

---

[15] I allow myself this sweeping generalisation based merely on my own experience, what others have told me, and what seems to be the usual portrait of the young in literature, especially in novels about coming of age. It may well be that this is not the case, or that it is only an empirical fact about our time and culture. My argument does not depend on the truth of this assertion.

the sublime, and the empirical claim that these phenomena are more readily experienced in youth. The person most susceptible to the feeling of the sublime is the one who is concerned with moral ideas, not someone who has a good disposition. Therefore can we assume everybody to have developed moral ideas, but they may lack the awareness of these ideas in the situation. This is still something that we demand from them in the situation, as part of the double demand involved in judgements of the sublime.

Thinking ideas and feeling the sublime

My claim has been that the Kantian analysis of the judgement of the sublime shows not only that the feeling presupposes knowledge of moral ideas, but that it has a revelatory function as well. What are revealed through the judgement of the sublime are moral ideas. At the same time, the required background of the subject for experiencing the sublime is not only the ability to act morally, i.e. according to, and motivated by, the moral law as expressed in the categorical imperative, but culture, i.e. development of moral ideas; particularly the idea of freedom. Every rational being has the ability to perform moral action, but we cannot assume everybody to have sufficient awareness of moral ideas for experiencing the sublime. Of course, the conscious awareness of the idea of freedom is not required for a person to be free.

If my interpretation of the exposition and deduction of the judgement of the sublime is accepted, this judgement must be the subjective aspect of an act of objective reflective judgement, which is a judgement in which the particular is given, and the universal (the concept or rule) is found. The objective aspect must be the reflection on rational ideas when the object of nature exceeds the limitations of imagination or contains some other feature making it relate to reason, such as a man apparently acting on a principle instead of being necessitated by inclinations. These ideas are not involved in the judgement of the sublime, but the objective aspect of the experience, or at least the potential for such an objective aspect, is necessary for there to be a subjective aspect. Awareness of moral ideas is necessary for someone to experience the sublime. There must be a reflective judgement according to an idea of reason, at least potentially, for the feeling of the sublime to occur, and the reflection on ideas as a result of a sensuous intuition, obviously requires some development of such ideas.

The judgement of the sublime has no moral function as such, just as the judgement of taste has no cognitive function. What is more, in the judgement of taste we can learn something new about the world, whereas the judgement of sublimity requires us to possess knowledge of the ideas involved in the cognition accompanied by the feeling prior to the experience. Apparently the result is that moral ideas take no part in the judgement as such, nor do we learn about *new* moral ideas. So what is left of the moral import of the sublime? Immediately it looks as if the moral significance of the experience is not in the feeling of the sublime but in the cognitive judgement and the subsequent reflection on ideas of reason. But then it is not the judgement of sublimity that is morally significant, but its objective counterpart. Besides, this is a reflection on ideas we already know, so we do merely repeat what we already are aware of.

The first suspicion can be countered without much difficulty. First, our failure to comprehend the infinite in its totality results in reflection on ideas of reason. Then the question arises how this changes our conception of nature and the freedom of man as a rational being. There is nothing in this transition from the world of appearances to the world of ideas that should affect our way of acting or the way we view man's freedom as a rational being. We remain within a theoretical perspective on reality. It is the feeling of negative pleasure, as Kant calls it, that makes us aware of the insufficiency of imagination and understanding, and our independence from the world as free, rational beings, capable of spontaneity in action as well as in theoretical reason. This feeling, resembling the moral feeling, stimulates our reflection on the significance of freedom from the world of appearances. It also accustoms us to the affection of sensibility by reason experienced as a humiliation and elevation, which is found in the feeling of respect. In this way we become more inclined to recognise this affection as real, instead of trying do discount it as an illusion.

The second suspicion mentioned above may appear to be more serious: We are led to reflect on moral ideas through the feeling of the sublime, but if we are familiar with these ideas already, is there any moral import in this at all? It seems as if we are just reminded of things we already know. But for this judgement to be morally significant, we must require that the subject be affected in some recognisable way. To be morally affected presumably involves changing some attitude that is expressed in action. The presupposition here is that Kant's moral theory is a virtue ethics, where the cultivation of character, including feelings, plays a central role. As Sherman puts it:

> Despite [Kant's] criticisms of Aristotle, he appeals to a project of virtue that, like Aristotle's, relies on the steady transformation of character through choice, experience, and critical practice over time.[16]

Even given this framework of Kantian virtue ethics it is unclear how the judgement of the sublime can contribute to this shaping of character.

When it comes to action, we can gain new insights concerning the significance of moral ideas through new applications for these ideas, but in the contemplative experience of the sublime it is more difficult to see how any knowledge can be acquired. This fits well with some recent works on the Kantian sublime, which downplay the moral significance of the judgement[17]. Several of these interpretations give moral ideas a role as a necessary basis for the judgement of sublimity, but deny this judgement any positive moral significance. I have already argued that Kant holds that the experience of the sublime is morally significant, and I think he is right. To show that, I will discuss his theory of the sublime in relation to his moral theory, as it is understood in several recent interpretations.

4. 3 Cultivation and conversion

Cultivation of feeling

The assertion that a developed knowledge of moral ideas is a condition for the occurrence of feelings of the sublime seems to imply that what we feel in this experience is what we already know; hence no moral lesson is learned. The obvious answer to this claim is that being made aware of something we already know can be important in several ways. Rational ideas are not like the concepts of understanding restricted to particular applications in intuition. Thus, these ideas cannot be understood and dealt with once and for all. On the contrary, they will always guide inquiry into practical matters in new situations, bringing out new aspects of the ideas of freedom under rational law. Exercising my freedom to refrain from lying in a situation where the lie would have brought me an undeserved extra piece of cake is quite different from using one's own body to block the way for the tanks rolling through the streets of Beijing immediately after

16 N. Sherman, *Making a Necessity of Virtue*, 162.

17 Among them are Lyotard, *Lessons*, 189 f., Pries, *Übergänge*, 60 ff., Hund, 'Kant and Lazaroff', 352, and (although his use of 'sublime' certainly is not Kantian) T. Weiskel, *The Romantic Sublime*, e.g. 28 f.

the massacre on the Tianmen square[18]. The realisation of the idea of freedom is not something fixed, and hence one cannot know what it is in the way one knows what an object is. Freedom as autonomy is an idea with no determined object, but with an unlimited range of different applications having one feature in common; they are acts according to law, motivated by respect for the law.

Knowing moral ideas and realising them in action on one hand, and having aesthetic feelings of pleasure in experiencing these ideas as transcending the world of appearances on the other, certainly are not the same. How does this aesthetic experience contribute to man's morality? Not every action we perform is an action based on meticulous deliberation about what duty prescribes in this context. Even if it were, our deliberation still would be based on general principles. We act from habit, on general dispositions, and thus the development of character is given a central role to play in ethics. Recent interpretations of Kant's ethics have drawn attention to the role of maxims in his theory of moral character. In the words of O'Neill:

> In adopting maxims of a morally appropriate sort we will not be adopting a set of moral rules at all, but rather some much more general guidelines for living. To have maxims of a morally appropriate sort would then be a matter of leading a certain sort of life, or being a certain sort of person. The core of morality would lie in having appropriate underlying principles rather than in conforming one's action to specific standards.[19]

The Kantian moral theory allows no short cut from the Categorical Imperative directly to action, as is often assumed. We have to go by way of maxims, which means that we are determined by the underlying principles of action. Thus the character of the subject becomes more important than the assessment of singular acts[20]:

---

18 Here I am taking for granted that these acts are morally motivated, which we are never in a position to know for sure. There is always the possibility that the unknown Chinese man preventing the advance of the tanks followed an ancient honour code or was in a bad mood and wanted to annoy someone. And refraining from lying can always be motivated by the fear of getting caught.

19 O. O'Neill, *Constructions of Reason*, 152. This is also clearly brought out in Kant's chapter heading "*Die Ethik gibt nicht Gesetze für die Handlungen (denn das tut das Ius) sondern nur für die Maximen der Handlungen*" (MS 388). O'Neill's interpretation is, however, not without problems, as is clear from Allison, *Theory of Freedom*, 91 ff.

20 This is a simplification, because maxims can have different levels of generality, see p. 203 ff. Thus we must also assess the maxim of each act as if arising from a state of innocence (R 41). I will attempt to deal with this apparent contradiction later.

> Man nennt aber einen Menschen böse nicht darum, weil er Handlungen ausübt, welche böse (gesetzwidrig) sind, sondern weil diese so beschaffen sind, daß sie auf böse Maximen in ihm schließen lassen. (R 20)

Given this picture, we can find several points of moral influence of the experience of the sublime. One is as a reminder of freedom, the basic principle for adoption of all maxims. The experience of the sublime is an aesthetic experience of the freedom in adopting maxims in keeping with the different formulas of the categorical imperative, rather than maxims promoting some version of self-interest. This fits well with Kant's own description of the moral significance of the feeling of the sublime, as we see from a passage quoted earlier:

> Also ist das Gefühl des Erhabenen in der Natur Achtung[21] für unsere eigene Bestimmung, die wir einem Objekte der Natur durch eine gewisse Subreption (Verwechselung einer Achtung für das Objekt statt der für die Idee der Menschheit in unserm Subjekte) beweisen, welches uns die Überlegenheit der Vernunftbestimmung unserer Erkenntnisvermögen über das größte Vermögen der Sinnlichkeit gleichsam anschaulich macht. (KU§27, 257)

When someone is aware, through the feeling of the sublime, of the superiority of his rationality to non-rational nature within and without, his tendency to act on maxims of morality rather than those of self-love is strengthened. The feeling of sublimity is a reminder of our duty to act according to our rational nature, instead of being ruled by heteronomous laws. This is no guarantee that we will act morally every time; most likely we will not, but the experience of sublimity may contribute to our *Haltung*, to our basic attitude regarding action.

Motivation for action must, as we have seen, include a feeling, and this motivation must be incorporated in a maxim which must either be in accordance with the Categorical Imperative or not. Thus there are basically two types of motivational feelings: the feeling of respect for the law and the feeling of self-love or lack of respect[22]. The feeling of respect is a result of being subjected to the moral law, and must be present in all rational beings. But Kant also says that we have an obligation to cultivate this moral feeling and "*durch die Bewunderung seines unerforschlichen Ursprungs, zu verstärken.*" (MS 399 f). My claim is that one element in this cultivation and strengthening of the moral feeling, is through

---

21 I find it reasonable here to assume that the term '*Achtung*' is used in a loose sense. If we interpret this as respect for the moral law, this feeling would not remain an aesthetic judgement, but would be assimilated to the field of ethics.

22 Self-love includes all inclinations, also positive and negative feelings towards others. It is not in itself contrary to the moral law if the law of self-love is subordinated to the moral law in the maxim (R 36).

experiencing the feeling of the sublime. This cultivating effect of the sublime has three interrelated aspects.

One is that the feeling of sublimity is analogous to the moral feeling, and it is a feeling we wish continued and repeated. The pleasurable part of the feeling is self-strengthening, as all pleasure. We want it to continue, and we want to repeat it. The pleasures of the sublime and of respect are peculiar, in that both have a cognitive basis, and both arise on the basis of displeasure. Thus, it is not merely *any* pleasure we want to relive, but this peculiar kind of pleasure, with a basis in the superiority of reason over sensibility. The feeling of the sublime is not the same as respect, but it is reasonable that the feeling of the sublime stimulates moral feelings in us due to their similarity. Both feelings have a negative and a positive component involving the humiliation of our sensuous nature due to the realisation of the superiority of reason. As Kant says in the third Critique:

> In der Tat läßt sich ein Gefühl für das Erhabene der Natur nicht wohl denken, ohne eine Stimmung des Gemüts, die der zum Moralischen ähnlich ist, damit zu verbinden. (KU§29, 268)

Feeling the sublime functions as a reminder of the feeling of respect for the moral law.

The second, and more important, aspect is that the judgement of the sublime is one way we can admire the inscrutable source of the moral feeling as quoted above. The feeling of respect is strengthened through the experience of the superiority of our rational capacity, which derives from its ability to resist the constraints of nature, and this is exactly what happens in the experience of the sublime. Kant claims, however, that this is exhibited most intensely in a purely abstract 'representation' which needs no sensible stimulation to affect feeling:

> Man darf nicht besorgen, daß das Gefühl des Erhabenen durch eine dergleichen abgezogene Darstellungsart, die in Ansehung des Sinnlichen gänzlich negativ wird, verlieren werde; denn die Einbildungskraft, ob sie zwar über das Sinnliche hinaus nichts findet, woran sie sich halten kann, fühlt sich doch auch eben durch diese Wegschaffung der Schranken derselben unbegrenzt. ... Es ist gerade umgekehrt; denn da, wo nun die Sinne nichts mehr vor sich sehen, und die unverkennliche und die unauslöschliche Idee der Sittlichkeit dennoch übrigbleibt, wurde es eher nötig sein, den Schwung einer unbegrenzten Einbildungskraft zu mäßigen, um ihn nicht bis zum Enthusiasm steigen zu lassen ... . (KU§29, 274)

The negative representation of our moral vocation is the judgement of the sublime that affects us most strongly. One should suspect that this means that an aesthetic representation of an object is an inferior way of strengthening our moral disposition.

I am not sure that such a conclusion is warranted. The moral feeling of respect is presumably present in all human beings, but not equally cultivated or developed. Those who have a developed feeling, tend to be more readily motivated by respect rather than by self-love. Such people, given that they exist, are already conscious of the source of these feelings, and take pleasure in the contemplation of these ideas. For these people, the contemplation of moral ideas certainly strengthens the disposition they already have developed. For the rest of us, however, this pure access to the moral law may be too abstract and too far removed from the life we lead. For such less developed people, the experience of the liberation of reason from nature through the feeling of sublimity may have a more significant educational effect. After all, it is through the subordination of natural inclinations we are able to act on the moral law, and these inclinations are usually strong forces within us. Thus I believe Kant's fascination with abstract thinking, and his ever increasing wonder and awe at the moral law within, might have misled him into overlooking the cultivating force of the starry heavens above; at least in this particular passage of the *Metaphysik der Sitten*.

A more significant conclusion one can draw from this quotation is that also purely rational representations give rise to the feeling of the sublime, showing that the experience of the sublime in nature and in abstract thoughts are the same; we do not have to choose between emotions and rationality in this question. Thus the admiration of the inscrutable source of the moral feeling that Kant says is a way to strengthen the moral feeling is a judgement of the sublime. This leads us to a third way, related to the second, in which the experience of the sublime can have a positive moral influence:

> Dieses Gefühl der Erhabenheit seiner moralischen Bestimmung öfter rege zu machen, ist als Mittel der Erweckung sittlicher Gesinnungen vorzüglich anzupreisen, weil es dem angeborenen Hange zu Verkehrung der Triebfedern in den Maximen unserer Willkür gerade entgegenwirkt, um in der unbedingten Achtung fürs Gesetz, als der höchsten Bedingung aller zu nehmenden Maximen, die ursprüngliche sittliche Ordnung unter den Triebfedern und hiermit die Anlage zum Guten im menschlichen Herzen in ihrer Reinigheit wiederherzustellen. (R 50)

This passage concerns the aesthetic contemplation of the real sublime, but as Kant repeatedly insists, the subreptive sublime also concerns man's moral vocation, so even the aesthetic sublime in nature should have the same effect on feeling. The feeling of the sublime works against the inversion of the good order of incentives in our maxims due to our propensity for evil, and by that stimulates the predisposition for the good in us. How does it work against this inversion of incentives? By showing through a feeling the superiority of rationality over sensibility. In the feeling of the sublime, sensibility is subordinated to reason, and this is the relation between the incentives found in a good disposition (R 36). Thus we are less prone to subordinate the feeling of respect to sensuous impulses.

This discussion of the morally cultivating force of the sublime might be concluded with a suitably moderate claim that diversity of experiences is an asset to moral education. Both the contemplation of moral ideas as well as the substitute sublime of nature contribute to this cultivation, and experiencing the power of these ideas in different circumstances and in varying ways in itself gives a firmer grasp of them, influencing the way we think human life should be led. This will again affect which underlying principles we select to guide our everyday life. To get the full picture of Kant's position on cultivation of character, we have to delve deeper into his theory of moral psychology. But before that, another possible effect of the sublime has to be explored.

Moral conversion

I will argue that the sublime can have an even stronger, more profound moral influence on our life; an amplified version of the cultivating effect discussed above. This moral effect has its source in the feeling of the sublime as a feeling exhibiting the two main opposing attitudes we can adopt in life, i.e. the same source as the effect of the sublime in contributing to character development. This interpretation of Kant's moral philosophy, which focuses on the dualistic nature of this theory, is, admittedly, somewhat simplified; but this simplification serves to explain the main features of the moral import of the feeling of sublimity, and it does not misrepresent Kant's theory. Although we have to assume that every rational being must possess the moral law, and all empirical, yet rational, beings must be capable of moral feeling, we also know that it certainly is not uncommon to act on maxims of prudence and even immediate desires rather than maxims of duty. We can assume most of us are motivated by some kind of self-oriented incentive rather than respect for the law in most of our actions.

If it is correct that we generally neglect the reality of the moral law and its claim on us, there is a possibility that the experience of the sublime could make us realise that our pattern of action is inferior to an autonomous one. This would be a case in which the feeling of the sublime, by reminding us of our true vocation, prepares the ground for a change in the maxims on which we act, from selfish, prudential maxims to moral ones. In this way this feeling can contribute to the moral equivalent of a religious conversion. Is this a plausible account of the way we can be morally affected by the sublime? Kant's almost religious rhetoric when talking about the moral law, and his description of the emotional effect of the sublimity of these abstract ideas suggests that a theory along these lines is reasonable (see KpV 77 and KU§29, 274 f).

What is required for a moral conversion theory is that man's moral character be able to be changed, not gradually, but more or less over night. In an Aristotelian theory of character this would be impossible because of the central role ascribed to habituation as a basis for rational deliberation[23]; our character is formed from early childhood into a stable state consisting of patterns of habits. Such states are acquired gradually, and have to be changed likewise. Kant's theory has an element allowing him to escape this conclusion, and that is the crucial role played by the autonomy of the legislative will. Although habits and conventions do affect our pattern of action, we still are free to disregard those influences and choose respect for the law instead. Kant states that even the worst scoundrel (as long as he has the habit of using reason) would wish to be able to follow good maxims rather than those based on his inclinations (G, 454)[24]. Aristotle too, would admit the possibility of the person of bad character being able to acknowledge the superiority of the good to some extent and to act on it, but would still hold that there is a point of no return in the development of bad character, disallowing any change to the better[25].

What is more important, however, is that the basis for action according to the Aristotelian conception is not the will but the character developed over the course of years, meaning that there is no absolute point of reference from which to test these habits. The ideals and the heroes one is raised to admire, become the final points of reference for the rational deliberation on how to act and who to be. If one's upbringing is focused on enjoyment and pleasure, there is no ground for the change of habits through insight into the greatness of the life of contemplation,

---

23 Aristotle, *Nicomachean Ethics*, 1103a14-b25.

24 In a footnote to the *Metaphysik der Sitten* he says that there is no human being so depraved as not to feel opposition when breaking the inner law (MS 380). In Religion he says that it is possible to overcome even the wickedness of the heart, where the incentives arising from the moral law are subordinated to non-moral incentives. (R 30, 37). Thus Kant emphasises very clearly the universal character of moral feeling; implying that insanity is the only way this feeling can be erased from human consciousness.

25 Aristotle, *Nicomachean Ethics*, 1114a13-21.

preferred by the schools of Plato and Aristotle. The character is based on custom (*êthos* meaning both custom and character in Greek[26]), and the good that one is to strive for is exemplified and determined by the character of the excellent (*ho spoudaios*). The fact that generally accepted opinion (*endoxa*) furnishes the premises of the dialectical discussion that determines what characterises the excellent and thus the paradigmatic example of good character, is a further indication of the close connection between custom and individual character[27]. There is no absolute principle in this ethical theory making possible a test of the underlying principles decisive for the character[28]. This again means that character can only be gradually altered, because you stand on the boat while you rebuild it. What is to be changed is the very thing that is the basis for the change, which means it can only be radically altered over a long time, and if the basic habituation has been wrong, there is little hope for a change towards the good.

Kant's conception of character allows such radical or profound changes because man has the tool for an evaluation of the underlying principles of his character in the absolute character of the moral law, expressed in the categorical nature of the imperatives grounded in this law, i.e. in man's rationality. This allows for more than gradual cultivation of character through the contemplation and admiration of this law. His theory allows for a sudden realisation that the maxims one is living by fall short of this ideal. Such a realisation could result in the reevaluation of the life one is leading and its basis, due to the accepted superiority of living according to the law of rationality rather than by laws made on the basis of natural inclinations. This again could be followed by a rejection of the maxims guiding life thus far, and the adoption of maxims where other incentives are subordinated to respect for the moral law[29]. This conversion could also take the

---

26 Liddell and Scott, *Greek-English Lexicon*, 303.

27 Main sources for this interpretation are Aristotle's *Topica*, I,i, *Nicomachean Ethics*, 1140a25-b27, and 1176a16-20.

28 Aristotle's theory is based on a certain conception of what a man is, giving a theoretical foundation for deciding the best human life, but this cannot give a non-relative basis for evaluating one's own character and practices. Life has to be realised in concrete action, and here only practical wisdom (*phronêsis*) can decide what is best. But *phronêsis* is based on character. Although there is a best human life, this can only be assessed from within that very same life, because the cognitive ability needed for the assessment is based on good character. This does not imply that there are several such 'best lives'; only that there are no outer criterion for testing one's life.

29 The religious conversion is well-known through examples as St. Paul, St. Francis of Assisi, and Siddhata Gotama, who became the Buddha. Moral conversions is found in literary characters as Scrooge in Dickens' *A Christmas Carol* (C. Dickens, *Christmas Books*, 5 ff.), and Raskolnikov in Dostoevsky's *Crime and Punishment*, 519 ff. A famous movie example is from *Casablanca*, where Rick's cynical slogan was "I don't stick my head out for nobody", but he chose to give up his love as well as his thriving

weaker form of being a wish to commit such changes in life, and a resolve to continue to let oneself be exposed to these ideals, with the gradual change of character in positive direction as the long-term result[30].

Frankfurt's concept of second-order desires is relevant here; second-order desires being desires concerning certain (first-order) desires.[31] This can be understood as some kind of evaluation of one's desires, and at the same time a self-evaluation. To rephrase it in Kantian terms, we can say that second-order desires are desires to adopt a certain set of maxims instead of the ones governing one's present life. Still, this seems barely sufficiently as a Kantian account. Desires usually are conceived of as inclinations, not rational motivations, and then they are incapable of having this second-order function within the framework of Kant's moral theory[32]. The main components of these second-order desires must be rational if we are to understand them as evaluative, as well as to account for their effect on adoption of maxims. This rational aspect is better captured within the Kantian context if we use the term 'second-order motivation' instead. Having such second-order motivation is, however, not sufficient for changing the pattern of desires. Although one has this motivation based on insight into the nature of the good, one often does not act on this second-order motivation, due to the strength of the established habits (compare G 454).

This weaker kind of conversion resulting in the motivation to acquire a new set of principles of action without actually changing anything in the way the subject acts, may not seem as much of a moral conversion, but it has some far reaching importance. First, it includes the adoption of a new hierarchy of values, or perhaps the reestablishment of a hierarchy earlier discarded, and the possibility of real change of character in the long run. When a person realises the demands of the

---

business to save the life of his rival who fought the good cause. (One could of course claim that this sacrifice showed his real character, and his earlier attitude was a pretence. There are also other possible ways to interpret his actions, for example that the reason for his sacrifices was his love for Ilsa, not respect for the good cause. At least this shows how difficult it is to know someone's motivation on the basis of their acts only.) Maybe an even better example of moral conversion (suggested to me by David Sussman) from the same movie is the police chief Renault, who acts in the same fashion throughout the story, and without changing his outer behaviour displays a real change of heart at the end.

30 Kant's theory of conversion contains both these elements. Conversion must be a timeless or, empirically speaking, instantaneous change of heart, but it is a gradual process of change of the empirical character. I return to this below.

31 The concept was introduced in H. Frankfurt, 'Freedom of the Will and the Concept of a Person'. My source is C. Taylor, *Human Agency and Language*, 15 f.

32 This is not a criticism of Frankfurt's account. The problem concerns only how to adjust his theory to a Kantian framework.

moral law, this will affect him emotionally both in action and in reflection on action. The range of moral feelings, including respect, conscience, and love, will exert their influence more effectively than when the awareness of duty is less clear. This can, in the long run, promote acting according to duty as effectively as can the cultivation of feelings resulting from the experience of the sublime described above. In this way there is not a sharp distinction between conversion and development of empirical character. Still, I will argue that the distinction is useful.

Character formation and conversion, the two main moral effects of the experience of the sublime, are based on certain contestable assumptions about Kant's moral theory. The basic assumption is that the Kantian moral theory emphasises the importance of moral character rather than merely focusing on rule-following, and that this character is constituted by a pattern of maxims rather than a pattern of habits. In short, I have to navigate between an interpretation holding that particular acts are the focus of Kant's moral theory, implying that the agent's deliberation is not seen as influenced by a variety of conditions, and an interpretation that habits are the major decisive factor in determining action, and allowing only gradual change of character. To develop this interpretation, I have to take a closer look at Kant's moral theory, guided by some recent interpretative works.

4. 4 Maxims and disposition

Maxims and character

Maxims are subjective principles of action, chosen by man's executive will (MS 226). Maxims can be in accord with or contrary to the moral law, and the same law can result in very different subjective principles (MS 225). Being human is connected to being rational in the practical sense, which means that each of us has to regard his or her acts as performed on the basis of some maxim. A maxim is not the same as what this person takes to be his intention, and he has no way of knowing for sure which principle he acts on "*weil die Tiefe des Herzens (der subjektive erste Grund seiner Maximen) ihm selbst unerforschlich ist*" (R 51).[33] This allows for a range of different maxims governing our actions without our being able to know our real motivation. We should be careful not to picture Kant

[33] O'Neill, *Constructions*, 130, says that we are opaque to ourselves since can never be sure the real basis of our actions.

as formulating some early version of psychoanalytic theory, though, because it is not as if we act on unconscious motives. The point is that we have no way of making sure that we act on the maxim we believe we act on.

It is also improbable that we in most circumstances consciously deliberate about which subjective principle to act on. In Herman's words:

> What I call moral deliberation is occasional, in the sense that something occasions it; moral judgment is routine. While all moral action requires moral judgment, we do not need to deliberate morally in order to act morally. We deliberate as a way of figuring something out.[34]

Normally we know what to do without having to reflect on right or wrong, and in these cases we need not be conscious of our maxim, nor be able to formulate it instantly. Being asked why we did something, we usually are able to produce a maxim, but the occasional problem of formulating it indicates that we did not deliberate on what to do prior to acting[35]. This indicates that we generally act on principles that we do not have to produce separately for each action, which supports O'Neill's interpretation of maxims as underlying principles. Deliberation is called for when we do not know what is the right action in the particular circumstances. The deliberation may concern both the principles we live by and how to realise these principles in life.

O'Neill makes clear that underlying principles are not rigid in the sense that they have to last for life; we are free to discard some of them and adopt new ones[36]. This is of course important for my interpretation of the moral effect of the sublime, because I argue that the sublime has its effect on one's general orientation rather than on single acts. There are, however, problems in claiming that the Kantian maxims must be such general, character-building principles only. Allison points out that some of Kant's examples of maxims seem to be formulated too

---

34 B. Herman, *The Practice of Moral Judgment*, 145.

35 The idea that freedom as spontaneity constitutes what it is to be a rational agent means that we have to presuppose that an agent acted on a maxim even when he is unable to state any. An agent can of course deny being aware that he has performed the deed, in which case the question of whether he was conscious or mentally sound at the time arises.

36 O'Neill, *Constructions*, 152. This is my interpretation of her claim that maxims are not "longer-term principles". Her choice of term for this claim may appear unsuitable. "Longer-term principles" cannot mean principles that we adhere to for a long period of time, because most of the principles we live by do that. A more reasonable interpretation is that maxims are principles that point beyond the nearest future, and are suitable for a lifetime. If I join a neo-nazi mob for two weeks before realising the morally rejectable principles that guide my conduct, the principles I live by for merely two weeks could have lasted for the rest of my life. Accordingly, I would say that maxims usually are longer-term principles but that these can be changed.

specifically to be called underlying principles[37]. Allison does not provide any examples, but a passage pointing in this direction might be the description of one of the maxims of deception in Grundlegung:

> wenn ich mich in Geldnot zu sein glaube, so will ich Geld borgen und versprechen, es zu bezahlen, ob ich gleich weiß, es werde niemals geschehen. (G 422)

This is certainly not an underlying principle, if that is supposed to be principles that contribute to self-understanding and character. The character would not be described as a money-borrowing-when-knowing-to-be-unable-to-repay kind, but as wilfully deceptive. We would use the borrowing as an example of the character, not as a description of a character trait. Kant calls this maxim a principle of self-love, which is the most general way of describing what kind of basic disposition is expressed in this maxim. And when he is describing how to test the morality of the maxim against the formula of universality of the categorical imperative[38], he concludes with an intermediate description:

> Denn die Allgemeinheit eines Gesetzes, daß jeder, nachdem er in Not zu sein glaubt, versprechen könne, was ihm einfällt mit dem Vorsatz, es nicht zu halten, würde das Versprechen und den Zweck, den man damit haben mag, selbst unmöglich machen, indem niemand glauben würde, daß ihm was versprochen sei, sondern über alle solche Äußerungen als eitles Vorgeben lachen würde. (G 422)

This is a description of a principle of deception, and fits well with an interpretation along the lines proposed by O'Neill.

But are the two other levels of generality described by Kant also maxims? The first is almost on the level of concrete action description, whereas the other names one of the two most general types of action motivation as we know them from the second Critique: respect for the moral law or self-love (KpV 74 ff). This most general formulation of the principle of the action is not a maxim in the ordinary sense, but rather a classification of that person's *Gesinnung*[39] into one of two

---

37 Allison, *Theory of Freedom*, 92 f.

38 In discussing maxims and the testing of them against the Categorical Imperative, the different formulas and their relevance for this test is a central problem. But since this is not a work primarily concerning Kant's moral theory, I shall assume his assertion of the equivalence of the formulas to be true, and that there are no problems in performing this test. An instructive discussion and solution to this problem is found in O'Neill, *Constructions*, 126 ff.

39 This concept has no good English equivalent. It means something like the most basic disposition, character, or temperament, understood as a ground for more specific attitudes and character traits and the choice of maxims. I will follow the tradition, and use 'disposition'.

kinds, good or evil (R 24). The first, action-specific, formulation certainly is more like a maxim, but the reason why I will reject it as a proper maxim is that the morally relevant feature of the action is captured in the description of wilful deception, not in the description of the act of promising to return borrowed money without intending to keep it. So the intermediate level of generality seems to be the best candidate for being described as the maxim we act on.

B. Herman argues that to single out underlying principles only for moral assessment has a serious drawback, in that this

> elides action and agent assessment in a way that ignores relevant particulars of deliberative activity. Where, for example, the moral problem with an action is incidental to the life-rule or underlying intention, it would not register in the agent's maxim and thus would be inaccessible to moral assessment.[40]

I understand her to be saying that if the agent fails morally and misapply her underlying principle, we are unable to assess this action if our assessment is only of maxims as underlying principles. I assume that the problem is not that the agent is unaware that the particular she ignores is a moral problem, i.e. that she does not recognise this as a morally salient feature of the act[41]. The problem is that the maxim is too general to capture these morally salient features of the act. This seems to be a serious objection if one thinks of underlying principles as one or a few unified rules. But then one presupposes that human character is not complex and contains different, to some extent contradictory, sets of underlying principles, which is what I will argue. Agents do not have just one underlying principle determining who they are, considered as empirical characters. Every agent has a range of such principles composing her character, and not all of these principles pull in the same direction. Some of them are regularly acted on, and these principles contribute to the dominant traits of the agent's character. But there are other principles she acts on in special circumstances, which do not influence her regularly. She may even act on these principles every time she has the chance, but she seldom encounters situations where the principles apply. Then we can say that she acts out of character, which I think is misleading. If she is conscious and mentally sound it is better to call it a flaw in her character, if we consider these principles to be bad. Still they are part of her overall character, in the sense that she must possess these underlying principles since she acts according to them.

---

40 Herman, *Moral Judgment*, 220.
41 Ibid. 77 ff.

Now this seems to contradict Kant's own description of human frailty, where the point appears to be exactly that the agent has an underlying principle of moral worth, which she fails to follow:

> Wollen habe ich wohl, aber das Vollbringen fehlt, d. i. ich nehme das Gute (das Gesetz) in die Maxime meiner Willkür auf; aber dieses, welches objektiv in der Idee (*in thesi*) eine unüberwindliche Triebfeder ist, ist subjektiv (*in hypothesi*), wenn die Maxime befolgt werden soll, die schwächere (in Vergleichung mit der Neigung). (R 29)

Apparently the agent has a maxim of moral worth, but the action, due to frailty, does not accord with this maxim. But on Kant's view, we cannot say that the action is not according to any maxim at all. If we are to understand an action as intentionally chosen, it must be an act on some maxim. Frailty describes a case where the agent does not act according to the most general maxim governing her life, which is her disposition, but on some other, more specified maxim that does not accord with this fundamental moral disposition. But this maxim she acts on is still regarded as one aspect of her character, as is frailty, although on a more general level. The empirical character of a human being is always complex and consists in many, partly conflicting principles[42].

The relationship between these conflicting underlying principles could be illuminated by an example: I usually pay for the bus ride to work because I think one should not cheat or steal. One day, as I am about to enter the bus, I discover that someone has stolen my wallet. Since I have an appointment with a student who is going to have an exam, I am in a hurry to get to work. I decide to catch the bus without paying (which is fairly easy). This act of cheating would certainly reveal a flaw in my character; it would not be a case of an inexplicable act contrary to the morally worthy principle which is defining my character. It would mean that my feeling of respect for the law had been thwarted by the feelings resulting from my need to get to work immediately and the internal arguments about the insignificance of the loss to the bus company. This again means that my underlying principle never to deceive had for once been replaced by another underlying principle of willingness to deceive for self-serving[43] purposes. But we cannot

[42] Kant draws a sharp distinction between intelligible and empirical character where the latter concerns how we appear to ourselves. Judged this way we are a mixture of good and evil, although that is impossible transcendentally regarded. (See R 24 f, note.)

[43] In this discussion I have disregarded the possibility that when I caught the free ride I acted on a morally worthy principle, but that is also a possibility. If I had promised the student to be there at a particular time my sole motivation for catching the free ride might have been this promise. In that case we apparently have a conflict of duty, something Kant claims is impossible (MS 224). Herman interprets this claim employing

conclude either that this does not express a real action-guiding principle inherent in my character, or that it shows that the only principle I live by is the one of self-interest. I performed the action, and it was based on a morally unworthy maxim, which tells that the maxim to deceive is also a part of my character. The fact that I usually act on a principle of non-deception motivated by respect for the law indicates that this is a more dominant action-guiding principle. But when assessing my character, we have to take into account that there are situations where a complex of motivations appears stronger than the feeling of respect, and I choose to act on a principle contrary to respect.

Despite this rejection of Herman's objection, there remains a problem with seeing maxims as underlying general principles of this kind, and that is the fact that Kant uses the word maxim also for 'action-specific' principles, as seen in the quotation above. This can be explained through two strategies: either by blaming it on Kant's imprecision in employing the word, or by Allison's suggestion that "one might think of maxims ... as arranged hierarchically, with the more general embedded in the more specific, like genera in species."[44] There are obvious advantages to this approach as an interpretation, because it is the one that allows for Kant's divergent uses of the term and it fits well with our conception of the complexity of moral judgement. Morality can be described on different levels of generality, each one bringing out salient features not easily discerned on the other levels. But even very specific descriptions of actions reveal the complex of underlying principles, if we think of maxims as a hierarchy with the more general embedded in the specific. Thus they also reveal the moral character of the subject.

Moral worth and disposition

What is the focus of moral evaluation? What are we really testing when we apply the Categorical Imperative? The rightness or the permissibility of the act, the moral worth of the underlying principle, or the character of the agent? One may

---

Kant's subsequent statement that what is in conflict are the *grounds* of obligation, when adopting a maxim. This results in the need for deliberation, in which one of the grounds are judged to be the strongest. The resulting maxim of action might result in new obligations (apologising for the promise that could not be kept, or apologising to the bus company and paying for the bus ride afterwards), but that is left for a new moral judgement or deliberation. My duty in the actual case is to act on the ground that is judged to be the strongest. If it is not in my power to satisfy both grounds of obligation, my obligation cannot include both. Herman, *Moral Judgment*, 164 ff.

44 Allison, *Theory of Freedom*, 93.

think that Kant's ethics, as a deontological theory, is concerned with whether the act I am about to perform is right or wrong, or, rather, permissible or not. But Kant stresses the importance of the attitude when acting, shifting the focus from the actual effect as well as the intention or purpose of the act to the motive:

> eine Handlung aus Pflicht hat ihren Wert nicht in der Absicht, welche dadurch erreicht werden soll, sondern in der Maxime, nach der sie beschlossen wird, hängt also nicht von der Wirklichkeit des Gegenstandes der Handlung ab, sondern bloß von dem Prinzip des Wollens, nach welchem die Handlung unangesehen aller Gegenstände des Begehrungsvermögens geschehen ist. (G 399)

The moral worth of the action is in the maxim, which means that we do well in turning our attention away from the deontological focus on the act itself[45]. Of course any action can be obligatory, permissible or impermissible (MS 223). When we are testing which of these categories an action falls into, we are concerned with the legality, not the morality of the act. (MS 219), i.e. we are concerned merely with its conformity to law. Actions have moral worth when the incentive for action arises from the consciousness of the law itself, and that is something we only can discover by assessing the maxim.

The conclusion is that what we ascribe moral worth to, is the principles we act on, and these are expressive of our will. The basic question is whether my will is good, as we can see from the first lines of *Grundlegung* (G 393)[46]. This does not necessarily mean that the will is object of the moral assessment, and the worth of the maxim is secondary to the goodness of the will. Since the will is embedded in maxims, the one cannot be evaluated in isolation from the other. If my will is good, this is expressed in morally worthy maxims. As human beings our will is not

---

45 I do not imply that deontology necessarily means judging actions as right or wrong; Korsgaard in *Creating the Kingdom*, 291, talks about deontological reasons as absolute principles of action, independent of consequences. But I believe it is misleading to call Kant's theory deontological, because the word usually is associated with acting according to specific sets of rules. In this rejection of deontology as a description of the central aspects of Kant's theory, I follow the arguments of O'Neill in *Constructions*, 152 ff. and Herman in *Moral Judgment*, 208 ff. Still, Herman qualifies her rejection of the classification in admitting that Kant's theory could be called 'weak deontology', because it rejects value maximising and takes the "distinction between doing and allowing, or intending and foreseeing, to be morally significant". Ibid 210, note 5.

46 One may object that the fact that Kant starts out with the notion of a good will is no proof that this is fiundamental, because the exploration of this concept leads him to the concept of duty (G 397). My defence is that although the idea of a good will is contained in the notion of duty, morality still is first and foremost dealing with the question about what is good without conditions, and Kant's answer to that involves the idea of freedom in acting from respect for the moral law.

only good, which means that it is expressed in maxims that are morally unworthy as well as in worthy ones.

Kant says that we call a man evil because of his evil maxims, not his evil deeds (R 20). But we know that maxims cannot be observed, Kant continues, so we have to deduce an evil maxim from this act that is contrary to law. But the deduction leads us even further to "*einen in dem Subjekt allgemein liegenden Grund aller besondern moralisch-bösen Maximen*" (R 20). There is a similar ground for morally good maxims, too, and this basic moral tendency of mind is the disposition [*Gesinnung*] of the agent. The disposition is the most fundamental ground of all maxims, and, thus of all acts. This is not a natural disposition or habit, but a disposition originating in a free choice, which is necessary if the agent is to be held accountable for the maxims based on this disposition (R 20 f). The paradoxical result is that we not only are responsible for our character, in the sense that we affirm the habits and values we have been taught, but in the sense that the character is our own free choice independent of natural dispositions and acquired habits. Such a free choice cannot be what we usually mean by character, which includes all habits and preferences, many of which are morally insignificant (at least within a Kantian moral conception).

Kant clearly states that man himself is the originator [*Urheber*] of this moral character, but then undermines that statement by adding that we must imagine this disposition to be present at birth (R 21 f), implying that this is "a timeless act of selfconstitution"[47], to use the words of Allison. This is not to be taken as a metaphysical claim, but as a statement of how an agent must think of himself. If the maxim I act on is freely chosen, the general disposition to choose that maxim must also be my own free choice. If not, the maxims would only be free relative to the options possible within a disposition I could not be responsible for. My freedom would be very restricted.

The disposition is the most fundamental ground for adoption of maxims. All maxims are motivated by one of two main types of motivation; respect for the law or self-love. These motivations have an emotional component, and express an agent's general attitude towards morality. If her respect for the law has the necessary motivational force, her general attitude is dominated by awareness of the demands of the moral law. If self-love is chosen as superior motive rather than the feeling of respect, the disposition is one in which the demands of the law are subordinated to self-love. Since all maxims can be classified according to their motivational source, they also tell something about the disposition or the character

47 Allison, *Theory of Freedom*, 137.

(in a restricted sense) of the agent. Because maxims are not independent of the disposition of the agent, we cannot suppose them to be the fundamental expression of freedom. They are chosen by an agent, and the agent is not constituted by this one maxim, but must be seen as its source. Thus the disposition of the agent must be regarded as the foundation of the maxim. A morally good maxim must originate from a good disposition, and generally an evil maxim must have an evil disposition as its ground, although there are exceptions to this[48].

This sounds reasonable, but it seems to lead to the unreasonable conclusion that if I do one good deed, i.e. a deed motivated by respect for the law, I am a virtuous person and all my maxims must be good. This does not correspond well with experience, and destroys the basic assumption in my example above, namely that a person who usually shows respect for the moral law, can in given circumstances act contrary to it, without changing his fundamental disposition. The day after acting contrary to law, the free rider again pays the bus fare because it is the right thing to do, as he usually does. Human beings are neither wholly good nor wholly bad, and Kant's theory on the disposition of man is sensitive to such moral ambiguity. Kant does, however, avoid the problematic conclusion that the act expresses the basic disposition.

Mankind is by nature good, or it has certain predispositions [*Anlagen*] for good, which includes (1) inclinations towards self-preservation, procreation, and community, (2) the rational ability to deliberate on how to satisfy inclination, which enables a judgement of my happiness as compared with that of other men, and (3) the receptivity for respect for the moral law, i.e. the ability to act rational motivated by rationality (R, 26ff)[49]. This shows that inclinations and self-love are taken by Kant to be good by nature[50], which means that the traditional interpretation of doing the good as a struggle to subdue our natural inclinations is misleading[51]. But the two first predispositions can be used contrary to their end, which means that they are employed to evil purposes.

---

48 Sometimes a good disposition results in bad maxims. The maxim to punish children physically when they behave badly may stem from a good disposition combined with faulty psychology.

49 Kant insists in a footnote that this moral law is not contained in the idea of rationality as such. Our executive will could be imagined as always needing some inclination to motivate action, i.e. that as rational we could still be unaware of the moral law as the highest incentive (R 26). The idea of morality cannot be deduced from the fact of practical rationality.

50 Self-love must always be under the control of reason to be good, though. Hence it is what Kant terms rational self-love that is good, not self-conceit (KpV 73).

51 Allison reads this as expressing a certain change in Kant's conception of the inclinations, which Kant saw as obstacles to good acts in the earlier moral works, see ibid. 149.

Evil is a human propensity (*Hang*), and is, unlike the predisposition for the good, to be regarded as acquired (R 28 f)[52]. Evil is not to be found in a desire to break the law, i.e. it is not a pleasure in acting contrary to the moral law, which is a devilish trait (R 35). The nature of evil is not to be found in a wish to do evil, nor in a blind adherence to man's animal nature, but in the way the maxim is structured:

> Also muß der Unterschied, ob der Mensch gut oder böse sei, nicht in dem Unterschiede der Triebfedern, die er in seine Maxime aufnimmt (nicht in dieser ihrer Materie), sondern in der Unterordnung (der Form derselben) liegen: welche von beiden er zu Bedingung der anderen macht. Folglich ist der Mensch (auch der beste) nur dadurch böse, daß er die sittliche Ordnung der Triebfedern, in der Aufnehmung derselben in seine Maximen umkehrt. (R 36)

A disposition is evil, not because the incentive to act according to the moral law is absent, but because it is subordinated to other incentives. The moral order would be the other way around, securing the moral law the upper hand. In this account of good and evil, Kant clearly shows that respect for the law must always be present in human acts, although its presence might always be as subordinated to the other incentives in the maxim. Since we have a predisposition for the good, our maxims are always related to respect for the moral law in one way or another. Acting means rationally deciding what to do on the basis of the present incentives. Among these we necessarily find respect for the moral law as an inherent trait in human nature (MS 399). The decisive question is whether respect is given the upper hand. In the opposite case, we act on incentives that are good in themselves, but serve evil because they are given more weight than respect for the law in the maxim we act on. Our propensity for evil is shown in a free choice of subordinating what we know is right to what we wish for ourselves or other people we care about[53].

As human beings we have this natural predisposition for the good, but also the propensity for evil, which, even though it must be regarded as freely acquired, is a

---

52 When evil is thought of as acquired, we can never escape our responsibility for these acts. Likewise the predisposition we have for the good consists of two elements that can be employed contrary to the good, and one element that is merely a receptivity to the good, all of which renders us free to choose, and responsible.

53 I am not implying that our personal relationships with people should be of no concern to us. Love for others make us pursue goals that are valuable. It is right to act on feelings for those close to us. But they lose value if they make us act contrary to morality. Wanting the best education for my daughter is good, but not if I bribe some corrupt teacher to alter her exam grade in order to secure her a place at the best university. My interest in her well-being should not outweigh moral considerations. For an illuminating discussion of this problem, see Herman, *Moral Judgment*, 41 ff.

part of human nature. Mankind as a species is evil (R 32) although we are, as we saw above, good from nature. This evil is radical, in the Latin sense of being rooted in human nature (R 37). But it is still possible for us to act on morally good maxims, indicating a good disposition. Although mankind as such is evil, we are not doomed to evil maxims, just like our predisposition for good does not guarantee that our maxims are good. Kant does explicitly reject these implications by distinguishing between the principles underlying human action and the empirical fact of these acts as performed by the single individual (see e.g. R 25 and footnote R 24 f). The propensity for evil is actually what secures our freedom and moral accountability[54]. Since the predisposition for respect is part of our inherent nature (which it must be if we are to explain the alleged fact of morality), freedom seems to disappear unless there is some reason for man not to give priority to the feeling of respect (something we know man does). Such reasons cannot be just that the incentives other than respect have a stronger force than respect, because that would leave us with a kind of stimulus-response model to account for maxims. The reason for us not always to act on respect for the moral law must lie in a free choice expressive of our character; i.e. we must have a freely chosen propensity for evil.

Now we can return to the question of character raised above. If I do a good deed, it must arise from a good disposition. Apparently a good disposition cannot result in evil deeds, and I must be incapable of such deeds. This is of course not Kant's conclusion, but he does not provide any clear account of how this is to be understood. It has often been pointed out that Kant's account of evil resembles Christian dogmas about man's evil nature. A comparison with St. Augustine's conception of evil can illuminate the relationship between disposition and character in Kant's theory. The Augustinian view on good and evil in the human will, as Coplestone paraphrases it, clearly foreshadows Kant's theory:

> The will itself is good, but the absence of right order, or rather the privation of right order, for which the human agent is responsible, is evil. Moral evil is thus a privation of right order in the created will.[55]

---

[54] The propensity for evil is of three kinds, frailty, impurity, and wickedness. The first is our failure to act on the good we have adopted in our maxim, the second the need for additional support from other incentives to do what duty requires, and the third the subordination of respect for the law to non-moral incentives (R 29 f). Perhaps only frailty is required to establish our freedom, but even frailty is described as a propensity for evil, and carries within itself the potential for wickedness.

[55] F. Coplestone, *A History of Philosophy, vol II*, 85.

This leads to the doctrine of the two cities, or the two basic character traits that dispose men towards or away from God (and the morally good). But these cannot merely be seen as dividing mankind into two separate groups, because the division goes through each person. In principle we belong to one or the other city, although we in reality have both traits struggling within us[56].

It is reasonable to ascribe a secularised version of this doctrine to Kant. Evil is inversion of the moral order, and although our disposition is good or bad in principle, we have both traits within us, and are capable of forming maxims from both kinds of disposition. A good maxim stems from a good disposition, but regarded empirically our disposition is never wholly good, although that is what we strive for. Neither is our disposition wholly bad either, since even the worst villain is influenced by moral feelings and is capable of reforming. Although a person's character has a main disposition, it is neither pure (be it good or evil), nor static.

Three kinds of maxims

A dualistic view of human action is the natural consequence of a theory of two basic kinds of dispositions. Morally worthy maxims stem from a good disposition, unworthy maxims stem from an evil disposition. The former maxims pass the test of the Categorical Imperative, whereas the latter ones fail the test. But not every action we perform is either good or bad, or at least that is not in keeping with common sense. I can choose to eat cereals for breakfast without deserving either praise or blame[57]. Kant is aware of this, as we see from the following passage:

> *Erlaubt* ist eine Handlung (licitum), die der Verbindlichkeit nicht entgegen ist; und diese Freiheit, die durch keinen entgegengesetzten Imperativ eingeschränkt wird, heißt die Befugnis (facultas moralis). Hieraus versteht sich von selbst, was *unerlaubt* (illicitum) sei. (MS 222)

Two dispositions result in three kinds of acts; obligatory, forbidden, and permitted. They are classified by the way their respective maxims relate to the categorical imperative, and thus the imperative functions as a test for maxims. If the maxim is such that I cannot will that it shall become a universal law, acting

---

56 Ibid.

57 Whether this line of action is permitted always seems to depend on the circumstances. If there is only one serving of cereals left, and the only alternative for breakfast is oranges, and the person I am having breakfast with is allergic to oranges, I ought to leave the cereals to him. I should eat oranges.

according to it is forbidden. If it does pass the test, it does not follow that the maxim is obligatory. That would lead to absurd consequences such as the obligation to pursue two mutually exclusive lines of actions simultaneously, since both pass the test. The maxims that pass the test must, accordingly, be permitted. A morally worthy maxim results in obligatory actions, and these are the ones that are opposite to the forbidden actions[58].

Now most actions do not have any opposite in the way for example hot is the opposite of cold, so maybe it is better to say that refraining from an impermissible act is obligatory: If I want a Rolex and lack the means to purchase it, I can just formulate the maxim of stealing and, seeing that it fails the test of universality, realise that I am obliged to refrain from taking what I want without paying. Although this is correct, it appears to be weaker than Kant's claim. We do not only have a duty to refrain from impermissible acts, but to act according to duty. But what kind of action that is obligatory depends on the circumstances, which means that this is a matter of judgement. This can be illustrated by another example: The maxim of honesty in business regardless of what I could gain from dishonesty and of my feelings about the person I am doing business with, has moral worth, and acting on it is obligatory. But being honest is not the same as disclosing all information in every case, such as letting the seller know the maximum amount I am willing to pay for a product in a situation of negotiations. So although the impermissibility of lying means that adopting a maxim of honesty is obligatory, the agent must still exercise judgement to decide how to apply this maxim in action.

Still this does not seem to answer all questions, because most of us go about our daily lives without encountering moral challenges on every street corner (or we believe we do not). But Kant's account of good and evil seems to require more than merely permissibility for an action not to be evil. The decisive question is which disposition is expressed in the maxim a person acts on, not in the passing of the moral test only. The previous discussion showed that having an evil disposition meant subordinating the moral motivation to the non-moral, which implies that also permissible acts can be morally evaluated. Apparently Kant does not think so in calling these permitted acts morally indifferent [*adiaphoron*] (MS 223), but his theory of disposition seems to negate that to a certain degree. Herman has provided a plausible account of this in her description of the motive of duty as a limiting condition for nonmoral motives:

> As Kant sees it, moral deliberation characteristically begins with a nonmoral interest or motive that prompts consideration of an appropriate course of

---

[58] See the discussion of this in Korsgaard, *Creating the Kingdom*, 60 ff.

> action. ... Once I am aware of what I want to do, I must consider whether it is morally permissible. If I have an effective motive of duty, I will act only when I determine that it is. I then act in the presence of more than one motive, satisfying both my nonmoral desire *and* the motive of duty.[59]

Here the motive of duty functions as a limiting condition, unlike in cases where it provides a sole motive for the action, and produces a morally worthy maxim. In the latter case I need not be nonmorally motivated at all. In the interpretation presented by Herman there is room for the inherent goodness in all our motivational sources, as described in *Religion*, because they are good as long as they are subordinated to the motive of respect for the moral law. These acts are regarded to be evil only when they are not limited by duty, i.e. by respect for the moral law.

Then we get the following picture of the relationship between the moral worth of maxims and the disposition of the agent in Kant's theory: An agent who is always conscious of the moral law will test the maxim he intends to act on against the Categorical Imperative. If his reason for pursuing the line of action is constrained by the passing of the test, his disposition is good. If he acts on the maxim regardless of the outcome of the test, or even without considering how the maxim fares when willed as universal law, his disposition is evil, even though his action is permissible. Only in the case when he acts *motivated* by respect for the law, not only constrained by it, is his maxim worthy. He can still have other motives for acting, but the moral motivation must in itself be decisive for acting, not merely constraining nonmorally motivated action. It is decisive in the sense that the agent would act on the good maxim not only if the nonmoral motive were absent, but even if some nonmoral motive opposed it. And the worth of the maxim increases with the strength of the opposing motivation[60].

4.5 Character, conversion and development

Kant's conception of character

Kant's conception of moral character can appear to be rather thin compared with traditional moral theories. If character merely deals with the choice between two basic dispositions that determine the maxims we act on, many idiosyncratic

---

59 Herman, *Moral Judgment*, 15.

60 I owe this interpretation of the relation between the motivation for action and the worth of the maxim to Thomas Pogge.

personal traits are irrelevant. Whether I am spontaneous, extroverted, and enjoy social gatherings, or reflective, silent, and solitary, is merely *adiaphoron*. It can be discussed to what extent this is a good or a bad aspect of his theory: it leaves room for moral goodness occurring in many forms, but at the same time excludes elements that are commonly regarded as morally important[61]. But when we turn our attention away from Kant's critique of practical reason to his actual theory of moral conduct, we face a different scenario.

The well-known examples from the *Grundlegung* of duties of beneficence, self-development, honesty, and refraining from suicide (G 422 f), show that this theory does have quite a lot to say about good states of character. Even more detail is added by the Metaphysics of Morals, as is shown by the following example where the argument is that we have a duty to behave nicely so as to promote good character in ourselves and others, even though the behaviour in itself only creates an illusion of virtue:

> Es ist zwar nur Scheidemünze, befördert aber doch das Tugendgefühl, selbst durch die Bestrebung, diesen Schein der Wahrheit so nahe wie möglich zu bringen, in der *Zugänglichkeit*, der *Gesprächigkeit*, der *Höflichkeit*, *Gastfreiheit*, *Gelindigkeit* (im Widersprechen, ohne zu zanken), insgesamt als bloßen Manieren des Verkehrs mit geäußerten Verbindlichkeiten, dadurch man zugleich andere verbindet, also doch zur Tugendgesinnung hinwirken; indem sie die Tugend wenigstens beliebt machen. (MS 473 f)

We do have a duty to be sociable to some extent; our social behaviour is not irrelevant to morality although duty does not prescribe a particular type of personality. An agent must find his own way to display these signs of reciprocity. The duty to fake virtue is not inconsistent with honesty because everybody knows it is just pretence, Kant thinks, and this is another Aristotelian aspect of his theory. By acting according to social rules, the real virtue is stimulated. The basic assumption in Aristotle's theory of moral education is that you yourself take on the moral character of your actions, and Kant's argument is related to this principle.

But Kant's emphasis on the spontaneity of the will prevents him from accepting the Aristotelian habituation theory, as we see from his rejection of habits that have the character of necessity, which makes them contrary to freedom (MS 407). A habit of always telling the truth is not tantamount to acting on a morally worthy maxim of truth-telling, and does not signify a good disposition. The habit of always helping others will almost certainly contradict duty in some cases, and is certainly not a moral habit. In this case, helping others has turned into an

---

[61] This is a common argument against Kant by neo-Aristotelians, see Nussbaum, *Fragility*, 5, note.

inclination, and the moral motive is always subordinated to this inclination in the maxim of the agent. Thus an evil disposition is displayed. This sounds unduly harsh, but it is an unavoidable consequence of Kant's basic assumption that the only good is a good will, and he has good reasons for this assumption. A habit that does not consist in principles, but is based on practice only, is vulnerable to new situations and new temptations (MS 383 f). If I help someone in distress because I feel sympathy for them, I risk refusing to help another because I do not feel the same way in his case, either because I do not like him, or because I do not like him enough, so my desire to go home and relax overpowers the feeling of sympathy. If my habit is to question what I could will should be a universal law, what I personally desire to do is checked by the answer to this question.

Kant is not hostile to the idea of habits as such, and values experience as necessary for achieving virtue:

> Die Tugend kann man also nicht durch die Fertigkeit in freien gesetzmäßigen Handlungen definieren; wohl aber, wenn hinzugesetzt würde, "sich durch die Vorstellung des Gesetzes im Handeln zu bestimmen", und da ist diese Fertigkeit eine Beschaffenheit nicht der Willkür, sondern des Willens, der ein mit der Regel, die er annimmt, zugleich allgemein-gesetzgebendes Begehrungsvermögen ist, und eine solche allein kann zur Tugend gezählt werden. (MS 407)

The 'habit' that is needed is the habit of choosing the idea of the universality of the law as the determining motive for action. This is not blind adherence to certain patterns of action (which is not Aristotle's idea of habit, either), but a continuous awareness of the claims of the moral law. One gets into the habit of evaluating one's proposed maxim in light of the categorical imperative, and this habit is the hallmark of a good disposition. Accordingly, the social fake virtues are ways of acting that support the duties associated with social life; being agreeable and showing tolerance and respect.

Kant conceives of character as having a core in the principle of freedom as autonomy, but this core must influence the character in a wider sense. Two general duties are derived from the requirements of the categorical imperative; to promote one's own perfection and the happiness of others (MS 385 f). There are two kinds of perfection, one natural and the other moral. The first kind illustrates that character in the wide sense is an essential part of morality, because we have a duty to develop our natural predispositions enabling us to realise whatever end we set ourselves, and thereby making ourselves human (MS 391 f). This is a wide obligation[62], which means that it does not prescribe particular acts (as for example the duty of truthfulness does) or to what lengths one should go in satisfying this obligation. This is left for one's judgement to decide. Both mentally and physically we have a duty to develop our natural talents, but the talents vary, as well as the situation one is born into, which means that there are no outer rules for how this is to be done (MS 444 ff).

Moral perfection requires developing the habit of being motivated by the law rather than the inclinations, which means strengthening the receptivity to respect for the law in us. This sounds like one single attitude, one virtue, but as we are empirical beings, acting from duty takes on different forms according to the position we are in:

> Was aber die Vollkommenheit als moralischen Zweck betrifft, so gibt's zwar in der Idee (objektiv) nur eine Tugend (als sittliche Stärke der Maximen), in der Tat (subjektiv) aber eine Menge derselben von heterogener Beschaffenheit. (MS 447)

The imperfect duty to self-perfection leaves room for a wide variety of possible characters, without making morality irrelevant. I can realise my humanity in many different fashions, according to what I like, what I am good at, what possibilities I have for education and work; but I have to strengthen my disposition for the good in this pursuit of happiness.

Added to this are the perfect duties towards oneself, such as avoiding excessive eating and drinking, allowing oneself necessary enjoyment, being truthful, having self-esteem, and similar action-guiding principles. Even several of these perfect duties leave ample room for judgement, showing more of the latitude accorded by Kant's theory, a latitude that still does not leave moral principles impotent, due to the procedure of testing maxims against the Categorical Imperative. Among these duties are also the ones to stimulate the right kind of natural feelings, those which serve morality, as is seen in the prohibition against cruelty towards animals:

> In Ansehung des lebenden, obgleich vernunftlosen Teils der Geschöpfe ist die gewaltsame und zugleich grausame Behandlung der Tiere der Pflicht des Menschen gegen sich selbst weit inniglicher entgegengesetzt, weil dadurch das Mitgefühl an ihrem Leiden im Menschen abgestumpft und dadurch eine der Moralität im Verhältnisse zu anderen Menschen sehr diensame natürliche Anlage geschwächt und nach und nach ausgetilgt wird … . (MS 443)

---

62 The distinctions between wide, narrow, imperfect, and perfect duties are not too clear in Kant's theory, and it is beyond the scope of this discussion to develop an acceptable interpretation of his theory on this subject. For an informative discussion, see T. E. Hill, *Dignity and Practical Reason*, 147 ff.

This shows Kant's awareness of the importance of cultivating our sympathetic feelings towards other living creatures because awareness of the suffering of others contributes to strengthening the moral feeling proper in us[63].

These sympathetic feelings are part of our natural inclinations related to other people, and we have a duty to share the feelings of others, which is regarded as a free act. And Kant says that we have an indirect duty to seek out places of human suffering in order to develop the sympathetic feelings (MS 457). The other duties of love (which is not to be understood as a feeling, but as a practical maxim) are duties of beneficence and gratitude. And Kant clearly states that we are free to judge how to fulfill these duties, and that we can choose to give priority to those closest to us without violating the universality of the maxim of benevolence (MS 452). The other part of our duties of others is according respect to others, due to their dignity as moral beings (MS 462).

These duties give a general direction for our moral development, i.e. for building character. For we cannot know how to adhere to these obligations without having experience and the knowledge about ourselves and others. In order to foster a good disposition, one which makes us act on moral motivation rather than other feelings, we can educate ourselves, studying nature and culture, and we can read poetry, listen to music, as well as indulge in other cultural activities. One of the elements contributing to this cultivation, which can be part of several of the activities mentioned above, is the experience of the sublime.

Kant's account of moral education supports my claim that acquiring a moral character involves development as well as conversion:

> [Die Tugenden] müsse durch Versuche der Bekämpfung des inneren Feindes im Menschen (asketisch) kultiviert, *geübt* werden; denn man *kann* nicht alles sofort was man *will*, wenn man nicht vorher seine Kräfte versucht, und geübt hat, wozu aber freilich die *Entschließung* auf einmal vollständig genommen werden muß; weil die Gesinnung (animus) sonst, bei einer Kapitulation mit dem Laster, um es allmählich zu verlassen, an sich unlauter und selbst lasterhaft sein, mithin auch keine Tugend (als die auf einem einzigen Prinzip beruhet) hervorbringen könnte. (MS 477)

Both development and conversion are needed to cultivate character, but there is one problem left here concerning conversion: the conversion Kant talks about is a transcendental "event", an act out of time.

---

[63] It is tempting to attribute to Kant a rudimentary theory of the importance of empathy as a kind of moral perception making us aware of the "weal and woe" of others, as developed in A. J. Vetlesen, *Perception, Empathy, and Judgment*, 215 ff. Vetlesen's traditional Kant-interpretation certainly does no justice to the role of moral feelings in Kant's moral writings, as is admitted and partly redressed in note 16, 369 f.

Empirical conversion

Cultivation of character is a gradual development and we do not perform good deeds on the basis of a conversion. In that respect we must think of the conversion as a principle behind every good deed. It is not as such an event in a person's history but a mysterious act of free will:

> Dieses ist nicht anders zu vereinigen, als daß die Revolution für die Denkungsart, die allmähliche Reform aber für die Sinnesart (welche jener Hindernisse entgegenstellt) notwendig und daher auch dem Menschen möglich sein muß. Das ist: wenn er den obersten Grund seiner Maximen, wodurch er ein böser Mensch war, durch eine einzige unwandelbare Entschließung umkehrt (und hiermit einen neuen Menschen anzieht) so ist er sofern dem Prinzip und der Denkungsart nach, ein fürs Gute empfängliches Subjekt; aber nur in kontinuierlichem Wirken und Werden ein guter Mensch … . (R 47 f)

Still, although this conversion is not something that has any direct effect on the shaping of character, and must be considered a timeless event, we must conceive of it as something that affects our self-conception and moral orientation in action. So although virtue is won through long and gradual improvement, and the conversion is only the principle underlying this, there must still be a link between the principle and our empirical character. Kant's theory must have room for an empirical aspect of the conversion. This is evident from his description of wickedness, or the corruption of the heart.

The gravest form of propensity for evil is the corruption or perversity of the heart, when the respect for the moral law has been subordinated to non-moral incentives (R 30). Kant emphasises that a man with a wicked heart and a man with a good heart may be indistinguishable by their conduct. What matters is their respective supreme maxims, i.e. whether the conformity to law is one of legality or one of morality. Only the latter is a case of good disposition, because he follows the spirit of the law rather than merely the letter. They both also act contrary to the law, the first due to wickedness, the latter due to frailty or impurity, or an maxim that has not included all morally salient features of the situation.

Now if conversion is possible, as Kant insists it is, this means that the way I think is changed. This change does not take place in time, Kant says, and is only cognisable by pure reason (R 31). Still this change of heart must affect our motivation for every single good act we perform as temporal beings. Even if a man never commits an evil act, we must still think of all his acts as resulting from a conversion from bad to good, because he has a natural propensity to evil (R 32) which is rooted in his nature (R 37). So even a man who always subordinates his nonmoral incentives to the respect for the moral law have to choose this subordination against his propensity for evil for every single act. This is an act of conversion, although each and every act he performs involves this subordination. He was good prior to this act, but the act is still conceived of as an act of conversion since he has a propensity for evil that he never can rid himself of.

But an empirical conversion must also be possible in the sense that at a certain point in time I freely choose to think differently about the way I act. Or, to weaken the claim: After this moment in time, I regard myself to be a person who used to act on what I found beneficial for myself and my beloved ones, and who now strives to do the right thing because it is right. This event is not an event in time in the sense that it is empirically caused. It is freely chosen, and as such only accessible to thought, but there is a change in my empirical character in the sense that my reasons for acting in conformity with the moral law is changed. My change of heart must affect me empirically in the way that I see myself as a new man in comparison with how I used to be, as we can see both from the quote above, and from this passage:

> Wenn aber Jemand bis zu einer unmittelbar bevorstehenden freien Handlung auch noch so böse gewesen wäre (bis zur Gewohnheit als anderer Natur): so ist es nicht allein seine Pflicht gewesen, besser zu sein; sondern es ist *jetzt* noch seine Pflicht, sich zu bessern: er muß es also auch können … . (R 41)

Although every act on a morally worthy maxim must presuppose conversion as a timeless act, conversion can also be a term for an event where there is a revolution in the way I arrange the incentives in my maxims. In this way can conversion also be thought of as an event in time.

The feeling of the sublime and cultivation of character

The sublime can contribute to the development towards moral perfection because it subordinates sensibility to reason, because it phenomenologically resembles the moral feeling of respect, and because it is a way we can admire the source of this feeling, as discussed above. These effects contribute to strengthening the respect for the moral law, and increase our tendency to structure our maxims according to the moral order, i.e. subordinate other incentives to the feeling of respect for the law. The feeling of the sublime also contributes by increasing our tendency to act on the perfect duties towards ourselves, by increasing our awareness of the supreme value of our autonomy as rational beings, which increases our wish to avoid degrading ourselves by not acting autonomously.

The feeling of the sublime can even strengthen our resolve to act on the duty to self-development, because increased awareness of the demands of the moral law leads to a related wish to realise moral perfection, which presupposes natural perfection. Our natural talents are the tools for freedom of action. An optimal development of these tools give us the widest range of options when deciding how to act, thus improving our abilities to act on morally worthy maxims. This claim must, however, be qualified, because Kant stresses the principle of "ought implies can", which means that I am not obligated to anything that I am unable to do. I assume that if I am able to do more, my obligations increase accordingly. Developing my natural talents increases my abilities, meaning that there is more I can do, and my duties increase accordingly. But my disposition does not necessarily improve, because my opportunities for acting contrary to respect for the law are also enhanced. Therefore developing natural talents is a duty. It can serve our moral perfection, but it need not serve it, since the possibility for transgressions increases, too. This is in keeping with the principle of spontaneous freedom. However much we strive to improve ourselves and the conditions for acting morally, each choice in itself is made under the principle of freedom, and can be evil. Still this does not alter the fact that the feeling of the sublime can be a motivating factor for seeking natural perfection as a duty.

On its own, the experience of the sublime can play a minor role only in this complex of factors contributing to the shaping of character. But it can play some role. Perhaps in some lives an insignificant one, while in others the decisive factor resulting in an empirical conversion. The important point is that this discussion has shown that it is possible to use Kant's aesthetic and moral theories to develop an account of the moral significance of the sublime. If we accept Kant's basic claims in his third Critique and in his moral works, the judgement of the sublime is not an aesthetic judgement only. The feeling of the aesthetic sublime can contribute to the improvement of moral character, through its connection with moral ideas and its similarity with the feeling of respect.

4. 6 The moral import of the beautiful and of the sublime

A brief comparison with how beauty may indirectly serve moral awareness may help to show the direct impact of the feeling of sublimity on man's moral development. Kant says that beauty is a symbol of morality, and by that he means that there is an analogy between the beautiful and the morally good. A symbol is the

> Übertragung der Reflexion über einen Gegenstand der Anschauung auf einen ganz anderen Begriff, dem vielleicht nie eine Anschauung direkt korrespondieren kann. (KU§59, 351).

For example, an animated body can symbolise a constitutional monarchy and a hand mill can symbolise a despotic state. (KU§58, 352) It is the way we think about these objects that is similar or analogous, not anything about the objects themselves. In the first example we think of the rules or principles of the monarchy as internally just as we do for a purposively arranged living organism. In the latter example there is an external will determining the rules. So when beauty is the symbol of morality this means that there is an analogy between the ways we reflect on judgements of beauty and on moral judgements. Kant mentions four points of analogy:

> 1. Das Schöne gefällt *unmittelbar* (aber nur in der reflektierenden Anschauung, nicht, wie Sittlichkeit, im Begriffe). 2. Es gefällt *ohne alles Interesse* (das Sittlich-gute zwar notwendig mit einem Interesse, aber nicht einem solchen, welches vor dem Urteile über das Wohlgefallen vorhergeht, verbunden, sondern welches dadurch allererst bewirkt wird). 3. Die *Freiheit* der Einbildungskraft (also der Sinnlichkeit unseres Vermögens) wird in der Beurteilung des Schönen mit der Gesetzmäßigkeit des Verstandes als einstimmig vorgestellt (im moralischen Urteile wird die Freiheit des Willens als Zusammenstimmung des letzteren mit sich selbst nach allgemeinen Vernunftgesetzen gedacht). 4. Das subjektive Prinzip der Beurteilung wird als *allgemein*, d.i. für jedermann gültig, aber durch keinen allgemeinen Begriff kenntlich vorgestellt (das objektive Prinzip der Moralität wird auch für allgemein, d.i. für alle Subjekte, zugleich auch für alle Handlungen desselben Subjekts, und dabei durch einen allgemeinen Begriff kenntlich erklärt). (KU§59, 353 f)

These four points cannot be taken to be independent and equally important ways of using beauty to symbolise morality, because the agreeable and empirical objects would then be suitable symbols of morality as well. The agreeable is liked directly, just as the beautiful is, and empirical judgements about objects of nature also contain a claim to universal validity. These analogies are not sufficient to turn the agreeable or empirical objects in general into symbols of morality. Presumably it is the combination in one judgement of all these four points that is decisive for the symbolic function of beauty.

Still it is not likely that these four points are equally important for the symbolic function of beauty. Clearly, the idea of freedom is the focal point in Kant's account. Guyer has pointed out two main ways in which beauty is a symbol of autonomy:

> Reversing the order of Kant's exposition, we may see him as saying, first, that the relationship between the freedom of the imagination and the lawfulness of the understanding which is the essence of the experience of beauty symbolizes the preservation and maximization of freedom both intra- and interpersonally by means of governance which is the positive essence of morality, and, second, that the naturally gratifying effect of the harmony between imagination and understanding on sensibility which is the explanation of the pleasure of aesthetic response symbolizes the ideal of achieving a harmony between reason and inclination … .[64]

Thus the freedom of acting in harmony with the law is the centre of the analogy, and without this focus, the similarities noted on the other points can be said to be neutralised by the differences Kant also points out. It is this connection between freedom and law that makes beauty a more suitable symbol than other, more anarchic, instances of freedom, such as the freedom in the movements of a butterfly.

It is important to stress in what way beauty serves as symbol. There is no link to morality in the judgement of beauty itself. It is only when we reflect on the characteristics of this judgement that we are able to discover the points of analogy between beauty and morality. Beauty can only function as a symbol in situations where we think or talk about beauty and morality, not in the actual aesthetic judging of a beautiful object. Here we find the major difference between the moral significance of beauty and sublimity. The pleasure of beauty is not founded on moral ideas and it is not connected to an expression of such ideas. The feeling is phenomenologically distinct from the moral feeling of respect, and cannot serve as a way of admiring the inscrutable source of the moral feeling. It involves no adjustment of sensibility to the demands of reason, either[65]. So when Kant talks about beauty as a symbol of morality, this does not indicate any moral content to the judgement of taste itself.

---

64 P. Guyer, 'The Symbols of Freedom in Kant's Aesthetics', 347.

65 Guyer points out as one aspect of the symbolic function of beauty the fact that it pleases immediately and thus illustrates the ideal of humanity as including the "*harmony* between duty and inclination" (Ibid. 349). It is, however, important to note that in morality this harmony is acquired through the adjustment of sensibility to the demands of reason, which means that this aspect of beauty as symbol stands in contrast to the free harmony between imagination and understanding displayed in beauty. In the first case, sensibility conforms to law, in the latter, the faculties of sensibility and concept harmonise freely.

This is not to say that the judgement of beauty has no direct connection with morality. My claim is merely that this moral connection is not found in the symbolic function of beauty. There is one section where Kant suggests some such connection, though. He seems to claim that beauty's symbolic function is the basis for the universality claim in the judgement of beauty:

> Nun sage ich: das Schöne ist das Symbol des Sittlich-guten; und auch nur in dieser Rücksicht (einer Beziehung, die jedermann natürlich ist, und die jedermann anderen als Pflicht zumutet) gefällt es mit einem Anspruche auf jedes anderen Beistimmung, wobei sich das Gemüt zugleich einer gewissen Veredlung und Erhebung über die bloße Empfänglichkeit einer Lust durch Sinneneindrücke bewußt ist und anderer Wert auch nach einer ähnlichen Maxime ihrer Urteilskraft schätzt. (KU§59, 353)

Apparently Kant says that only in the light of the symbolic relation between beauty and morality, which we demand from everyone as a duty, does the beautiful please with a demand for universal assent. This is very problematic because it seems to replace the epistemological justification for the judgement of taste by one connected to the function of beauty as a symbol for the morally good. Even more problematic is this as Kant, as we saw above, mentions the claim to univeral validity as one of the factors in the symbolic function of beauty. The result is a vicious circle, where beauty is a symbol partly due to the intersubjective validity of the judgement of the object, and the judgement is intersubjectively valid due to the symbolic function of beauty. In addition, Kant nowhere provides a justification for the claim that this symbolic relation between beauty and morality must be recognised by all.

An alternative reading of the passage cited above may make Kant's connection between beauty and morality more in keeping with the account of taste in the Analytic. When Kant says "*...nur in dieser Rücksicht (einer Beziehung...)*" he may refer to the relation between beauty and morality in general, rather than the symbolic relation between them in particular. This is also the implication of Pluhar's liberal interpretation of this passage:

> Now I maintain that the beautiful is the symbol of the morally good; and only because we refer [*Rücksicht*] the beautiful to the morally good (we all do so [*Beziehung*] naturally and require all others also to do so, as a duty) does our liking for it include a claim to everyone else's assent … .[66]

[66] Pluhar's translation of *The Critique of Judgment*, 228. The additions in the text are Pluhar's own. This indicates the distance between the original and the translation in this particular case.

The point here is that some kind of reference to morality is involved in the justification of the universality demand in the judgement of taste. It is not the symbolic relation between the two phenomena that is the “only” reason for the claim to everybody’s assent in our pleasure in the beautiful, but the fact that there is a relation independent of this symbolic relation. This solves the problematic circularity in the symbolic relation between beauty and morality, but it does not solve the problem of connecting this passage to the analysis and deduction of judgements of taste. My suggested solution to this problem requires a look at another related passage in the Dialectic and comparison of this with the interpretation suggested in chapter 2.

The solution to the antinomy of taste involves a relation between taste and morality. Kant says that the judgement of taste is based on the indeterminate concept of the supersensible substrate of appearances (KU§57, 340 f). Prior to that he also indicates that the basis of the judgement may lie in the supersensible substrate of humanity. This squares well with the interpretation based on Pluhar’s translation of the problematic passage concerning beauty as a symbol of morality: if the judgement of taste is based on an indeterminate concept of the supersensible substrate of humanity, this must mean that the universality demand in judgements of beauty has a necessary reference to morality. The supersensible substrate of humanity must necessarily be connected to man’s vocation, which is moral autonomy.

I do not think that the moral turn of the Dialectic means that Kant gave up the epistemological grounding of the judgement of taste. The connection of the judgement of taste to the supersensible ground of appearances and the supersensible ground of humanity can be explained within the interpretative frame I have developed in chapter two. The antinomy that is presented in the Dialectic is that a judgement of taste on the one hand must refer to a concept since it contains a claim to universal validity, but on the other hand cannot refer to a concept since we cannot discuss this kind of judgement (due to its subjectivity) (KU§56, 338 f). The solution is that the word concept is used in different ways in these two theses. There is some concept involved because judgements of taste issue a demand to universal validity for themselves. This concept cannot be one of understanding, though, because then the claims of taste could be argued. The concept must be an indeterminable one of reason (KU§57, 339 f).

We have seen that the universality demand in taste is connected to this judgement as a feeling of the proportionate attunement of the cognitive powers in free play. The attunement of the faculties is based on the form of purposiveness of an object, because it is the subjective aspect of an objective judgement according to purposes, i.e. a teleological judgement. The principle of the purposiveness of nature is a principle contained in judgements of taste and is guiding teleological judgement. But still this is a principle that is indeterminable because we can provide no adequate intuition for it (KU§57, 340). This principle merely expresses the presupposition that nature is a purposively arranged system. The application of the idea of purposiveness to concepts in teleological judgements fails to connect an adequate concept to the given intuition. But the idea of a purposively arranged system as well as the teleological judgement of the totality of nature (KU§67, 379) carries with it the idea of an ultimate purpose of nature, which is man as an end in himself (KU§83-84, 431 ff).

This means that the autonomy of man as a moral being is the unconditioned we are led to when reflecting under the principle of the purposiveness of nature. The judgement of taste issues a universality demand due to its function as the subjective basis for judgements according to purposes. But these judgements carry with them the idea of nature as a purposively arranged totality, which ultimately is connected to the realisation of man's purposes as a moral being. The supersensible substrate of humanity must be understood as the realisation of the highest good, i.e. of morality (KrV 119). Thus this principle also must be related to the supersensible basis of appearances, because the idea of purposiveness must necessarily refer to the ultimate end of this purposive system.

We see from this short analysis of the relation between judgement of taste and morality that the connection between these two kinds of judgement are indirect. It is only because the idea of purposiveness is contained in judgements of taste and this idea leads us to the idea of moral freedom, there is a relation between morality and taste. This indirect relationship is the basis for the main aspects of the function of beauty as a symbol. Thus the symbolic function of beauty is not the basis for the universality demand in taste. The conclusion is that both the moral foundation of taste as layed out in the dialectic and the symbolic function of beauty, indicates that the connection between taste and morality is merely indirect. It is only when reflecting on the basis of the judgement of taste we can discover its partly hidden link to morality. One can even say that this connection is difficult to discover without a critique.

Likewise, we do not discover the symbolic function of morality merely by being exposed to beautiful objects. Although Kant says that this is a common way of regarding objects, the examples he gives of how we express this analogy is hardly convincing as regards its usefulness:

> Wir nennen Gebäude oder Bäume majestätisch und prächtig, oder Gefilde lachend und fröhlich; selbst Farben werden unschuldig, bescheiden, zärtlich

> genannt, weil sie Empfindungen erregen, die etwas mit dem Bewußtsein eines durch moralische Urteile bewirkten Gemütszustandes Analogisches enthalten. (KU§59, 354)

As evidence for the connection between beauty and morality, this weakens rather than strengthens Kant's case. First of all, these concepts used by Kant exemplifies a very wide notion of morality; much wider than the rather narrow idea of morality as freedom from inclinations under rational laws indicated in the four points of the analogy. In addition, the concepts are derived from our sensations rather than from a disinterested contemplation with an ensuing reflection on the object in question. Furthermore, the characterisation of the buildings and trees as majestic and magnificient is clearly related to sublimity rather than to beauty. Even more problematic is the description of the colours as innocent, modest and tender, which recalls Kant's discussion of whether colours can be subject to a pure judgement of taste. Apparently Kant's conclusion was that colours are an agreeable addition of charm to the proper object of the judgement of taste (KU§14, 224 ff). The implication is that pure colour cannot be a free beauty and is unsuitable as a symbol, since the judgement of it does not involve freedom, universality, or disinterestedness. In fact, all we are left with from Kant's examples of beauty as symbol of morality is the cheerful and gay plains. So, if one is able to imagine cheerful plains, and one chooses to regard cheerfulness as a concept relevant for Kantian morality[67], one has at least one example of beauty as a symbol of morality. The inadequacy of these examples indicates how little importance Kant ascribed beauty as a symbol of morality.

In the preceding discussions I have attempted to show that judgements of taste refer to the unconditioned indirectly, whereas those of sublimity are directly connected to the unconditioned. Beauty is connected to morality as a symbol, which means that the moral significance of beauty is not found in the judgement, but in our reflection on the judgement. Thus the moral significance of this judgement is merely indirect. The moral significance of the sublime on the other hand, is in the judgement itself. Merely judging a sublime object aesthetically is morally significant because it stimulates our reflection on moral ideas, and makes us susceptible to the moral feeling of respect. The pleasure in beauty has no such direct moral influence, and the moral function of beauty is not even a necessary part of the judgement of taste (although its moral basis is). An indication of the

---

67 Cheerfulness may presumably be included among the the virtues of social intercourse, which plays a peripheral role in Kant's moral system as a short appendix to the Doctrine of Virtue (MS, 473f).

relatively modest moral importance of beauty as a symbol is the fact that it plays no role in Kant's moral works, and the reason is clear:

> Hieraus folgt, daß das intellektuelle, an sich selbst zweckmäßige (das Moralisch-) Gute, ästhetisch beurteilt, nicht sowohl schön als vielmehr erhaben vorgestellt werden müsse, so daß es mehr das Gefühl der Achtung (welches den Reiz verschmäht) als der Liebe und vertraulichen Zuneigung erwecke; weil die menschliche Natur nicht so von selbst, sondern nur durch Gewalt, welche die Vernunft der Sinnlichkeit antut, zu jenem Guten zusammenstimmt. (KU§29, 271)

Beauty is pleasant and lovely, and although it is elevated above the agreeable, it is still directly connected to sensible nature only, not to the supersensible. Therefore it has merely a symbolic function that can influence only in a minor degree our susceptibility to respect for the moral law.

Guyer argues that the moral significance of beauty is greater than that of the sublime. His claim is based on two mistakes. The first is that he assumes that the sublime also functions as a symbol of morality[68]. But Kant explicitly says that in the experience of sublimity we *feel* a power to resist nature within ourselves. The sublime can also function as a symbol (as indicated in the examples of majestic and magnificent trees and buildings), but that is not a possibility Kant elaborates. It would probably be less suitable as symbol than beauty, both because it already is directly connected to morality, which makes it a confusing symbol, and because it represents no harmony between freedom and law. Guyer's second mistake lies in his claim that the sublime "is a symbol of our freedom merely negatively conceived"[69]. This means that the sublime shows the freedom of the will as independent from other causes than itself, but not that this freedom consists in adherence to the moral law. Guyer argues that Kant in the exposition of the dynamically sublime does not refer to practical reason. But when Kant talks about the feeling of the sublime as revealing our mind's vocation, our intellectual ability, as elevated above nature (KU§28, 262) it is difficult to see what that could mean unless this is also connected to lawfulness. And in the next section this feeling is even said to have reference to practical reason (KU§29, 267). Unless the idea of autonomy as the ability to self-legislation is presupposed, we cannot experience the sublime.

In short, the sublime has a greater moral significance than beauty because (1) it is directly connected to a reflection on moral ideas, (2) it stimulates the cultivation of moral feeling, (3) it involves an aesthetic appreciation of the inscrutable ground

---

68 Guyer, 'Symbols of Freedom', 342 f.
69 Ibid. 342.

of this feeling, and (4) it represents a subjectively necessary connection between aesthetic judgement and morality.

5. The sublime in art and literature

Before I can apply my Kantian account of the moral significance of the sublime to my interpretation of Beckett's *Molloy*, I need to analyse one last major area of Kant's aesthetic theory: his theory of art. My interpretation of Kant's theory of aesthetic reflective judgement consists of two major components: (1) The disinterested feeling claiming its own universal validity must be regarded as the subjective aspect of the cognition of an object of nature, and (2) the basis for the claim to universal validity is the necessity of judging objects under the principle of purposiveness in order to supplement determinative judgements under the categories of understanding. Judgements of taste are based on the feeling of a mental state which is a subjective condition of cognition of an object as a totality and of the interrelations between objects. The judgement of sublimity is a special kind of aesthetic reflective judgements, one which concerns objects that are not subsumed under the principle of the purposiveness of nature, but under the principle of the purposive use of nature for man's freedom as a rational subject.

My discussion starts with the problem of how to apply the principles for judging nature to intentionally created artifacts. Since art is an intentional product, it is purposive, but that does not mean that we can judge it reflectively under a principle of the purposiveness of nature. This principle guides reflective judgements of nature under the hypothetical assumption of its purposive arrangement. Judgements about real intentions are determinative. To explain how these objects also can be subject to aesthetic reflective judgements, Kant's perspective changes from the question of how the subject judges the object to how the object is produced. His answer is that these objects do have non-intentional aspects that must be judged reflectively. Judging these aspects requires that we regard art as if it were nature, i.e. as non-intentionally produced, but we must still be aware of its artificial origin.

We are justified in judging fine art this way, Kant claims, because the non-intentional aspects have their source in a natural talent called genius. Genius is a natural disposition over which the artist has no rational control, and through which nature gives the rule to art. Thus genius produces exemplary works. Genius is the ability to express aesthetic ideas. I understand aesthetic ideas to be those aspects of a representation of an object (either of art or of nature) that give rise to the free play of the cognitive powers. Thus aesthetic ideas are the products of the activity of imagination. They give rise to many thoughts, Kant says, and I argue that these ideas enable us, in the objective aspect of the reflective judgement, to find a concept for the object. Every work of fine art is an intentional product, and having genius is not sufficient to become an artist. One must also be able to present aesthetic ideas in a suitable way. That requires 'academic' training in the appropriate skills combined with the use of taste to refine the work. In this chapter, I argue that for the creation of sublime works of art, not only genius, trained skills, taste, but also a feeling for the sublime are required.

Several commentators have understood Kant to claim that art cannot be sublime. This is strange, considering the number of sublime works of art described in Kant's works. I offer a different interpretation of the crucial passages, as saying that in a critique of the judgement of sublimity, sublime objects of art are not suitable examples because they are also intentionally produced. I then discuss some of the examples of sublime art in Kant's work that show that both architecture and poetry, according to him, can be sublime. I argue that, according to his theory, there is nothing that prevents works of painting, sculpture, and music, from being sublime. Also, novels should be included among works of fine art as Kant defines it. I claim that novels are, just like poems, suitable vehicles for giving rise to the feeling of the sublime.

I then turn to the problem of how a bounded form like the novel can be sublime. I discuss and reject a proposal that the sublime in art is the non-determinable aesthetic ideas presented within a bounded, beautiful form. I suggest that we must distinguish between 'form' and 'content' as used in art criticism, and 'form' and 'material' of the object of aesthetic assessment as understood by Kant. Aesthetic reflective judgement is always concerned with the form of the object understood as the structuring activity of the cognitive powers, but the material that is structured encompasses both the form and content of the work as discussed in art criticism. What we judge in the pure aesthetic judgement of the work of art is how we feel when cognising the object. This is just one of the many perspectives under which we can judge a work of art, but it is a necessary aspect of every work of fine art.

5. 1 Art and purposiveness

Intentional production and aesthetic judgement

The last part of the Analytic of Aesthetic Judgement (KU§§43-53) introduces a new aspect of Kant's Critique; aesthetic reflective judgements of art. Obviously this causes problems for an interpretation that takes the assumed purposiveness of nature to be the guiding principle of aesthetic reflective judgements. The principles guiding aesthetic judgements about art can hardly be identical with those guiding aesthetic judgements about nature, because there are significant differences between nature and art, as also Kant emphasises:

> *Kunst* wird von der *Natur*, wie Tun (facere) vom Handeln oder Wirken überhaupt (agere), und das Produkt, oder die Folge der erstern als *Werk* (opus) von der letztern als Wirkung (effectus) unterschieden. (KU§43, 303)

Works of art are intentionally produced, i.e. they are the results of actions with particular ends. Now any conscious human action is directed towards an end, and therefore Kant distinguishes art from science (which enables one to produce the desired effects immediately) and craft (where the attraction lies only in the utility of the product) (KU§43, 303 f). A work of art is an intentionally produced object[1] which requires skill, not only theoretical knowledge, and which pleases on its own account and not due to its usefulness.

By this introduction to his discussion of the aesthetic judgement of art, Kant's perspective has changed from being almost solely concerned with the subject's judgement of her own mental state to a focus on the object and the source of its production. This remains the main perspective throughout the discussion of art, although discussed within the context of aesthetic reflection on these objects. The earlier analyses of the judgements of taste and sublimity are clearly presupposed. Why this change of perspective? The answer lies in the difference between art and nature. When we make conceptual judgements of nature under the principle of purposiveness, this purposiveness cannot be more than a subjective assumption we must resort to, because of our limited cognitive capacities. Then the judging subject must require that everybody should share her mental state if this judgement is going to have more than private validity. But when the object of judgement is

---

1 'Object' is used in a wide sense here. Obviously there are problems in calling symphonies, poems or novels objects, but this is not a problem I have to deal with in this context. In a Kantian frame of reference, an aesthetic object is something that we judge by disinterested pleasure. The ontological status of the aesthetic object is irrelevant.

intentionally produced, then the judgement is based on a real, not an assumed purposiveness, since we must assume that a real purpose is the reason for the existence of an artifact. This is a determinative judgement, which means that it is objectively valid. Since the judgement is universally valid objectively it follows that the mental state is one that everybody must share (KU§8, 215), and no assumption about the merely subjective universal validity of the mental state is necessary. The intentional origin of artifacts means that these objects cannot immediately be judged according to the principle of purposiveness without purpose since they have real purposes[2].

To avoid the unacceptable conclusion that a work of art cannot be subject to aesthetic reflective judgement, Kant has to discuss the creation of works of art to find out how they can be subject to judgements of taste despite being intentionally produced. The condition is that there be something about these works that cannot be thought of as an effect of the artist's intentions. These objects are intentionally produced to be judged aesthetically, and to achieve that, the artist must intentionally create a work containing features not controlled by his intentional purpose. This is a common feature of all (good) works of fine art: a description of these works as intentionally produced cannot grasp all relevant aspects of them. We must resort to reflective judgement to achieve cognition of the object as a whole.

This problem of intended purposes does not occur in judgements of natural objects, but has to be solved when it comes to artifacts. Therefore some of Kant's main questions and answers in his discussion of the aesthetic reflective judgement of fine art are: 1. How can intentional products be judged according to a principle of purposiveness without purpose? As we shall see his answer is that the work of art must be judged as (partially) non-intentional (KU§45, 306 f). 2. How can the artist intentionally produce something that is non-intentional? By releasing a creative force that is not controlled by his intentions: genius (KU§46, 307 f). 3. What is involved in this talent called genius? The exhibition of aesthetic ideas (KU§49, 312 f). 4. Can this talent be expressed in other artifacts beside objects of fine art? Yes (KU§48, 313). He also discusses the relation between genius and taste, and which art forms are to be included among the fine arts. The change of perspective in the discussion of the judgement of art represents no departure from his general aesthetic theory as expounded in the earlier parts of the Critique. It is

2 When judging an artifact, we may be uncertain about the purpose of the object, but that is not the issue here. When making a determinative judgement, a claim to objective validity is made, i.e. a truth claim is made, which does not necessarily express the truth. See Allison, *Transcendental Idealism*, 72.

necessary to justify his claim that we judge these intentional products under the formal principle of the purposiveness of nature. Then the deduction of judgements of taste is valid for the judgement of objects of art in the same way as it is for the judgement of objects of nature.

I have mentioned earlier Kant's view that there are three ways in which a natural object can be pleasing: as agreeable, as beautiful, or as good. Kant uses the same tripartite division for works of art, which are classified as agreeable art, fine (literally: beautiful) art [*schöne Kunst*] (KU§44, 305), or are which is judged according to the perfection of the object (KU§48, 311 f). Kant's main concern here as in the main part of the previous discussion, is the pure judgement of taste, and therefore fine art becomes the focus of the discussion. He does, however, contrast to fine art with agreeable art, and has some problem drawing the line between the two forms of art, especially in his discussion of music (KU§51, 325). In the end he settles on the moral significance of art as the feature that distinguishes fine art from agreeable art that only pleases the sensations:

> Doch in aller schönen Kunst besteht das Wesentliche in der Form, welche für die Beobachtung und Beurteilung zweckmäßig ist, ... nicht in der Materie der Empfindung (dem Reize oder der Rührung), wo es bloß auf Genuß angelegt ist, welcher nichts in der Idee zurückläßt, den Geist stumpf, den Gegenstand nach und nach anekelnd, und das Gemüt, durch das Bewußtsein seiner im Urteile der Vernunft zweckwidrigen Stimmung, mit sich selbst unzufrieden und launisch macht. Wenn die schönen Künste nicht nahe oder fern mit moralischen Ideen in Verbindung gebracht werden, die allein ein selbständiges Wohlgefallen bei sich führen, so ist das letztere ihr endliches Schicksal. (KU§52, 325 f)

The last sentence says that fine art must be connected, closely or remotely, with moral ideas if dullness of the spirit and disgust with the object of art is to be avoided as the long-term result. Kant apparently means that if a work of art is not thus connected with moral ideas, the pleasure the spectator takes in the object is merely that of charm and emotion. This pleasure is one that in the long run affects the spectator negatively. My suggestion is that fine art is closely connected with morality in our judgement of sublime objects, and remotely in our judgement of beautiful objects. In the judgement of the sublime, the feeling is related to a purposive use of the object for the supersensible, i.e. moral, vocation [*Bestimmung*] of human beings, and is directly connected to the reflection on moral ideas. Beauty has a remote connection with moral ideas both because it is as a symbol of morality and because the judgement of taste is a judgement under the principle of purposiveness. This principle is ultimately said to be an indeterminate concept of the supersensible substrate of humanity (KU§57, 340 f)[3].

When it comes to the distinction between fine art judged as free and as accessory beauty, the picture is less clear, since Kant appears to demand that every aesthetic reflective judgement of art must accord with a concept of the object's perfection, which seems to imply that it is not pure.

> Wenn aber der Gegenstand für ein Produkt der Kunst gegeben ist, und als solches für schön erklärt werden soll: so muß, weil Kunst immer einen Zweck in der Ursache (und deren Kausalität) voraussetzt, zuerst ein Begriff von dem zum Grund gelegt werden, was das Ding sein soll … . (KU§48, 311)

This passage, where Kant seems to claim that all aesthetic judgement of art is applied (i.e. judging the object as accessory beauty), is somewhat obscure. Is 'thing' here the work of art or is it the object(s) represented in the work of art? If the latter is the case, then our judgement would not concern the object of art, but the content represented in it. That would require all art to be representational, which seems to be what Kant means when he states that artistic beauty is a beautiful representation [*Vorstellung*] of a thing (KU§48, 311). On the other hand, he uses ornamental designs and music without words to exemplify free beauty because they represent nothing (KU§16, 229) which shows that Kant does not hold art to be necessarily representational, at least not in the strong sense suggested in §48. Thus, the concept involved in a judgement of art is not a concept of the represented object, since not all fine art is representational.

The concept that is needed is a concept of the work of art itself. But do we need just the awareness of it as fine art by contrast with other intentionally produced artifices, or a more specific concept? My suggestion is that we need a concept of the intentions behind the art work, for if we first determine the intentional form and content of the work, then we are able to determine what is purposive *without* being intended by the artist. And that is what is required for us to make a pure aesthetic judgement of the object.

Purposiveness without purpose in works of art

The key to judging art under the principle of merely formal purposiveness, is to regard the art work as not completely determined by human intention, i.e. we regard it as if it were nature:

---

3 See chapter 4.6.

> Die Natur war schön, wenn sie zugleich als Kunst aussah; und die Kunst kann nur schön genannt werden, wenn wir uns bewußt sind, sie sei Kunst, und sie uns doch als Natur aussieht. ... Also muß die Zweckmäßigkeit im Produkte der schönen Kunst, ob sie zwar absichtlich ist, doch nicht absichtlich scheinen; d.i. schöne Kunst muß als Natur *anzusehen* sein, ob man sich ihrer zwar als Kunst bewußt ist. (KU§45, 306 f)

In the first sentence Kant suggests a reciprocal relation between art and nature, in that nature must look like art to be beautiful and art must look like nature to be beautiful. In determinative judgement, nature is regarded as mechanistic, in terms of causal laws, whereas in reflective judgement we judge nature under the principle of purposiveness, seeing organic objects as purposive wholes, as well as all of nature as composing a purposive totality. In this technical (drawing on the Greek term *techne*, meaning both art and other productive skills) judgement we regard nature as an intentionally created whole, i.e. as art. Aesthetic reflective judgement as the subjective aspect of teleological judgement presupposes this idea of nature as art, and (assuming the correctness of my interpretation) Kant refers to this principle when he says that nature is beautiful when it looks like art.

The latter sentence is concerned with the fact that products of art are always intentionally produced, and we are usually aware of, and concerned with, this intention when we experience these objects. Then it seems as if our judgement is not pure, because there is a real purpose in the principle of purposiveness; i.e. the judgement is conceptual, not aesthetic. Guyer has however pointed out that since the intention in the creation of fine art is the production of disinterested pleasure, this is no problem:

> Because what the concept of fine art requires is only the intention to produce pleasure through the free play of the cognitive faculties, there is no way in which the recognition of the intention alone can determine the response to a work of fine art; yet precisely where that intention is successfully accomplished, it will also be the case that no mere concept alone can be seen as fully determining the response to the work. ... in a crucial respect a work of artistic genius does not merely *look like* a work of artistic genius but is one, and thus has no need to look like one at all.[4]

Guyer correctly says that intention to give disinterested pleasure must be contained in the concept of fine art. The problem with his account is that this is not sufficient to distinguish between a failure and a success in producing fine art. And it is the aesthetic judgement, not the production, of objects that is Kant's concern. This means that Kant wants to capture with his definition only objects that can be

---

4 Guyer, *Claims of Taste*, 355 f.

judged as *fulfilling* the intention involved in creating art, i.e. objects that actually lead to someone taking pleasure in the purposiveness of the form of these objects.

If an artifact is to be judged as fine art, there must be something more about it than just the intention to produce disinterested pleasure, namely that there is something about the object that does appear purposive without being intentionally created. In this sense the object must look like nature, i.e. it must be purposive without this purposiveness being part of the intention. We should not take 'look like' in a literal sense. What it means is merely that the object must be such that we judge it not only according to what we know or assume to be the artistic intentions, but also as a product of nature. Art does not have to imitate nature, but must be nature in the sense that we judge it at least partially to display the same non-intentional purposiveness that is found in nature. Guyer is right when he points out that defining something as a work of art means defining it as something that is produced with the intention to produce pleasure. He is wrong when he claims that this intention makes the requirement that art must look like nature superfluous. The artifact is a work of art only when the intention is successfully accomplished, and this is only the case when the object looks like nature.

To make a pure judgement of art, a particular attitude is required, which disregards all interest and feelings based on concept (such as the pleasure in the good). We have already encountered this requirement in the discussion of the aesthetic judgement of nature, but now another element is added to the appearances, concepts and feelings involved in the experience of an object. The aesthetic judgement of an art work is made by disregarding the intention involved in producing the object. This disregard allows the judgement to be pure. We achieve this attitude when we regard the object as if it were a product of mere nature, although we are still conscious of its artificial origin (KU§45, 306). When we judge art as if it were nature, the subject's mental state must be one of free play of the cognitive powers and we demand that everybody should share this mental state.

Accordingly, the connection between taking nature as art and art as nature is more than a mere word play, but there is a significant difference in the meaning of the words as they are used in these two relations. The first relation deals with what principle we have to assume to make any pure aesthetic reflective judgement, whereas the other deals with what attitude we have to take to be able to judge this particular object (of art) according to the principle assumed in the first relation. Thus there is no real reciprocity between the two expressions; the latter is dependent on the assumptions of the former, whereas the opposite is not the case.

5.2 Genius and aesthetic ideas

Genius and non-intended purpose in art

How can intentionally produced art be judged under the principle of the purposiveness of nature, when it is not part of nature? The justification for the subjective necessity of an aesthetic judgement of nature is based on it being a judgement of the subject's mental state when making a teleological judgement, a state we require everybody to share. But this claim to universal validity for our feeling is only required as long as there is no real purpose[5] in the object we are judging, because knowledge of the real purposiveness of the object would give us a conceptual basis for judging the object determinatively. When such a conceptual basis is available, then a shared state of mind is not a necessary presupposition for the judgement.

In art there is a real purpose in the sense that the artist creates the object intentionally, and we are entirely justified in ascribing real purposiveness to the object. But if Kant's account of the aesthetic reflective judgement is to be successfully transferred from nature to art, the work of art cannot be completely explained by the deliberate intentions of the artist. There must also be a purposiveness without a real purpose which means that we cannot fully determine the object as being created according to a particular plan accounting for every single element and relation within the finished product. If we could, there would be no point in a demand to universal assent for our state of mind when cognising the object. Then the object would not be judged according to the principle of purposiveness, but determined conceptually according to the known purpose (as we can do when judging commercial products such as pop music or so-called soap operas on television), and the art would not be fine, but mechanical (KU§45, 306).

Beautiful art must not only be intentionally produced, but must also contain elements that can be judged under the heuristic principle of a purposiveness of nature. These non-intentional elements must have a source different from the intentional, conceptual aspects of the work, a source Kant calls genius:

---

5 When we judge the action of a person, we always judge it as directed towards an end, i.e. as being based on a purpose. This judgement issues a claim to objective validity. This is distinguished from the *heuristic* judgement of nature under the concept of real purposiveness (KU VIII, 193), which is merely a device for making sense of nature for our judgement. This kind of real purposiveness can be represented only by reflective judgements with intersubjective validity.

> *Genie* ist das Talent (Naturgabe), welches der Kunst die Regel gibt. Da das Talent, als angebornes produktives Vermögen des Künstlers, selbst zur Natur gehört, so könnte man sich auch so ausdrücken: *Genie* ist die angeborne Gemütsanlage (ingenium), *durch welche* die Natur der Kunst die Regel gibt. (KU§46, 307)

Fine art is defined as the art of genius. When the rules of art are given by a natural disposition, we have no access through rational means to the rules determining art, and we have no way of knowing the real purpose in an object of art. We cannot even claim there to be any such purpose behind the rules of the work of art, because that would be tantamount to asserting a real (intentional) purpose in nature's apparently purposive regularities. We are no more warranted in claiming real purposiveness for this lawfulness than for any other of nature's empirical regularities.

Although we can say that art is intentionally produced, and we can find out everything about how the artist planned and executed the creation of a work of art, we have no possible access to the essential factor in the creation of art, the factor that makes fine art into an object of disinterested pleasure. This factor is not even accessible to the artist himself, because it is a talent whose operation cannot be described in rules[6]. The decisive element in fine art is its exemplary originality in the sense that it does not follow rules but creates them, so that they can be discovered and followed by others (KU§46, 307f). Because fine art cannot occur except as the result of the creative talent called genius, nature is the basis for the rules of art (compare KU§57, 344).

The creative work of genius cannot be rational in the sense of expressing the autonomy of man, as the ability to judge, both practically and theoretically, does.. But it must be accessible to rational judgement, i.e. it must be possible to see it as being as law-governed as any other natural phenomenon. Since genius is not rational in the first sense, it must be part of man understood as nature, as subject to the regularities of nature. Man viewed as nature is man governed by causally determined physical and psychological laws. Not all of man's actions can be completely explained according to the principles of determinative judgement even if regarded solely from the empirical point of view, and perhaps the most important phenomenon that escapes our capacity for determinative judgement is

6 Kant's view of the inspired, non-rational basis of the creative arts has a striking similarity with Plato's understanding of poetry in e.g. *The Republic*, 607B-608B, as is pointed out in D. Crawford, 'Kant's Theory of Creative Imagination', 176 ff. Crawford argues that this similarity stops at the assessments of the value of art, in that Kant emphasises its moral significance, whereas Plato wanted to banish poetry from the ideal state due to its attractive irrationality.

the creative element in fine art. However much we understand of man's psychology, we seem unable to explain the causality of the creative process, presumably because its fundamental characteristic is originality, and we must instead judge it reflectively under the principle of the purposiveness of nature.

Kant does not express this connection between the judgements of art and nature explicitly, but there are several passages supporting this interpretation. He states that art is purposive on its own (KU§44, 306), i.e. it is not created to serve some other goal we can determine conceptually. Furthermore, there are several elements in the description of genius pointing in the same direction:

> Man sieht hieraus, daß Genie 1) ein *Talent* sei, dasjenige, wozu sich keine bestimmte Regel geben läßt, hervorzubringen: nicht Geschicklichkeitsanlage zu dem, was nach irgend einer Regel gelernt werden kann; folglich daß *Originalität* seine erste Eigenschaft sein müsse. ... 3) Daß ... der Urheber eines Produkts, welches er seinem Genie verdankt, selbst nicht weiß, wie sich in ihm die Ideen dazu herbei finden, auch es nicht in seiner Gewalt hat, dergleichen nach Belieben oder planmäßig auszudenken und anderen in solchen Vorschriften mitzuteilen, die sie in Stand setzten, gleichmäßige Produkte hervorzubringen. (KU§46, 307 f)

It is impossible to describe the rules of the products of genius, because otherwise one could learn to have genius. But one can describe the rules of each single work of art. Thus it is possible to copy fine art without being a genius, but without being able to determine the last, and decisive factor in the production of art: How to create art? The creative element, the element that is the defining characteristic of fine art, is impossible to determine causally. Even the artist himself cannot plan the production of it. If this element had been determined, then the creative process could have been repeated in new situations by anybody who had acquired the skill. Therefore we have to judge the creative element of a work of art as a purposive product of nature while recognising that this judgement is only valid for human judgement; it does not have objective validity. In this sense, the judgement of art is part of our judgement of nature, and accounts for the claim to subjective universality for our feeling when cognising the object.

This particular attitude of regarding art as if it were nature is not the same as regarding art in the same way as we regard nature. On the contrary, the attitude must include the awareness of the intentionality of the art work, an awareness that enables us to disregard this intentionality in the pure aesthetic judgement of the work. This intentionality we can describe as conceptual purposiveness, to contrast it with the purposiveness of genius, and it includes didactic elements, imitation of objects and events, creation of narratives, expression of wit, as well as structural features belonging to the different genres of art. Kant emphasises the importance of expressing the material provided by genius in a proper form (KU§47, 311). In a total aesthetic assessment also the question of the intentions expressed in the work is of interest, as well as its moral content, its complexity, its originality and so forth. The pure aesthetic judgement is an integral, and even essential, part of this judgement (KU§52, 326), but it is clearly not Kant's view that pure aesthetic judgement alone is adequate for a proper assessment of a work of art[7]. But if we do not take this judgement into account, our assessment of the object of art lacks an essential component, a component that is an element in Kant's basic description of fine art:

> Schöne Kunst dagegen ist eine Vorstellungsart, die für sich selbst zweckmäßig ist und, obgleich ohne Zweck, dennoch die Kultur der Gemütskräfte zur geselligen Mitteilung befördert. Die allgemeine Mitteilbarkeit einer Lust führt es schon in ihrem Begriffe mit sich, daß diese nicht eine Lust des Genusses, aus bloßer Empfindung, sondern der Reflexion sein müsse; und so ist ästhetische Kunst, als schöne Kunst, eine solche, die die reflektierende Urteilskraft und nicht die Sinnenempfindung zum Richtmaße hat. (KU§44, 306)

Kant's claim is that the pleasure we take in art, if it is to be reckoned as fine art and not mere enjoyment, must be a universally communicable feeling, which is the basis for aesthetic reflective judgement. Thus we cannot assess a work of fine art as a work of fine art without judgement of taste or sublimity being a part of the assessment, but that requires an awareness of how we are affected by the work in other ways as well.

Expression of aesthetic ideas and the purpose of art

Genius includes the ability to express aesthetic ideas (KU§49, 317), and Kant says that

---

7 To distinguish the pure judgement from the accessory judgement and other conceptually based pleasures in the object, we must be able to determine these different feelings, i.e. we must clarify the possible ways to judge the object aesthetically (by feeling). Furthermore, in the discussion of pure and accessory judgement of nature, Kant states the moral value of judgements of accessory beauty (KU§16, 230 f), and finds the development of taste to be part of the moral project of cultivating humanity in ourselves (KU§60, 355 f). The connection between aesthetic judgements in general and moral development is a large topic, which, regrettably, I cannot discuss adequately within the context of this work.

> unter einer ästhetischen Idee aber verstehe ich diejenige Vorstellung der Einbildungskraft, die viel zu denken veranlaßt, ohne daß ihr doch irgend ein bestimmter Gedanke, d.i. *Begriff* adequät sein kann, die folglich keine Sprache völlig erreicht und verständlich machen kann. (KU§49, 314)

An aesthetic idea is defined as a special kind of representation in the imagination of the subject experiencing the object. This representation induces much thought, without one determinate concept being adequate to the imagined material. In this case imagination must be free, since it cannot be determined by a particular concept. When this representation of the imagination leads to many thoughts, this relation between the cognitive powers is a relation of free play. My conclusion is that genius is the ability to create an object that is such that it expresses aesthetic ideas. Aesthetic ideas are those aspects of an object that give rise to a free play between the cognitive powers in the representation of the object. Kant accordingly says that both natural and artistic beauty is expression of aesthetic ideas (KU§51, 320).

This interpretation deviates considerably from other interpretations. Guyer, for instance, who takes as his point of departure Kant's statement that an aesthetic idea is the counterpart to an idea of reason, in that the first is a representation of the imagination to which no concept can be adequate, and the latter is a concept to which no intuition can be adequate (KU§49, 314). He takes an example (KU§49, 315) as paradigmatic, and finds that in the production of art there must be three elements involved; first, a rational idea which is the content of the work and second, an indeterminate amount of particular images (e.g. Jupiter's eagle). He continues:

> Third, intervening between these two elements, is the aesthetic idea properly so called, the idea of the imagination that suggests the idea of reason on the one hand and the indeterminate array of images on the other. In this case that would be nothing other than the imaginative idea of Jupiter himself as the embodiment of majesty or sublimity.[8]

There are two problems with this interpretation. First, if Kant, by calling aesthetic ideas the counterparts to rational ideas means that rational and aesthetic ideas belong together in the sense that every aesthetic idea is the embodiment of a rational idea, the consequence is that there would be an image adequate to this rational idea, and a concept adequate to this aesthetic idea. That contradicts Kant's own definitions of rational and aesthetic ideas. I find it more plausible that Kant in this passage gives his reason for calling these representations of the imagination

[8] Guyer, *Claims of Taste*, 358.

'ideas'. Since these images cannot be conceptualised, and rational ideas cannot be intuited, they both differ from concepts of the understanding, but in opposite ways. Kant says this is the main reason for calling these representations ideas, although he also says that aesthetic ideas strive towards something that lies beyond the bounds of experience (KU§49, 314). But he does not say that this something is an idea of reason; it may well be just another nature. I take Kant to mean that the imagination can create fictitious worlds, such as the one found in fairy tales, science fiction, or fantasy literature. Ideas of reason and aesthetic ideas are counterparts because they are defined as opposites. They do not come together in pairs, nor can the aesthetic ideas be captured in any concept. The image of Jupiter can be conceptualised through the descriptions of him in Roman mythology, which means that this image cannot be an aesthetic idea as Kant defines it.

The other problem is that Guyer's reading attaches art too strongly to ideas of reason. According to Kant, judgements of the sublime involve ideas of reason, whereas judgements of taste are connected to cognition, and thus, concepts of understanding. On the basis of this distinction between the two kinds of aesthetic reflective judgements, the implication of Guyer's reading is that all art is sublime rather than beautiful[9]. With beautiful works of art such as Leonardo da Vinci's *Mona Lisa,* Michelangelo's *David,* or a pastoral poem, there are no ideas of reason of which these works are the embodiments, since they are artistic depictions of a particular person (notwithstanding the mythical character of the Biblical David) or event. If these images embody any concept, it must be empirical concepts of the objects they represent. The examples Kant uses to illustrate aesthetic ideas mostly involve ideas of reason, making Guyer's interpretation reasonable. But leading up to these examples we find a passage that indicates that this connection is just one of the two ways we use the creativity of imagination:

> Die Einbildungskraft … ist nämlich sehr mächtig in Schaffung gleichsam einer andern Natur aus dem Stoffe, den ihr die wirkliche gibt. Wir unterhalten uns mit ihr, wo uns die Erfahrung zu alltäglich vorkommt; bilden diese auch wohl um: zwar noch immer nach analogischen Gesetzen, aber doch auch nach Prinzipien, die höher hinauf in der Vernunft liegen ... wobei wir unsere Freiheit vom Gesetze der Assoziation ... fühlen, nach welchem uns von der Natur zwar Stoff geliehen, dieser aber von uns zu etwas ganz anderem, nämlich dem, was die Natur übertrifft, verarbeitet werden kann. (KU§49, 314)

The first part of the second sentence deals with the creation of art according to laws analogous to those of nature, whereas the latter part deals with art involving

9 Crawford, 'Theory of Creative', 173 f. takes aesthetic ideas to be symbols of ideas of reason. This interpretation suffers from the same problems as Guyer's.

ideas of reason. My claim is that the first part describes the creation of beautiful art, which follows the rules of nature in some way or another, and the latter deals with sublime art, which involves ideas of reason. This is a parallel to the distinction between the boundedness of the beautiful and the unboundedness of the sublime (KU§23, 244). We can read the passage as a transition from a general discussion of aesthetic ideas, to a more specific concern with the sublime. In the discussion following this passage, Kant is concerned with sublime poetry, which is evident both from the example discussed by Guyer, as well as from the poems cited later in the section (KU§49, 315f).

Thus there must be some concept(s) involved in the expression of aesthetic ideas, but they do not have to be ideas of reason. The relation between the expression of aesthetic ideas and these concepts can be understood in parallel with the interpretation of the judgement of nature under the principle of purposiveness, where the aesthetic judgement is based on the subjective aspect of a conceptual reflective judgement. When we make a reflective judgement, imagination structures the represented material in many ways under the principle of purposiveness, resulting in a rich variety of thoughts. This free play is experienced through our disinterested feeling, which is judged aesthetically. The cognitive goal is to find concepts which enable us to make sense of the object, but the feeling is as such independent of this cognitive determination in teleological judgement. When Kant talks about the concepts or ideas involved in art, his concern is with this cognitive aspect for which the aesthetic aspect is a subjective condition. The play with aesthetic ideas is the basis on which the cognitive judgement is exercised.

But if this model is relevant for the judgement of art as well, the question is: what kind of teleological judgement is involved? Art seems to have no aim beyond giving rise to the pleasure in the free play of the faculties, and does not result in any conceptual judgement of purposiveness. The solution may lie in the rule-giving function of genius. Genius displays an exemplary originality which gives the rule to art:

> Weil aber das Genie ein Günstling der Natur ist, dergleichen man nur als seltene Erscheinung anzusehen hat: so bringt sein Beispiel für andere gute Köpfe eine Schule hervor, d.i. eine methodische Unterweisung nach Regeln, soweit man sie aus jenen Geistesprodukten und ihrer Eigentümlichkeit hat ziehen können: und für diese ist die schöne Kunst sofern Nachahmung, der die Natur durch ein Genie die Regel gab. (KU§49, 318)

Not only in practical freedom do human beings give rules directed towards an end; but we do so even as subject to the laws of nature. These rules are expressed in art, and can be found by reflective judgement under the principle of purposiveness, i.e. in teleological judgement. The rules of the art work are conceptually expressed, and lack objective validity. We cannot subsume these rules under causal laws of understanding, and they have only subjective validity like all merely reflective judgements. Still, they contain a demand for intersubjective validity, since they are based on a mental state we require everybody to share. Human creativity issues rules that are determined under the principle of the purposiveness of nature, and the subjective aspect of this objective judgement is the intersubjectively valid feeling underlying aesthetic judgements of the art work.

The purposive formation of the work of art

Kant is careful to emphasise that the inspired, free imaginations of genius is not sufficient to make a work of fine art. A work of art that is not properly structured cannot be an example of fine art:

> Das Genie kann nur reichen *Stoff* zu Produkten der schönen Kunst hergeben; die Verarbeitung desselben und die *Form* erfordert ein durch die Schule gebildetes Talent, um einen Gebrauch davon zu machen, der vor der Urteilskraft bestehen kann. (KU§47, 310)

Here Kant makes a distinction between form and matter that is different from the better known one in the critical philosophy, where the distinction deals with the empirical matter and the a priori form of appearances in experience (KrV A86/B118). This distinction also differs from the distinction drawn between form and matter of the object in aesthetic judgement, where aesthetic reflective judgement is a judgement of the form of the object. Kant held that all thinking was characterised by the distinction between form and matter (KrV A266/B322), which accounts for the several different senses of this pair of concepts in his works[10]. The distinction he draws at this point cannot be the one that is common in all art criticism, either, the distinction between what is expressed in the work, and how these expressions are organised or structured to be presented in the most adequate way, a distinction that can be understood several ways:

> Some art critics use the word "form" to mean approximately the *composition* of a painting – "It is a pointillist painting" would not be a form-statement in this

[10] See the discussion of the different senses of form and matter in Longuenesse, *Capacity to Judge*, 147 ff.

> usage. Others, to mean the whole design, in contrast to what the painting *represents* – "It contains a red patch" would be a form-statement in this usage. Others, to mean "how" the objects are arranged on the picture-plane – "thickly" and "gracefully" would be form-terms in this usage. And there are other varieties.[11]

Regardless of how we define this distinction, it is not the one Kant has in mind. Both the form and the content (in such uses of the words) of a work of art can be subject to pure aesthetic judgement, as Guyer points out:

> Genius thus lies in the ability to produce both form and content and the "happy relation" between them which makes the former especially successful for the expression of the latter.[12]

This understanding of Kant's view is related to the marriage of form and content as presented by Nussbaum[13], regarding form in the traditional sense to be an integral part of the content.

We must look for yet another meaning of form and matter in this context. Since producing the form requires training, it must have to do with those elements that are conventionally accepted, i.e. the elements that are already known and determined. These can be formal features, e.g. rhythmical patterns or rules of proportion; conventions for expressing content, e.g. symbols and allegories; as well as material for content, such as Biblical and traditional stories, historical events, natural phenomena, and so forth. These elements are mechanical, in the sense that one can be trained in the presentation of them within each art form. In the actual context, form comprises all these non-original elements that together encompass all the intentional aspects of the object of art. The content consists of the non-intentional creative elements that Kant calls aesthetic ideas, which are recognised by their original exemplary nature.

Thus it is clear that no object of art can be the product of genius only, but must always intentionally be presented in a frame of rules and conventions. We can judge the object on several levels, then: (1) As an object, it is judged determinatively according to the laws of nature. (2) As a human artifact, it is judged according to the intention we must presuppose as the ground for its production, i.e. it is judged as intentionally purposive. (3) As a work of fine art, we must judge it as a work of nature through genius, and (4) the subjective aspect of this judgement is the pure aesthetic judgement of the work. But these perspectives are not independent aspects of the total experience of the object; to see it as an

[11] M. C. Beardsly, *Aesthetics*, 166.
[12] Guyer, *Claims of Taste*, 360.
[13] Nussbaum, *Love's Knowledge*, 3 f.

artifact (2) we must see it as an object (1), and to judge it as a work of genius (3,4) we must see these creative imaginations as arranged within an intentional whole (2). In the passage cited above, the matter is the product of genius and the form is the intentional work of art when this creative element is disregarded. The distinction I have drawn between judgements under the principle of the purposiveness of nature and those about intentional purposes is the same as the distinction Kant draws between the material of genius and the conventional academic form. He is concerned with our pure aesthetic judgement as an element in human judgement of the world, a context of which art is only a part. His central perspective on art is as the rule-governed product of man as part of nature, not as a free, rational agent.

The work of art cannot consist of the material of genius only. If these imaginations are not presented in a properly constructed form, there will be nothing to judge:

> man weiß nicht recht, ob man mehr über den Gaukler, der um sich so viel Dunst verbreitet, wobei man nichts deutlich beurteilen, aber desto mehr sich einbilden kann, oder mehr über das Publikum lachen soll, welches sich treuherzig einbildet, daß sein Unvermögen, das Meisterstück der Einsicht deutlich erkennen und fassen zu können, daher komme, weil ihm neue Wahrheiten in ganzen Massen zugeworfen werden, wogegen ihm das Detail (...) nur Stümperwerke zu sein scheint. (KU§47, 310)

If a work of art is to be judged, it must be a structured or designed presentation of the material. Although a work of art can have 'contents' other than the products of genius, Kant's concern is merely with how this material of genius is organised. And this structuring is not an inspired product of genius; it is the result of hard labour in finding the correct form through trial and error (KU§48, 312). Kant is not clear on how this structuring comes about, because he says, as quoted above, that the ability to form the material into fine art requires academic training, but at the same time he says that taste (and the power of judgement in general) disciplines genius (KU§50, 319). But the capacity for taste is part of the power of aesthetic judgement, not only a skill acquired in school or an activity (KU§48, 313). The power of judgement requires the presence of an object, an event, an action, or at least some potential actions or objects if it is to be exercised. Judgement cannot give rise to objects or actions, be they imaginary or real. In this respect, judgement is a passive faculty, even though it is active as a self-legislating faculty. Thus taste must guide the artist in finding the right form for the material that is to be expressed. But how can taste guide the artist? Kant seems to think that the artist attempts to find a suitable form for his ideas through making a sketch or a model, and judges this form in order to decide to what extent it is suitable for his purpose:

> Diese Form aber dem Produkte der schönen Kunst zu geben, dazu wird bloß Geschmack erfordert, an welchem der Künstler, nachdem er ihn durch mancherlei Beispiele der Kunst, oder der Natur, geübt und berichtigt hat, sein Werk hält, und, nach manchen oft mühsamen Versuchen, denselben zu befriedigen, diejenige Form findet, die ihm Genüge tut: daher diese nicht gleichsam eine Sache der Eingebung, oder eines freien Schwunges der Gemütskräfte, sondern einer langsamen und gar peinlichen Nachbesserung ist, um sie dem Gedanken angemessen und doch der Freiheit im Spiele derselben nicht nachteilig werden zu lassen. (KU§48, 312 f)

If the model does not express the ideas the artist aims to present, a new version of the work is produced, and again judged, and this process continues until the artist has found the optimal way of expressing her aesthetic ideas.

This shows why an academically trained talent is necessary to create works of art. Giving the right form to the creations of the imagination cannot be a case of fooling around without knowing how to gain the effects one is seeking. The artist must know how to use the instruments of each particular art to succeed to the satisfaction of her own and other people's taste. This skill is a question of understanding the rules of the art (besides having some physical abilities that are necessary in some arts, notably music and the visual arts) and how to apply them in general, but finding the right application in each concrete case is a question of taste. The rule-governed activity requires a concept of the purpose of the product and is performed by the faculty of understanding, which is the faculty of concepts and, accordingly, rules (KU§49, 317). Thus, when the elements of imagination, understanding, and genius (spirit [*Geist*]) are balanced to the satisfaction of taste, a product of fine art is produced (KU§50, 320). The academically trained skills, guided by imagination and understanding, are employed in producing a product according to an intentional end. This involves a concept of what the work of art is going to be, but still this is no complete determination of the end product. To become a work of fine art, it must be a product of genius as well, and this aspect of the work cannot be judged according to what we take to be the calculated purpose of the work. It can only be judged reflectively under the principle of purposiveness, where our knowledge of human intentionality is of little help, due to the non-rational character of genius.

Kant's sketch of the creative process appears sound when applied to beautiful art. But when the material that is to be presented is sublime, not beautiful, it is not obvious that taste is called for at all since taste is not involved in the judgement of sublimity. On the other hand, the sublime work of art too is given an intentional and purposive presentation, so perhaps taste has a role to play even in these works of art. There are two possibilities here: 1) The production of a sublime work of art requires taste to supply the work with the correct presentation even though its content is sublime, and also calls for judgement of taste. 2) The production of the sublime work of art requires feelings for the sublime rather than taste and what are needed in the creation of such a work of art are imagination, understanding, genius, and feeling[14]. Besides, the faculty of reason must be involved, too, since the conceptual aspect of the judgement of the sublime is ideas of reason.

Option 2) gains support from the Kantian discussion of the relation of genius to taste, where Kant seems to be singularly preoccupied with fine art as the art of beauty and pays no heed to the sublime (KU§48, 311 f and §50, 319), which perhaps is natural given that fine art [*schöne Kunst*] in German is literally the art of the beautiful. We could say that Kant was concerned with the production of beautiful art when discussing genius, and if he had cared to discuss the sublime (a mere appendix, as we recall), he would have substituted it for taste in his account of the faculties involved in the creation of fine art. This attempt will not work, though, because Kant would have taken care to use 'aesthetic reflective judgement' (or just 'judgement' as an imprecise abbreviation) rather than 'taste' if he did not think that judgement of taste was necessary for the production of sublime art. This is supported by the sublime poems referred to in the section between the two sections connecting genius and taste (KU§49, 315 f) and by Kant's emphasis on the special role of taste in the creation of fine art:

> Der Geschmack ist, so wie die Urteilskraft überhaupt, die Disziplin (oder Zucht) des Genies. (KU§50, 319)

This is not decisive evidence for the conclusion that Kant meant that taste is necessary in the production of sublime art as it is in the creation of beautiful art, but it clearly supports that conclusion. In the Anthropology we find another passage indicating that Kant did hold that taste is necessary in the creation of sublime works of art:

> *Das Erhabene* ist zwar das Gegengewicht, aber nicht das Widerspiel vom Schönen: weil die Bestrebung und der Versuch, sich zu der Fassung (apprehensio) des Gegenstandes zu erheben, dem Subjekt ein Gefühl seiner

[14] Kant calls the ability to judge the sublime 'feeling', just as the ability to judge the beautiful is called 'taste': "Denn, so wie wir dem, der in der Beurteilung eines Gegenstandes der Natur, welchen wir schön finden, gleichgültig ist, Mangel des *Geschmacks* vorwerfen: so sagen wir von dem, der bei dem, was wir erhaben zu sein urteilen, unbewegt bleibt, er habe kein *Gefühl*." (KU§29, 265)

> eigenen Größe und Kraft erweckt; aber die Gedankenvorstellung desselben in *Beschreibung* oder Darstellung kann und muß immer schön sein. (A 243)

If the presentation of the sublime in art must be beautiful, taste must be a necessary faculty in making this work of art.

I am left with option 1), but this can also be divided into two different assertions: i) Judgements of taste and judgements of the sublime are both necessary in the creation of sublime art, or ii) the creation of sublime art require the same faculties as the creation of beautiful art, which means that no judgement of sublimity is necessary in its production. The latter suggestion gains plausibility from the grounds mentioned above, i.e. Kant was concerned with the sublime when writing these paragraphs so it is implausible that he should have forgotten to mention this judgement in case it was necessary. Besides, the presentation of the sublime in a work of art is the presentation of an *illusion* of infinity or overwhelming force, as we have seen above, and this illusion must be presented as a form (i.e. as bounded) to be cognised. Although the work of art is judged sublime, the presentation of these sublime images can only be made in a bounded form, and need only the reflective aesthetic judgement of objects of form, which is taste, in its production.

The problem with this is that if the aesthetic ideas that genius is expressing are sublime, how can the artist recognise the proper form by taste? The artist has these images that he wants to express, and through his artistic skill he sets himself a goal. Take W. B. Yeats' *The Second Coming* as an example. Yeats' aesthetic ideas needed a form, and he chose a rather short poem rich in thought-provoking imagery of a world in disarray and the threat of subsequent terror. He found some words expressing the ideas he already had imagined. But how could he know that these words expressed the images he tried to express unless he felt them himself when he read his drafts at different stages? Or how could he know that an early draft did *not* express these images, without judging the poem according to the principles of the sublime? Although creating a work of art requires a bounded form, one cannot decide that this form is rightly judged as sublime unless the judgement of the sublime is involved in the creative process. Thus, in producing a sublime work of art the following faculties are required: imagination, understanding, reason, genius, judgement of taste, and judgement of the sublime. My conclusion is that any sublime work of art requires both kinds of aesthetic reflective judgement, not only in the process of producing the work, but in the judgement of the finished work, as well, if it is to be cognised in all aspects[15].

5.3 The sublime in art

Sublime objects of art

In his discussion of the sublime Kant mainly employs examples of natural objects, and he says that the sublime in art[16] is always restricted by the conditions of an agreement with nature (KU§23, 245). This warrants the assumption that art can be sublime, but one can easily get the impression that the sublime in art is merely an appendix to the sublime in nature, and even in some sense inferior. But as we have already seen, Kant does not avoid sublime art altogether; he uses both the pyramids and St. Peter's in Rome as examples in his exposition. Thus it is an exaggeration when Guyer claims that "works of art seem to have no part in Kant's image of the sublime"[17]. Kant suggests in his discussion of genius that poetry can be sublime just as nature:

> So sagt z.B. ein gewisser Dichter in der Beschreibung eines schönen Morgens: "Die Sonne quoll hervor, wie Ruh aus Tugend quillt". Das Bewußtsein der Tugend, wenn man sich auch nur in Gedanken in die Stelle eines Tugendhaften versetzt, verbreitet im Gemüte eine Menge erhabener und beruhigender Gefühle. (KU§49, 316)

Even more convincing as an illustration of Kant's inclusion of the sublime in the aesthetic judgement of poetry is a passage from the first Critique:

> Die unbedingte Notwendigkeit, die wir, als den letzten Träger aller Dinge, so unentbehrlich bedürfen, ist der wahre Abgrund für die menschliche Vernunft. Selbst die Ewigkeit, so schauderhaft erhaben sie auch ein Haller schildern mag, macht lange den schwindligen Eindruck nicht auf das Gemüt; denn sie *mißt* nur die Dauer der Dinge, aber *trägt* sie nicht. (KrV A613/B641)

---

15 Remember the pyramids that were judged sublime when regarded from the right distance. They must be judged by taste when seen from further away or at close range. But we need not judge the pyramids under both principles, as the leading constructors (in this connection they must have been the artists) had to do in order to create these sublime constructions.

16 Kant says that art (i.e. fine art) is produced through freedom (KU§43, 303), presupposes a purpose in its cause (KU§48, 311), and pleases on its own account unlike craft which pleases on account of its effect (KU§43, 304).

17 Guyer, *Experience of Freedom*, 264.

The important point here is that it is Haller's *poetical depiction* of eternity that is sublime, not the fact that we think the idea of eternity when reading his poetry, although this fact explains why our judgement must be sublime. Poetry can lead to ideas of reason just as objects of nature do, and apparently there is no difference in the way they bring about the aesthetic feeling of the sublime.

There is an apparent contradiction between this claim and Kant's statement that the sublime in art must conform to that of nature, if the latter claim means that the sublime in art is in some way secondary. On the other hand, my interpretation of aesthetic reflective judgements as based on a principle of purposiveness or purposive use of nature seems to put objects of nature in a suitably privileged position when compared with objects of art. Objects of art must be regarded *as if* they were objects of nature to be subject to a pure aesthetic judgement. This attitude means disregarding the intentionally produced elements of the object and focusing on the creative elements that are produced by genius.

If I am correct to assume that these principles of purposiveness are subjectively necessary for aesthetic reflective judgements, his claim that there is a requirement of conformity to the sublime of nature for sublime objects of art is explained. But we need to know how this claim to conformity can be understood. To say that fine art requires the originality of genius, and that genius is a natural talent that cannot be determined according to the rules of understanding, is not the same as saying that art has to meet certain conditions to be in harmony with nature. To decide whether the only condition that sublime art must meet is production by the natural talent for originality called genius, it can be useful to examine Kant's use of examples in the exposition of the sublime.

Kant is clearly reluctant to furnish his exposition of the sublime with examples of works of art. Rather than this being a consequence of an *impossibility* of pure judgements of sublime art, I believe it is due to Kant's wish to avoid misleading examples on a rather complex issue. Support for this assumption can be found in Kant's rejection of using sublime objects of art in his exposition:

> Ich ... bemerke nur, daß, wenn das ästhetische Urteil *rein* (*mit keinem teleologischen* als Vernunfturteile *vermischt*) und daran ein der Kritik der *ästhetischen* Urteilskraft völlig anpassendes Beispiel gegeben werden soll, man nicht das Erhabene an Kunstprodukten (z.B. Gebäuden, Säulen u.s.w.), wo ein menschlicher Zweck die Form sowohl als die Größe bestimmt, noch an Naturdingen, *deren Begriff schon einen bestimmten Zweck bei sich führt* ... , sondern an der rohen Natur ... , bloß sofern sie Größe enthält, aufzeigen müsse. (KU§26, 252 f)

Crowther mistakenly assumes this to mean that judgements about the sublime in art are of secondary importance to Kant since they "involve teleological considerations and would thereby lack 'pure' aesthetic status."[18] Literally Kant is only saying that he is looking for a suitable example for a critique and in that context art products as well as objects with a known purpose in nature should be avoided. My suggestion is that Kant holds these to be unsuitable examples because the reader could misunderstand what kind of pleasure Kant is talking about if he used examples where feelings of sublimity, feelings of pure or accessory beauty, as well as moral and other non-reflective feelings could be present. Kant's reason for using primary examples from crude nature is to avoid misunderstandings, not to label judgements of the sublime in art secondary to those of nature. Thus we have the capacity to make pure aesthetic judgements concerning the sublime in objects of art.

Kant wanted to avoid art and purposive nature when providing examples of the sublime, because in these cases our judgement (understood as the aggregate of our assessments of the work) includes concepts of the purpose of the object, contradicting the counterpurposiveness that characterises the sublime. This problem is relevant even for those movements within modern art that aim to undermine determinable meanings and purposes in the work, e.g. surrealism, the theatre of the absurd, abstract expressionism, including novels such as *Molloy*. Producing a work of art is in itself a purposive action. Using works of art to discuss the judgement of sublimity was even more problematic at Kant's time, when works of art generally were considered to be representations of objects. Even Kant seems close to this position, as is evident in his distinction between natural and artistic beauty:

> Eine Naturschönheit ist ein *schönes Ding*; die Kunstschönheit ist eine *schöne Vorstellung* von einem Dinge. (KU§48, 311)

Although Kant's definition of fine art is connected to his analysis of aesthetic reflective judgements rather than to art as representation of natural objects, the requirement that the work of art must look like nature or be viewable as nature (KU§45, 306f) also points in the direction of a theory of representation. If we consider the most clearly mimetic art forms, sculpture and painting, works within these art forms are, or used to be, static and restricted in size. It seems to follow that works within these art forms had to be judged as beautiful (or, at least, non-sublime) representations. The restrictions on size made a representation of the

[18] Crowther, *Kantian Sublime*, 152.

mathematically sublime difficult, just like the static nature of these art forms led to problems in the representation of the dynamically sublime[19]. On the other hand: painting is defined by Kant as sensible illusion (KU§51, 322 f) and attempts by painters to create illusions of infinity or of overwhelming force had become standard in the so-called sublime landscape painting of the eighteenth and nineteenth centuries[20]. This illusion is, however, never complete because the spectator must be conscious of the artificial character of the object, which draws his attention to the purposive character of the art work. Thus the illusion is broken and even the presented object is seen as a purposive creation, and not as counterpurposive for cognition which is a condition for the experience of the kinds of sublimity mentioned here.

One could object that the artistic imitation of a beautiful object of nature would be subject to the same kind of interference from the consciousness of the artistic intention, and that is of course correct. This explains why Kant mentions ornamental designs and music among the free beauties, along with flowers and some kinds of birds (KU§16, 229). He may think that we do not judge these works according to purpose (i.e. intention), but that would be a rather dubious claim[21]. I think that his idea is that these objects are not immediately connected with a particular purpose, so it is easier to avoid confusing the pure and the applied aesthetic judgements of them. When we see a horse, our idea of a beautiful horse is shaped by a conventional ideal of a healthy, lean, strong racehorse. It is difficult to disregard this ideal, but we have to disregard all feelings based on this ideal if we want to judge the horse as a free beauty. So when there is no such purpose or ideal immediately associated with the object, it is much easier to make a pure judgement of taste. Therefore abstract art forms are better when we want to avoid that our pure judgement is confused by feelings arising from the concept of the artist's intentions.

There is an important difference between works of art used to exemplify judgements of taste and works of art used to exemplify judgements of the sublime. The object is seen as purposive for cognition when it is judged to be beautiful or ugly, a purposiveness that is compatible with the intentional purpose of the work of art. Both are kinds of purposiveness connected to the act of cognition, whereas

---

[19] The dynamically sublime can be static, though, as is the case with Kant's bold, overhanging rocks (KU§28, 261).

[20] Prime examples can be found in the work of J. M. W. Turner.

[21] He also seems to be in trouble when he says that birds and flowers cannot be determined as to their respective purposes, since he states that all living organisms must be judged according to the principle of intrinsic purposiveness (KU§66, 376)

the purposiveness of the sublime is connected with the object's counterpurposiveness for cognition. Thus the two aspects we can judge the object under (as an intentionally purposive work of art and as sublime object), contradict each other.

This explains the problems involved in art works creating an illusion of the sublime. When an illusion of infinity or overwhelming power is created, the represented object must also be given a physical form which must not only be part of a purposive work of art, but also be a cognitively purposive object for merely reflective judgement. An illusion of something infinite is not, in fact, infinite. It just looks infinite. The representation of a starry night in van Gogh's famous painting is not unlimited like the starry heavens Kant calls sublime. The sublime in representational art must always be both purposive and counterpurposive for cognition, and in this latter aspect must be a purposively created illusion. This explains why Kant found sublime works of art in general not to be suitable examples of the sublime in his exposition. Experiencing the sublime in representational art is not in any way ruled out by its unsuitability for didactical purposes, though. Still one can say, as a general rule, that the more aspects an object can be experienced under, the more difficult it is to make a pure aesthetic judgement about it, especially when this judgement requires the simulation of something unlimited within a limited presentation.

Sublime art in the Critique of Judgement

Kant thought that art could be sublime, as his examples show. Even in Kant's time, not all kinds of art were thought of as mere imitations of the physical world as painting and sculpture were supposed to be (KU§51, 322 f), although the rule was that art should imitate life. As we will learn from the following examples of sublime art mentioned in the third Critique, his main focus is not representation, but how the subject is affected.

Poetry is called a play with ideas (KU§51, 321) and is deemed the highest form of art apparently because it expands nature:

> [Die Dichtkunst] stärkt das Gemüt, indem sie es sein freies, selbsttätiges und von der Naturbestimmung unabhängiges Vermögen fühlen läßt, die Natur, als Erscheinung, nach Ansichten zu betrachten und zu beurteilen, die sie nicht von selbst, weder für den Sinn noch den Verstand in der Erfahrung darbietet, und sie also zum Behuf und gleichsam zum Schema des Übersinnlichen zu gebrauchen. (KU§53, 326)

The free production of poetry is clearly not restricted to imitation of nature, but includes images or illusions that cannot be experienced in nature. The creation of poetry is almost entirely the result of genius, as Kant says in a parenthesis prior to the sequence cited. This claim is rather odd, since poetry also requires skill in shaping images, and has until the twentieth century been shaped a rich variety of rules and conventions. These images can be accompanied by the feeling of the sublime, as Kant indicates when he says that poetry lets the mind feel its ability to use nature as a schema of the supersensible. But he declares in the following sentence that the understanding can also use the illusions of poetry purposively. The implication is that poetry can be both beautiful and sublime.

Representations in poetry are free from determination by nature, but they certainly have some basis in the forms of nature, since they can be used by the understanding or can be employed like some objects of nature to give rise to the feeling of the sublime. This explains why poetry, unlike the pictorial arts, can provide didactic examples of the sublime, since the poetical play with ideas does not necessarily represent objects of nature, but rather something that is both particular and incapable of being subsumed under determinate concepts. A painting or a sculpture (for Kant), on the other hand, contains an imitation of a particular object:

> Die ästhetische Idee (Archetypon, Urbild) liegt zu beiden in der Einbildungskraft zum Grunde; die Gestalt aber, welche den Ausdruck derselben ausmacht (Ektypon, Nachbild) wird entweder in ihrer körperlichen Ausdehnung (wie der Gegenstand selbst existiert) oder nach der Art, wie diese sich im Auge malt (nach ihrer Apparenz in einer Fläche) gegeben. (KU§51, 322)

The two centuries succeeding this text have of course changed these art forms completely, first by the early nineteenth century interest in depicting both mathematically and dynamically sublime landscapes, and later by the introduction of non-mimetic, abstract painting and sculpture, which for Lyotard exemplifies the aesthetics of the Kantian sublime applied to modern art.[22] Kant's frame of reference explains why he does not discuss sublime visual arts.

Kant says that poetry has the highest aesthetic value (KU§53, 326). The reason may be that poetry enables us to combine the beautiful and the sublime within one work, a combination that may make fine art even more artistic [*noch künstlicher*] (KU§52, 325). Kant's examples of poetry exhibit such combination, although their

---

22 Lyotard, *The Postmodern Condition*, 77 ff. I think Lyotard is simplifying both Kant's theory and the aim of contemporary painting in this short argument, but he has a point.

artistic value can be doubted. One is written by Frederick the Great and translated from French, apparently by Kant himself:

> Laβt uns aus dem Leben ohne Murren weichen und ohne etwas zu bedauern, indem wir die Welt noch alsdann mit Wohltaten überhaüft zurücklassen. So verbreitet die Sonne, nachdem sie ihren Tageslauf vollendet hat, noch ein mildes Licht am Himmel, und die letzten Strahlen, die sie in die Lüfte schickt, sind ihre letzten Seufzer für das Wohl der Welt. (KU§49, 315 f)

The other is by Withof, of whose work Kant cites just a single line and takes the liberty of altering a word[23]: "die Sonne quoll hervor, wie Ruh' aus Tugend quillt" (KU§49, 316). Both poems combine the beautiful with the noble sublime, i.e. the image of virtuous conduct, and seem to be chosen more for political reasons than for their suitability in this context. More in keeping with Kant's exposition of the sublime is the famous footnote attached to this passage:

> Vielleicht ist nie etwas Erhabneres gesagt, oder ein Gedanke erhabener ausgedrückt worden, als in jener Aufschrift über dem Tempel der *Isis* (der Mutter Natur): "Ich bin alles was da ist, was da war, und was da sein wird, und meinen Schleier hat kein Sterblicher aufgedeckt." (KU§49, 316)

The main lesson to learn from this is that poetry and other literary expressions are very well suited to the sublime, and that the sublime also can be presented in combination with the beautiful. Considering the distinction between the beautiful object as bounded and the sublime as connected to the representation of unboundedness, it is a bit odd that one aesthetic object can be judged as being both. On the other hand, the sublime is connected to the way we experience an object, and Kant provides many examples of bounded objects that we judge sublime, for example in architecture.

The only objects of art used as examples in the analytic of the sublime proper are the pyramids and St.Peter's Basilica in Rome. I believe this use of examples from architecture can be explained by the particular status of architecture as compared with other fine arts:

> [Die Baukunst] ist die Kunst, Begriffe von Dingen, die *nur durch Kunst* möglich sind, und deren Form nicht die Natur, sondern einen willkürlichen Zweck zum Bestimmungsgrunde hat, zu dieser Absicht, doch auch zugleich ästhetisch-zweckmäßig, darzustellen. Bei der [Baukunst] ist ein gewisser *Gebrauch* des künstlichen Gegenstandes die Hauptsache, worauf, als Bedingung, die ästhetischen Ideen eingeschränkt werden. (KU§51, 322)

---

[23] See KU§49, 316, note 50 in Pluhar's translation.

Architecture does not imitate forms of nature; it is the art of creating forms determined by purposes. A building is meant for a particular use, something that should lead us to expect that Kant would classify it as belonging to craft [*Handwerk*] rather than fine arts, since the distinction between these activities is that the first is attractive through its effect, whereas the second pleases on its own account. But Kant qualifies the classification by stating that this is not the only relevant distinction between these activities, and that he does not want to discuss whether all of the seven fine arts really belong in that group (KU§43, 304). I suppose that a more detailed classification of the arts would result in the division of architecture into two groups; one primarily oriented towards utility, the other towards the expression of beauty and grandeur[24]. Kant emphasises that in every fine art there is a basis of craft knowledge, exemplified by the correctness and richness of language as well as of prosody and meter required in poetry (KU§41, 304). This means that the practical orientation of architecture has to be considered even when the artistic purposes are primary.

It is evident that Kant's examples of sublime architecture are buildings in which the craft aspect is subordinate, even though both are examples of superior craftsmanship. St. Peter's and the pyramids are built to honour divinities, and size, material, and the labour of building and decoration go far beyond their uses as church and tombs. The purpose of these buildings is to signify the real sublime[25]. Signifying the real sublime in art is an exercise in contradiction: The real sublime is supersensible, i.e. it cannot be imagined or conceptualised according to the laws of understanding, but representing an object or idea is an act of imagination, and signifying the real sublime in art should be impossible. On the other hand, exploiting the purposive use of the contra-purposive aesthetic sublime may be the way to navigate around this problem. Then the construction involves creating the illusion of something that is beyond the comprehension of the imagination. Since it is created by activities of the imagination, it cannot actually be non-comprehensible, but, as described by Kant, these buildings succeed in creating exactly this feeling of being of a size that exceeds the power of imagination. This explains the particular suitability of architecture in exemplifying the mathematical

---

24 Perhaps the most influential tradition in architecture of the twentieth century, functionalism, saw the ideal of architecture in the combination of these two aspects of the art: Beauty in construction was determined by the function of the building.

25 The real sublime for Kant is, as we have seen the autonomy of rational beings; but the worship of the divine can be seen as a recognition of the superiority of the supersensible. It is only when we are conscious of our own worth that we can at the same time worship God in the right way, i.e. in repectful devotion without fear (KU§28, 263).

sublime. Traditionally it is the only art form that creates works of a size that can make them appear to be without limit (when regarded from the right perspective)[26]. And it is reasonable that this impressive architecture was reserved for expressions of the power of the divine.

Kant does not mention another element common to medieval cathedrals of Europe that also can be regarded under the heading of the sublime: the figures of devils and monsters used as ornamentation on both outer and inner walls. These figures can be regarded as an attempt to add a dynamically sublime element to the mathematically sublime size of the building. In *The Name of the Rose*, Eco attempts to imagine the psychological effect of this on a young monk in the thirteenth century[27], and the description is clearly one of the feeling of the sublime. Perhaps the Enlightenment philosopher Kant found these images mainly to express superstition, and thus not something that could be judged as sublime (compare KU§40, 294)?

The concept of the sublime is very often invoked to describe particular works of music or passages within such works, but Kant does not seem to think of music in those terms. He is not sure whether it is a fine art (subject to aesthetic reflective judgement) or merely an agreeable art (a free play of sensations without any cognitive function) (KU§44, 305). After arguing for both views he seems to conclude that since there is an objective, mathematical basis for the sensations and since there appears to be definite limits, common to all human beings, to our ability to distinguish tones, music is subject to reflective judgement and is a fine art. In the final sentence of the paragraph, however, Kant seems to leave the question open whether music is a pure fine art or a mixture between fine and agreeable art (KU§51, 325)[28]. The latter option is probably explained by the secondary qualities of the single tones. If the single tones have a subjective component, this subjectivity must also be part of the relation between the tones in a composition[29].

Thus it is clear that whatever reason Kant had for arguing against the aesthetic value of music he does not give it the credit it is due as an art form. Weatherstone discusses this inadequacy and shows one of the most decisive deficiencies in

26 Today there are made sculptural works of this scale, such as some kinds of land art. Christo's *Running Fence* and *Surrounded Islands*, for instance.

27 U. Eco, *The Name of the Rose*, 41 ff.

28 Later he has changed his mind and says that music is more an agreeable than a fine art, KU§54, 332.

29 This is suggested in a footnote by Pluhar in his translation, n.62, 195.

Kant's account to be his failure to see that pieces of music are appreciated as formal unities, not as single tones, and that tones have two aspects:

> If Kant had analysed tone into *pitch* and *timbre*, he would have found it much easier to see how musical forms are cognized, and he would not have been so ready to equate tones and colours. The pitch of any note in a musical composition is meaningful only in relation to the other notes of the composition[30]. By the interrelation of pitches within a composition, a composer is able to create clear formal structures.[31]

When attention is directed to melody, rhythm, harmony and other formal elements, we have a way to distinguish between fine and agreeable art in music in the same way as in visual art and poetry, a distinction Kant appears to have difficulty in making when his main focus is on single notes.

To create music, the originality of genius is required, as in other arts, and when music is a fine art in this sense, there are good reasons to believe it can be both beautiful and sublime. Examples of sublime music might be the painful 'noise' of the religious music of Tibet, the Indonesian Gamelan music, or Arvo Pärt's use of silence and dynamical movement in his music. The judgement of music is the judgement of a purposive whole in which the purpose of this whole escapes us, since there is an element of creative originality, of genius, which cannot be explained as an effect of a plan or describable intention. This is not altered by the fact that this creativity must be presented within a frame of rhythm and rules of harmony. That music can be sublime as well as beautiful Kant seems to admit indirectly in his discussion of how the fine arts can be combined:

> Auch kann die Darstellung des Erhabenen, sofern sie zur schönen Kunst gehört, in einem *gereimten Trauerspiele*, einem *Lehrgedichte*, einem *Oratorium* sich mit der Schönheit vereinigen; und in diesen Verbindungen ist die schöne Kunst noch künstlicher. (KU§52, 325)

In the oratorio, the elements of beauty and sublimity are united, but whether both elements are expressed in the music, or Kant means that the religious text is the sublime element and that music contributes beauty is difficult to tell. I assume the first reading is plausible on the ground that he says that the sublime is *united*, not merely combined, with beauty in these art forms. But if he is willing to go that far, he should also admit that music as a fine art can be sublime on its own.

---

30 It is interesting that even colours have a relational character, changing appearance according to the colour(s) of their surroundings.

31 M. Weatherstone, 'Kant's Assessment of Music in the Critique of Judgement', 64.

Sublime novels

Kant held that art could be sublime, as is evident from his own use of sublime poetry and architecture. He did not provide any examples of sublime visual art and music, and I have suggested that the reasons for this deficiency need not be any inherent trait in these art forms preventing them from being sublime. But to apply Kant's theory of the sublime to Beckett's *Molloy*, it must also be possible for novels to be sublime. The novel, understood as a narrative fiction of a certain length, had developed into a separate genre at Kant's time[32], but he was not likely to know it in any form that would make it natural to include it among the fine arts. Since the novel, as it has developed, long ago has been accepted as a form of art, we can take as a tentative assumption that it can be included within fine art in the Kantian sense.

Music and the visual arts are experienced perceptually, and as such they are like any other object of experience; we cognise them by subsuming the sensible under concepts. Judging literature is more complex, in that we start with concepts that evoke images in us when we read the text. Basically, these images are connected to what Beardsley calls the cognitive import of the text, i.e. its capacity to convey information. Together with the emotive import of the text, i.e. its capacity to affect the hearer's feeling, this is how we are affected by a work of literature or any other linguistic expression.[33] Furthermore one can argue that literature is an institutional concept, defined within a practice:

> There are no syntactic, semantic, or even more loosely 'rhetorical' features of a text that define it as a literary work. A text is identified as a literary work by recognizing the author's intention that the text is produced and meant to be read within the framework of conventions defining the practice (constituting the institution) of literature.[34]

Lamarque and Haugom Olsen says that the constitutive conventions giving a literary work aesthetic value reside in the imaginative and the mimetic dimensions of the work[35]. It is the first of these dimensions Kant takes to be constitutive of works of art, through the notion of aesthetic ideas.

Maybe Kant would agree with the institutional foundation of this theory, since he claims that many artifacts should have the form of fine art, but we do not call them fine art on that account (KU§48, 313). To have the form of fine art, an object

32 P. Lamarque and S. Haugom Olsen, *Truth, Fiction, and Literature*, 268.
33 Beardsley, *Aesthetics*, 117 f.
34 Lamarque and Haugom Olsen, *Truth, Fiction*, 255 f.
35 Ibid. 261.

must express aesthetic ideas, but, since objects of nature do that as well, such expression is not sufficient to call an object art. Fine art is the art of genius, which means that it is created for no other purpose than to express aesthetic ideas, but if such an expression is to be possible, there must exist conventions that enable us to recognise the work as a work expressing this kind of intention. The institution of art is a condition for the recognition of the object as one made with the intention of being a work evoking aesthetic ideas. But the institutional account would not satisfy Kant completely, because he would hold that the mere intention to produce a work of fine art is not enough; the intention must be successfully realised for the artifact to become a work of art. The work must actually produce the imaginative free play called aesthetic ideas, for it to be a work of art.

The understanding of literature as presented above is broad enough to include both poems, short-stories, and novels, and since this conception does not go beyond Kant's definition of fine art as artifacts produced for the purpose of evoking aesthetic ideas in the audience, literature in this sense is a fine art. Now poetry was a primary vehicle for expressing the sublime in art, but it does not follow that the same is the case with prose fiction. But if we consider what kind of ideas that are included in sublime poetry, it is clear that these ideas underlie a significant portion of the grand tradition of prose fiction, as well:

> Der Dichter wagt es, Vernunftideen von unsichtbaren Wesen, das Reich der Seligen, das Höllenreich, die Ewigkeit, die Schöpfung u.d.gl. zu versinnlichen. (KU§49, 314)

The finitude of human life in contrast with eternity has been a central theme of Western literature, along with other themes associated with the sublime. This is clearly the case if one reads the canon suggested by Bloom, which starts with Dante and ends with Beckett, containing works selected for "their sublimity and for their representativity"[36], including both poetry, plays, and prose fiction. The role of the sublime in Conrad's *Heart of Darkness* or Kafka's *The Process* may be less direct than in the poetry of Blake or T. S. Eliot, but is decisive for the way in which the reader experiences the work.

Indirectly, we can gain further support for the claim that there can be sublime novels from Kant's discussion of the combination of fine arts in works such as tragedies written in verse and oratorios, both of which can display the sublime combined with beauty (KU§52, 326). These art forms have a narrative structure just as novels have, and warrant the conclusion that the bounded structure of

---

[36] Bloom, *The Western Canon*, 2.

narratives does not prevent them from exhibiting the sublime. The decisive point is whether these works lead the reader to a reflection on ideas of reason.

Purposive form and sublime content

A sublime work of art must be both beautiful and sublime, but how do these two aspects relate to each other in the judgement about the work? In the case of the pyramids and St. Peter's Basilica, the answer seems rather straightforward if one allows for some simplification. The buildings are sublime when regarded from some particular distances or perspectives; from all other points of view they appear restricted and are judged by taste. The same is the case for medieval cathedrals like the one in Chartres, situated in the middle of a town with narrow streets that force the spectator to see it from a perspective that shows it as sublime, and the similar case of New York skyscrapers. But when we experience a sublime painting or poem, there is no equivalent to the distance that can be called the sublime perspective of architecture (unless there are paintings that are exceptions to this general point, like gigantic murals or other large-scale paintings).

Kirk Pillow has provided an original interpretation of this problem by suggesting that in a work of art, the sublime content is situated within a beautiful form[37], and we judge both the form and the content in an aesthetic judgement. This interpretation has several elements in common with my understanding of Kant, since Pillow shows that Kant's theory allows for sublime works of art, and he locates the sublime in aesthetic ideas as produced by the imagination of genius. Pillow also argues that the sublime must be presented within a work that is judged by taste. Immediately it appears as if this interpretation can solve my problem of how a bounded work of art can be sublime, but the details of Pillow's theory are in some ways problematic. The main argument is that a work of art has a form that is judged by taste, and that form is "the spatial and temporal form of objecthood, as Kant has retained it from the first *Critique*, combined with a generous conception of the imagination's free play"[38]. This form is the medium for the expression of aesthetic ideas which, according to Pillow, must be the sublime content of the work of art, since the "hallmark of the aesthetic idea is the *inexhaustibility of its content*"[39]. This means that the aesthetic idea cannot be (aesthetically) comprehended in the same way as the mathematically sublime cannot be

---

37 K. Pillow, 'Form and content in Kant's aesthetics', 444 f.
38 Ibid. 448.
39 Ibid. 453.

comprehended (KU§26, 251 f). Therefore this content is judged according to the aesthetic reflective judgement of sublimity. The aesthetic judgement of art is two judgements in one, one judgement of taste for the form, and another judgement of the sublime for the content, with a smooth transition between them[40].

Nowhere does Kant indicate that all objects of art are sublime, and Pillow solves this possible challenge by interpreting Kant as saying that not all beautiful works of art present aesthetic ideas,[41] but the passage he refers to does not say exactly that:

> Reich und original an Ideen zu sein, bedarf es nicht so notwendig zum Behuf der Schönheit, aber wohl der Angemessenheit jener Einbildungskraft in ihrer Freiheit zu der Gesetzmäßigkeit des Verstandes. (KU§50, 319)

Claiming that a work of art does not have to be rich and original in ideas is not the same as saying that no aesthetic ideas are needed. If Kant means what Pillow suggests, he contradicts his own definition of art as the product of genius (unless he contradicts his definition of genius as the ability to express aesthetic ideas, a definition which entails that every product of genius manifests this ability and hence must express or contain ideas, KU§49, 317). A picture, a poem, or a piece of music that lacks either taste or genius is called a would-be [*seinsollenden*] work of fine art (KU§48, 313), a clear indication that beautiful forms cannot lack aesthetic ideas altogether, and still be classified as art. If we accept Pillow's interpretation, all proper works of art must be sublime, and that is contrary to Kant's position (KU§45, 306 f).

I will also question the claim that aesthetic ideas are sublime just because they are inexhaustible in content and cannot adequately be comprehended in a concept, since the mathematical sublime involves the inability to comprehend a totality in imagination. The sublime involves the short-coming of imagination, whereas in aesthetic ideas it is understanding that fails to provide an adequate concept, and aesthetic ideas seem to be a sequence of loose associations not necessarily involving any demand for the imagination of the totality of these ideas.

The claim that all aesthetic ideas are sublime is even more questionable when we consider the fact that this interpretation is based on the aesthetic reflective judgement of the *content* of a work of art. 'Form' may mean different things in different contexts in Kant's works, and the same can be said about 'content' or

---

40 Ibid. 457.

41 Ibid. 458. Pillow says that "not all beautiful form presents aesthetic ideas", but for his argument to be successful, he must also claim that objects of art can be beautiful without presenting aesthetic ideas at all, which is why I have specified his claim this way.

'matter', but since aesthetic reflective judgement is explicitly said to deal with the form (or even the formlessness as is the case with the sublime) of the object, one should clarify in what sense this content can be regarded as having a form, or being formless. One possibility implicit in Pillow's account is that the aesthetic idea is a separate object of judgement, which makes the aesthetic judgement concern the form (or formlessness) of *this* object (i.e. the aesthetic idea). On this reading, I must presuppose that the form of the aesthetic idea is not identical with the form of the object of art, a supposition that is highly problematic.

Aesthetic ideas are the product of imagination when not guided by determinate concepts, and they must be present in all reflective aesthetic judgement, be it of nature or art:

> Man kann überhaupt Schönheit (sie mag Natur- oder Kunstschönheit sein) den *Ausdruck* ästhetischer Ideen nennen: nur daß in der schönen Kunst diese Idee durch einen Begriff vom Objekt veranlaßt werden muß, in der schönen Natur aber die bloße Reflexion über eine gegebene Anschauung, ohne Begriff von dem was der Gegenstand sein soll, zur Erweckung und Mitteilung der Idee, von welcher jenes Objekt als der *Ausdruck* betrachtet wird, hinreichend ist. (KU§51, 320)

Kant here says that the judgement of taste (and presumably the judgement of the sublime) in nature as well as in art always includes the experience of aesthetic ideas expressed by the object. A reasonable supposition is that these ideas are the creations of imagination in the effort to find a concept for the representation under the principle of the purposiveness of nature. And as argued earlier, the form of the object is our mental state in this cognitive process under the principle of purposiveness. It is important to note that Kant says that the object is *regarded* [*betrachtet*] as an expression of aesthetic ideas, which means that there is no claim about the real properties of the object, but only about the creative structuring of the object by imagination (which of course raises the problem of how to separate the object from the cognitive structuring of it in Kant's account). Now we can say that the difference between objects of art and natural objects does not consist in art's ability expresses aesthetic ideas (since both art and nature do that), but in the intentionality that lies behind the creation of art.

If we assume that this interpretation is correct, Pillow's suggestion faces further problems. If objects of nature have content consisting of aesthetic ideas, which, as Pillow argues, are formless and thus sublime, then all objects have sublime content. Instead of the traditional Kantian problem of everything being beautiful, this account entails that everything is sublime. This unhappy conclusion can only be avoided by severing the connection Pillow establishes between aesthetic ideas and the sublime. On my interpretation, Kant holds that aesthetic ideas must be present in beautiful objects, in ugly objects, and in sublime objects, as well as in those that are judged as both beautiful and sublime. Then Pillow's main point contradicts Kant's view on the connection between an object's expression of aesthetic ideas and its suitability for pure aesthetic judgement.

I have argued above that Kant's notion of the form of objects is not equal to form as the word is used in art criticism. Aesthetic ideas can be expressed both in the form and in the content of the work of art ('form' and 'content' are here understood in the art criticism sense), and both form and content belong to the material of the object. The aesthetic judgement is not concerned with this material, but with the form of the object, which is the structuring activity of imagination and understanding. This structuring activity of aesthetic reflective judgement can be called a production of aesthetic ideas in accordance with the object, but we are not judging these ideas, but merely the state of mind, i.e. our feeling, when performing this creative activity. Even in the 'objective' (teleological) aspect of reflective judgement we are unable to know the aesthetic ideas, since there are no objects adequate to these intuitions (KU§49, 314); they are not cognisable. But we must consider the teleological judgement to be the cognitive result of this creative imaginative process.

Pillow holds that aesthetic ideas must be sublime since they are not determinable, and because they are said, in one important passage, to lead to the reflection on rational ideas (KU§49, 315). This passage is the same as the one Guyer discussed when concluding that aesthetic ideas stand in a direct relation to ideas of reason. I believe that the argument I used to question Guyer's view also is valid against Pillow. The full context of the passage, although obscure, indicates that aesthetic ideas do not have to be accompanied by ideas of reason. These ideas are only involved in the production of sublime art. In beautiful art, the artist draws on his experience of nature and still creates a work expressing aesthetic ideas.

There remain promising suggestions in Pillow's interpretation of Kant, since the sublime in art must be presented within a humanly made form and accordingly be restricted by man's natural capacities, which means that the work of art cannot be formless even though we judge it to be so. The suggestion that the sublime can be the content within this form, combined with the point that a visual object of art can be sublime from some perspectives and beautiful or ugly from other, allows for the possibility that an object of art can be judged in several ways. When judged as a totality, the object always has a form that must be judged by taste, even if it is an object that is incomplete or deliberately breaks the rules of completeness by (in narrative literature) lacking beginning or end in the conventional sense, or (in poetry or music) by breaking any possible establishment of a rhythm. Every aesthetic trick of that kind will be unable to evade the establishment of the work as a totality, which is what Kant probably means when he says that for judging an object of art we must base the judgement on a concept of what the thing is meant to be. This is related to the hermeneutic assumption that a text as a whole is meaningful and that this is the basis for understanding[42], a principle that can be extended to all meaningful material, including art.

But there are other perspectives on art, which we can call judgements about its content. In these judgements, we are not concerned with the totality as such, but with different aspects of the work considered in isolation. These aspects can be either sublime, beautiful or both (or ugly or aesthetically indifferent for that matter). It must be noted that talking of aesthetic reflective judgements of the content of a work of art requires caution; we are still judging the form of the object in Kant's sense, i.e. the mental state we are in when cognising the object. We are not really judging the object or an aspect of it, but the feeling of the subject who experiences the object. But we nonetheless judge an aspect of the object in that we do cognise the different aspects of the object, and the aesthetic judgement is a judgement of our mental state when cognising these aspects. This mental state will vary according to which object or which aspect of an object we are experiencing, and will be a judgement of taste if it is the subjective aspect of a conceptual judgement[43] under the principle of purposiveness, and will be a judgement of the sublime if it is the subjective aspect of a conceptual judgement under the purposive use of the object for man's supersensible vocation.

If we return to Yeats' *The Second Coming*, his images of things falling apart and loss of meaning can be judged by taste as part of a purposive totality[44], although this totality can hardly be described as beautiful. But the threatening end describing the beast slouching towards Bethlehem, taking the place of the expected saviour, is an image associated with evil conquering good and thus an image of the powerlessness of man. The image of the beast belongs to the dynamically sublime and represents a different aspect of the poem from the first, already apocalyptic

---

[42] Gadamer, *Wahrheit und Methode*, 271.

[43] It is, as argued in chapter two, sufficient that we have a potential cognition of the object under this principle, i.e. that the object *can* be judged under this principle.

[44] Destruction is only possible against the background of something constructed, and is also associated with the hope of a new beginning. Kant also stresses the value of judging the apparently disagreeable, and thus, counterpurposive under the principle of purposiveness (KU§67,379). This sense of counterpurposive is not the same as the principle associated with the sublime, where the object is counterpurposive because it is not overtaxing our cognitive capacities, not because we do not see its function within the totality.

part. This second, sublime part is not possible without the first part as a background, since the first part builds up towards a solution, a salvation which is denied. These parts must be judged under the two principles of purposiveness and purposive use of nature (genius) respectively. These are two aspects of the poem, and they belong to the purposive totality of the poem, purposive in the sense that it is an object, since it has limits and structural elements that together create a whole.

A work of art has a many-faceted content formed in certain ways to express this content. The pure aesthetic judgement can either be a judgement of the work as a whole, where all aspects contribute to this purposive totality, or it can concern one of its aspects. We can judge both this totality (of content) as well as one or more of its aspects (of content) aesthetically, but in both cases we judge the form of the object, i.e. our feeling when cognising the object under teleological principles. The form of the work of art, i.e. its structure and style, is in a way inseparable from the content in the aesthetic judgement, since both are parts of the conceptual judgement of the object of art, of which the aesthetic judgement is the subjective aspect. Thus the discussion of the art critic's form belongs to the conceptual analysis of the work of art, which is necessary to disentangle the various judgmental aspects of the work of art such as its pure aesthetic, applied aesthetic, conceptual, moral, and entertaining features. That Kant holds that the work of art gives rise to several such kinds of judgements is clear from his brief but very rich discussion of the feelings of gratification, approval and disapproval, games and play, humour, respect, and naivety in the comment that ends the Analytic of Aesthetic Judgement (KU§54, 330 ff). We can find further support in his assertion that moral treatises and sermons, too, should display taste (KU§48, 313)[45]. These factors indicate that human artifacts (in a wide sense) can be judged in many ways, and that a work of art does not have to be exclusively an object of pure aesthetic reflective judgement.

Aesthetic, cognitive, and moral judgements of art

If I am right in my reading of Kant, his theory opens the way for pluralistic interpretations of art. A work of art can be judged in several different, even

[45] If moral treatises can be subject to pure aesthetic judgement, it does not follow that works of art can be subject to moral judgements, but it shows that the aesthetic and the ethical do not necessarily belong to different spheres, and that the same work can be judged according to both principles. Whether the work belongs to the genre of moral treatises or that of narrative literature should not make any difference.

contradictory ways, without that necessitating a rejection of one of the contradicting positions. Kant's discussion of the relation between free and accessory beauty shows one aspect of this pluralism:

> Ein Geschmacksurteil würde in Ansehung eines Gegenstandes von bestimmtem innern Zwecke nur alsdann rein sein, wenn der Urteilende entweder von diesem Zwecke keinen Begriff hätte, oder in seinem Urteile davon abstrahierte. Aber alsdann würde dieser, ob er gleich ein richtiges Geschmacksurteil fällte, indem er den Gegenstand als freie Schönheit beurteilte, dennoch von dem andern, welcher die Schönheit an ihm nur als anhängende Beschaffenheit betrachtet (auf den Zweck des Gegenstandes sieht), getadelt und eines falsches Geschmacks beschuldigt werden, obgleich beide in ihrer Art richtig urteilen: der eine nach dem, was er vor den Sinnen, der andere nach dem, was er in Gedanken hat. (KU§16, 231)

It is worth noticing that this pluralism is not in any way relativistic; both judgements are right, and both could have been wrong, and we are warranted in claiming universal assent for both kinds of aesthetic judgement. I argued above that these two kinds of judgement can and should be supplemented by further aspects, and further support can be gathered from Kant's examples of poetry, where the importance of their moral messages is underscored (KU§49, 315f), and his inclusion of didactic poems within fine arts (KU§52, 325). One could say that I am spending time on the obvious by proving that Kant meant that works of art should be both interpreted as meaningful expression as well as judged by disinterested feelings, but Kant's focus on the pure aesthetic judgement has led commentators to think that he held this to be the only genuine way to assess art:

> Some philosophers of art who have argued for a theory very like the Presentational theory (Kant, Fiedler) have, it is true, stipulated that we should free ourselves from all concepts when we approach art: but it is hard to attach much sense to such an extreme demand.[46]

Such misunderstandings used to be common, and perhaps have even been among the causes of the formalist preoccupation of twentieth century theories of art, including a sceptical attitude to ethical and political interpretations of art[47]. Besides, my aim is to show how the Kantian sublime can be part of the judgement of literature, and to decide its role vis-à-vis different conceptual interpretations of such works. Therefore it is important to show that Kant's theory at least implies a pluralistic theory of interpretation.

---

46 R. Wollheim, *Art and its Object*, 61.
47 Booth, *Company*, 36 f.

The main conclusions of my discussion of Kant's fragmented theory of art can be summed up as follows: (1) Fine art is a human artifact with the purpose of expressing aesthetic ideas, which are the qualities that are judged by pure aesthetic reflective judgements. (2) This requires genius, an inspirational ability that is not rationally guided, and as such a part of man as nature. (3) Also human artifacts that do not have the expression of aesthetic ideas as their primary purpose can express aesthetic ideas, and thus display genius. (4) Fine art, including novels, can be sublime.

6. *Molloy* and the Kantian sublime

I have shown that Kant held that art can be sublime in the same way as nature, and that novels too must be included among these possibly sublime forms of art. Now it is time to return to the analysis of Beckett's *Molloy*, to see whether my Kantian theory is relevant for this work. I begin by noting that it is by thwarting not the attempt to understand the text, but the attempt to create a fictive world in imagination that the work gives rise to the feeling of the sublime. And although the judgement concerns the feeling of the subject, not any feature of the object, it is still possible to point out features that give rise to this feeling, as Kant often does in his exposition.

I suggest three factors that contribute to the experience of *Molloy* as sublime. The first is the formal feature of self-doubt or self-negation. This is mathematically sublime since it allows an apprehension of all the different images of the story but prevents the aesthetic comprehension of them as a totality. The second is the dynamically sublime characters of Molloy and of Moran when he disintegrates. They follow principles blindly and disregard all personal desires or interests. Since these are not moral principles, the affects or lack of affects that drive the characters to follow the principles, belong to the terrifying, dynamically sublime. The third sublime feature of this novel is found in poetical passages that combine the mathematical and the dynamical mode. Here paradoxical images of eternal, unchanging, and continuous destruction are evoked in the reader. Since these passages are connected to the recurrent theme of the murmur or sound underlying the voices of the narratives, the sublime becomes the underlying feeling of the whole work.

I then go on to argue how this approach can be combined with the cognitive approach suggested by Nussbaum. The requirement is that we should be able both to be engaged in the lives and emotions of the characters, and to judge the work by disinterested, non-engaged feelings. I show how there is room both in Kant's and Nussbaum's theories for this combined attitude when experiencing a work of art. But when the feeling of the sublime is connected to stories of evil acts containing human suffering, we seem to have a more difficult case. Feeling pleasure in an action or event that is reprehensible and calls for sympathy appears to be morally wrong. I argue, by referring to Kant's discussion of the French Revolution, that so long as we feel the appropriate feelings of loathing and sympathy, we can also take aesthetic pleasure in such stories without dulling our natural feelings.

6. 1 Forms of sublimity in Molloy

Text, imagination and feeling

My initial analysis of *Molloy* tried to point out some features of this work that give rise to the feeling of the sublime in the reader. I supplemented that analysis with a discussion of critical assessments of the work that I hold can be understood as calling attention to a sublime impact of the work. According to Kant's analysis of the sublime, calling an object sublime is the same as claiming that the object is such that it gives rise to a particular kind of feeling in the subject experiencing the object. When the object in question is a literary work, this means that we cannot locate the sublime in some particular feature of the text, but in the way the reader judges this work. This means that the focus of my attempt at analysing *Molloy* as a sublime work of literature cannot be the structure, the narrative, or the way the characters are described, but rather how these features are judged aesthetically, i.e. by disinterested feeling.

I have exaggerated slightly in saying that we cannot point to any features of the work that make it sublime. Kant's exposition of the sublime is, as we have seen, very much concerned with the objective aspect of the reflective judgement of the object. It discusses at length how different characteristics, such as immense size, the impression of irresistible force, and the unswerving pursuit of principles are objective counterparts to the subjective judgement of sublimity. The aesthetic reflective judgement of these objects does involve not only the lawfulness of understanding, but also that of reason, because sublime objects have characteristics which make us search for concepts of reason in addition to, or instead of, concepts of understanding. In the following I will attempt to point out some characteristics of *Molloy* that can account for the sublimity of this novel.

Understanding requires interpretation, and a literary work is constituted by the reader as a narrative within a fictive world:

> A reader's task is to reconstruct this world by identifying and weighing the aspectival (connotative, evaluative, etc.) qualities in the fictive descriptions. This involves much more than accepting as true, or as 'known fact', what is

> explicitly reported. Information about narrative worlds is presented through a series of narrative filters.[1]

A text is, to put it rather crudely, the material out of which the imagination and the understanding create a story. Thus there is a creative work involved in reading literature that is different from the representational activity involved in the cognition of real objects. The text provides the concepts by which understanding gives the rules for the imagination's shaping of the imagined world of the story. When Molloy describes the encounter between A and C (M 9 ff), the reader forms an image of these two men in greatcoats walking towards each other, halting, exchanging a few words, then walking on, one towards a town, the other with uncertain steps in the opposite direction. The text is only the basis for the imagination of the landscape and the event, which is created through the imaginative work of the reader. In addition to the text, the reader draws on her experiences of the real world as well as other stories she has read or heard. This is what Kant means when he says the imagination creates another nature out of the material that is provided by actual nature (KU§49, 314).

So my concern is with the text of *Molloy* as it gives rise to images that not only create another nature on the basis of the actual nature, but as it gives rise to images that are free from the law of association which create something that surpasses nature (KU§49, 314). These images are not determined by a concept, nor are they images that give rise to concepts of understanding when we reflect on these images in our thought on them. The concepts on which the images are based give rise to thoughts that involve ideas of reason:

> Wenn nun einem Begriffe eine Vorstellung der Einbildungskraft untergelegt wird, die zu seiner Darstellung gehört, aber für sich allein soviel zu denken veranlaßt, als sich niemals in einem bestimmten Begriff zusammenfassen läßt, mithin den Begriff selbst auf unbegrenzte Art ästhetisch erweitert, so ist die Einbildungskraft hierbei schöpferisch und bringt das Vermögen intellektueller Ideen (die Vernunft) in Bewegung, mehr nämlich bei Veranlassung einer Vorstellung zu denken (was zwar zu dem Begriffe des Gegenstandes gehört), als in ihr aufgefaßt und deutlich gemacht werden kann. (KU§49, 314 f)

When the concepts of the text are represented by the imagination in a way that leads to many thoughts including concepts of reason, this means that the imagination is in a state of free play with reason, and this representational activity is judged by the subject through a feeling of the sublime. This does not mean that *only* ideas of reason are involved, although that is often the case. We may well

---

[1] Lamarque and Haugom Olsen, *Truth, Fiction*, 93.

conceive of representations of the imagination that involve both concepts of understanding and ideas of reason. This is the case for sublime affects, where the action according to principles rather than impulses of the senses (KU§29, 272) may also be explained psychologically with reference to the subject's own prudential aims, mass psychology (as in the case of enthusiasm), or with reference to a craving for social recognition. In this case, imagination may involve both understanding and reason, although not simultaneously, since the explanations of the action under either concepts of nature or principles of freedom are mutually exclusive. We cannot regard the courageous, self-disregarding attack of the soldier at the same time as expressive of psychological conditioning due to military training and as expressive of his free choice to defend the principles of the constitution of his country. Regardless of whether the reflective judgement of an object or event involves understanding or reason, we demand that everybody should represent it the same way, which means that everybody should feel the same as we do when we cognise the object.

The mathematically sublime form

I will explore the sublime in *Molloy* assuming that it can involve both mathematical and dynamical modes, and that it can display both the terrifying and the noble sublime. I will also tentatively assume that the sublime can be found both in the form as well as in the content of the work. When I say that the form of *Molloy* is sublime, I mean that the narrative is told in a way that gives rise to the feeling of the sublime. As Nussbaum and many others have emphasised, the form-content distinction has limited value, because the way a story is told influences and changes the content of that story, so that one can say that form is part of the content[2]. On the other hand, a distinction between form and content is valid when discussing how different works deal with the same story, such as the different ways the story of Orestes' return to Electra is dealt with in tragedies written by Aeschylos, Sophocles, and Euripides respectively[3]. A suitably wide definition focuses on the unifying character of the form:

> Using the distinction between form and subject[4], we can say that the aesthetic value defined by the creative-imaginative aspect of the concept of literature is

[2] Nussbaum, *Love's Knowledge*, 3 ff.

[3] Lamarque and Haugom Olsen, *Truth, Fiction*, 262 ff.

[4] The subject of a literary work is "its settings and scenes, its characters, the actions of its characters", ibid. 259.

> constituted by the imposition of form on a subject. Imposing form on a subject is to impose coherence on a complexity of elements: a manifold of elements is in construal both identified and recognized as forming a unity. An *expectation* of a complex and coherent form is thus one central element in the literary stance; and appreciation, the mode of apprehension defined by the literary stance, aims at identifying the complex and coherent form of a literary work of art[5].

This definition can be used as point of departure for discussing how the form of *Molloy* can contribute to the overall assessment of the work as sublime.

One of the features most frequently discussed in the secondary literature on *Molloy*, is the way the narrative contradicts itself, or at least how the narrator doubts his own account of what did take place: "A and C I never saw again. But perhaps I shall see them again? But shall I be able to recognise them? And am I sure I never saw them again? And what do I mean by seeing and seeing again?" (M 15) When we compare this self-doubt, which prevents a clear and coherent story from unfolding, with the definition of form above, we find that this self-questioning form does the opposite of what a form is supposed to do. The subject or content in *Molloy* can be described as a "complexity of elements", but only in a very wide sense of 'coherence' can the form be said to impose coherence on this complexity. The reader's attempt to create coherence to the complexity of elements is prevented by these self-referring questions and negations.

Since the form of this work fails to provide this coherence, the reader's expectation of such coherence is not fulfilled. And this expectation is no simple convention or habit the reader has acquired. It is the way we relate to any object or meaningful text we encounter. We assume that the work is given as a meaningful and, thus, coherent unity, and this is a basic form of human understanding, as Gadamer points out:

> Die Antizipation von Sinn, in der das Ganze gemeint ist, kommt dadurch zu explizitem Verständnis, daß die Teile, die sich vom Ganzen her bestimmen, ihrerseits dieses Ganze bestimmen. ... Einstimmung aller Einzelheiten zum Ganzen ist das jeweilige Kriterium für die Richtigkeit des Verstehens. Das Ausbleiben solcher Einstimmung bedeutet Scheitern des Verstehens.[6]

This does not mean that the text we strive to understand must be coherent throughout. Often we bracket some elements, try to explain them away, or deliberately alter them to make them fit with our pre-judgements. But these ways of avoiding contradictions only serve to show the importance of coherence when

---

5 Ibid. 265.

6 Gadamer, *Wahrheit und Methode*, 296.

we try to make sense of a text. This kind of unity and hence meaningfulness is denied us in the reading of *Molloy*.

Here it is tempting to draw attention to the fact that Kant refers to the lack of form [*Unform*] (KU VII, 192) of sublime objects or describes them as being formless [*formlos*] (KU§23, 244), which may suggest that *Molloy* is sublime just because it is formless. The reader's attempts at grasping the unity of the work, the coherence provided by the form, is made impossible by the self-negations. But that would be to simplify the problem we are facing here, because form in the sense defined by Lamarque and Haugom Olsen is the structuring of the subject (or content), whereas form and formlessness in the context of Kantian aesthetics refers to the activity of imagination. The implication would be that any incoherent or partially contradictory narrative would be sublime, and that is highly implausible. Rather than feel the pleasure of sublimity, most people become annoyed when they discover such incoherences in narratives. Or, as already indicated, we try to overlook these inconsistencies and recreate the unified work.

The text of *Molloy* puts more obstacles in the way of coherent creation of the work than texts that happen to have some inconsistent elements. The self-negations and the misuses of conventional phrases and of philosophical and religious language *deliberately* prevent the creation of a coherent unity of both the narrative and the world in which it takes place. The novel effectively prevents the reader from creating a meaningful totality, i.e. a coherent form for the work, by disregarding these contradictions or interpreting them in a way that makes such coherence possible. Furthermore, the self-negating style is not arbitrary in a way that allows the reader to regard the work as a failure in form. This contradictory style is the form of the work, and cannot be overlooked or explained away. So the question is, to return to the Kantian approach: how does this affect the creation of images on the basis of the text?

When the reader co-creates the work on the basis of the textual material and her own experiences of the actual world, she strives for creating a unified whole out of this material. This assumption Kant shares with Gadamer, Iser, Nussbaum, and Lamarque and Haugom Olsen. The imagination creates a fictional world mirroring the actual world by association. When the reader's imagination creates a story and a world on the basis of the text of *Molloy*, the text itself undermines the images that are formed. Repeatedly, the reader finds that no sooner has a picture of the events been formed than the material of the text denies or questions what he has already brought to fictional life. No image replaces the one that is destroyed. Scruton cites a passages ending in the sentence "But perhaps I'm remembering things" (M 9) and describes the reader's experience thus:

> Here the prose moves under the apparent pressure of a great emotion, straining after words as though trying to match them against a recalcitrant reality. What we are given, however, is not so much an object of dramatic feeling as a huge, still, isolated image, detached from the narrative and ending with the typical Beckett device of a cliché ('perhaps I'm remembering things') stunningly altered with its literal meaning laid bare: 'perhaps I'm remembering things'; the implication being, perhaps I'm not. It is as though the narrative has been dissolved, released from the control of any dramatic meaning, and the reader condemned to search for the emotion with which to match the image in the text.[7]

But there is no stable image left with which to match an emotion. The image created when reading Molloy's self-doubting words ("Perhaps I'm inventing a little, perhaps embellishing, but on the whole that's the way it was" (M 9)) is not simply removed as if it had never been there. The self-negation eradicates the particular image, but not the need to have an image. As Scruton points out, even self-contradictions may tell us something. He goes on to point out one of the main narrative functions of Beckett's style of self-negations: "In this way a literary language may evolve which, while it creates no fictional world independent of itself, conveys, nevertheless, quite precise states of mind."[8]

If we read these passages from Scruton (whose main point is very different from mine) against the background of Kant's analysis of the sublime, we find several of the basic components from Kant's exposition of the sublime: (1) failure of the imagination to provide an image of the object, and (2) a mental state is still present, despite the inadequate image, (3) a feeling replaces the image as the representation given. So if we accept this description of the effect of *Molloy*, the aesthetic judgement of the work under this description is a judgement of the sublime rather than a judgement of taste. But under which mode of the sublime should this 'object' be classified? The reference to 'a huge, still, isolated image' indicates the mathematically sublime. This does not seem completely right, though. The problem is not primarily that we are unable to encompass in imagination the object described in the text, but that the text withdraws the statements on which the initial images were formed, which makes these images inadequate in the representation of the given text. But the dynamically sublime is an even more unlikely candidate for classification of the sublime form of *Molloy*. There is nothing powerful, fearful, or admirable about this sublime.

Despite its difference from the paradigmatic form of mathematical sublimity, the form of contradictions as found in *Molloy* should be classified as

---

7 Scruton, *Aesthetic Understanding*, 197.
8 Ibid.

mathematically sublime. It is a different kind of mathematical sublimity when compared to the one described by Kant. That the form of this work must be classified as mathematically sublime becomes clear if we take into account the basic foundation for distinguishing between the two modes of the sublime. It is the distinction between theoretical and practical reason (KU§24, 247). Since these self-negations of *Molloy* influence our ability to form images, i.e. our contemplation of this fictive world, it is theoretical reason that is involved in the difficulty we encounter when attempting to form images of the events and world of *Molloy*. Therefore the form of this novel must be said to be mathematically sublime, not due to its overwhelming size, but to its elusiveness. It does not follow, however, that this self-negation has no connection with the dynamically sublime. The self-negations also show something about the narrators of the two parts of *Molloy*, and in this respect it is possible that it influences our aesthetic judgement of their character. To what extent the self-negations contribute to our judgements of the characters of the narrators as dynamically sublime, I discuss below.

Now my analysis calls for some specificity: How can this form of self-negation give rise to the feeling of the sublime? An important condition is that the fictitious world of the novel is assumed to be a totality. If the novel is presented or read as a formal experiment or as an argument in a debate concerning narrative conventions, we do not read it as a work of fiction, but according to its formal arrangements or as an argument in disguise. Then the work will not require the same kind of imaginative representation or the same narrative coherence. It is the formal structure itself, or the demand for argumentative coherence that becomes the focal point. I may take an interest in the formal aspects of Joyce's *Finnegans Wake* and analyse for example the use of Norwegian words and phrases in the work, or count its references to Dante's *The Divine Comedy*. Then a lack of narrative coherence, or of the comprehensibility required for such coherence, is not important for my reading. It is when I read the work as telling a story and as creating a fictitious universe through this story, and therefore presuppose coherence of the narrative and of the fictitious world, that the destruction of this coherence can be judged sublime. Then I try to grasp the story as a meaningful unity, on models provided by the actual world and other narratives.

It is reasonable to hold that Kant's theory of the appreciation of art was not created with the intention to include narratives. It is also clear that the actual world in which we live is not structured as a narrative. Still our self-understanding can be said to be narratively structured. This has consequences for an application of Kant's theory of the sublime to works with a narrative form. Kant says that the fictitious world created by the imagination in a work of art is based on material from the actual world, not only the actual world, but other narratives provide material for creating a fictitious world on the basis of a narrative. This is pointed out by, among others, MacIntyre:

> [M]an is in his actions and practice, as well as in his fictions, essentially a story-telling animal. He is not essentially, but becomes through his history, a teller of stories that aspire to truth.[9]

I am not sure that Kant would agree. He would probably go one step further than MacIntyre in grounding the necessity of a narrative approach to the understanding of ourselves and the world in which we live. Although narratives do not tell the truth about how the world is structured, man's tendency to understand the world through stories is not a mere fact about what we have become through history, either. It is our rationality that is such that when we try to understand a phenomenon that cannot be explained through the mechanism of nature, we must resort to a teleological explanation. And teleology provides a basic fundament for all narratives. Thus our status as story-telling animals is one of the basic features of our understanding, as Kant presents it. So when we try to make sense of an object, a chain of events, or a story we must understand it as a goal-oriented unity, because that is how we structure the phenomena of the world. Not because the world *is* structured teleologically, but because the understanding of man is.

When a unified, coherent totality is denied the reader, without allowing her to explain this as a result of the incompetence of the author, since it is a necessary element of the form of the work, then the aesthetic comprehension of the work fails. The reader can describe or paraphrase the events, but cannot imagine them as they are described. Aesthetic apprehension, the imagining of the separate elements of which the work is made up, is possible. We can imagine the separate images of the following passage where Molloy tells about his possible encounter with a woman on the beach, but when we have to take into account the self-doubts and all possible sources of mistakes mentioned, no unambiguous image is left:

> I think one of them one day, detaching herself from her companions, came and offered me something to eat and that I looked at her in silence, until she went away. Yes, it seems to me some such incident occurred about this time. But perhaps I am thinking of another stay, at an earlier time, for this will be my last, my last but one, or two, there is never a last, by the sea. However that may be I see a young woman coming towards me and stopping from time to time to look back at her companions. Huddled together like sheep they watch her recede, urging her on, and laughing, no doubt, I seem to hear laughter far away. Then it is her back I see, as she goes away, now it is towards me she looks

9 MacIntyre, *After Virtue*, 216.

> back, but without stopping. But perhaps I am merging two times in one, and two women, one coming towards me, shyly, urged on by the cries and laughter of her companions, and the other going away from me, unhesitatingly. (M 74 f)

We have no difficulty in forming a picture of this incident or incidents as they are described. But when he starts to doubt whether he has merged two separate occasions into one, the sequence of events is not clear-cut anymore. If he has described two events, what happened to the woman of the first event after she had approached Molloy, and where did the woman of the second event come from when leaving him? And were the group of laughing women there on both occasions? Or maybe both events belong to earlier stays at the seaside, and do not belong to the story Molloy is telling. And a few pages earlier Molloy introduces the stay at the beach in a way that makes it impossible to know whether he was there at all:

> And to saying what became of me, and where I went, in the months and perhaps the year that followed, no. For I weary of these inventions and others beckon to me. But in order to blacken a few more pages may I say I spent some time at the seaside, without incident. (M 68)

Did Molloy spend time at the seaside, did he meet a woman there, did that encounter happen in the way he told it? We cannot, on the basis of the story as it is told, answer these questions, although we can form images of the separate events in isolation. Therefore what Kant calls aesthetic apprehension is possible, but our imagination cannot comprehend the totality aesthetically (KU§26, 251 f).

Now since the power of imagination is inadequate in forming an image of these events as recounted, it cannot get into any free play with the understanding because there is no representation of an image for which to find a concept. But the inadequacy of imagination gives rise to a feeling of purposiveness, because the object can be used for the purposes of reason (KU§27, 257 f). What matters is not that the object is modest in size, but that it overtaxes the power of imagination by a particular way of presenting the material. The negation of the stated course of events does not leave an emptiness as if nothing was said. It leaves a void, or as Beckett expressed it twelve years before publishing *Molloy*:

> At first it can only be a matter of somehow finding a method by which we can represent this mocking attitude towards the word, through words. In this dissonance between the means and their use it will perhaps become possible to feel a whisper of that final music or that silence that underlies All.[10]

---

10 Cited from H. Bloom, *Ruin the Sacred Truths*, 201.

This feeling is a feeling of the sublime, but the paradox is that according to Kant, it is our own capacity for words, or concepts, that we feel. Kant would not accept that this feeling is achieved by using a method, as Beckett seems to think in this early period. The effect is dependent on the creative talent genius, which cannot be rationally controlled, although it also involves rationality.

The dynamically sublime characters

The second way Beckett's *Molloy* gives rise to the feeling of the sublime, is through the portrayal of narrators and characters of the novel. When discussing the sublimity of the form of this work, a problem was the development of fine art after Kant. The features that make *Molloy* sublime in form were not part of the picture of fine arts drawn up by Kant. When it comes to the content, the portrayal of the narrators through the narrative, we are closer to Kant's own description of the dynamically sublime human affects, as discussed in chapter three[11]. Kant holds that affects that conquer the impulses of sensibility are sublime, because they have their source in ideas. In this case, it does not matter whether the ideas are moral ideas (KU§29, 271 f). Thus the sublime affects are either noble, when they have a basis in respect for moral ideas, or terrifying, when they have a basis in some non-moral idea or express a non-moral relation to a moral idea or principle (B 212).

When Kant says that even moral depravities and moral failings may appear sublime so long as they are not tested by reason, it is clear that it is within this category we find the narrators of *Molloy*. The scant traces of moral language in Molloy's story are just as misunderstood or misused as the other conventions the narrator employs. And when he goes into a discussion of moral principles, it turns out that he has only one, and this is not the categorical imperative:

> But imperatives are a little different, and I have always been inclined to submit to them, I don't know why. For they never led me anywhere, but tore me from places where, if all was not well, all was not worse than anywhere else, and then went silent, leaving me stranded. So I knew my imperatives well, and yet I submitted to them. It had become a habit. It is true they nearly all bore on the same question, that of my relations with my mother, and on the importance of bringing as soon as possible some light to bear on these and even on the kind of light that should be brought to bear and the most effective means of doing so. (M 86)

---

[11] See p. 149 ff.

This is Molloy's project, and it is not a moral project in any ordinary (or Kantian) sense of the word. The imperatives he follows are pointless in the sense that they bid him to do something that it is impossible to accomplish. As Molloy says: "Charming things, hypothetical imperatives" (M 87). He cannot alter anything in relation to a mother with whom it is impossible to communicate, if she is still alive. He also says that he has gone to her many times on the basis of such imperatives and he always left her without accomplishing anything (M 87).

This is sublime in Kant's sense, because Molloy continues to follow these principles through great pains and sufferings, and always subordinates his own well-being to act according to these imperatives. He does not display affects such as enthusiasm in his adherence to these imperatives, which goes well together with Kant's emphasis on the sublimity of *Affektlosigkeit*. Still he goes to such lengths that when he is unable to walk on his crutches to get to his mother, he starts to crawl (M 89). And he leaves the relative comfort of Lousse's home to continue his quest (M 59) despite her attempts to persuade him to stay. So although Molloy is a foreigner to us when it comes to the imperatives he acts on and the way he understands our language and conventions, we still find something strangely heroic in his relentless pursuit of meaningless principles. He has something in common with Don Quixote who also pursued principles and ideals that seemed inappropriate and misunderstood in relation to the situations he encountered. But in the case of Don Quixote we can recognise both what drives him and the principles he acts on. We can also understand his mistakes. Molloy is a stranger. His principles are not ours, just as his notions do not resemble ours, as he says, but are "all spasms, sweat and trembling, without an atom of common sense or lucidity" (M 68). But he is nonetheless heroic in the sense that he is acting on principles at the cost of his own well-being, and that we do recognise.

Now I am in a position to return to the problem of why early critics as Bataille and Esslin explained an apparently similar aesthetic judgement of the work as resulting from mutually exclusive causes[12]. Esslin is representative of early critics many of whom regard Molloy as a dignified hero displaying courage and noble stoicism, whereas Bataille regards Molloy as representing the borderline between the human and the non-human, attractive and terrifying at once. In a sense, they both point to elements in the complex basis for the sublimity of the character Molloy. Molloy is following principles instead of succumbing to the concern for everyday matters, but this does not make him noble and dignified in the traditional sense of these words. He is not pursuing the immutable [*unwandelbar*] principles

[12] See p. 48 ff.

of pure reason. Such pursuit is, according to Kant, the hallmark of the noble sublime (KU§29, 272). The imperatives Molloy follows appear arbitrary and irrational, given that they demand something that it is impossible to do, namely to establish a new relation with a mother with whom he is unable to communicate. Still they are principles, and Molloy suffers greatly for their sake, and in this sense his act is sublime. We cannot make sense of his action by turning to nature in the form of understandable psychological mechanisms. This means that the imagination involves reason in the attempt to make sense of this phenomenon.

Bataille does not make Molloy a hero in the way Esslin does, and he is probably closer to pinpointing the reasons for the sublime attractiveness of this character. Molloy is no exhibition of the noble sublime but of the terrifying, adventurous sublime, to use Kant's pre-Critical classification:

> In der menschlichen Natur finden sich niemals rühmliche Eigenschaften, ohne daß zugleich Abartungen derselben durch unendliche Schattierungen bis zur äußersten Unvollkommenheit übergehen sollten. Die Eigenschaft des *Schrecklich-Erhabenen*, wenn sie ganz unnatürlich wird, ist *abenteuerlich*. [Accompanying footnote:] In so fern die Erhabenheit oder Schönheit das bekannte Mittelmaß überschreitet, so pflegt man sie *romanisch* zu nennen. (B 213 f)

The character of Molloy is as such a variation on the idea of acting according to duty. He represents the terrifying sublime, because his principles are not founded on respect for humanity, neither in himself nor in others. This lack both of respect and compassionate sympathy for others is most plainly displayed in his encounter with the charcoal-burner who fails to understand Molloy's question about the way out of the forest, and holds him back when he tries to move on.

> So I smartly freed a crutch and dealt him a good dint on the skull. That calmed him. The dirty old brute. I got up and went on. But I hadn't gone more than a few paces when, and for me at this time a few paces meant something, when I turned and went back to where he lay, to examine him. Seeing he had not ceased to breathe I contented myself with giving him a few warm kicks in the ribs, with my heels. ... People imagine, because you are old, poor, crippled, terrified, that you can't stand up for yourself, and generally speaking that is so. But given favorable conditions, a feeble and awkward assailant, in your own class what, and a lonely place, and you have a good chance of showing what stuff you are made of. And it is doubtless in order to revive interest in this possibility, too often forgotten, that I have layed over an incident of no interest in itself, like all that has a moral. (M 84 f)

I have left out the detailed description of the maltreatment of the charcoal-burner, but it is given in the same neutral, descriptive tone as the rest of the passage. As a contrast: all details are completely left out of Moran's story of how he kills a passer-by, although he remarks that the story of this event would be worth reading. But, as he says, "it is not at this late stage of my relation that I intend to give way to literature" (M 152). Both stories are devoid of any moral concerns, and therefore they belong to the terrifying sublime, as described by Kant. Now we may of course find these episodes only morally repulsive and not sublime at all, but in that case we are not concerned with the aesthetic judgement of these works. The absence of moral judgement in this analysis does not mean that moral judgement of the work is not legitimate within a Kantian context. I return to a discussion of how to unite aesthetic and moral judgement of a literary work below.

It is this terrifying mode of the sublime in the description of the character Molloy that is captured in Bataille's account of him as being on the border of humanity due to his lack of moral concern and attachment to other human beings. Just in this adherence to principles, be it to principles that we cannot share and that cannot be universalised, do we find the sublimity of Molloy. He is a negative hero, or the inversion of a moral hero. He does not yield to his inclinations but his principles are not moral principles. And the effect of the terrifying sublime, be it of nature or of man, is generally stronger than the effect of the noble sublime. There is something more shocking about this power that calls on our virtual resistance than the display of a power that we admire and wish to imitate, although Kant thinks that the latter is judged by feelings of a more permanent kind (KU§29, 272).

Moran does not display the same sublime character, although he is much more concerned with principles and reflects on them. But his principles are those of a self-righteous petty bourgeois, suspiciously controlling his surroundings rather than himself with these principles. Thus these principles do not check his self-love, but are a vehicle for satisfying it. So we see Moran as an all too human character, sharing our own worst moral deficiencies and lack of insight in our own nature. Only when he lies down to think of his inner Molloy (M 112 ff) does the story take on a sublime character, but that is due to the images of the wild Molloy crashing through the jungle of open country, who "hastened incessantly on, as if in despair, towards extremely close objectives" (M 113). That is until he is abandoned by his son and disintegrates while he grows "gradually weaker and weaker and more and more content" (M 163). From then on, he undergoes a moral conversion, not from self-conceit to moral goodness, but from self-conceit to this strange enthusiasm or despair also found in Molloy. Thus Moran too in the end, is driven by affects that are experienced as dynamically, terrifying sublime.

The murmur and sublime poetry in *Molloy*

The third way this work displays the sublime, is in certain poetical passages, which may appear as key passages if read in conjunction with the description of the kind of experience Beckett was seeking to evoke by his writing. He wanted "to represent a mocking attitude to the word, through words" to enable us to feel the silence or whisper underneath everything. The narrators throughout the *Trilogy* repeatedly return to the murmur that is there instead of silence:

> In reality I said nothing at all, but I heard a murmur, something gone wrong with the silence ... . (M 88)

> And it is then a little breath of fulfilment revives the dead longings and a murmur is born in the silent world, reproaching you affectionately for having despaired too late. (MD 278)

> ... the words fail, the voice fails, so be it, I know that well, it will be the silence, full of murmurs, distant cries, the usual silence, spent listening, spent waiting, waiting for the voice ... . (U 417)

When the voice fails the result is not silence, but a murmur, an undefinable sound that underlies the talking, just as the negation of the stories told does not result in a mere withdrawal of the initial claim, as if nothing had been said at all. There is always at least a feeling that something has been told, although one cannot say for sure what this something is. Likewise, the silence when the voices of the narrative stop talking, is not a silence but an indistinct sound; a murmur. This is probably what Beckett refers to as the "whisper of that final music or that silence that underlies All". Thus he describes in the narrative the kind of experience he is aiming at for the reader of the narrative. This is a feeling of something that is not expressible in words.

This recurrent theme is not in itself sublime, although it may be a description of an experience of the sublime. It is not sublime because we can easily imagine a voice going silent so that all we hear is a murmur. What I want to draw attention to is that this reference to murmur, together with the compulsion to narrate and the wish to end the narrative, are recurrent themes throughout the *Trilogy*. These elements are therefore important factors in the reader's experience of the work as a whole. The murmur or underlying sounds also feature in two poetic, mystical passages that I said were central in the initial discussion of *Molloy*, and which I now will return to and discuss in the light of Kant's theory of the sublime. Both passages describe experiences that Molloy has while staying at Lousse's house.

The first starts out with a reflection on the sciences Molloy has spent time on, and how it was magic that in the end "had the honour of my ruins" (M 39). He talks about this ruin as some particular place he sometimes seeks out, but then changes his mind:

> And the thing in ruins, I don't know what it is, what it was, nor whether it is not less a question of ruins than the indestructible chaos of timeless things, if that is the right expression. It is in any case a place devoid of mystery, deserted by magic, because devoid of mystery. (M 40)

Already here we have two of the words that associate this passage closely with the Kantian analysis of the sublime: chaos (KU§24, 246) and timeless things (KU§26, 254, B 210). The chaos is even indestructible, which in its contradictory way enhances the impression of total chaos that cannot be structured. There is a transition in the passage from describing this as a place, a thing, and as being in ruins, to describing it through the ideas of indestructible chaos of timeless things. There are images corresponding to the first set of concepts (place, thing, ruins), but not to the second. But due to the transition, we cannot treat the latter as abstract ideas, but strive to form images of these concepts. The impossibility of this representation is, if Kant is correct, accompanied by the feeling of the sublime.

The description of this place, or maybe state of mind is more appropriate, continues with Molloy's assertion that he does not go there gladly, although more gladly than to other places. But then he finds that when he says that he goes there, it appears as a state he seeks out voluntarily:

> But it is not the kind of place where you go, but where you find yourself, sometimes, not knowing how, and which you cannot leave at will, and where you find yourself without any pleasure, but with more perhaps than in those places where you can escape from, by making an effort, places full of mystery, full of the familiar mysteries. I listen and the voice is of a world collapsing endlessly, a frozen world, under a faint untroubled sky, enough to see by, yes, and frozen too. (M 40)

Again the description invites the imaginative representation of things that cannot be imagined. We are able to imagine things collapsing, maybe even worlds collapsing, but not that they collapse endlessly. Like any destruction, a collapse must come to an end. And the task of the imagination is made even more impossible by the additional information that this world is frozen, which means that it is motionless. In this section the mathematically sublime images[13] of

[13] It may be more correct to say that 'non-images' rather than images are produced by the cognitive powers of the reader of such passages, since, according to Kant, these concepts cannot be constructed by the imagination. I still choose to use 'image' as a

timelessness and chaos are supplemented by the dynamically sublime images of collapsing worlds. The reason why these words are sublime and not nonsensical has to do with their apparent meaningfulness and the way they contribute to the totality of the narrative.

This sublime passage takes on a greater significance for the work as a whole, since it is connected to the recurrent theme of the murmur underlying the voices of the narrative, as we continue with the subsequent sentence:

> And I hear it murmur that all wilts and yields, as if loaded down, but here there are no loads, and the ground, too, unfit for loads, and the light too, down towards an end it seems can never come. For what possible end to these wastes where true light never was, nor any upright thing, nor any true foundation, but only these leaning things, forever lapsing and crumbling away, beneath a sky without memory of morning or hope of night. These things, what things, come from where, made of what? And it says that here nothing stirs, has ever stirred, will ever stir, except myself, who do not stir either, when I am there, but see and am seen. Yes, a world at an end, in spite of appearances, its end brought it forth, ending it began, is it clear enough? (M 40)

The association between the murmur and these sublime images may follow the reader in later passages where the murmur is mentioned. Thus when she reads "it's the last words, the true last, or it's the murmurs, the murmurs are coming" (U 418) from the last page of *The Unnamable*, the murmurs are not ordinary sounds in the background, but the sounds of frozen worlds collapsing endlessly and indestructible chaos. Then these passages describe what we can call the underlying tone of the narratives of the *Trilogy*, which is that of the sublime.

There is a seriousness to the description that makes it resist the attempt to read this as another mockery of efforts to give meaning to human life. Although this description has affinities with mystical experiences, it does not employ the language and metaphors of mysticism. Besides, there is no attempt to negate the words uttered here, nor any misuse of conventional phrases. In a way these paradoxical sentences display the practice of self-negation in condensed form. These concepts cannot be represented by the imagination, and the effect of this text on sensibility is basically to put the reader in a particular mood or feeling, connected to this failed representation.

A few pages later we find a description of another, somewhat similar experience:

---

more loose term, indicating the activity of imagination that is central to our judgement of this part of the novel.

> And that night there was no question of moon, nor any other light, but it was a night of listening, a night given to the faint soughing and sighing stirring at night in little pleasure gardens, the shy sabbath of leaves and petals and the air that eddies there as it does not in other places, where there is less constraint, and as it does not during the day, when there is more vigilance, and something else that is not clear, being neither the air nor what it moves, perhaps the far unchanging noise the earth makes and which other noises cover, but not for long. For they do not account for that noise you hear when you really listen, when all seems hushed. And there was another noise, that of my life becoming this garden as it rode the earth of deeps and wildernesses. Yes, there were times when I forgot not only who I was, but that I was, forgot to be. Then I was no longer that sealed jar to which I owed my being so well preserved, but a wall gave way and I filled with roots and tame stems for example, stakes long since dead and ready for burning, the recess of night and the imminence of dawn, and then the labour of the planet rolling eager into winter, winter would rid it of these contemptible scabs. (M 48 f)

Here too the background sound is associated with sublime images such as the noise of the earth and its "deeps and wildernesses", as well as the more classical image of the giving up of the self and the unity with dead nature, ready for destruction. Again the underlying sound is not merely the absence of voices talking, but is given content in the form of images connected with infinity and destruction, which give rise to the feeling of the sublime. Just like the passage discussed above, the association between the background noise or murmur and the feeling of the sublime contributes to making this novel a sublime work of art in the Kantian sense.

Are we morally affected by this sublime? Yes. I argued in chapter four that the feeling of the sublime contributes to moral conversion as well as cultivation of moral character. The sublime resembles the moral feeling of respect phenomenologically because it subordinates sensibility to reason. The feeling also involves the admiration of the source of this feeling, which is the moral law. The sublime thus contributes to the strengthening of our respect for the moral law, and increases our tendency to subordinate other incentives to the feeling of respect for the law. The feeling also increases our tendency to act on the perfect duties towards ourselves, by making us more aware of the supreme value of our autonomy as rational beings. When we do not act autonomously, we degrade ourselves, and this we wish to avoid. In chapter five, I argued that there is no fundamental difference between the feeling of the sublime in nature and in art, and that narratives, like other art forms, can be sublime. The preceding analysis of this chapter combined with the arguments of chapters four and five warrants the claim that the aesthetic sublime of *Molloy* is morally significant.

6. 2 Aesthetic judgements and other judgements of literature

Ethical literary theory and aesthetic reflective judgement

When I apply my interpretation of Kant's theory of the sublime to Beckett's *Molloy*, I do not intend to say that this is the only valid way to approach this work, nor that it excludes other approaches. On the contrary; this theory can explain just one significant aspect of the work, namely that aspect which makes it an object of aesthetic appraisal. By aesthetic appraisal I mean the judgement of the work as beautiful or sublime, which is a judgement based on a particular kind of feeling. This judgement gives us no access to the way we identify (or fail to identify) with the protagonist and share his feelings, thoughts, and experiences. It does not involve the reader's appreciation of the humour of the novel or her interpretation of its fictitious universe. Likewise, the formal features of the work, or its ethical and epistemological arguments are of no interest in the pure aesthetic judgement. But all these and many other ways of relating to a novel are important aspects of the general judgement of the novel, i.e. the reader's experience of it. The aesthetic judgement is most important in assessing the underlying mood of the work, and that which makes it a work of art instead of merely a piece of entertainment; that is, if we accept the main outline of Kant's theory.

I have shown that Kant's aesthetic theory does not exclude other approaches to judgement of a literary work, it *requires* other such approaches to supplement the aesthetic reflective judgement concerning the subject's mental state when reading the work. There is a problem in connection with this claim, though, since the aesthetic reflective judgement is fundamentally different from other kinds of assessment of art works. One can choose to focus, for example, on the ethical argument implicit in the novel, or on the description of psychological conflicts, or on the time conception expressed in the text, or on the role of emotions in description of the main characters, and so forth. All these aspects can be isolated and discussed in separation from the others, although some of them may involve the same material, and in some of the discussion a disregard of other possible interpretative approaches may result in a deficient analysis. As I indicated in the first chapter, a failure to take into consideration the use of humour in Beckett's text may result in a too naive an interpretation of the view on sexuality expressed there. But by and large these different perspectives from which we can assess the text can be treated in isolation from each other.

The aesthetic reflective judgement of a work of art is, according to Kant, not connected to any of these different interpretative strategies, and at the same time potentially present in all such judgements. Because the judgement does not concern particular features of the object, but the subject's mental state when representing the object, she can always judge this state by her feeling of it. Thus this state pervades all judgements of this work of art, because our classification of it as art is based on the judgement that this is a work made with the intention to give rise to this kind of feeling in those who experience it. At the same time, the reader is not constantly aware of this feeling, because she is deliberately focusing on the object and not on her own response to the object. But she can make both aesthetic and cognitive judgements simultaneously: "Akira Kurosawa's movie *Ran* has a beautiful battle scene that shows the meaninglessness of war". Thus there is nothing in Kant's theory preventing the combination of an aesthetic reflective judgement with a judgement based on the ethical literary theory proposed by Nussbaum.

There is one difficulty in relation to this acceptance of a pluralistic approach to the judgement of literature that has to been solved. In a way, this difficulty is related to Nussbaum's questioning of the coherence of an account of disinterested pleasures. According to her, criticism and reading of novels both require a deeply felt involvement in the novel's characters:

> It is, in fact, criticism that focuses exclusively on textual form to the exclusion of human content that appears to be unduly narrow. For it appears to take no account of the urgency of our engagements with works of literature, the intimacy of the relationships we form, the way in which we do, like David Copperfield, read "as if for life", bringing to the text our hopes, fears, and confusions, and allowing the text to impart a certain structure to our hearts.[14]

This means that, in order to grasp significant aspects of a novel, one must take an emotional interest in the novel as something that matters in one's own life. But we remember at the same time that Kant says that to make an aesthetic reflective judgement, one must separate from the interested feelings of the agreeable and the good (KU§8, 216). Thus in a sense an interpretation of the kind suggested by Nussbaum, where the grasping of the ethical significance presupposes an interested attitude to the novel, is exactly what we have to rid ourselves of when we make a disinterested aesthetic reflective judgement of it. Thus there is an incompatibility between these two approaches that seems to imply that I cannot experience the full ethical depth of the novel if I judge it aesthetically, or I have to disregard its aesthetic qualities (in the Kantian sense) if I am to "read for life".

---

[14] Nussbaum, *Love's Knowledge*, 22.

This problem has two possible solutions; either we explain it by a two-aspect theory or we assume that we simultaneously can be both engaged and disinterested when judging art. To start with the first one: these two approaches are two different aspects we can judge the novel under. Both are legitimate points of view, although we have to disregard one while we focus on the other. So when I read for life, I do not really experience the beauty and the sublimity of the novel as a novel. I may recognise beauty in it, in cases where the protagonist experiences beauty or the narrator describes some beautiful object or event, but I do not enjoy the aesthetic pleasures of the work itself. For such a reader, *Molloy* as a whole is not sublime, but the passage describing the place of endlessly collapsing worlds is sublime for the reader as it is for the implied author[15] and the narrator. So it is only *through* my interested engagement in the narrative that I can experience disinterested pleasure of beauty or sublimity, so the disinterested pleasure in the novel as a work of art is impossible from this perspective.

If I want to make this kind of aesthetic reflective judgement of the novel, I have to disregard my interested engagement with the novel. I must purge the experience of all emotional interest and feelings related to value judgements. Still, I can make cognitive judgements of almost every aspect of the novel, including moral judgements of the kind: "When Molloy kicks the unconscious charcoal-burner, he is acting contrary to all moral principles, including Kantian, Utilitarian, Aristotelian, and those of everyday morality." But I have barred myself from feeling the repulsiveness of the deed and of the neutral, descriptive language in which it is related. I can of course switch between these two aspects when reading the novel, although probably not altogether according to my own wishes. If I could switch at will to the disinterested stance, I would also be certain that I made a pure aesthetic reflective judgement, a certainty Kant repeatedly says that we cannot have (e.g. KU§8, 216; §32, 282; §38, 290, note).

That we do this kind of switching back and forth between these aspects is possible, but hardly plausible. Aesthetic judgements are made more or less continuously, although we are not equally aware of them all the time. It is not as if this flower were beautiful now because of my switching to the aesthetic mode. The flower is beautiful all the time and I am more or less aware of it. Even when I

15 "Even the novel in which no narrator is dramatized creates an implicit picture of an author who stands behind the scenes, whether as a stage manager, a puppeteer, or as an indifferent God, silently paring his fingernails. This implied author is always distinct from the "real man" – whatever we may take him to be – who creates a superior version of himself, a "second self", as he creates his work." W. Booth, *The Rhetoric of Fiction*, 151.

consider a meadow for property development, I can see the beauty of the flowers there, although probably not as attentively as when taking a recreational walk. So I will suggest a not quite as simple theory for how a Kantian pure, disinterested aesthetic approach to literature can be combined with an emotionally involved and interested approach of the kind set forth by Nussbaum. This account assumes that we are able to distinguish feelings according to their quality and cognitive content although they occur simultaneously. If this assumption is correct, then we can have interested and disinterested feelings at the same time when reading a novel. We will also have the ability to distinguish between these different kinds of feeling. In the next section I will say why I think that this is not only a way to solve the present problem, it is a consequence of Kant's theory.

This solution to the problem of how the reader can simultaneously be engaged and enjoy disinterested aesthetic pleasures suggests that although we do engage in "reading for life", at the same time we are constantly aware that what we read is a work of art (or perhaps that it is an unsuccessful attempt to create a work of art). This is not the same as the awareness, which we also must have, that the novel is a work of fiction, implying that the events depicted should not be assessed the same way as real life events. Literature as fine art (as understood by Kant) does not for example include pulp fiction, although literature both as fine art and as pulp fiction is a work of fiction. I think the difference between these two kinds of fiction is one variety of the distinction Kant draws between fine and agreeable art:

> [Ästhetische Kunst] ist entweder *angenehme* oder *schöne* Kunst. Das erste ist sie, wenn der Zweck derselben ist, daß die Lust die Vorstellungen als bloße *Empfindungen*, das zweite, daß sie dieselben als *Erkenntnisarten* begleite. (KU§44, 305)

These are two different judgements that presuppose the fictionality of literature. There also are novels that can be classified neither as agreeable nor as fine art, such as didactic literature of the religious, moral, or political kind. In this case our emotions in the novel are only of the engaged kind, but still the reader is conscious of the fictionality of the work. The awareness of the novel as a work of art includes the thought that it is a work of fiction, but this is just one element of this awareness. The particular attitude[16] we take when regarding something as a

[16] Aesthetic attitude is usually understood as expressing a concern with formal features of the work: "If you are interested in learning facts about natural and artificial selection, or the history of biological theory, you are taking a practical attitude [to Darwin's *Origin of the species*]. But, if you wish, you can read it as an enormously patient and sustained argument, or as a masterpiece of style, or as the record of a dedicated and selfless pursuit of an important truth about the world. In that case you are after its "aesthetic qualities", and considering it not *qua* biological treatise, but *qua* literary work."

work of art makes us especially sensitive to our disinterested feeling in relation to it.

The reader is aware that story she is reading, is a work of fiction and a work of fine art, and this awareness affects her judgement of it. The reader's engagement in the characters and the events related is different from the engagement in real persons and real events. She is therefore simultaneously free to regard the novel as a work of art and thus a source of disinterested pleasure. The engagement is in this respect disengaged, because the reader can both be repulsed by Molloy's lack of compassion and at the same time find it sublime. This is not contrary to Nussbaum's theory, because she emphasises the value of the fictionality of novels because the reader is engaged without being too personally involved:

> As [Henry] James frequently stresses, novel reading places us in a position that is both like and unlike to position we occupy in life: like, in that we are emotionally involved with the characters, active with them, and aware of our incompleteness; unlike, in that we are free of certain sources of distortion that frequently impede our real-life deliberations. Since the story is not ours, we do not find ourselves caught up in the "vulgar heat" of our personal jalousies or angers or in the sometimes blinding violence of our loves. Thus the (ethically concerned) aesthetic attitude shows us the way.[17]

Although Nussbaum's notion of aesthetic attitude is broader than the Kantian one, and ethically concerned too, this at least shows that also on Nussbaum's view the partially disengaged aspect of our involvement with art is important. The Kantian addition I suggest is just an extension of this kind of outsider's perspective that is already a significant part of Nussbaum's theory.

So when we read a novel we are emotionally involved with the characters, but at the same time we judge the novel aesthetically, taking disinterested pleasure in its beauty or sublimity. And this disinterested pleasure, I have argued, has its own moral significance, in particular when the novel is characterised by the sublime. The moral import of this judgement is not more or less important than the ethical significance of novels as presented by Nussbaum. It is a different aspect of the moral significance of literature; more important in some contexts, less in others. This Kantian theory points out a way we are affected by literature and other forms of art that cannot as readily be explained within the approach developed by

---

Beardsley, *Aesthetics*, 62. I use 'aesthetic attitude' in a narrower sense, as that attitude you take when you focus on your aesthetic reflective judgement of the object. This attitude is especially relevant when judging things that we take to be works of art, because such objects are intentionally created to produce the pleasures of beauty or sublimity.

17 Nussbaum, *Love's Knowledge*, 48.

Nussbaum. The theory of the moral significance of the sublime in literature is a supplement to the ethical literary theory developed by Nussbaum.

Human suffering, evil, and moral judgement of sublime art

If we accept that it is possible to have these two qualitatively distinct kinds of 'feeling-based' judgements of a novel at the same time, this raises one problematic question: How can a story that includes morally repulsive and condemnable acts still be considered not only a source of aesthetic pleasure, but even a pleasure that contributes to the development of a good moral character? The immediate answer is that the acts described in novels are not real and there is nothing wrong in taking pleasure in fictitious events, be they morally repugnant or not. This answer is too simple and will not be acceptable in the context of the virtue theories of ethics developed by Aristotle and Kant.

Aristotle says that development of character includes the habituation of feeling so that we take pleasure in the right sort of action. We learn to take pleasure in the good by doing the good[18]. So a good character, one that includes a concern for the well-being of others, must take pleasure in the well-being of others and feel pity when they suffer. In this respect there is no difference in our reactions to actual and to fictitious events. This is evident from Aristotle's discussion of the purpose of tragedy, as stated in his famous definition of the art:

> Tragedy, then, is mimesis of an action that is elevated, complete, and of magnitude; in language embellished by distinct forms in its sections; employing the mode of enactment, not narrative, and through pity and fear accomplishing the catharsis of such emotions.[19]

The point of the tragedy is this *katharsis*, convincingly argued by Nussbaum to mean psychological and cognitive clarification[20], which we achieve by being engaged in the fate of the main character(s) of the story. Thus the feelings produced by engagement with fiction are no different from other feelings when the question is their role in building a stable disposition. Feeling pity for the suffering of good, but not flawless, people[21] in fiction makes us feel the appropriate way

---

18 Aristotle, *Nicomachean Ethics*, 1104b10-1105b12.
19 Aristotle, *Poetics*, 1449b23-28.
20 Nussbaum, *Fragility*, 388 ff.
21 In *Poetics*, 1454a16-21, Aristotle says that the portrayed character should be good, but in 1453a7-10 he emphasises that the person should not be "preeminent in virtue and justice" and his misfortune should be due to some error or mistake [*hamartia*].

towards other people in real life. And conversely, if I take pleasure in the suffering of innocent people, this contributes at least to a weakening of my potential for perceiving the suffering of other people as something that should engage me.

Kant also emphasises our duty to develop sympathetic feelings towards others, although the argument is somewhat different:

> Obzwar aber Mitleid (und so auch Mitfreude) mit Anderen zu haben, an sich selbst nicht Pflicht ist, so ist es doch tätige Teilnehmung an ihrem Schicksale, und zu dem Ende also indirekte Pflicht, die mitleidigen natürlichen (ästhetischen) Gefühle in uns zu kultivieren und sie, als so viele Mittel zur Teilnehmung aus moralischen Grundsätzen und dem ihnen gemäßen Gefühl zu benutzen. – So ist es Pflicht: nicht die Stellen, wo sich Arme befinden, denen das Notwendigste abgeht, zu umgehen, sondern sie aufzusuchen, nicht die Krankenstuben oder die Gefängnisse der Schuldner und dergl. zu fliehen, und dem schmerzhaften Mitgefühl, dessen man sich nicht erwehren könne, auszuweichen: weil dieses doch einer der in uns von der Natur gelegten Antriebe ist, dasjenige zu tun, was die Pflichtvorstellung für sich allein nicht ausrichten würde. (MS, 457)

We should cultivate the natural sympathy (or pity, as Aristotle says) for the suffering of others, because this feeling contributes to our acting according to duty. Kant does not say anything about the effect of exposure to suffering in fiction, but there is no reason to assume that his theory of natural sympathy differs from that of Aristotle. Sympathetic engagement in the sufferings of the characters in novels also contributes to the cultivation of this feeling. And again, if we reverse the coin, the exposure to suffering that we do not share has a negative effect even if this suffering is only that of the narrated David Copperfield or the enacted Oedipus. This we see from Kant's prohibition of the maltreatment of animals because it weakens our sympathetic feelings towards other human beings:

> In Ansehung des lebenden, obgleich vernunftlosen Teils der Geschöpfe ist die gewaltsame und zugleich grausame Behandlung der Tiere der Pflicht des Menschen gegen sich selbst weit inniglicher entgegengesetzt, weil dadurch das Mitgefühl an ihrem Leiden im Menschen abgestumpft und dadurch eine der Moralität im Verhältnisse zu anderen Menschen sehr diensame natürliche Anlage geschwächt und nach und nach ausgetilgt wird … . (MS 443)

When we expose ourselves to the pain of animals without being affected, which must be the case if we maltreat them, our natural sympathy for the sufferings of other human beings is dulled. I find it reasonable that there is a similar parallel between the sufferings of fictional characters and the sufferings of human beings. If I take pleasure in the pain of a fictional character, in the long run my sympathy for real human beings who suffer is dulled.

Kant must also have a similar theory of the appropriate response to evil deeds, although his main focus is the subject's attitude towards his own deeds, not those of others. I cannot influence the perfection of another person, he alone can do that, and therefore my focus should be on my own perfection and the happiness of others (MS 385 ff). Just as the cultivation of sympathy is a duty, so must the cultivation of loathing for evil be a duty. This loathing cannot include hatred or wish for vengeance (MS 461), but still it is a feeling that evil acts are contrary to the humanity in us. Kant mentions several such loathsome vices. The first group concerns the hatred of others and includes envy, ingratitude, and malice (MS 458 ff). The second group concerns the lack of respect for others and includes arrogance, defamation, and ridicule (MS, 465 ff). So if the feeling in connection with the experience of such vices does not encompass a loathing of them, the effect on our own character presumably would be the same as the failure to feel sympathy for the suffering of others. Our love and respect for our fellow human beings is dulled. My claim is that this is the case even in our response to fictional renderings of these vices.

My ability to take a disinterested attitude toward evil or sufferings described in fictional literature, and even to take pleasure in this, affects my ability to resist evil in myself and to sympathise with human suffering in the real world. Does this mean that we should not, for moral reasons, take pleasure in this kind of sublimity? I do not think so. I do not think this would be Kant's position, either, at least not when formulated in this general fashion. But there are two conditions for the acceptability of evil and human suffering as part of the sublime in a novel, conditions that we can deduce from Kant's aesthetic and moral theory. The first one is that this must be a work of fine and not of agreeable art. We should not, on Kant's view, waste much time on agreeable art at all, since it has no connection to culture and moral development (KU§52, 326). Kant's position on moral improvement is clear: if I do not progress, I deteriorate (MS 409). Now there may be occasions when an entertaining novel or a harmless soap is a good alternative to medical treatment, be it for insomnia or depression, but this kind of diversion is addictive (as most of us have discovered) and should be consumed sparingly and with caution. This is how I understand Kant's view. And when this entertainment, which in itself dulls the spirit, portrays evil action and suffering, i.e. presents evil and suffering as entertaining rather than loathsome or pitiable, then there certainly can be no justification for spending time on it. So unless thrillers and westerns involve some product of genius, Kant must think that we are better off without them.

The second condition is that the suffering must be presented so that the pleasure we take in the sublimity or beauty of the novel is not of a kind that prevents our simultaneous sympathy with the sufferer. The terrifying sublimity of the torture machine in Kafka's '*In der Strafkolonie*'[22] must not become an obstacle to our natural pity for the officer and horror at the absence of any sympathy in the spectators to the apparatus. Even fiction affects us, as Aristotle points out, and we should not ignore this if our goal is to become virtuous. Kant held that we can at the same time take pleasure in an event or, more precisely, in a description of the event, and recognise it as containing morally objectionable elements. This is evident from his discussion of the French Revolution, which, according to Kant, reveals the moral tendency in humankind, not in the events themselves, but in the reaction it awakens in the spectators:

> Die Revolution eines geistreichen Volks, die wir in unsern Tagen haben vor sich gehen sehen, mag gelingen oder scheitern; sie mag mit Elend oder Greueltaten dermaßen angefüllt sein, daß ein wohldenkender Mensch sie, wenn er sie zum zweitenmale unternehmend glücklich auszuführen hoffen könnte, doch das Experiment auf solche Kosten zu machen nie beschließen würde, - diese Revolution, sage ich, findet doch in den Gemütern aller Zuschauer (die nicht selbst in diesem Spiele mit verwickelt sind) eine *Teilnehmung* dem Wunsche nach, die nahe an Enthusiasm grenzt, und deren Äußerung selbst mit Gefahr verbunden war, die also keine andere als eine moralische Anlage im Menschengeschlecht zur Ursache haben kann. (SF 85)

The Revolution is rife with horrors and misdeeds, but still the observation of it fills people with hope, a feeling Kant not only accepts but even says expresses a moral predisposition in humankind. This shows that, according to Kant, there is no contradiction between feeling repulsion from evil and sympathy with those who suffer and at the same time taking pleasure in what one observes. And if this is acceptable concerning a real life event, it certainly also must be so when the event is part of a fictional account.

Does Kant think that the Revolution itself is a sublime event? The pleasure of the spectators is not described as a pure aesthetic judgement, but as a pleasure in the good. It is possible that this response must be called a judgement of accessory beauty because it is an pleasure connected to a teleological judgement[23]. The spectators judge the Revolution under the idea of the progress of humankind, and

---

22 F. Kafka, *Das Urteil und andere Erzählungen*, 98 ff.

23 It is actually both a moral and a teleological judgement. Kant says that this enthusiasm for the Revolution derives both from the moral right to a constitution and from the purpose of the republican constitution, which is to secure (negatively) the progress of humankind (SF 85 f).

this is the source of their pleasure, Kant says. Thus this is not, according to him, a pure judgement of taste, and certainly not a judgement of the sublime. One can of course ask, since the judgement concerns the purpose of humankind, whether it is not an applied judgement of sublimity rather than of taste. After all, the idea involved is the purpose of man as a moral being, not the purpose of man as part of nature. However this may be, I think that Kant should, on the basis of his own description of the Revolution, recognise its sublimity. The enormous power of the masses of people united in a common resolve to change the order of society is a phenomenon that cannot be subsumed under causal explanations or under the idea of the purposiveness of man as nature. This leads to an inadequacy of our imagination that involves reason rather than understanding in reflection. Thus the feeling of this relation has the quality of the sublime, and since it involves the reflection on moral ideas, such as freedom and justice, it must belong to the dynamical mode. So the Revolution itself, with the enthusiasm of its participants, is the subject of a judgement of the dynamically sublime. We see this event in terms of the purpose of man, which lies in his moral vocation. So although the spectator realises that the Revolution involves horrible misdeeds and atrocities, she still judges it to be sublime. But the pleasure of the sublime clearly must never make us blind to our natural compassion with the sufferers or to the reprehensibility of the atrocities committed in the name of this Revolution.

Although Kant overlooked or did not want to emphasise the sublimity of the Revolution itself, he does recognise one kind of aesthetic reflective judgement of sublimity in this passage from *Der Streit der Fakultäten* that is of interest for my present discussion. He says that the participation of the spectators of the French Revolution borders on the feeling of enthusiasm. We remember that enthusiasm was the paradigmatic sublime affect in Kant's discussion. So when we regard the enthusiasm of the non-participating adherents of the Revolution, this is judged by us, the spectators of the spectators, as a sublime affect. Also here a simultaneous *moral* assessment of this affect is required, according to Kant:

> Dies also und die Teilnehmung am Guten mit *Affekt*, der *Enthusiasm*, ob er zwar, weil aller Affekt als ein solcher Tadel verdient, nicht ganz zu billigen ist, gibt doch vermittelst dieser Geschichte zu der für die Anthropologie wichtigen Bemerkung Anlaß: daß wahrer Enthusiasm nur immer aufs *Idealische* und zwar rein Moralische geht, dergleichen der Rechtsbegriff ist, und nicht auf den Eigennutz gepfropft werden kann. (SF 86)

Although Kant says that the affects deserve moral blame, while the sublime lack of concern for the subject's own interests and desires expressed in these affects deserves praise, I will add that the political context of this enthusiasm should be part of the moral assessment. There is a morally significant difference between the enthusiasm for the bloody *Khmer Rouge* revolution in Cambodia and the enthusiasm for the 'Velvet Revolution' in Czechoslovakia, but both kinds of revolutionary enthusiasm express sublime affects.

It follows that a novel like *Molloy* which involves descriptions of violent and cruel acts as well as characters who show no sign of compassion or communal feelings, can be regarded a source of aesthetic pleasure within a Kantian theory. This is the case despite the fact that part of what makes this novel sublime is depiction of morally reprehensible acts. But it can be a source of aesthetic pleasure only if (1) the novel is truly sublime, which is indicated by the feelings of the sublime being accompanied by reflection on rational ideas, and (2) the aesthetic feeling does not displace sympathy with those who suffer and a parallel antipathy for evil, which is appropriate even in regard to fiction. There may even be cases where the feeling of the sublime is impermissible, because the only appropriate response is a reaction on moral grounds. In that context, we may talk of a primacy of the practical. In some cases, for example gross maltreatment of innocent, defenceless children, *only* moral condemnation is appropriate. The reason would be that any other feeling on that occasion would lessen the compassion for the victim and the loathing for the evil deed that we ought to feel. Then the moral basis and effect of the sublime cannot outweigh the negative direct effects on our character. But in normal fictional accounts, the sublime can involve accounts of evil deeds and human suffering, so long as we feel the appropriate engaged sympathy and loathing alongside the pure aesthetic delight of the sublime.

6. 3 Molloy*, the sublime, and ethics*

The point of departure for this book was the question of how a work like Beckett's *Molloy* could be morally significant. Based on my own experience of reading literature, the assumption was that the many-faceted and very interesting theoretical work on literature and ethics of the last ten years or so has overlooked one kind of moral import of some works of literature. These works made me feel, rather than think, that I was presented with something real transcending the limits both of the novel's imagined universe and the actual world of my own experience. This quasi-religious feeling stimulated a reflection on my own life and values, which had the character of moral reflection. This feeling of transcendence has in the tradition been called the feeling of the sublime, and the most elaborate theory connecting this feeling to morality rather than psychology, as Burke does, or religion, as Pseudo-Longinus[24] and Harold Bloom[25] in their different ways do, is found in Kant's aesthetic theory.

Although Kant finds the basis of the sublime in man's morality and indicates that this experience is morally significant, he nowhere states explicitly how this feeling can make a morally relevant difference in human lives. My aim has therefore been to develop a Kantian theory of the ethical significance of the reader's aesthetic response to some works of literature. I hope at the same time to have made this something more than an interpretation of Kant by developing this account in relation to a reading of Beckett's *Molloy*, and by the reading of *Molloy* to have shown that Kant's aesthetic theory can be relevant for literature very different from the kind he could have imagined. I have also argued that the Kantian theory of the moral significance of the sublime in literature is not an alternative but a complement to the existing theories of literature and ethics, such as the one developed by Nussbaum.

So the result of my Kantian exploration is a theory that can account for the experience of *Molloy* as described by several critics: despite its nihilistic and despondent picture of existence, *Molloy* is a source of aesthetic attraction - it is even taken by some to be a positive reaffirmation of the value of human life. The main features of this Kantian theory of the morally significant aesthetic sublime of literature are:

1) Judgements of taste are based on a feeling of a free play of the cognitive powers of imagination and understanding in the representation of an object. We claim subjective universal validity for this feeling because it is the subjective aspect of an objective reflective (teleological) judgement of nature under the principle of the purposiveness of nature for our cognitive capacity.

2) Judgements of sublimity are based on feelings qualitatively different from the feelings involved in taste. The feeling of the sublime is a complex simultaneous attraction and repulsion based on a free play between imagination and reason because the imagination fails to represent the object under a principle of purposiveness of nature. Instead the object is judged under the principle of the purposive use of nature for man's supernatural vocation. This judgement claims subjective universal validity conditional on the presence of moral feeling and acquaintance with moral ideas in everyone.

3) There are two modes of the sublime depending on whether theoretical or practical reason is involved. The mathematically sublime concerns objects that

---

24 Longinus, *Sublime*, 35, 1-5.
25 Bloom, *Ruin the Sacred*, 200 ff.

appear great beyond comparison, and the dynamically sublime objects that appear overwhelmingly mighty. The latter can also concern human affects such as enthusiasm, anger and apathy, when the sources of these affects are principles and not the concern for one's own interest. Both modes are connected to moral ideas, the dynamical directly, and the mathematical indirectly because theoretical ideas also involve the moral ideas of the spontaneity and autonomy of human reason.

4) The real sublime is not found in objects of nature, Kant says, but in human freedom as self-legislating rational beings, which is superior to the greatest or mightiest object of nature or art. When we experience the ambivalent feeling of the sublime in the encounter with a great or mighty object, what we really feel is the superiority of our own free will to act according to the moral law.

5) The aesthetic judgement of sublimity can affect us morally in the sense that it can contribute to a positive development of moral character in the subject. I suggest that the feeling of the sublime can be one of many factors stimulating moral conversion or cultivation of moral character, basically due to its phenomenological similarity with the moral feeling of respect, and because it involves moral ideas.

6) Fine art can also be subject to aesthetic reflective judgements under the principles of the purposiveness or the purposive use of nature. Unlike other human artifacts, these art works are made to be judged aesthetically, as purposive without purpose, something that is possible if they contain elements produced by the talent called genius. This talent is not under rational control, nor can the lawfulness of its products be explained by reference to causal necessity. These products must therefore be explained reflectively, which is only possible on the condition of a free play of imagination with the power of concepts. Thus we must judge them by taste or as sublime. This means that fine art, including novels, can be sublime.

By applying this Kantian theory of the aesthetic sublime and its moral significance to Beckett's *Molloy* I have given one possible explanation of the fact that so many of its readers, including myself, are affected by this work in such a profound way. This Kantian approach to the sublime can also be used in the interpretation of other sublime works of literature. But because the basis for the interpretation will be aesthetic judgement, one cannot define on beforehand which textual elements that will lead to the feelings in the judgement of something as sublime. This is a consequence of the singularity of aesthetic judgements.

Thus, the aesthetic experience in reading the literary work will be the only source for deciding whether this is a sublime work of art. On the basis of that judgement it is possible to analyse the text to try to point out the elements that is counterpurposive in a way that can give rise to the feeling of the sublime. One can never proceed the other way by starting with finding "sublime" elements, and then move from these elements to the requirement that we ought to have a complex feeling of pleasure through displeasure when reading this text. And if the reader of Beckett's *Molloy* does not experience the sublimity of this novel, and perhaps finds it to be "almost unendurably boring" as Toynbee did, no textual analysis or theories of the kind presented here can suffice to change their mind. The only way someone can discover the sublimity of a work of art and perhaps be influenced by it is through his own experience of the work.

Bibliography

Adorno, Theodor W. *Noten zur Literatur*, Frankfurt am Main: Suhrkamp, 1994.

Allison, Henry E. *Kant's Theory of Freedom*, Cambridge: Cambridge University Press, 1990

Allison, Henry E. *Kant's Transcendental Idealism. An Interpretation and Defense*, New Haven: Yale University Press, 1983.

Allison, Henry E. 'Pleasure and Harmony in Kant's Theory of Taste' in Parret (ed.), 1998, 466-483.

Ameriks, Karl 'How to Save Kant's Deduction of Taste' in *Journal of Value Inquiry* 16, 1982, 295-302.

Aquila, Richard 'A New Look at Kant's Aesthetic Judgments' in Cohen and Guyer (eds.), 1985, 87-114.

Aristotle *Metaphysics*, Oxford: Clarendon Press, 1972.

Aristotle *Nicomachean Ethics*, Cambridge, Mass.: Harvard University Press, 1982.

Aristotle *Poetics*, Cambridge, Mass.: Harvard University Press, 1995.

Aristotle *Politica*, Oxford: Clarendon Press, 1972.

Aristotle *"Art" of Rhetoric*, Cambridge, Mass.: Harvard University Press, 1982.

Aristotle *Topica*, Cambridge, Mass.: Harvard University Press, 1989.

Ayala, Francisco J. 'The Distinctness of Biology' in Weinert (ed.), 1995, 268-285.

Baron, Marcia 'Was Effie Briest a Victim of Kantian Morality' in *Philosophy and Literature*, 12, 1988, 95-113.

Bataille, Georges 'Molloy's Silence' in Gontarski (ed.), 1986, 131-140.

Beck, Lewis White *A Commentary on Kant's Critique of Practical Reason*, Chicago: The University of Chicago Press, 1963.

Beckett, Samuel *Molloy. Malone Dies. The Unnamable* [*Trilogy*], London: J. Calder, 1994.

Beckett, Samuel and Duthuit, Georges 'Three Dialogues', in Esslin (ed.), 1965, 16-22.

Beardsley, Monroe C. *Aesthetics. Problems in the Philosophy of Criticism*, Indianapolis: Hackett, 1981.

Bernstein, Jay M. *The Fate of Art*, Cambridge: Polity Press, 1993.

Bloom, Harold *Ruin the Sacred Truths*, Cambridge, Mass.: Harvard University Press, 1991.

Bloom, Harold (ed.) *Samuel Beckett*, New York: Chelsea House, 1985

Bloom, Harold *The Western Canon. The Book and School of the Ages*, London: Macmillan, 1995.

Bloom, Harold 'Introduction', in Bloom (ed.), 1985, 1-5.

Booth, Wayne C. *The Company We Keep. An Ethics of Fiction*, Berkeley: University of California Press, 1988.

Booth, Wayne C. The Rhetoric of Fiction, London: Penguin Books, 1991.

Budd, Malcolm 'Delight in the Natural World: Kant on the Aesthetic Appreciation of Nature. Part III: The Sublime in Nature' in *British Journal of Aesthetics*, 38, 3, 1998, 233-250.

Burke, Edmund *A Philosophical Enquiry into the Origin of our Ideas of the Sublime and the Beautiful*, Oxford: Oxford University Press, 1990.

Bøe, Solveig, Molander, Bengt, and Strandhagen, Brit (eds.) *I første-, andre- og tredjeperson. Festskrift til Audun Øfsti*, Trondheim: Filosofisk Institutt NTNU, 1999.

Cavell, Stanley *Must We Mean What We Say?*, Cambridge: Cambridge University Press, 1995.

Cohen, Ted and Guyer, Paul (eds.) *Essays in Kant's Aesthetics*, Chicago: The University of Chicago Press, 1985.

Cohn, Ruby *Back to Beckett*, Princeton: Princeton University Press, 1973.

Cohn, Ruby *Samuel Beckett: the comic gamut*, New Brunswick: Rutgers University Press, 1962.

Coplestone, Frederick *A History of Philosophy. Augustine to Scotus*, New York: Image Books, Doubleday, 1985.
Crawford, Donald W. *Kant's Aesthetic Theory*, Madison: The University of Wisconsin Press, 1974.
Crawford, Donald W. 'Kant's Theory of Creative Imagination' in Cohen and Guyer (eds.), 1985, 151-178.
Critchley, Simon *The Ethics of Deconstruction*, Oxford: Blackwell, 1992.
Critchley, Simon *Very Little...Almost Nothing*, London: Routledge, 1997.
Crowther, Paul *The Kantian Sublime. From Morality to Art*, Oxford: Clarendon Press, 1991.
Danto, Arthur C. *The Philosophical Disenfranchisement of Art*, New York: Columbia University Press, 1986.
Davies, Paul 'Three novels and four *nouvelles*: giving up the ghost to be born at last' in Pilling (ed.), 1994, 43-66.
Dickens, Charles *Christmas Books*, Oxford: Oxford University Press, 1988.
Diffey, T. J. 'Natural Beauty without Metaphysics' in Kemal and Gaskell (eds.), 1995, 43-64.
Dostoevsky, Feodor *Crime and Punishment*, New York: Norton & Co, 1964.
Dostoevsky, Feodor *The Brothers Karamazov*, Chicago: Great Books of the Western World, Encyclopædia Britannica, 1990.
Eagleton, Terry *Literary Theory. An Introduction*, Oxford: Blackwell, 1996.
Eco, Umberto *The Name of the Rose*, London: Picador, 1984.
Eldridge, Richard *On Moral Personhood. Philosophy, Literature, Criticism, and Self-Understanding*, Chicago: The University of Chicago Press, 1989.
Esslin, Martin (ed.) *Samuel Beckett. A Collection of Critical Essays*, Englewood Cliffs: Prentice-Hall, 1965.
Esslin, Martin 'Introduction' in Esslin (ed.), 1965, 1-15.
Fletcher, John *The Novels of Samuel Beckett*, London: Chatto and Windus, 1970.
Foster, Paul *The Beckettian Impasse: A Zen Study of Ontological dilemma in the Novels of Samuel Beckett*, University of Heidelberg, 1980.
Fricke, Christel *Kants Theorie des reinen Geschmacksurteils*, Berlin: de Gruyter, 1990.
Frye, Northrop 'The Nightmare Life in Death', in Bloom (ed.), 1985, 17-25.
Gadamer, Hans-Georg *Wahrheit und Methode. Grundzüge einer philosophischen Hermeneutik*, Tübingen: J.C.B. Mohr, 1990.
Gerhardt, Volker and Herold, Norbert (eds.) *Perspektiven des Perspektivismus. Gedenkschrift zum Tode Friedrich Kaulbachs*, Würzburg: Königshausen und Neumann, 1992.
Ginsborg, Hannah 'Kant on the Subjectivity of Taste' in Parret (ed.), 1998, 448-465.
Ginsborg, Hannah 'Lawfulness without a Law: Kant on the Free Play of Imagination and Understanding' in *Philosophical Topics*, 25, 1, 1997, 37-81.
Ginsborg, Hannah *The Role of Taste in Kant's Theory of Cognition*, New York: Garland, 1990.
Gontarski, Stanley E. 'Literary Allusions in *Happy Days*', in Gontarski (ed.), 1986, 308-325.
Gontarski, Stanley E. (ed.) *On Beckett: Essays and Criticism*, New York: Grove Press, 1986.
Graver, Lawrence and Federman, Raymond (eds.) *Samuel Beckett. The Critical Heritage*, London: Routledge& Kegan Paul, 1979.
Guyer, Paul (ed.) *The Cambridge Companion to Kant*, Cambridge: Cambridge University Press, 1992.
Guyer, Paul *Kant and the Claims of Taste*, Cambrige: Cambridge University Press, 1997 [First edition: Cambridge, Mass.: Harvard University Press, 1979].
Guyer, Paul *Kant and the Experience of Freedom. Essays on Aesthetics and Morality*, Cambridge: Cambridge University Press, 1993.
Guyer, Paul 'The Symbols of Freedom in Kant's Aesthetics' in Parret (ed.) 1998.
Harpham, Geoffrey Galt *Getting It Right. Language, Literature, and Ethics*, Chicago: The University of Chicago Press, 1992.

Henrich, Dieter *Aesthetic Judgment and the Moral Image of the World*, Stanford: Stanford University Press, 1992.

Herman, Barbara *The Practice of Moral Judgment*, Cambridge, Mass.: Harvard University Press, 1996.

Hill, Thomas E. *Dignity and Practical Reason in Kant's Moral Theory*, Ithaca: Cornell University Press, 1992.

Hudson, Hud 'The Significance of an Analytic of the Ugly in Kant's Deduction of Pure Judgments of Taste' in Meerbote and Hudson (eds.), 1991, 87-103.

Hund, William B. 'Kant and A. Lazaroff on the Sublime' in *Kantstudien*, 73, 3, 1982, 351-355.

Iser, Wolfgang *The Act of Reading. A Theory of Aesthetic Response*, Baltimore: The John Hopkins University Press, 1980.

Jonsen, Albert R. and Toulmin, Stephen *The Abuse of Casuistry*, Berkeley: University of California Press, 1988.

Kafka, Franz *Das Urteil und andere Erzählungen*, Frankfurt am Main: Fischer, 1952.

Kant, Immanuel *Anthropologie in pragmatischer Hinsicht*, Stuttgart: Reclam, 1983.

Kant, Immanuel *Beobachtungen über das Gefühl des Schönen und Erhabenen* in *Kants Werke II*, Berlin: de Gruyter, 1968 [*Observations on the Feeling of the Beautiful and Sublime*, Berkeley: University of California Press, 1991. Translated by John T. Goldthwait].

Kant, Immanuel *Erste Einleitung in die Kritik der Urteilskraft*, Hamburg: Felix Meiner, 1990 [*Critique of Judgment. Including the First Introduction*, Indianapolis: Hackett, 1987. Translated by Werner S. Pluhar].

Kant, Immanuel *Grundlegung zur Metaphysik der Sitten*, Hamburg: Felix Meiner, 1965

Kant, Immanuel *Kritik der praktischen Vernunft*, Hamburg: Felix Meiner, 1990 [*Critique of Practical Reason*, New York: Macmillan, 1993. Translated by Lewis White Beck].

Kant, Immanuel *Kritik der reinen Vernunft*, Hamburg: Felix Meiner, 1976 [*Critique of Pure Reason*, London: Macmillan, 1978. Translated by Norman Kemp Smith].

Kant, Immanuel *Kritik der Urteilskraft*, Hamburg: Felix Meiner, 1990 [*Critique of Judgment. Including the First Introduction*, Indianapolis: Hackett, 1987. Translated by Werner S. Pluhar].

Kant, Immanuel *Die Metaphysik der Sitten*, Frankfurt am Main: Suhrkamp, 1968 [*The Metaphysics of Morals*, Cambridge: Cambridge University Press, 1996. Translated by Mary Gregor].

Kant, Immanuel *Prolegomena zu einer jeden künftigen Metaphysik*, Hamburg: Felix Meiner, 1976.

Kant, Immanuel *Die Religion innerhalb der Grenzen der bloßen Vernunft*, Hamburg: Felix Meiner, 1990 [*Religion within the Limits of Reason Alone*, New York: Harper, 1960. Translated by Theodore M. Greene and Hoyt H. Hudson.]

Kant, Immanuel *Der Streit der Fakultäten / The Conflict of the Faculties*, Lincoln: University of Nebraska Press, 1992. Translated by Mary J. Gregor.

Kemal, Salim *Kant's Aesthetic Theory*, New York, St. Martin's Press, 1997.

Kemal, Salim and Gaskell, Ivan (eds.) *Landscape, natural beauty and the arts*, Cambridge: Cambridge University Press, 1995.

Koppe, Franz (ed.) *Perspektiven der Kunstphilosophie. Texte und Diskussionen*, Frankfurt am Main: Suhrkamp, 1991.

Korsgaard, Christine M. *Creating the Kingdom of Ends*, Cambridge: Cambridge University Press, 1996.

Kulenkampff, Jens *Kants Logik des ästhetischen Urteils*, Frankfurt am Main: Klostermann, 1978.

Lamarque, Peter and, Haugom Olsen, Stein *Truth, Fiction, and Literature. A Philosophical Perspective*, Oxford: Clarendon, 1996.

Lazaroff, Allan 'The Kantian Sublime: Aesthetic Judgment and Religious Feeling' in *Kant-Studien* 71 (2) 1980, 202-220.

Lemons, John, Schrader-Frechette, Kristin, and Cranor, Carl 'The Precautionary Principle: Scientific Uncertainty and Type I and Type II Errors' in *Foundations of Science*, 2, 1997, 207-236.

Levy, Eric P. *Beckett and the Voice of Species*, Dublin: Gill and Macmillan, 1980.
Liddell and Scott *Greek-English Lexicon* [Abridged version], Oxford: Oxford University Press, 1990.
Longinus *On the Sublime*, Cambridge, Mass.: Harvard University Press, 1995.
Longuenesse, Béatrice *Kant and the Capacity to Judge. Sensibility and Discursivity in the Transcendental Analytic of the Critique of Pure Reason*, Princeton: Princeton University Press, 1998.
Lyons, John *Semantics*, Cambridge: Cambridge University Press, 1977
Lyotard, Jean-Francois *Lessons on the Analytic of the Sublime*, Stanford: Stanford University Press, 1994.
Lyotard, Jean-Francois *Om det sublime*, København: Akademisk Forlag, 1993.
Lyotard, Jean-Francois *The Postmodern Condition: A Report on Knowledge*, Minneapolis: University of Minnesota Press, 1991.
MacIntyre, Alastair *After Virtue. A study in moral theory*, London: Duckworth, 1985.
Makkreel, Rudolf A. *Imagination and Interpretation in Kant. The Hermeneutical Import of the Critique of Judgment*, Chicago: The University of Chicago Press, 1990.
Matthews, Patricia 'Kant's Sublime: A Form of Pure Aesthetic Reflective Judgment' in *The Journal of Aesthetics and Art Criticism*, 54, 2, 1996, 166-180.
McCloskey, Mary 'Review of P.Crowther, *The Kantian Sublime*' in *Philosophy*, 65, July 1990.
Meerbote, Ralph 'Reflection on Beauty' in Cohen and Guyer (eds.), 1985, 55-86.
Meerbote, Ralph and Hudson, Hud (eds.) *Kant's Aesthetics*, Atascadero: Ridgeview Publishing, 1991.
Mooij, J. J. 'Literature and Morality: The Primacy of Ethics' in Tysdahl (ed.), 1992, 99-114.
Murphy, P. J. 'Beckett and the philosophers' in Pilling (ed.), 1994, 222-240.
Myskja, Bjørn 'Intersubjectivity in Kant's Third Critique' in Bøe et al. (eds.), 1999.
Nadeau, Maurice 'Critique in *Combat*' in Graver and Federman (eds.), 1979, 50-54.
Nadeau, Maurice 'Samuel Beckett: Humour and the Void' in Esslin (ed.), 1965, 33-36.
Nozick, Robert *The Examined Life*, New York: Simon and Schuster, 1989.
Nussbaum, Martha C. *The fragility of goodness*, Cambridge: Cambridge University Press, 1986.
Nussbaum, Martha C. *Love's Knowledge*, Oxford: Oxford University Press, 1992.
Nussbaum, Martha C. 'Non-Relative Virtues: An Aristotelian Approach' in *Midwest Studies in Philosophy*, 13, 1988, 32 – 53.
O'Neill, Onora *Constructions of Reason. Explorations of Kant's Practical Philosophy*, Cambridge, Cambridge University Press, 1989.
Otto, Rudolf *The Idea of the Holy*, Oxford: Oxford University Press, 1958.
Parret, Herman (ed.) *Kants Ästhetik. Kant's Aesthetics. L'esthetique de Kant*, Berlin: de Gruyter, 1998.
Pilling, John (ed.) *The Cambridge Companion to Beckett*, Cambridge: Cambridge University Press, 1994.
Pillow, Kirk 'Form and Content in Kant's Aesthetics: Locating Beauty and the Sublime in the Work of Art' in *Journal of the History of Philosophy* 32: 3, 1994, 443-459.
Plato *The Republic*, Cambridge, Mass.: Harvard University Press, 1982.
Pluhar, Werner S. 'Translator's Introduction' in Kant, 1987, xxiii-cix.
Pogge, Thomas W. 'Kant on Ends and the Meaning of Life' in Reath, Herman, and Korsgaard (eds.), 1997, 361-387.
Pries, Christine 'Einleitung' in Pries (ed.) 1989, 1-30.
Pries, Christine (ed.) *Das Erhabene. Zwischen Grenzerfahrung und Größenwahn*, Weinheim: VCH, Acta Humaniora, 1989.
Pries, Christine *Übergänge ohne Brücken. Kants Erhabenes zwischen Kritik und Metaphysik*, Berlin: Akademie Verlag, 1995.
Pries, Christine and Lyotard, Jean-Franscois 'Das Undarstellbare – wider das Vergessen' in Pries (ed.), 1989, 319-347.

Reath, Andrews, Herman, Barbara, and Korsgaard, Christine *Reclaiming the History of Ethics. Essays for John Rawls*, Cambridge: Cambridge University Press, 1997.

Recki, Birgit 'Ästhetische Einstellung und moralische Haltung: Die Perspektiven der Vernunft im Gefühl des Erhabenen' in Gerhardt and Herold (eds.), 1992, 161-183.

Robbe-Grillet, Alain 'Samuel Beckett or "Presence" in the Theatre' in Esslin (ed.), 1965, 108-116.

Roll-Hansen, Nils 'The Meaning of Reduction in Biology' in Suárez (ed.), 1996, 125-148.

Rushdie, Salman 'Is Nothing Sacred?', The Herbert Read Memorial Lecture, February 6, 1990.

Sartre, Jean Paul *Existentialism & Humanism*, London: Methuen & Co, 1994.

Schaper, Eva *Studies in Kant's Aesthetics*, Edinburgh: Edinburgh University Press, 1979.

Schaper, Eva 'Taste, sublimity, and genius: The aesthetics of nature and art' in Guyer (ed.), 1992, 367-393.

Scruton, Roger *The Aesthetic Understanding. Essays in the Philosophy of Art and Culture*, South Bend: St. Augustine's Press, 1998.

Sherman, Nancy *Making a Necessity of Virtue. Aristotle and Kant on Virtue*, Cambridge: Cambridge University Press, 1997.

Strawson, P. F. *The Bounds of Sense. An Essay on Kant's Critique of Pure Reason*, London: Methuen & Co, 1966.

Suárez, José Tojo (ed.) *1st International Conference on Philosophy of Science*, Vigo: University of Vigo, 1996.

Taylor, Charles *Sources of the Self. The Making of the Modern Identity*, Cambridge: Cambridge University Press, 1989.

Taylor, Charles *Human Agency and Language. Philosophical Papers 1*, Cambridge: Cambridge University Press, 1995.

Toynbee, P. 'Critique in *Observer*' in Graver and Federman (eds.), 1979, 73-76.

Tysdahl, Bjørn (ed.) *Literature and Ethics. Proceedings from the Symposium "Skjønnlitteratur og etikk"*, Oslo: The Norwegian Academy of Science and Letters, 1992.

Vetlesen, Arne Johan *Perception, Empathy, and Judgment. An Inquiry into the Preconditions of Moral Performance*, University Park: Pennsylvania State University Press, 1994.

Weatherstone, Martin 'Kant's Assessment of Music in the Critique of Judgment' in *British Journal of Aesthetics*, 36, 1, 1996.

Weinert, Friedel (ed.) *Laws of Nature. Essays on the Philosophical, Scientific and Historical Dimensions*, Berlin: de Gruyter, 1995.

Weiskel, Thomas *The Romantic Sublime: Studies in the Structure and Psychology of Transcendence*, Baltimore: John Hopkins University Press, 1976.

Wellmer, Albrecht 'Adorno, die Moderne und das Erhabene' in Koppe (ed.), 1991, 165-190.

Wetlesen, Jon *Selverkjennelse og frigjøring. Et buddhistisk perspektiv*, Oslo: Universitetsforlaget, 1983.

Williams, Bernard *Ethics and the Limits of Philosophy*, Cambridge, Mass.: Harvard University Press, 1985.

Williams, Bernard *Moral Luck*, Cambridge: Cambridge University Press, 1997.

Wittgenstein, Ludwig *Philosophical Investigations*, Oxford: Blackwell, 1992.

Wittgenstein, Ludwig *Tractatus Logico-Philosophicus*, London: Routledge & Kegan Paul, 1996.

Wollheim, Richard *Art and Its Object*, Harmondsworth, Penguin, 1970.

Wyller, Truls *Etikkens historie. En systematisk framstilling*, Oslo: Cappelens Akademisk Forlag, 1996.

Zammito, John H. *The Genesis of Kant's Critique of Judgment*, Chicago: The University of Chicago Press, 1992.

Index